Ocean Racing &
Offshore Yachts

Ocean Racing &

Peter Johnson

Offshore Yachts

DODD, MEAD & COMPANY   NEW YORK

Published in the United States of America by
Dodd, Mead & Company, Inc.

Composed in 11 on 12 pt Baskerville
and made and printed in Great Britain by
The Camelot Press Limited, London and Southampton

Acknowledgements

MY THANKS are first of all due to Peter A. G. Milne, who has so excellently interpreted my ideas by means of the line drawings. His own knowledge of the sea has been of great value in this respect. Numerous firms have very kindly made information available and their names are usually mentioned in connection with the product where it occurs. Among those who have spent time in amplifying their own fields have been John Powell of Sparlight Ltd., David Sanders of Westerly Marine Construction Ltd., Richard Gatehouse of Brookes and Gatehouse Ltd. Information has come too from W. A. Souter & Son Ltd., Marine Construction Ltd., South Coast Rod Rigging Ltd., Yacht Tests Ltd., Lewmar Marine Ltd., Hurrell and Johnson Ltd., Paceship Ltd., Sovrel Marine Inc., Martec Inc., Norseman Ropes Ltd., Jensen Marine Inc., Goiot S.A. and Campbell-Sheehan Inc.

Points about sails have been assisted by Bunty King of Hood Sailmakers Ltd. and Ken Rose of Bruce Banks Sails. Thanks are due to the hospitality of numerous clubs in different countries which aid offshore racing and where I have obtained data. In particular David Colquhoun and Richard Hood of the JOG, Joseph Low, National Commodore of the MORC and John Daniell of the MORF of Southern California have been helpful. Our yachting magazines reflect the current scene and for allowing the reproduction of an appendix and some background material thanks are due to Charles Jones, Editor of *Yachting and Boating Weekly*. Bernard Hayman, Editor of *Yachting World* has kindly allowed the use of opinions expressed in articles and I have also made use of this authoritative journal as a historical record of the last two decades. Designers in various parts of the world have been most helpful in supplying information and drawings and have spoken to me about their work. These include Olin Stephens, Dick Carter and Alan Gurney in U.S.A., Philippe Harlé, Dominique Presles and Michel Dufour in France, Per Bröhall in Sweden, Ricus van de Stadt in Holland and in England Angus Primrose, Fred Parker, Michael Henderson, Kim Holman, Donald Pye, John Illingworth, John Sharpe, Raymond Wall, Rod Macalpine-Downie and Ian Hannay.

Others who have helped with verbal, written or photographic material are Robin Glover, Basil Wood, John Pearson, George Stead, Dick Pitcher, Valerie Roberts, Eileen Ramsay, Pierre Fouquin and Denis de La Noüe.

Contents

B

Diagrams

Plates

PHOTOGRAPHIC CREDITS

Pierre Fouquin 1, 19a, 21

Hon. Ambrose Greenaway 17, 18

Peter Barlow 25, 26

La Noüe-Bateaux 6, 20, 32, 49, 50

Eileen Ramsay 5, 7

Campbell-Sheehan 27, Jensen Marine 24, Lewmar Marine 31

Newbridge Boats 51

All other photographs are by the author.

·1·

THE OFFSHORE SCENE

It seems not at all a foolish hope that the ocean racing yachts of the future may set a standard which will bring about an improvement in the form of cruising yachts. I believe that we shall see the development of a class of yachts more efficient in combined speed and seaworthiness than those which have hitherto been built in any class.—E. G. MARTIN, founder of the Royal Ocean Racing Club, in 1928

As THE progress of science and industry grows, the need for the mature use of leisure increases as well. More reliance on complicated electromechanical aids ranging from typewriters to space craft has undoubtedly produced a reaction to spend effort on more simple and perhaps more satisfying concepts of life.

Sailing small boats is widely quoted as an occupation which enables you to "get away from it all", but those who sail on the sea know that this negative aspect is only an introduction and that yachting can be immensely absorbing in its own right. At one end of the scale is the simple relaxed few hours, while at the other is all the endeavour of a long cruise or a campaign of international racing. Between these extremes come numerous forms of sport on the water, some competitive and others merely making pleasurable use of wind and sea, but yacht racing can be classified into three major types: dinghy racing, keel-boat racing and cruiser racing.

In the racing field the term "cruiser" is used to distinguish it from the other two, and one might define it as a yacht with accommodation for some or all of the crew and facilities for them to live on board. One of the problems is exactly what to call such boats, when they appear on the racing scene. One of the pioneers of ocean racing in the 1930s, Cutty Mason, wrote: "Although almost every other noble sport is dignified with some suitably concise title, generally consisting of a single word, that is not the case with amateur deep sea yacht racing under sail; and, as a consequence, those who engage in it are customarily referred to by means of some clumsy, and often inadequate, string of words or epithets. . . ."

The majority of cruising yachts which race are under 35 ft. on the waterline, the range of size going down to around 17 ft. LWL. In these pages we are confining ourselves to boats of around 30 ft. LWL and below. The question of where the lower end of the scale becomes impracticable for racing is dealt with in due course. Note that I have referred to the yacht by her waterline length (l.w.l. or load waterline). This practice is used throughout this book, though the size of yachts is often spoken of elsewhere in other ways, notably length overall or some form of tonnage. These other terms are favoured by builders and designers, one of the reasons being that they make the yacht sound at its largest, but if comparing rating, accommodation or speed with a single dimension, LWL is the most significant. I am aware that it is not always possible to be sure of the exact LWL of a particular boat, but it is the most serviceable comparison for different designs. So here, where the length of a yacht is mentioned in feet and inches, this is the LWL unless otherwise stated.

More and more races for habitable yachts are held all over the world and the most important events are such established courses as the Fastnet and Bermuda races in England and USA respectively, and classics of the same or greater length in the waters of Australia, South America, the Far East and the Mediterranean, besides regular events across the Atlantic and Pacific.

In addition, there are numerous shorter events, which demand less time from the crews of the yachts and for this reason can be sailed regularly throughout the season instead of only annually or biennially.

The term "ocean racing yacht" is generic and does not denote that the particular yacht races across oceans. "Ocean racing" has become the word for a type of racing and not a specific undertaking. If we do wish to indicate the crossing of an ocean, it is now necessary to use descriptions such as "trans-ocean racing" or "deep sea" or "blue water" racing. For shorter events in open water "offshore" or "passage" racing is more modestly descriptive. In the terms "cruiser racing" or "handicap racing", the implication is that it is other than dinghy and keel-boat class racing. The ocean racing yacht can also give excellent sport inshore, that is on a day course round buoys, and in its design some thought may well be given to this aspect. But if a class of yacht is used solely for this type of sailing, it will develop into an inshore boat not fit to take on the open sea. The Dragon class was originally intended for Baltic cruising as well as racing, but after thirty years has become a refined racing boat, the diminutive cabin top only remaining to comply with the rules. The 12-metre has sleeping accommodation and a galley to comply with its rules, but for nothing else until outdated for racing and converted for cruising. Rules will never ensure the development of equipment but the open sea will. Bunks which are comfortable at sea, chart tables and galleys which work, are aboard ocean racers because they are needed to sail the boat offshore and not because the rules call for them. A recent trend for ocean racing yachts is the combined inshore and offshore series. It consists of perhaps three inshore events and one or two ocean races, with a points system arranged to give an overall result to an individual yacht or a team. This gives the close racing of inshore courses, but means that the yachts must be fit for the open sea.

Length of races   The characteristic of an ocean race is not so much of the length as in the nature of the course. An offshore event can be as short as 50 miles if it has the greater part of its length over exposed waters. Each step up in the distance sailed for a race gives it a different quality and typical lengths are as follows:

50 miles. This is an offshore race if in open water, but it can be finished in daylight except in light weather. Races under 40 miles must be considered inshore races for any type of yacht, because it is impossible to make any leg very far from the start and finish.

100 miles. This distance is often quoted as the average sailed by an ocean racer in twenty-four hours (i.e. just over 4 knots), but whatever the likely speed of yachts, given some windward work or light patches, it is the sort of race that starts on one day and finishes on the next. The very apt American term is "an overnight race".

250 miles. The Royal Ocean Racing Club have many of their regular events of this distance or a little shorter to fit the week-end. It gives plenty of scope for legs long enough to make the navigator worried and time for the weather to give surprises. The crew of a 30 ft. yacht hope to get around the course in thirty-six hours and a 22 ft. yacht in forty-eight hours, but it more often takes them both longer.

600 miles. This is the approximate length of races such as the Fastnet, Bermuda race and Sydney–Hobart. Members of the crew will need a week's holiday to do these, apart from the time required in preparing the yacht and sailing her home from the place of the finish.

2500 miles. Races of this order are the great trans-ocean events. The race committee will lay down many conditions for a course of this sort, one of which will be the minimum size of yacht that can compete. While very small yachts can take part safely, there is always the time factor to be considered. In transatlantic races under the Royal Ocean Racing Club or Cruising Club of America, 24 ft. is the minimum that has so far been permitted. Such races are undoubtedly the great landmarks in ocean racing and the seal on the ability of small yachts to go offshore, yet their strength lies in the fact that they are sailed by the sort of boats and crews which also engage in week-end events and day racing in their own countries. A word here on the recent single-handed races across the Atlantic and Pacific, which are also ocean races. As the main trophy is not awarded on a rating system, but goes to the first boat home, the tendency is for huge yachts, limited only by the ability of one man to control them, to take part. The smaller yachts involved tend to be an assorted bunch dictated mainly by the whims of their owners and although each is interesting in herself, they are thrown off from the main trend of cruiser racing. The big boats are sponsored, because of the nature of the publicity which these events attract, and this does nothing towards an economic ocean racer. A very good small yacht, which might be of great interest to thousands of racing men, cannot by reason of its size hope to win. The notion of limiting size by the number of the crew has been a failure and shows that, for regular ocean racing a proper handicap rule is essential, leaving the number of crew to the discretion of the owner.

Since races of, say, 250 miles and upwards are bound to cross a high proportion of open water, it remains to chart out the characteristics of the shorter offshore course. It can be considered to have the nature of an ocean race, if not more than twenty per cent, though preferably a little less, is in sheltered water and this will normally be at the start and finish. If half the race is in the Solent or Long Island Sound, it is not an ocean race. There should be a night at sea or, in high latitudes where the nights are short, at least some darkness during the race. There should not be so many short legs that navigation becomes pilotage; even in a 60-mile event there should be one leg of not less than 25 miles. Nor should the race keep too much along a shore, for although this can be tough enough, and sometimes more dangerous than open water, it does not leave the boats "on their own". Besides it is not that offshore sailing is more demanding—I have taken part in a number of round-the-buoys events which have been more physically exhausting than an ocean race—but it is a different type of race.

Rating Rules   Much of the increase in the use of cruising boats for racing since 1946 is attributable to excellent rating rules being available to measure any yacht and give her a handicap to compete against a whole range of types and sizes; thus small fleets can quickly become established with a season's programme. Rating rules are continually referred to in the chapters which follow and are considered in detail later. The rating rules mentioned in these pages are those of the Royal Ocean Racing Club, the Cruising Club of America and the International Offshore rule. Until 1969, the first two evolved each under its own authority, the RORC rule being used in Europe, Australia, the Far East and other parts of the world except the Americas. In the United States the CCA rule was pre-eminent, but there have been a number of others, many smaller groups using a modified CCA rule or their own system. Every rule suffers from necessary small amendments year by year, but the last major revision of the RORC rule was in 1957 and sometimes the "1957 RORC rule" is mentioned and when discussed it is this rule as amended to 1969 that is meant. The International Offshore rule was adopted in 1969 and represents the best of the two main rules, many of the principles of the hull measurement are those of the 1957 RORC rule, while the sail area system is akin to that of the CCA. Where the expression "rating rules" is used, it signifies that all the rules apply on a certain topic; where "the rating rule" is mentioned this can be taken to mean the International Offshore rule, unless otherwise indicated.

The progress of ocean racing   Ocean racing has not always been in the approved position that it is today and even in terms of the history of yachting its progress has been rapid, with an almost indigestible build-up of clubs, boats and events in the nineteen-sixties. With such world-wide expansion the many interesting events are difficult to get into focus, but it may be useful to pick out some of the landmarks which have led us to the current scene. In the nineteenth century, yachting was conducted in vessels which we would today consider very large and their racing was done in the regatta style. They had largely professional crews, and though well able to cross the open seas and oceans, any competitive racing was inshore. At the end of the century a number of people were cruising in smaller yachts and Joshua Slocum made the first ever single-handed circumnavigation of the world in the 37 ft. *Spray* in 1895–98. While there is much yachting history of interest and influence on the ocean racing yacht, these events are certainly included:

1866   December. *Henrietta, Fleetwing* and *Vesta* (all about 106 ft. l.o.a.). take part in first transatlantic race for yachts.
1880   Royal Cruising Club formed for yachts under "10 tons".
1904   New York–Marblehead race, 330 miles, organized by Thomas Fleming Day. All yachts under 30 ft.
1906   First New York–Bermuda race. Three yachts take part, all under 40 ft. l.o.a.
1922   CCA founded and begins to run regular Bermuda race.
1925   First Fastnet race is held in ordinary cruising yachts (minimum 30 ft.). RCC shows no interest and competitors form RORC (then "the ocean racing club").
1931   *Dorade* (Rod and Olin Stephens) designed by Sparkman and Stephens of New York, specifically as an ocean racer, wins the Fastnet by a large margin. Other designs for ocean racing follow in Europe.
1932   CCA draws up its own rating rule basically different to RORC.
1945   First Sydney–Hobart race.
1947   Light displacement *Myth of Malham* (John Illingworth), 33 ft. 6 in. begins three years of consistent success in RORC racing.
1950   *Cohoe* (Adlard Coles), only 25 ft., wins transatlantic race.
         Samuel Pepys (Erroll Bruce), 24 ft., is second.

Sopranino (Patrick Ellam), 17 ft. 9 in., races from England to Spain and Junior Offshore Group is formed as a result. Similar clubs to sail midget ocean racers follow later in USA, France and elsewhere.

1951 Following on the success of the transatlantic race the RORC makes Fastnet lower limit 24 ft. LWL.

1956 Severe gale hits regular RORC fleet racing in English Channel; there are numerous incidents but no one is lost.

1957 First Admiral's Cup starts. Similar inshore/offshore type of series begin some years later in USA and Australia.

1957–64 World economic conditions cause unprecedented expansion of yachting not least in ocean racing yachts.

1965 First One Ton Cup races for offshore yachts, started by Cercle de la Voile de Paris.

1969 International Offshore Rating (IOR) rule initiated.

MAINLY TO WINDWARD

*What a glorious thing the sea is! Sometimes smooth and silky with hardly a ripple;
then gay and sparkling in the sunshine with white horses; then, grey, grim and menacing,
with huge terrifying waves. But, even at its worst and most awe-inspiring, one cannot
but be impressed and wonder at the majesty of it, and it is a highway for those who have
the temerity to use it.*—E. F. HAYLOCK

IN THE days before the ocean racing yacht had transformed the sailing scene, and
especially in the early days of the Bermudian rig, the great difference in ability between
cruisers and racers was their windward showing. The history of rigs is dominated by this
gradual betterment in sailing against the wind. The modern Bermudian rig is the furthest
the design of efficient windward sailing rigs have yet gone. There are numerous variations
and some aspects of the design are influenced by the requirements of other points of
sailing, such as the need to set the best type of spinnaker. But basically the rig is a windward
instrument.

Cruising and racing needs   This is the place to get quite clear the needs of the offshore
racer and the coastal cruiser. When this book surveys the small ocean racer it also does
the same for cruising yachts. The basic requirements are the same; only the degree to
which they are taken differs. The ocean voyager, sailing with following winds for which he
has picked a route, may not be so interested in getting to windward, though at some stage
in his voyage he is going to be glad of every knot he can make to weather. The coastal
cruiser on the other hand must reckon on winds from all points of the compass over the
period of a season. Assuming she can sail within 45 degrees of the wind, and that even 60
degrees from the true wind is akin to windward sailing, then one-third of the potential
courses demand windward ability (Fig. 1). And this is not all, for in this large sector
where tacking or at least close-hauled work is called for the speed is slower than running or
reaching. Thus the actual *time* spent in this sector is greater.

It is a theoretical way of looking at the problem of the cruiser, but it is valid and
demonstrates that the cruiser's needs are along the lines of those of the ocean racing yacht.

When cruising in a high performance racing yacht I can confirm the pleasure which
you will get from her performance on her own or when sailing near other yachts. This is
particularly so on the wind, when actual speed and ability to point close can leave an
inferior performer standing.

Safety on the sea   In recent years there has been a tendency to specify that ocean racers
must carry more and more safety equipment. This is quite reasonable with the rapid
expansion of the sport. It is considered further on, but what is true safety at sea? The perils

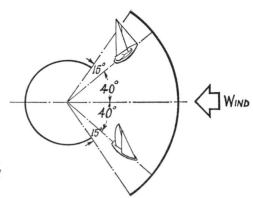

FIG. 1. *If the wind direction blows at one time or another from every point of the compass, then one-third of the time windward ability is required.*

that can befall a yacht can be divided into structural failure and danger of position. By structural failure is meant such events as dismasting, being stove in by a floating object, and fire. By "danger of position" is meant stranding due to a navigational error or being caught on a lee-shore. This is the second big aspect of windward ability, and a very great factor in the safety of an ocean racer: the quality of being able to beat off a lee shore in bad weather. This is more basic than any amount of emergency equipment such as life-rafts and flares, and it can even be argued that if the yacht is encumbered with too much emergency equipment on deck, her performance will suffer and she will be less safe. This is especially so in the smaller sizes. Royal Ocean Racing Club regulations call for "Storm sails capable of sailing *to windward* in heavy weather". Junior Offshore Group safety rules state: "To be suitable for JOG racing a boat should possess sufficient *windward* ability to enable her to get off a lee shore in bad conditions and boats must have draft of at least 60 per cent of (16 per cent LWL plus 2 feet)". What this draft should be is shown in the Table (Fig. 2).

Speed to Windward Whatever the conditions, the object must be to make the best speed to windward. Increased speed of the yacht through the water is not profitable if it results in a smaller speed to windward, conventionally known as VMG. In Fig. 3, VS gives the best VMG and though the yacht is romping along at VB she is not making up to windward so effectively. At VA she is closer to the wind but the loss in speed will be obvious enough. VS will vary for different wind strengths, different boats and different states of sea, and can only be found for one particular set of circumstances. Indeed, as conditions change from minute to minute the critical course to windward reverts to the brain and hand of the helmsman. At any instant there is an ideal VS which may or may not be found.

On the helm One or more really good helmsmen who can take the yacht to windward are worth more than many electronic instruments, or the latest in sails that can be put aboard the yacht. Some people seem unable to master the technique. Others can be depended on to keep the yacht going. It is easier to describe the yacht being sailed badly than well. The bad helmsman lets her come too near to the wind and the luff of the headsail

c

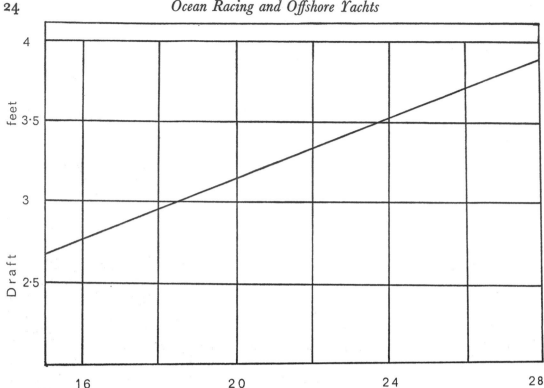

FIG. 2. JOG MINIMUM DRAFTS

LWL of yacht	Minimum draft allowed under JOG rules
ft.	ft. in.
16	2 9
20	3 1
24	3 6
28	3 11

Minimum drafts of various waterline lengths permitted under the rules of the JOG. Ocean racers in the higher sizes invariably exceed these drafts, but some small standard cruisers may fail to comply with this minimum. Most designers of ocean racers would consider greater draft desirable.

begins to lift; then he is away picking up speed but too far off the wind. When she is too near the wind and a sea is running her speed is lost. The most difficult conditions are those with little wind but some sea running. It is here the good helmsman is able to keep the yacht eating out to windward, not being stopped or slowed by every awkward sea.

What is the best way to sail any yacht to windward? First, complete concentration is called for. No one must speak to the helmsman except for essential remarks. For a few seconds' distraction, a few yards are lost, this is indisputable. So there must be no distraction; but where should the concentration be?

The answer is, on ocean racers, no one place. Watching a successful helmsman recently offshore, it was noticeable that his eyes were everywhere, on everything that

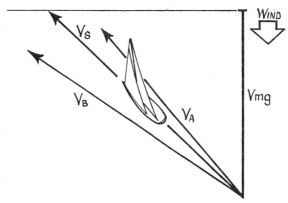

FIG. 3. *Speed made good to windward is known as VMG and this is achieved by sailing course VS. Course VB is faster through the water and course VA is closer to the wind, but neither is optimum windward sailing.*

FIG. 4. *Steering from weather side enables an eye to be kept on luff of headsail and seas to windward.*

mattered. These included the sea, the racing flag, sails, instruments and other yachts racing. The sails are the main guide and in particular the luff of the headsail. There is a point where the luff just begins to break and there is a point which cannot be visually detected, but becomes *known* by experience just before it begins to break—this is the place to be. The racing flag will blow out about along the line of the headboard which will be to leeward of the angle of the boom owing to twist in the sail. It is not so sensitive, but a useful guide, if only after tacking or rounding a mark for bringing the boat into the correct angle to the wind, while perhaps the sails are still being sheeted in.

When racing under RYA rules a rectangular racing flag which must not be less than one-third of the height of the sail number along any side has to be carried, but a windsock does not "flap" and gives a far more useful indication. It can be combined on one pole with a racing flag if desired.

The mainsail is not a guide when sailing to windward; its trim is important but that is another matter. So the helmsman's position should be where he can see the headsail and the racing flag. He will want to see the seas as the yacht takes them on the weather bow and this applies in fresher breezes. It may be preferable to sit to leeward in light weather with the genoa fully in sight. As the breeze freshens, whether there is tiller or wheel steering, the leeward side will be less comfortable, the tiller less easy to control. On the smallest boats the weight of everyone will be beneficial to windward. With the yacht heeled the headsail can then be looked at along the weather side (Fig. 4). In this position the approaching seas can be seen, and any behaviour of yachts to windward noted for clues on approaching wind effects.

Sails, seas, flag are being noted, so we still have the instruments to watch. The position of the sea or even the flag or sails on the yacht cannot be placed specially to suit the helmsman, but the instruments can and their siting will be considered in detail later. At the moment assume that they can easily be seen by the helmsman in any of his steering positions.

Instruments   The instruments which may be in use when sailing an ocean racer to windward are:

> The compass.
> Wind direction indicators (coarse and fine).
> Wind speed indicator.
> Water speedometer.

Other dials which may be in operation such as the measures of depth and distance are not the concern of helmsmen in relation to sailing the yacht to windward.

The use of the *compass* when sailing to windward is typical of the differences found between offshore and inshore racing. Its correct use depends on understanding between the navigator and the helmsman. If the yacht is beating to windward then the compass course is merely the best windward course on either tack. In this case the helmsman should not allow himself to be distracted by it, but sail the yacht on the indications discussed above. What he will do is glance at the compass course at intervals to see what is the course steered. If the navigator's ordered course is near to this (e.g. the yacht can lay the course on one board), then the helmsman should still concentrate on actually sailing the yacht, but then he will have to note if he can either no longer point on it, in which case the situation reverts to that just mentioned, or if he can sail higher. In this event the navigator has to be called in because there will be tactical and other considerations. The yacht may be sailed higher close-hauled, or the sheets may be eased. What is wrong is to stay on the compass course without any other action.

In practice the wind continually varies in different cycles. The pattern may be variations of up to 5 degrees every fifteen seconds and then something larger, say 6–8 degrees every ten minutes. The yacht is being coaxed to windward in relation to the wind, but difficulty arises in reporting the mean compass course over a period of half an hour. There is also an unavoidable tendency for the helmsman to report the course the navigator has indicated. The solution is frequent logging of the course reported to be steered and an understanding by the helmsman of the navigator's problem on the point of sailing.

Enough has been said here to emphasize that sailing the ocean racer needs a feel for the whole technique of getting the boat along. The navigator of an aircraft or steamer cannot apply his knowledge directly and helmanship, tactics and navigation are inseparable. In the chapters which follow we have had often to consider them apart, but when the yacht is racing it will not be possible to say where one ends and another begins.

The *water speed indicator* is a real aid in windward sailing. Very small changes in the speed of the yacht are not perceptible to the helmsman but a falling off in speed is at once apparent on a sensitive speedometer. Usually there will be a reason for this: dying wind, sailing too close, change of sea pattern. The helmsman must understand what this is so that he can either correct or accept it. On the other hand there could be an increase in speed if the yacht is sailed too free and this could be just as much a warning. The speedometer on this point of sailing can give a calm assurance that there is consistency in the helmsmanship.

On any point of sailing, it must be remembered that instruments are only aids. Now this has been said before, but it needs illustrating. For instance, a speedometer should be instantly disregarded if the reading is suspect. It may have weed on the impeller. The point is that the helmsman knows the instrument is, as it were, following his actions. When it reacts, he is in tune with it: thus it aids his helmsmanship. This line of thought should apply to all electric aids to navigation. The opposite of this is to be hypnotized by a row of dials.

The *wind direction indicator* is to be seen aboard well-equipped racing yachts today. Some inshore classes have banned these devices, which are expensive, but offshore at night they are useful even when cruising and therefore within the spirit of ocean racing. The apparent wind is shown at an angle to the ship's head on a dial in front of the helmsman and there is often a fine scale to give the accuracy within one or two degrees. Helmsmen will develop their own techniques for using these. By day the presentation supplements the other indications of wind direction. An inexperienced helmsman will be immensely assisted. On taking over the helm, it speeds up those first few minutes of getting the feel of her, because to start with the wind angle can be kept at the same reading as the recent helmsman has found to be optimum. When sails are being changed or reefed and thus some of the normal indications are missing and there are distractions on deck, it enables a consistent course to the wind to be held.

At night the advantages are considerable for then the luff of the genoa and the racing flag cannot be seen. Emerging on deck it take time to get used to the feel of steering and the indicator is an immediate check. In bad weather with spray flying and steering difficult it is again very helpful and on going about the new course can be picked up quickly.

Wind speed is the easiest instrument to understand, being shown on a dial in knots, and operated by a masthead anemometer. It is, of course, the apparent wind speed that is shown. It has various uses not all specially relevant to helmsmanship.

With all these instruments it is possible with the help of a specially made slide-rule type calculator to find the value of VMG. To do this, yacht speed, apparent wind angle and wind velocity are needed. Different wind angles can be steered to give the best theoretical VMG, but it requires the assistance of the skipper or navigator to undertake this: the helmsman should be concentrating on his own job.

Sail Trim   In considering the problem of the helmsman we have so far ignored sail trim, which is not just a matter of hardening everything in as much as possible! With the masthead rig it must be appreciated that the headsail is the most important sail, and it thus must be trimmed "first". It must be possible to winch the genoa in without undue strain and disorganization in the cockpit. As the breeze freshens a well-cut genoa will be sheeted just as flat as it will go. The cut of the sail will ensure that there is some desirable curve in it. The effect of a sail that is too full will be to cause undue heeling and lack of forward drive.

In lighter winds the opposite holds good and a sail that is over-flattened will lack any ability to keep the yacht moving. Sheet lead is very important in any wind and all yachts must have a complete choice of sheeting positions along a considerable length of track. Too often these are limited and if the genoa lead is not in the ideal position the rest of the effort that goes into setting it is wasted. The first crude check is that either the leech or foot is not unduly tight or, more noticeably, loose and shaking. If the leech appears to be shaking the lead must come forward and vice versa. With this settled, check that when beginning to luff the headsail begins to lift along its entire length or at least first near the centre. If it begins to break at top or bottom, the lead is still not right.

The further forward the lead is needed—for instance on a smaller jib with a shorter foot—the more inboard it will come. For this reason some yachts are laid out with tracks which go from the covering board and forward and inward towards the forestay.

One small piece of equipment which can prove irritating is the leech line. If tightened, leech curl can result, which is most undesirable as it prevents the wind leaving the sail cleanly. If the leech is flapping unduly a gentle tension can be taken up on the line, but this is a temporary measure and the sail really needs attention from a sailmaker.

With the genoa trimmed for windward work, the mainsail deserves attention and though less important in the masthead rig going to windward it has more variations in handling. Mainsail design and fittings are discussed later and the various adjustments depend on the equipment available (Fig. 5), but in any case the clew outhaul must be adjusted for the strength. Take up on it in heavy breezes to flatten the sail and bring the draught forward. If the draught or belly of the sail is allowed to remain it will edge aft and lose all effectiveness to windward. Luff tension must also be hardened for a fresh wind. If zippers are in use along the foot, it will be learnt by experience what strength of wind calls for these to be closed. The same applies to a Cunningham hole if used. A most important aspect of trimming the sail is to find the correct position on the track for the mainsheet slider. The general rule is to have it further out as the wind increases and at the same time harden down the sheet. The result of this is to tighten the mainsail with

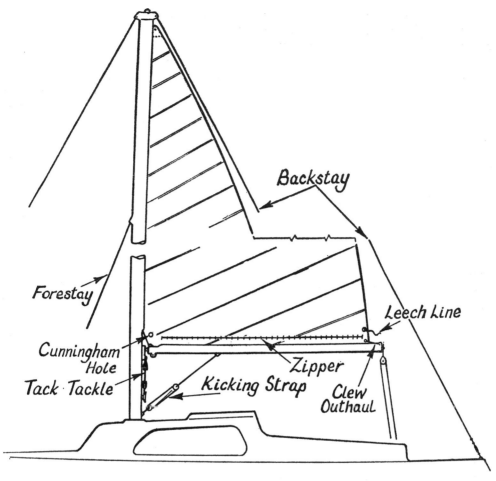

FIG. 5. *Eight aids to controlling the shape of the mainsail.*

minimum twist. To bring it in the centre line also hardens the leech unduly. However, it is important to experiment with the slider position and the mainsail tension, both of which vary with the boat and her mainsheet layout. In smaller boats the slider on the mainsheet track can be played in windward sailing, rather than the sheet itself.

A bending boom has the blocks so arranged that the curvature increases with the tension of the mainsheet. There may be more than one track. It is important to see that in light weather the boom returns to nearly a straight line to restore fullness to the mainsail. Pains should be taken to move the blocks so that the curvature is what is required.

One further adjustment should be made when going to windward. The backstay needs tightening in a fresh breeze to counteract the greater tension of the forestay caused by the masthead genoa and also to relieve to some extent the tension on the leech of the mainsail. It is not a question of just bending the mast, the value of which is dubious when the headsail is the important sail. Dinghies do this, but their rig is quite different. The mast will be bent, but the object is to bring the masthead a little aft.

Stiffness and heavy weather   As the wind increases so a yacht heels and this can have several results. There will be less sail area projected to the wind. In a way this is self-compensating for the increased wind velocity and pressure. (The pressure of the wind is proportional to the square of its velocity.) It means that the lee deck may frequently drag in the water presenting anything but a smooth surface—stanchion bases, tracks, foot rails and sheets. There will be an effect on balance causing a pull on the tiller in the form of weather helm. This is caused by the shape of the hull: most yachts being finer forward than aft tend to turn towards the direction from which they heel. Naturally, the helm applied to counteract this causes significant drag.

So heeling is undesirable, but the yacht must be driven at her maximum speed and as much sail as possible carried. Perhaps not "as much as possible", but as much as optimum. Before discussing this aspect, it will be seen that a stiff yacht will be at considerable advantage as soon as the breeze freshens. She can hang on to her canvas and drive to windward while others are reefing. Later we consider the ways to give a yacht this important quality of stiffness, but if she does start to put her rail in frequently the time has probably come to reduce canvas.

Actual length and displacement have a big effect on the power of a yacht, as this is often called. A larger yacht has the advantage in heavy weather. Sailing to windward in strong breezes is the most continuously punishing test an ocean racer has to face. Conditions are not pleasant. Spray will fly back into the sails and stream down to the deck in sheets. Frequently the crew in the cockpit will receive the same treatment. It is almost impossible, however clever the design, to prevent damp getting below; nor has foul weather clothing been developed that will keep inner garments dry in really bad conditions. This is when boats and crews who can stand this sort of treatment find themselves in the prize list.

Helmsmanship is not easy in such circumstances but a modern yacht will go to windward surprisingly well. Heading up to big seas can result in the yacht being nearly stopped, so it is better to sail the course to windward and let broken tops find their own way across the boat. It may pay to "fence" a particularly ugly looking one that looks as though it is going to break solid. However, at night it would not be seen, anyway. Short spells at the helm are preferable in heavy weather. At this stage much depends on the forethought that has been lavished on the strength and design of deck gear, and its ease of handling by the crew.

Balance and Trim   A yacht should be trimmed quite vertical athwartships, and it is worth checking in still water before racing. Trim fore and aft is a less easily decided matter and is another area where experiments will need to be made. A common fault in small yachts is for gear to accumulate in the after-part of the vessel, where it is ready to hand and, when racing, the majority of crew may be in the cockpit. Such factors tend to put the yacht down by the stern, adversely affecting performance. Being bow light to windward means slightly more windage in the wrong place and the excess buoyancy forward will be an additional cause of pitching. More important, in light to moderate weather the wetted surface will be increased as the sections are wider aft than forward. To avoid this situation the crew must be distributed over the length of the vessel (Fig. 6). For instance, with a crew of five, at least two of them should be on the weather deck or at the foot of the mast. When offshore and keeping watches, or in dirty weather, those not occupied will be better

1. *Shewolf*, a Half Ton Cup yacht designed by Sparkman and Stephens racing off La Rochelle. The author in the weather shrouds trims the double mitre cut spinnaker.

2. *Left:* Sailing to windward in the open sea. An Arpege class yacht in the Bay of Biscay.

3. *Below:* Heavily reefed yachts head out to sea in gale conditions at the start of a Royal Ocean Racing Club event.

4. The helmsman's concentration is of no avail due to lack of trim: note boot top below waterline aft. A Contessa class yacht.

5. Sailing to windward. The position of the crew is important in this yacht of 18 ft. 10 in. LWL. The mainsheet is at the end of the track. The other dimensions of this Emeraude class yacht designed by Dominique Presles are LOA 26 ft. 8 in., beam 8 ft. 7 in., displacement 1·77 tons.

6. The Australian Half Ton Yacht *September* designed by her owner Douglas Gilling reaching hard under spinnaker and using a bearing out spar.

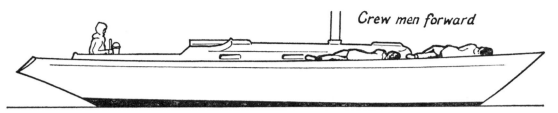

FIG. 6. *In light weather the weight of the crew must be in the correct place on an ocean racer's deck. Slightly more weight than usual forward will help in these conditions.*

below and they must be well forward, say just aft of the mast, and the accommodation must allow this.

There will be circumstances where other weight distribution is acceptable or desirable. Running hard in a short sea, it could be envisaged that the yacht trimmed down by the stern would be beneficial, reducing the tendency to roll and broach. Such use of weight in ocean racers depends on the individual boat, but the point is that experiments must be made. In exceptional cases the ballast keel may need its proportions altered to bring the ballast forward or aft. If so, there has been a design error and the alteration will need the advice of a yacht designer.

Trimming by the stern is sometimes recommended in elementary seamanship for eliminating weather helm, but is not desirable for reasons just explained and a racing yacht should balance or carry the slightest weather helm in a 10-knot breeze with biggest genoa. As the boat heels weather helm is liable to increase. It is then that it becomes advisable to balance it out. So reducing sail has a two-pronged effect: causing less angle of heel and so less helm, and also reducing this helm by redistributing the sail area.

Two aids in this business of keeping the yacht standing on her feet and driving to windward should be noted. Trapezes as commonly used on racing dinghies can be used to support several members of the crew out to windward. Their weight will be of increasing effect in the smaller boats. Many clubs ban this practice, such as the RORC whose rules state "no member of the crew may be stationed outboard of the life lines". But it is worth checking to see if trapezes are allowed, though under a recent IYRU rule this has to be specifically stated. It is not suggested that they should be used offshore for hour after hour but there might be a right moment, perhaps approaching the finish with seconds making a difference between success and failure in the race. Then one or two men on trapezes might add that extra power to make that difference. Many skippers will doubt that on their boat such measures will make any difference, taking into account the gear to be rigged to the mast, the interruption to other work on deck and the windage of the man outboard. There is a tendency for clubs to legislate rather hurriedly sometimes when such techniques first appear on ocean racers. Perhaps it would be better to allow new ideas of dubious value a free rein, either to die out of their own accord or develop into something more practical which cannot immediately be foreseen.

The other aid to windward ability which is seen from time to time is the trim tab. Explained crudely it is an additional narrow rudder on the after-edge of the keel with the main rudder being further aft on its own skeg, or independently hung. It can be used to set in a little weather helm on the keel and therefore increase lift to windward on each tack,

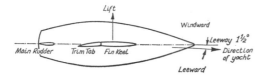

FIG. 7. *The use of a trim tab in sailing to windward. The resulting asymmetrical shape tends to lift the yacht to windward and can also relieve weather helm on the main rudder.*

while enabling the main rudder to have zero helm (Fig. 7). On some larger yachts it can be coupled to the main rudder control to give exceptional turning ability. Generally, for offshore racing it must be remembered that "extras" such as trapezes and trim tabs can be a distraction and there is considerable virtue in simplicity.

Stronger winds Once the yacht becomes hard pressed the decision has to be made to reduce canvas. Often this is left too late, but there must be some time lag for the skipper to decide whether the fresh breeze has come to stay and whether he is going to have to lose time (this is inevitable however well drilled the crew) in changing sail, so there is a natural reluctance to do so. Each yacht will have developed a sequence of sail reduction when going to windward. First of all, the sails must be flattened by those devices with which they are equipped, as already mentioned. Assuming a flat enough genoa is carried, the first reduction of sail will be to reef the mainsail. Now the yacht can continue to sail to windward under the headsail while the crew reefs the mainsail. If there is roller reefing, the main should be slacked well off and one man should wind the reefing handle while another eases away on the halyard. Care should be taken to avoid the mainsheet fouling whether on a claw ring or a swivel at the boom end. How to get a really smooth setting sail with roller reefing is a problem and it is not so easy to haul the leech aft in heavy weather with the boom eased off. The best advice is to watch the sail as it rolls down, and not be satisfied the first time if it is very uneven.

For slab reefing there is little option in the amount to be reefed: it will be a single or double reef. Reefing will take longer, but a slightly better looking sail may result; the other advantages of slab reefing concerns the gear which can be left permanently rigged on the boom.

Other rigs besides the masthead sloop will reduce accordingly. A yawl's mizzen will usually be handled before anything, while a cutter, which is rare now among small ocean racers, can change her genoa for two headsails before reefing the main.

How much mainsail should be reduced before changing to a smaller headsail? It is worth trying a double-slab reef or with roller reefing, one-third of the luff length reduction. The criterion though is the balance of the yacht. It depends on the characteristics of each yacht, but by reducing the main in this way the weather helm is eliminated and so the main can be further reefed until there is even a slight tendency to lee helm. At or just before this point is reached reductions should begin on the headsails—smaller genoas, followed perhaps by more mainsail reduction, and smaller jibs.

Finally, there may be set a storm jib by itself or perhaps with a trysail. The trysail should be sheeted independently of the main boom and on the quarter—the spinnaker sheet block anchorages should be strong enough. The mainsail track should be used, but there should also be eyes in the luff of the trysail to thread lacing in case the track has been damaged.

Gale conditions   The modern ocean racer has the reputation of being able to keep going to windward in a gale as long as the crew can stand it. Yachts of over 24 ft. can beat to windward under shortened canvas in winds of 35 knots (Force 7 to 8). The main punishment on a well-found boat will be on the crew. It will be difficult as mentioned to keep any clothing dry even under the best foul-weather suit and some water is bound to get below to the galley, chart table and accommodation. When off watch the motion will be violent and sleep impossible. With a mean wind of 40 knots (Force 8 to 9) in open water, few yachts under 24 ft. will make to windward at all. Such wind strengths are rare in most waters where an ocean racing season is in progress, but are never impossible. Many modern hulls will actually reach across the wind under bare poles, which is in effect lying a-hull with the helm slightly down being counteracted by the force of wind on the hull and mast. There is still no danger to the ocean racer in this wind strength or even higher, *provided* she has ample sea room and is not damaged. The first is more important, because the second can possibly be put right.

This question of sea room is one of the main dangers to a small yacht in a race. If threatened by bad weather on a lee shore when cruising, the best plan is to get up to windward so that when the 40-knot gale arrives there is acceptable room for drift. But, when racing, this course of action may not be acceptable tactics and there is never any certainty that the severe conditions will materialize. The ocean racer then is going to accept more risk than the cruiser, and this is an additional reason for windward ability, apart from purely racing considerations. Damage to gear, especially the rig, sails or steering can turn a difficult position into a dangerous one and this should be borne in mind when equipment is considered (see later chapters). Before a race the skipper looking at the course can see on it the likely difficult waters in the event of a severe gale from a certain direction. For instance, year after year, the Royal Ocean Racing Club, runs its Cowes to Dinard race across the English Channel and into the Gulf of St. Malo open to the full force of a north-westerly gale and littered with rocks and reefs. The course passes close to the Minquiers, an area of islets and rocks, through which navigation is impossible. Yet yachts who have had to seek assistance in these waters have been limited to those who have suffered damage, usually a dismasting or rudder failure.

Downwind in heavy weather, if the course of the race means the gale is aft, the considerations are little different from cruising boats. Most trouble will occur with carrying the spinnaker too long, as discussed later. Except on races of great length, the danger in the mind of the skipper concerns how long the gale will last. At its heaviest he may be reduced to running under bare pole. In these circumstances there is presumably a mark to leeward which the yacht is making for and this may have a lee shore behind it. He therefore hopes that before it is neared, the weather will have moderated enough at any rate to make to windward on rounding it. There is also the difficulty of finding it, depending whether it is a buoy or other seamark in the prevailing conditions. If at the end of the leeward leg, conditions are as bad or worse, then the situation is the same as envisaged with the windward sailing considered above and the course of action will depend, as always, on the state of crew and yacht, the geographical position and the actual weather pattern and prospects.

·3·

OFF THE WIND

A SIGH of relief goes up when, after a long period close-hauled, a mark is rounded and the sheets can be eased. The yacht comes away from the acute angle of heel, the forward motion becomes more effortless and the desired course can be sailed in a straight line once more. And the crew can relax—or can they? The answer is: certainly not; for, off the wind, the concentration of helmsman and routine of the crew is as important as when close-hauled. Many of the principles from the previous chapter where the yacht was hard on the wind apply. Here all other points of sailing are considered.

The present-day ocean racing rig is influenced by two main points of sailing: close-hauled and sailing under spinnaker. As soon as the wind is no longer near the close-hauled position, the question will be: "When can the spinnaker be set?" For the spinnaker will provide an immense increase in sail area and even with the genoa lowered, it will mean around 75 per cent more sail in a masthead sloop. The tendency will be to set the spinnaker whenever possible: it follows that the attempt is made to make spinnakers suitable for reaching and gear must be provided to handle the sail when it is set shy in this way.

But it will not always be possible to set the spinnaker. The problem is looked at again later, but the consideration may arise whether to run off enough to set the spinnaker and gain extra speed. This is very much a matter of tactics, because it is seldom that the time spent in sailing a longer course even under spinnaker will be shorter than on the direct route. In fresh winds the difference is small enough to rule out this line of thought, but it is a possibility in light weather (Fig. 8). Assuming we cannot set the spinnaker there are plenty of other things to do when the yacht is close fetching, close reaching or reaching.

Reaching sails   More sail area can be carried than when close-hauled in an equivalent wind and a problem is posed in fresh conditions, if the wind frees slightly from close-

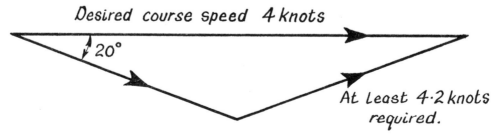

FIG. 8. *If making 4 knots it could pay to sail off 20 degrees if this resulted in an increase of speed of over 0·2 knots.*

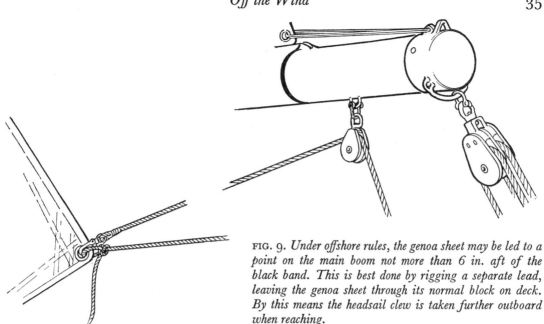

FIG. 9. *Under offshore rules, the genoa sheet may be led to a point on the main boom not more than 6 in. aft of the black band. This is best done by rigging a separate lead, leaving the genoa sheet through its normal block on deck. By this means the headsail clew is taken further outboard when reaching.*

hauled allowing the sheets to be started. Should a bigger headsail be set and, if it is, will the wind head again and make it unsuitable? This sort of problem in sail carrying continually crops up in ocean racing and does emphasize the usefulness of a yacht which is not too sensitive to her canvas—stiff, in fact.

Given the right area of canvas, what is the right sail? In North America, reaching sails are popular, but experience in Europe tends to confirm that they are seldom of use and the appropriate genoa is more useful. A reacher is cut rather higher in the foot and a low-cut genoa can scoop up enough water to burst itself. If the wind is so far forward that in light weather the spinnaker cannot be set, then the chances are that it will draw even further forward at times so a genoa is needed anyway. The genoa is an excellent reaching sail if certain things are done to it. The sheet lead can come aft along the track, the broader the point of sailing the further aft the block. If the weather is light, a special light-weather sheet should be rigged in Ulstron. This is not so necessary close-hauled where the clew is close to the block. On some sails the leech line can be taken up a little: if this is needed excessively it means that the block may have been moved too far aft or the sail is out of shape.

Ocean racing rules allow the genoa sheet to be led to the end of the main boom (not more than 3 in. aft of the black band without penalty under the IOR rule) and advantage can be taken of this, though it does not suit the modern low-cut genoa so well. The most satisfactory way may be to lead another line, perhaps the weather sheet in this way, leaving the existing genoa sheet in position (Fig. 9). Adjustment can then be made between the two.

A problem that occurs between the close-hauled and reaching position is getting the foot of the genoa over the life-line. The sheet lead in respect to the life-lines may be

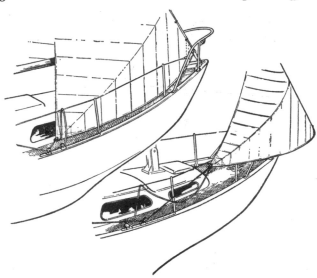

FIG. 10. *Changing the genoa from close-hauled to reaching trim is made easier by having different sliders and sheets. When headsail is eased away for a reach, the sheet for this point of sailing already lead outside rail is brought into use. Extra sheet winches are useful for this sort of thing.*

different and involve re-leading the sheet completely. It is the kind of thing so often over-looked at the design stage, yet very important in terms of time wasted and tiring work for the crew (Fig. 10). The important thing is to ensure that the clew is not pulled inboard by the sheet straining over the top life-line, but that the air can come off the leech cleanly.

In order to make these changes without difficulty, the genoa track should have two or three sliders. There may be more than one track available and this also facilitates accurate sheet leads. It will pay to mark the points which are found right for each headsail on the principal points of sailing.

Mainsails reaching and running   In the modern masthead sloop the mainsail is more important reaching than either close-hauled or running. Yachts which have tried to reduce rating by cutting away mainsail area, usually along the foot leaving a "ribbon" of a sail, are found to perform close-hauled nearly as efficiently as with the larger main. The owners of the yacht *Twister*, after a number of successful seasons, tried this. Their first race with the new cut-down mainsail involved a good proportion of reaching. The reduction in performance of the yacht was marked.

On a reach the proportion of work done by the main is high, but as the yacht comes further off the wind and the spinnaker is set, then even on a count of actual area the main reverts to a subsidiary role as the chute becomes the big driving force. So the mainsail needs to be given attention on a reach and the same applies to the mizzen on two-masted rigs. A kicking-strap, still infrequently seen on cruising yachts, is the most important piece of equipment on this point of sailing. It should have an ample purchase to operate without the assistance of having to push down the main boom. Cams on one of the blocks or a cleat on deck, the end being led from the block on the mast, assist in immediate control (Fig. 11).

A really tight kicking-strap will enable the mainsheet to be eased and the secret of sail trim when reaching is to ease the sails as far as possible. I can remember several instances where I have sailed clean past other ocean racers on a reach because their sails were pinned in: when running, the kicking-strap enables the mainsail to go further out before it touches the shrouds. It is assumed that modern yachts will have a kicking-strap permanently rigged—dinghy fashion. Hauling the boom down to the rail means adjustment every time the sheets are altered, which on a reach will be often.

In light weather it will be necessary to ease the kicking-strap, but mainly to correspond with easing of the halyard. It is not a method of putting curve into the sail. Paul Elvstrom has raised an interesting point that a tight kicking-strap on a close reach could cause additional weather helm as it "sheets in" the top of the sail. For ocean racing it seems to me that it would be better to reduce weather helm by other means, such as easing the main or even reefing.

One effect of the kicking-strap is not only to flatten the sail, but to alter the tension in the luff of the mainsail. Some device for forcing the gooseneck up or down can be useful, instead of only the more usual tack downhaul. The 1967 America Cup contenders had tackles for gooseneck downhauls and uphauls. A simple system of the same type would be useful on small ocean racers.

A mainsail on a run needs different adjustment from other points of sailing. The clew may be eased a bit to make it fuller and even the leach line brought in. Rolling may now become a problem and to prevent an involuntary gybe and to keep the main from spilling its wind, a main boom foreguy or "preventer" should be rigged in most weather offshore. It must be led from the end of the boom to as far forward as possible. Offshore yachts should have permanent provision for this by way of a snatch block and line taken aft to a cleat. A tackle should not be needed in small yachts because the mainsheet can be hauled in on its own tackle to tighten against the pull of the foreguy. If the latter can be left permanently on the boom when not in use, this will save having to haul in the mainsheet to rig it. When gybing it has to be brought back inboard but need not be disconnected from the boom end.

With a short, high boom in normal conditions, when there is no danger of the boom end being rolled into the sea, a short tackle from somewhere in the middle of the boom to the rail may be more convenient. It will be possible to lead a preventer or "go-fast" of this type to an eye on a stanchion base. When the boom is squared well off, the tackle will have to lead forward of the shrouds.

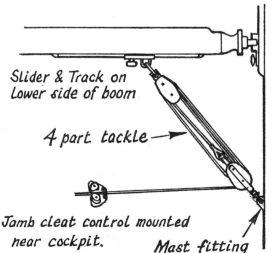

Slider & Track on Lower side of boom

4 part tackle →

Jamb cleat control mounted near cockpit.

Mast fitting

FIG. 11. *The kicking strap, an essential item, and its control.*

Trimming on a reach   The ocean racer will be on a compass course on a reach or going for a visual mark. Especially in light or moderate weather, all sheets must be constantly trimmed for maximum performance. In light weather the varying speed of the yacht means the apparent wind will alter direction every time the true wind alters its strength. Even offshore the genoa sheet should not be cleated, but turned round the winch and hand-held. The same goes for the mainsail where a jamb cleat can be of value. The sails must be eased in as they approach the point of luff flutter. But continual trimming in this way really pays. Depending on the number of crew, a man on the foredeck to "tell the genoa" will be useful.

A yawl is at her best on a reach when the sails do not interfere with each other and a mizzen staysail which is free under the rating rule can be set between the masts. The trouble with the yawl under 30 ft. offshore is that it requires most of the crew to man the sheets to obtain the best advantage, and this may not be possible. This is one reason the yawl rig is of doubtful advantage, though in larger yachts the factors are different.

Shortening sail off the wind   In strong winds if a yacht comes on to a free course after a close-hauled leg, the crew will be shaking out reefs. With roller reefing this is simple, provided the sail is kept off the shrouds. Pulling down a reef on a broad reach or when running means that the wind is of significant force to press the boat to such an extent on these points of sailing, that if rounding up to reef conditions will be quite bad.

With strong reefing gear, it will be possible to reef without rounding up, but this will also depend on whether slides or a groove is used on the luff and the smooth operation of the swivel or claw ring, if used. With slab reefing the boom will have to be brought inboard to reach the leech cringle, and tie down all the reef points.

The kicking-strap will need to be re-rigged when the sail is rolled. One system is to use a strip of canvas which holds into the rolled sail by friction. Unless this is very long, do not roll it in too early or it will all disappear! It can be adapted by means of snap shackles to go on to the normal kicking-strap tackle.

Setting the spinnaker   How close to the wind the spinnaker can be set in different wind strengths must be found for each yacht. With a modern ocean racer it is worth trying with the apparent wind up to 15 degrees ahead of the beam in light winds. (Some spinnakers will actually set with the boat hard on the wind, though they will not do any good.) If this is successful and the yacht's speed increases the apparent wind is going to move, say, 20 degrees ahead, and this must be appreciated before the spinnaker is hoisted.

Instruments are useful here, first to check the wind angle over a period prior to hoisting and to compare speed before and after hoisting. The spinnaker may fill with the wind forward of the beam and still not increase speed. Alternatively the helmsman may keep it filling by bearing away from the desired course. Apart from the time lost due to these factors, the actual hoisting and lowering operations are not conducive to maintained speed. So it is frequently a nice decision as to when to hoist a spinnaker.

All the spinnaker gear, sheets, foreguys and so on should be in position throughout a race and the halyard should be snapped on the pulpit, though it may be taken aft to the mast when close-hauled to save interfering with the genoa's clear air. On small ocean racers some form of turtle will always be used and the sail can be hoisted from the pulpit, or in the lee of the mainsail with spinnaker systems where the guy runs free through the end of the spinnaker boom.

Spinnaker trim The rules for trimming spinnakers are the same in offshore racers as in other types of yacht. Measurement rules limit the length of the spinnaker pole and height to which its heel may be raised on the mast. The pole must be at right angles to the wind, and its end should be in the same horizontal plane as the clew of the sail. The heel on the mast must be moved so that the pole is perpendicular to the mast to give maximum reach. With these matters looked after, the sheet should be trimmed by easing as much as possible. When the luff of the spinnaker collapses the sheet is hardened, but eased again as soon as possible. This technique has been mentioned for other sails off the wind and the spinnaker is treated in the same way.

Light weather difficulties But the spinnaker is not as simple as other sails, being held only at three corners, so collapse results if it is not kept full. In light weather it can fail to fill and droop round the forestay. Particularly bad conditions for the sail are heavy rain and next to no wind. One remedy is to station a man on the topping lift and as the clew begins to drop, the end of the pole should be lowered as well. This matches the rule of keeping the tack in the same plane as the clew and is often effective. Besides rigging a light weather sheet, I am sure that it does not always pay to have the largest spinnaker in light weather. The modern broad-shouldered sails are fine when there is a wind to fill them, but offshore, especially with a sloppy sea and little wind, they are liable to collapse. On *Summertime* we had a spinnaker not quite full size and rather meaner at the top than is usual, which was hoisted in these particular conditions.

Running by the lee should be avoided at any time, but in light weather it is particularly detrimental to speed. Maybe with a mark ahead, there is a temptation to hang on and fetch it, but I can remember doing just this on one occasion in the Round-the-Island race and boat after boat passed us. There is only one thing for it—get the crew moving and gybe her! Even on the correct gybe, a dead run may be a sluggish affair and it may be advisable to sharpen up 5 degrees or more to increase the speed. On a long leg this will involve tacking down wind, but more likely circumstances are the wind altering direction or hardening: then to have kept moving in the light air from astern, though eating out to weather a little, will have been sound sailing.

One further tip in a light air is to "over square" the pole 10 or 15 degrees, rather than keep it dead at right angles to the wind. This prevents the top part of the spinnaker from sagging forward away from the pole and helps it fill.

Heavy weather difficulties The spinnaker halyard should be provided with a winch to control it if it fills on the way up. If the spinnaker has a twist in it when hoisted this is usually removed by really hardening in the sheet and if necessary jerking it as well. Futile little tugs on the edge of the sail itself are a waste of time.

With the wind well aft, rolling becomes a problem, slowing the boat and being hard on the crew whether on deck or off watch below. Apart from edging closer to the wind, which may not be a desirable course, an attempt to reduce rolling can be made by easing the pole forward from the right angle position. An additional line or the lazy guy (if used) can be taken from the clew to a snatch block on the rail just forward of the mast, and then

D

lead aft where it is held by one of the crew, with the aid of a winch on larger boats. When rolling starts to become bad, haul in hard on this line. It stabilizes the spinnaker and has an immediate effect on the yacht. By using this method rather than taking the whole sheet forward, the lead of the sheet is unimpaired when the downward force is no longer required. The sheet can be taken forward from its usual position on the quarter and sheeted near the genoa track amidships, but the strain can carry away the normal genoa block, so haul it down a separate line using a snatch block.

When anything other than running dead in strong winds, broaching can develop. This is more marked in these days of large foretriangles. Early response with the tiller is the cure, and to get out of the broach may entail letting off the sheet: it should be coiled ready to run from the cockpit. When the situation really gets out of hand and the yacht is broaching frequently, it is unlikely she will be sailing her optimum along the course. A small heavy weather spinnaker could then be very useful.

In these conditions spinnakers are going to get torn, pulling out clews and so on. For this reason if only one spinnaker is carried on a long race, the yacht might be at a disadvantage when more moderate weather returns, having earlier taken in a torn spinnaker in a blow. Repairs on board may be possible but take time.

Offshore yachts should have more hefty spinnaker poles than inshore craft, but even so poles can be broken if allowed to press against the forestay. This especially applies if a "penalty" pole (i.e. a pole longer than the base of the foretriangle) is carried. To help withstand compression on the spar in heavy weather, lower the inboard end to bring it into the same plane as the guy: this will ease the loads at the end of the pole, where the topping lift is pulling against a downward component from the spinnaker guy.

Auxiliary sails   Under the spinnaker there is a big empty space and the usual technique is to fill this with the spinnaker staysail—"save-all" or "sneaker". It is best set abaft the forestay tacked down to weather; on one system it is on its own halyard and, of course, not hanked on to a stay. It is of little use for a dead run, when it is best cleared away in case of a gybe. The size, especially length of luff, is limited by the rating rule. On smaller boats it is simpler to use the normal genoa halyard, and if a spinnaker staysail is not carried, a short hoist genoa may be enlisted for the purpose.

Some skippers seem adept at carrying the full genoa with the spinnaker very frequently, but it is not easy to stop the sails spoiling the set of each other. On *Sunmaid V* a speciality was made of this, but Owen Parker, a spinnaker trimmer of high reputation, estimates that the point of sailing where this never pays is with the wind exactly abeam. On a close or broad reach it can be done, and the technique is to *ease* the genoa when it adversely affects the spinnaker. The spinnaker should be eased as much as possible in the usual way. Every time the genoa has to be sheeted in, it must be eased away again as soon as possible. If this can be made to work, it is certainly a way of piling on sail area.

Spinnaker aids   It is useful to summarize the various equipment which can be used to aid spinnaker work.

(i) *Pulpit boom rests*. These are designed into the pulpit and the distances to the mast are critical. They are particularly useful with a double pole gybe. Care must be taken to ensure that they do not contravene life-line regulations.

FIG. 12. *Suitable design for a spinnaker guy bearing out spar. Piston fitting clips to side of mast, guy passes over sheave and pole has tangs for its own topping lift and downhaul.*

(ii) *Bearing-out spar or jockey pole* (Fig. 12). This can be snapped on the weather side of the mast and out by the shrouds to hold the spinnaker guy off them and the life-lines. Because of the control it gives in winching back the pole off the forestay it is recommended. It is easy to stow away and can be simply rigged with a down-haul to the rail.

(iii) *Spinnaker net.* Some form of device must be used to stop a wrap up. Going aloft on a dark night to unshackle the top of the spinnaker in order to unwind it from the forestay is not recommended! Many cruising boats now have lines which drop down the forestay when the headsail is lowered, but their permanent position near the masthead may not be acceptable on grounds of windage. Spinnaker nets them-selves are unpopular because it is difficult to stow them without a tangle, but different coloured tapes and some special stowage arrangement can assist. With an inner forestay a "Hawe" line was used on *Summertime* and is simple and most effective. The windage of a single thin line down the mast is acceptable (Fig. 13). With these last two devices watch the lead of the spinnaker boom topping lift.

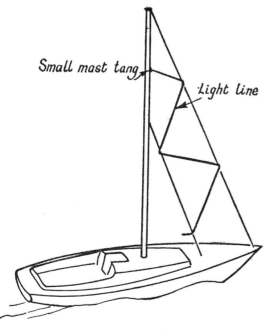

Small mast tang

Light line

FIG. 13. *An effective aid to prevention of spinnaker wrap. The Hawe line is normally kept close to the mast, but when in use is passed round the inner and outer forestays several times. A very thin synthetic line is sufficient: it is not possible without an inner forestay.*

(iv) *Other aids*, which are almost standard today, are spinnakers permanently folded and packed in turtles ready to hoist, top hinging snap shackles for sheets, but not for halyards, snatch blocks in preference to other types wherever used, for easy releading of sheets.

Spinnakers are hard on all their gear and for offshore use it must be strong. Smaller yachts are frequently seen with fittings which cannot take the loads. The quarter-block anchorages for the sheet and guy should be large and well fastened and the eyes on mast sliders must be heavy or a cone-type fitting used instead.

Single or twin poles   The detail of spinnaker gear, a favourite area for continual improvement by manufacturers, is looked at later, but the offshore man can really only decide for himself what system he can use by experience. Remember the boat may be bouncing about, rolling or tending to broach when the spinnaker is being handled and whatever system is used it must cope with all these unnerving conditions.

The sailing dinghy system of unclipping the spinnaker pole from the mast and on to the clew and then removing the other end from the tack and snapping it back on the mast is a non-starter offshore! It might be permissible in the smallest JOG boats where J (i.e. the length of the pole) is 7ft. or less, but even here it relies on the balance and manual ability of a man on the foredeck.

So single-pole systems offshore involve dipping the pole under the forestay while leaving one end attached to the mast. This will not be possible on a cutter or a yacht with an inner forestay. A spinnaker net or a headsail set under the spinnaker will also interfere with this system. Double poles mean more gear but since one pole is not removed from the sail before the other is secured they mean that control is maintained over the spinnaker. It is in any case advisable to carry two poles in case of damage, and so there is no question of surplus weight.

Double pole system   The now well established double-pole system involves two sheets and two guys, the latter being made of wire; under about 27 ft. this is too elaborate and the layout can be simplified. *Sunmaid V*, the successful English yacht designed by Sparkman and Stephens to the One Ton Cup rule and particularly well known in her own sailing waters for spinnaker handling, used this method. When in use the wire guy runs through the trigger-sealed end of the pole while the rope sheet on the tack is idle. On the other corner of the spinnaker, the sheet is in use and the wire guy leads slackly to the foredeck, through the end of pole not in use, and back to the cockpit (Fig. 14a).

To gybe, the out of use pole is brought up on its topping lift and the tension taken up on its wire guy and eased on the sheet. At the original tack, the wire guy is eased and tension taken on the rope sheet and the old pole swung inboard, its end remaining threaded through the now slack wire (Fig. 14b).

To hand the spinnaker, the operative pole is brought near the forestay and by means of the topping lift lowered to within reach of a foredeck hand. One man is on the spinnaker halyard and one or more on the sheet. The foredeck hand releases the snap shackle at the tack and the spinnaker flies to leeward like a flag. It is hauled in rapidly under the main boom by means of the sheet and then by its edge. The usual technique is to get it down the main hatch and away from the cockpit and deck as soon as possible. This method of

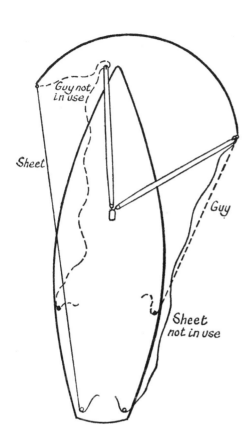

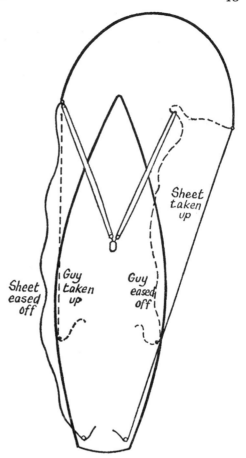

FIG. 14. (a) *Double pole gybe. Guy and sheet each side with guys led through end of pole.*

FIG. 14. (b) *In the act of gybing. Port hand pole being swung into use by its guy: starboard pole is brought inboard by foreguy (not shown).*

lowering holds valid for all systems with minor variations. Although the sail is said to fly away "like a flag", there is in fact considerable load on it as it flaps and the halyard should be kept turned on cleat or winch until the tension is manageable. Care should be taken not to gather in too much sail at the bottom, so causing it to fill again in the top half.

For the double-pole system just described the advantages and disadvantages can be summarized.

Advantages.   Minimum hands forward of mast when gybing. Very positive control throughout.

Disadvantages.   Two winches per side required. Weight of two lines and connecting snap shackles on clew in light weather. Maximum amount of gear and leads. With two lines per side it is difficult to dispense with the one not in use; with the sheet in use, the slack guy trails in the water, but if the slack is taken up it can itself prevent the sail from running out when the sheet is eased off quickly

When the guy is being taken up and the sheet eased away, it is usually not possible to see what is happening from the cockpit and the hands there are working blind, directed by the foredeck hand.

Sometimes the "new" sheet with the load on it blocks the path of the "dead" pole on its way down. This can be obviated by ensuring that the sheet when idle is *over* the pole; the topping lift tang brought further inboard on the pole can also contribute to this correct lead of the sheet. Wherever wire is mentioned, it is often preferable to use synthetic rope, for both sheets and guys.

Simplified double-pole system   These disadvantages are really telling for boats of about 30 ft. downwards and a simplified double-pole system is probably the best of all for offshore yachts from 25 ft. and up to 35 ft. The actual gear that is developed for it can make it easy or troublesome, but here the working only is mentioned. From a distance it resembles the method just described, but instead of wire guys, an outhaul is used on each pole. It is snapped to the sheet and leads along or inside the pole. Topping lift and foreguy are secured to the pole near its end (Fig. 15). When the spinnaker is set the outhaul of the pole in use is hauled taut and secured out through the pole near the mast to a cleat on the pole. The pole not in use remains on deck, its outhaul leads slackly out to the clew of the spinnaker.

To gybe, this pole is topped up and its outhaul tautened to bring it out to the clew. This will entail easing the spinnaker sheet. Now the spinnaker has two poles. Then the "old" pole has its outhaul eased away and it is lowered to the deck by using its topping lift and downhaul. If another gybe is not expected the lazy outhaul can be removed from the "new" clew.

Lowering sail is as in the previous system. When the tack is let go, the spinnaker boom remains near the forestay held by foreguy and topping lift, while the taut outhaul is continuing to hold the spinnaker guy, connected to it, at the end of the boom. This gear can be dismantled after the spinnaker is in and the yacht sailing again under genoa.

> Advantages. As in previous system, but only one pair of winches needed in cockpit.
> Disadvantages. It can be difficult to get sufficient manpower on the outhaul to take it up fully, especially when the pole is high up on the mast. If an internal outhaul is used with a simple cone end to the pole, then if one pole is damaged it is not easy to adapt to another gybing system.

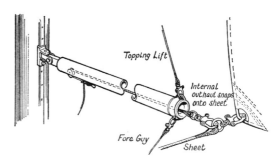

FIG. 15. *Double-pole spinnaker system with internal outhaul in each pole. The sheet becomes the guy when the pole in use is hauled out to it.*

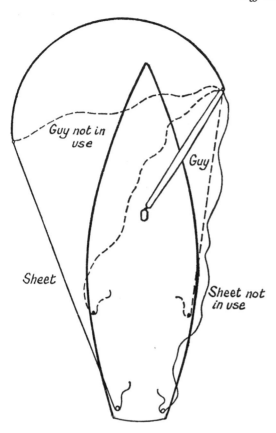

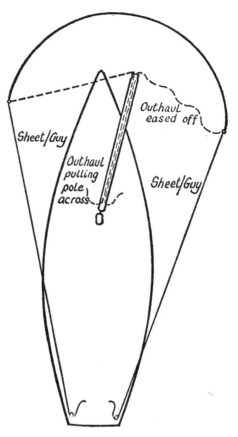

FIG. 16. *Single-pole system with sheet and guy on each side.*

Fig. 17. *Single-pole system with internal outhauls in spinnaker pole. Diagram shows pole being hauled across to port side.*

More simplification On some yachts the outhauls are not used, but ordinary trigger end poles are used double and simply snapped on to the "new" tack and released from the "old" one. It will be found if there is any weight in the wind that it will take two men to perform the task of getting the clew into the end of a pole. On smaller yachts it will obviously be easier, but these are the craft in which it is important to keep weight out of the ends. If you have a strong crew it may be worth trying this in the interests of simplicity. Large steel rings in the corners of the spinnaker will be helpful. It is not recommended in yachts over 23 ft.

Single pole system As mentioned, single-pole systems cannot be used where there is an inner forestay or other gear to prevent the pole being dipped across under the main forestay. In the larger yachts, as with the first double-pole system, each corner of the spinnaker has a wire guy and rope sheet. In the single-pole system both guys lead from aft and *both* run through smooth ends in the spinnaker pole. With the spinnaker set, there is a lazy guy and a lazy sheet (Fig. 16).

To gybe, the guy in use is slacked away and the pole lowered to dip under the forestay. Now the spinnaker is held by the two rope sheets. The "new" wire guy is tightened and the pole takes up to the "new" tack, as the sheet on the same corner is eased off.

A simplification of the same system is only to have one lazy line rigged at a time. As the pole is dipped under the forestay, a foredeck hand disconnects the old guy and substitutes the new one on which the pole is hauled out to the "new" tack.

Another variation of this takes a spinnaker outhaul from each of the bottom corners of the sail from where they lead into the mouth of a single pole. To describe a gybe is easy; lower the pole, ease away on the outhaul in use and take in on the other, as the pole dips under the forestay (Fig. 17). In all the above systems only one snap shackle should be attached to the sail and the outhaul to a ring near this snap shackle. Only in this way can the tack be instantly released.

In these operations teamwork is essential and a sequence has to be worked out among the crew of each yacht.

> Advantages. Completely spare pole can be carried. No hand need go forward of mast.
> Disadvantages. Spinnaker has no pole at all for a few moments. Heel of pole may have to be pushed up and then down again to enable it to dip.

A further single-pole system   This is a variation of the dip-pole system with no outhauls along the spinnaker pole, but one extra line is needed to gybe. It was used in *Sootica*, a 24 ft. WL boat which had a penalty spinnaker pole, one which was longer than the base of the foretriangle. When in operation the topping lift and foreguy are connected near the end of the pole in the usual way. The sheet is snapped on the clew, but the guy is snapped on the tack and then leads through the closed plunger at the end of the pole (Fig. 18).

To gybe, a lazy sheet has to be attached by hand to the clew and then hauled in to give slack on the "first" sheet, which is then taken in a bight on to the foredeck. The pole-end trigger is released and the pole dipped, using the topping lift. The trigger is then closed

FIG. 18. *Single-pole spinnaker system using guy threaded through end fitting with plunger.*

7 (a). Rolling on a dead run. This S31 class yacht begins a gentle roll. There is no main boom foreguy rigged. 7 (b). A heavy roll to windward causes the boom to fall across and nothing can be done to prevent a gybe. Note the striking wave at the stern.

7 (*c*). *Top left:* The result is a heavy broach, and the spinnaker trimmer (author) can do little but hold on. Note the height at which spinnaker sheet crosses the main shroud.

8. *Bottom left:* Spinnaker is brought in under the main boom on board an S & S 34. A moulded in instrument panel is over the hatch box.

9. *Right:* Spinnaker anti-fouling device. When the headsail is hoisted the lines are taken up with it.

10. *Below:* Where tactics count: approaching a mark of the course after several days at sea. The Fastnet Rock.

11. A compass mounted on the coachroof with an effective guard over it.

12. The Davis rangefinder.

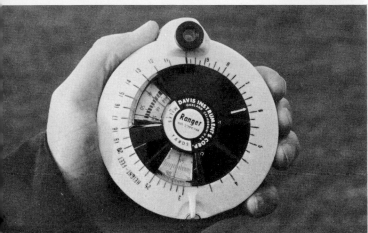

13. *Below:* Navigating with all instruments easily to hand and the data pinned round the chart table. Note athwartships book case.

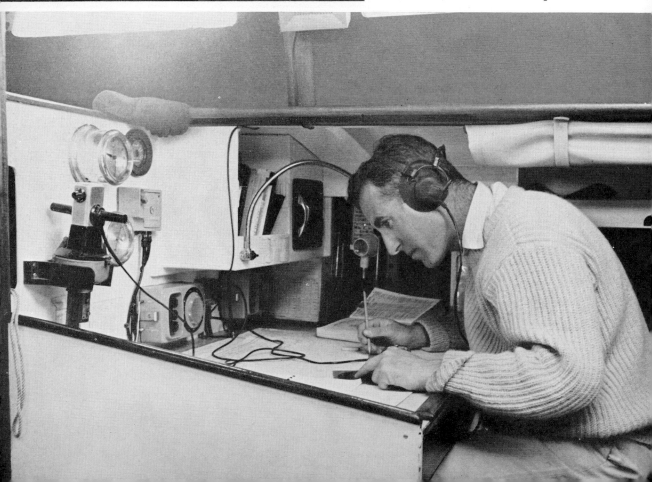

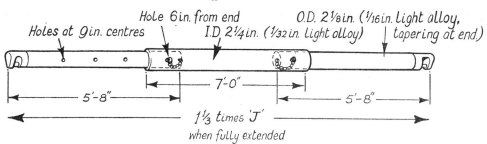

FIG. 19. *Telescopic pole for booming out genoas and jibs. It can be kept ready on deck or stowed below in three sections.*

over the bight of the sheet (the new guy) and the pole hoisted. Ease the lazy sheet and take in on the new guy, and the sail is now filling on the new gybe.

To hand the spinnaker, the guy is checked to see there are no kinks nor stopper in the end and it is made free for running. The guy is released and runs through the end of the spinnaker pole and the sheet is gathered in, while the halyard is eased away.

> Advantages. Lowering does not require anyone forward of the mast. No elaborate gear on pole. Sail can be hoisted in lee of mainsail and then pulled by the guy on to pole as required.
>
> Disadvantages. It may be difficult to snap on lazy guy and an additional winch or other means could be needed to get enough tension on it.

Light-weather sheet   Terylene is best for spinnaker sheets, but its weight, and especially the weight of snap shackles and rings, will pull down the clew in light airs when it is hard to keep the spinnaker drawing. A light-weather sheet of Ulstron or similar light-weight synthetic cordage should be available. Remove the snap shackle in the clew with the standard sheet and any lazy lines, and tie in the light-weather sheet. Problems can arise as the wind freshens and perhaps a gybe then becomes necessary and it is found that the gear needed for gybing is not connected. So the light sheet should always come off as soon as it is no longer required.

For maximum effectiveness the corners of spinnakers should not be fitted with heavy rings, but only a clew fitting to take one snap shackle. It is not necessary to have a light-weather spinnaker guy, because the weight of the gear shackled to the tack is taken by the boom supported by its topping lift.

Booming out a headsail   In heavy weather when the spinnaker has been damaged or conditions make it wise not to carry it, a genoa or jib can be boomed out to windward. Especially for yachts under 24 ft. travelling at their maximum speed this is more practical than a storm spinnaker. It is worth checking on IYRU rule 54 in full, but note "Any headsail may be attached to a spinnaker boom provided a spinnaker is not set". In larger boats this is sometimes difficult owing to the thrust on the pole, which if taken off the mast-fitting under load can push its way through the mainsail. A genoa is too long in the foot for it to set properly on a spinnaker pole of length J. The JOG, who feel small yachts may wish to have an alternative to a spinnaker in heavy weather, allow "a bearing out spar of any desired length" to boom out a headsail, when the spinnaker is not set. This pole should be telescopic, consisting of a centre alloy tube and two pieces with spinnaker end fittings (Fig. 19). It should extend to $1\frac{1}{3}$ times the base of the foretriangle. Yachts not under JOG rules will find that a working jib sets satisfactorily from the end of the spinnaker pole.

Where the spinnaker system has an outhaul on the pole, this is very useful to haul the pole end to the clew of the jib. When taking it in, by slacking off the outhaul, the heavy thrust on the pole can be eliminated before removing it from the mast. In any case even this apparently simple rig needs thought on the technique to be used (Fig. 20).

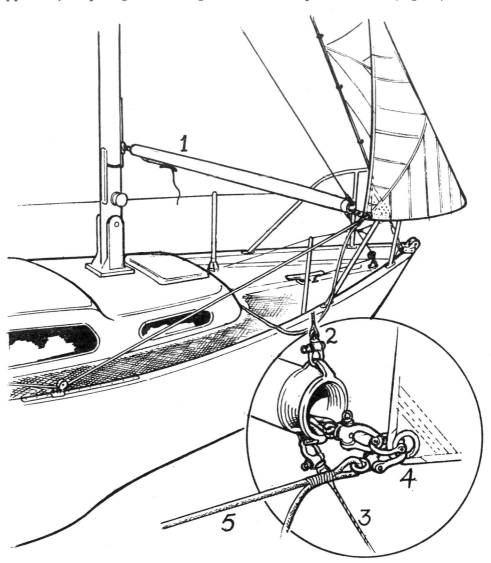

FIG. 20. *Booming out a jib in heavy weather may require care. If a pole with internal outhaul is available* (1) *the problem is simplified. It will still be necessary to use a topping lift* (2), *foreguy* (3) *and possibly an extra shackle in the clew* (4) *to take the normal spinnaker snap shackle. Normal jib sheet* (5) *is used.*

·4·

OFFSHORE TACTICS

In many offshore races the intervals between the yachts finishing is quite marked and the normal application of handicapping to give corrected times still fails to narrow many of the results. The leading boats are often only minutes or seconds apart but in a large fleet it is apparent that some yachts have been sailing quite "different races". What has happened is that they have used widely differing tactics, a number of which are afterwards discovered to have been mistaken. During an inshore race, say three times round a triangle, a move which has not succeeded on the first round is at once apparent and can be changed on a subsequent one, but offshore it is possible to make several moves which lose places, one after the other, with no means of discovering this until the moves of all yachts are compared some time later.

This question of analysing mistakes is worth getting into perspective if lessons are to be learned. (For "Race Analysis", see Chapter 21.) A skipper who loses a race or a place by a few minutes is tempted to ascribe this to a particular snarl-up or failure to steer the correct course for one reason or another for a short period. This is the "seconds count" theory, and while I am not suggesting for one moment that seconds should be wasted in racing, I do believe that, in the final analysis of the performance in the race, it is periods of, say, twenty or forty minutes that have been lost. Consider, for instance, running into a flat spot when approaching the finishing line: just check the clock over the period when the line is in sight until enough wind arrives to pull the yacht across. It is longer than you think. Failure to change to the correct amount of canvas, or a tack put in at the wrong moment—these are the incidents which can lose an equal number of minutes. Therefore, it is not possible to say that the race would have been won if a certain mistake had not been made. The rival's mistakes must also be discounted. In fact, the few minutes by which the yacht was beaten is the final arithmetical sum of the several time-consuming mistakes of both competitors. Our opponent wasted, say, 47 minutes and on our boat two or three incidents cost us an estimated 51 minutes: result, beaten by 4 minutes. The time question can be looked at another way, putting on the positive side, those moves which have saved time over the rest of the fleet. Of course, such an analysis can seldom be made, but the whole point is that offshore we are sailing against the clock and the final loss of a place is not attributable to the actual minutes which separate the boat ahead.

This is in contrast to inshore and dinghy sailing where in one-designs the actual time does not matter as long as the place ahead of the next man is retained. Offshore, other boats are in view from time to time. Often it is the same one or two throughout the race. Usually there is the nagging question as to where a third party is, just over the horizon perhaps, but exactly where? Other boats in view may indicate that you are doing well or badly in a general way, but you must know exactly who they are. I can recall a particular Class I boat, which must of course be nameless, which appeared to us (in a Class III) after twenty-four hours' sailing on at least two occasions. Less experienced members of the crew rejoiced that we were in with a Class I boat, but others knew that to sight this particular yacht meant very little as she was prone to trail her class.

The start   Tactics, then, are against the sea, the weather and the clock, and this is one of the fascinating aspects of ocean racing. You fight the sea to win the race. One exception to this is at the start when the yachts are for a short time close together and the circumstances are little different to inshore racing. Everyone likes to make a good start, though on the results of races over 40 miles there is little relation to the excellence of the start in the finishing order, though no doubt the well sailed yachts which come in early will also make a competent start. A few seconds lost do not matter, but the position of starting in relation to other yachts does. A considerable time can be wasted if the yacht is pinned to leeward of another boat or bunch of boats and this is a situation from which it is difficult to break free. A clear wind is therefore important and this means being well up on the line. The effect is thus the same as inshore racing for slightly different reasons.

Offshore races often begin on a run or reach, unlike inshore courses which are usually arranged to give a windward first leg. Especially on a reach there will be crowding at a weather mark and care should be taken to see that the anti-barging rule is not infringed (Fig. 21). If the weather mark is very crowded the best hope is to spot a gap in the fleet and make for that. To get a clear wind by this technique will require the yacht to be well up on the line as, if she lags, she will be blanketed by the body of the fleet to windward (Fig. 22).

These rules go by the board if there is a tidal differential along the line. With a foul tide and an onshore wind the stream is liable to be weaker near the shore and the leeward boats are at an advantage (Fig. 23). When the wind draws well aft, spinnakers will be hoisted at the gun and then the leeward end of the line has advantages. If the wind is light, it is possible to reach out slightly from the leeward end and increase speed, while those up

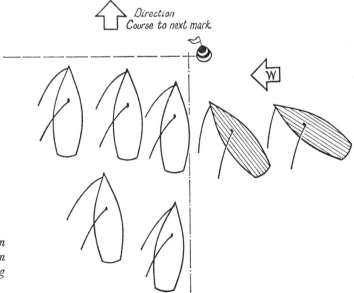

FIG. 21. *Reaching starts are likely in offshore races and care must be taken not to be shut out by the anti-barging rule* (as shaded boats).

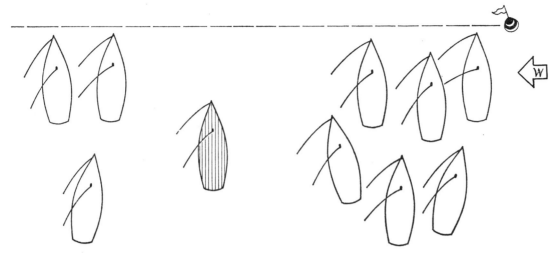

FIG. 22. *Finding a gap in the line on a reaching start is sound so long as the yacht is well up at gun fire. Here the shaded yacht is not far ahead enough to clear her wind.*

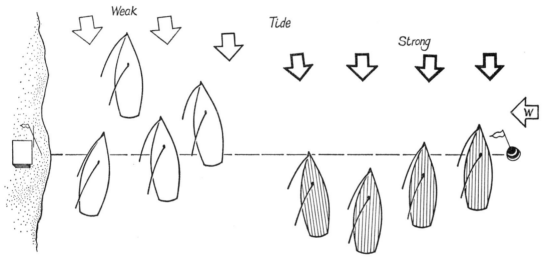

FIG. 23. *A reaching start with a foul tide and a line from the shore. Though the shaded yachts are to windward, they are not able to prevent the leeward boats getting ahead in the weaker tidal stream.*

to windward are liable to be sluggish. The leeward boat also has right of way and this is important under spinnaker where responding to a luff can cause difficulties. If there is a marked slack area near the shore when the start is of this type, the race committee should undoubtedly lay an inner distance mark to avoid trouble. At the beginning of the 1963 Fastnet race many of the boats tried to cheat the tide along the shore close to the starter's box in this way. In the resulting scrum there was a collision involving one of the boats in the ultimately victorious British Admiral's cup team. The result of the 605-mile race hung on the protest which ensued: a port and starboard tack dispute with the port tack boat claiming right of way having called for water close to the shore.

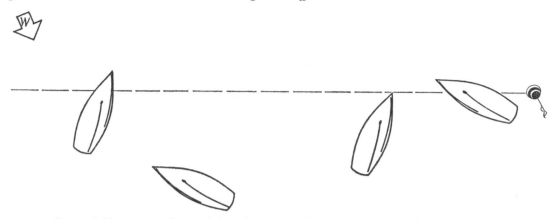

FIG. 24. *Port tack bias: port tack start is best for the mark in these conditions and the boat at the port end of the line has passed ahead of her near rival on starboard tack. The boat at the starboard end of the line will have to tack to clear the right of way starboard tack yacht.*

There have, in fact, been a number of collisions at the start of the Fastnet race, which is often begun under difficult conditions with strong winds against tidal streams. It is possible that the tension generated among crews at the start of an event of this nature has something to do with it. In this case an "unhurried" start without worrying about the actual seconds saved on the line would seem to be indicated.

Windward starts will more closely resemble inshore races and the advantages of the starboard tack can be worked out. One aspect that should be looked for is when the line is biased to give advantage to the port tack (Fig. 24). To take advantage of this the yacht should be well up on the line, otherwise she will be forced about by a starboard tack boat. When on the starboard tack shortly before the gun with a view to tacking just before crossing the line, the difficulty will lie in finding a place to tack in time: if it is left too late, it will mean the yacht is caught without way on when the gun goes (Fig. 25). This also emphasizes the point that displacement boats in general must start with plenty of way on. The point is made because of the practice with dinghies and light craft of remaining near the line with sails shaking until gunfire.

When there is an appreciable tidal stream at the start, there are always several boats who underestimate this. When the stream is foul, they are late for the gun and when it is fair they are at the line too soon. This tendency is accentuated in light weather. With the foul stream, you are unlikely to be over early. It is only necessary to bear away from the line and the yacht is soon carried back. The time taken to reach the line should be found and it will surprise by the number of minutes it takes to cover the ground. In practice, the yacht is carried away from the line when she is manoeuvring, perhaps adjusting sails or with the crew preoccupied with work on deck. If the helmsman is not alert he will suddenly look up to see that he has lost a lot of ground, and it is going to take some time to return to the proximity of the line. My own experience is that this happens with quite well-established skippers and is all too easily done.

Planning tactics   A study of the course well before the race can show various courses of action for likely circumstances. It is not possible to plan for every eventuality, but general

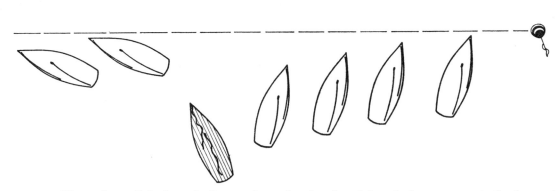

FIG. 25. *The yachts sailed along the line on the starboard tack and have broken away on to the favoured port tack. Two at the port end of the line are still on starboard tack. The shaded boat is tacking a few seconds before the gun, and will not be sailing fast at gun fire.*

ideas are useful for certain conditions. Once sailing, if the crew is tired or the skipper pre-occupied, there may be a reluctance to take the correct course of action. For instance, a simple case when tacking down a coast would be to make for the shore on the foul tide to avoid the worst of its strength. If this has been decided beforehand and unless there are some circumstances which make such a plan inadvisable, then the skipper is ready for this and it is one less decision to have to deal with at sea. Possibly it is best to look at this in a more general light. All the factors that can be foreseen are studied in charts and sailing directions, so that much of the work has been thought out ahead.

It should be pointed out that there is an element of luck in offshore sailing. The best boat does not always win, for sometimes there are dead patches in the wind that are quite haphazard or tidal predictions are not fulfilled to the advantage or disadvantage of individual yachts. This does not mean that calm areas cannot be avoided with skill or knowledge generally brought into play by some skippers to avoid what others would mistakenly write off as bad luck. But nevertheless there is this element of chance. The border line between chance and a hunch that pays off is narrow. In the 1967 Morgan Cup race there were variable winds on the leg from CH 1 buoy off Cherbourg to the Royal Sovereign lightship. After rounding the buoy many of the fleet had a foul tide and they duly laid on the port tack in the then moderate north-easterly wind. When the tide turned fair, boat after boat went about to stand across a fair tide, which would be the best manner to work such a situation. The Swiss One Ton yacht *Joran*, a Dick Carter design, however kept going on to the eastward. The boats that had turned north now ran into very calm weather from which they were unable to extricate themselves. *Joran* found the wind to the eastward where she had sailed, finally went about when she could lay the Royal Sovereign and got there hours before anyone else, winning the race. The skipper may have had his own reasons connected with the weather forecasts and other factors but the element of luck was demonstrated when in the One Ton Cup races later the same season and on the same leg, which was part of an offshore course, the same yacht tried similar tactics. This time there was no advantage and boats working up the eye of the wind towards the Royal Sovereign did better.

Weather　Many of the tactical decisions made depend on the expected change in the weather pattern. A close knowledge of meteorology as it affects yachts should be part of the equipment of all skippers. There is not space to cover the big subject of weather forecasting here, except to say that it should be given the fullest study. Before the race the latest information, including, if possible, a forecast chart, should be obtained. Reeds Nautical Almanac and similar publications contain a list of radio weather forecasts from a number of countries and languages and on different systems. These should be obtained three or four times a day and written down as they are heard. Suffice it to say that nothing like total reliance should be placed on any forecasts. They must only be regarded as a likely occurrence, always with the possibility of the unexpected happening. Therefore even if the tactics decided on are the correct ones for expected conditions, they may be thrown out by the wind failing to follow the change or maintain the strength or direction that was judged. If sailing in one region, it will be seen after some time which type of forecast is most reliable. The forecasts may be less reliable when the wind is from a certain direction. My own experience with the shipping forecasts for the British Isles and surrounding waters, is that they are most reliable after a certain weather pattern has set in, especially if it is from the Atlantic where there are weather ships and other reports for the forecasts to be based on. When the wind is easterly the forecast, particularly of wind strength, is very much less certain. The most difficult prediction of all seems to be a change in the weather type, for instance from a prevalent anti-cyclonic condition to a situation where depressions begin to affect the area. Much of this difficulty lies in the timing, because weather systems coming in from an ocean slow up at different rates as they approach a continent. A close watch on sky and barometer using your knowledge of weather becomes essential.

Navigation　Navigation and pilotage are dealt with in the next chapter. The relationship between these and tactics is close. Tactics assist navigation by knowing with accuracy where the yacht is at any moment, so that a correct tactical decision can be made. Frequent plotting is of service here. The rest of the crew or at least the person in charge of each watch should be briefed on the general plan for the next move so that he can take intelligent action on a change of conditions. Obviously the skipper will be consulted, but those on deck must know in what circumstances to alert him. In a small yacht there will be less difficulty in the skipper or navigator and crew working together in this way.

Tactics to windward　It will be found very useful to know through what angle the yacht tacks in various conditions of wind and tide. The important element in tactics to windward is to be on the correct tack at any given moment. When it is necessary to work out the alternatives, an accurate knowledge of the tacking angle is a great help. Frequent observation of the compass will give this information. With the modern ocean racer, it will seldom pay to free off in the hope of obtaining more speed. The yacht must be sailed "in the groove" and freeing off may even make the modern boat designed for windward work go slightly slower. Certainly the extra distance sailed will not be recovered due to speed.

　　　At any moment the yacht should be on the "best" tack, that is the tack which makes the least angle to the mark. In Fig. 26 when the yacht is at position A, tack Y is closer to the mark, the angle y being less than x. When position B is reached the option is open with

FIG. 26. (right). *Making up on the best tack to a mark.*

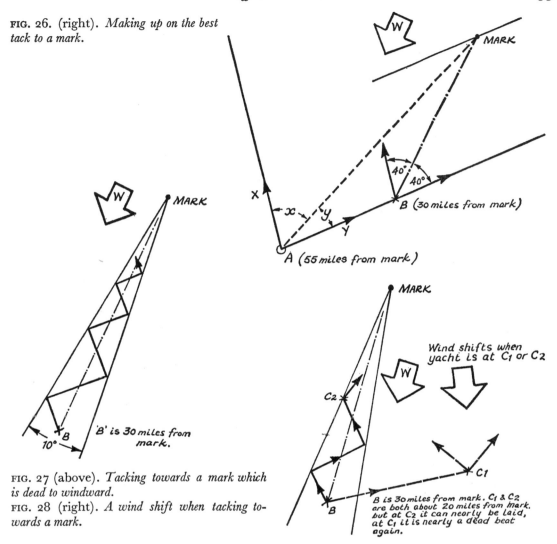

FIG. 27 (above). *Tacking towards a mark which is dead to windward.*
FIG. 28 (right). *A wind shift when tacking towards a mark.*

each tack being the same angle to the ideal course to the mark. Of course, once the yacht begins to sail along one of these tacks, it makes the alternative more favourable. So in practice, the technique is to work towards the mark in short tacks. By remaining in a 10-degree band (Fig. 27), there is an additional important advantage. In the event of a wind shift, the yacht is not so badly placed as she would be had the wind altered at the end of a long tack (Fig. 28). The key to windward tactics is related to this: responding and anticipating the change in direction of the wind.

The classic situation is when a frontal system passes through the race area causing at some stage a veer in the wind. This is not easy to predict because, as already remarked, the weather forecast is only a rough guide especially for a wind shift and even if a veer is expected the amount may be small. The RORC Cowes to Dinard race frequently gives this sort of situation. In Fig. 29 the beat from the Nab Tower to the Casquets begins with

E

a south-westerly with the prospect of a veering wind. The technique in such a situation is to make for where the wind is expected to come from and if the amount of the wind shift is uncertain, it is best to tack down the next arc of 10 degrees. When the wind alters it may well be possible to lay the course to the Casquets. On this particular case, the tides are strong off the Casquets and it frequently pays to go further to the west than into the next 10-degree arc for this reason. An area of strong tidal streams is better entered on the tack which clears the mark (Fig. 30) in preference to making short tacks in a strong foul current. This demonstrates that the theoretical way of approaching a mark on a beat to windward is immediately affected by the practical considerations, in this case a particularly strong tidal stream area.

When sailing in a wind which is slowly changing in direction, the skipper will have to watch the course continually, hoping to be able to tack at the optimum moment. In the 1967 Fastnet in *Summertime*, the W.N.W. wind tended to force yachts on the starboard tack further and further out into the Channel. We went with them. The classic Fastnet technique is to stay close to the English shore, but the forecast, which seemed worth giving a try, warned that the wind would *back*. During the night the W.N.W. wind began to fade and after some uncertain minutes returned as a light south-westerly. We were immediately able to go about and head on a course to clear Start Point. Boats that went close to Portland and into Lyme Bay had to beat out.

When the course can be laid   When the next mark can just be laid with the yacht close-hauled, there are few options. Apart from tidal considerations the yacht must be sailed on the one tack until the mark is reached. The tactics at any moment should be considered in relation to the route from where the yacht is at that instant, to the next mark. The course from the last mark is of no interest, and the tendency to think in terms of this should be avoided. If a mistake has been made or a course has been taken well away from the track between marks the problem should be looked at freshly, always assuming that the exact position is known (a navigational function.)

To return to the case of just laying the mark, the problem arises when the wind frees slightly, allowing sheets to be eased. Should you keep "up to windward" before starting to ease sheets and sailing the direct course? The answer is almost always "yes", at least when the wind first shifts. First, the wind shift may be only temporary and it may return, enabling you merely just to lay the course again or even find yourself headed slightly. So it is best to make some ground to windward. Secondly, the wind may head again much later nearer the mark. Most marks are near a shore and are just in the place where the wind begins to alter its direction. Thirdly, if the yacht was just laying the course, the chance is that due to helmsmanship, possible leeway in bad weather or sheer optimism, the mark will not after all be laid on the tack. We have already pointed out that the modern yacht will not gain speed through the water for the first 5 degrees of bearing away from the close-hauled aspect. Naturally if the wind frees enough to become a close reach, the direct course to the mark should be taken and windward tactics no longer apply.

When beating in light weather that becomes fluky, try to stick to the principles mentioned above. In practice, it will be hard work, frequently tacking to lay the nearest tack to the mark. Remember that on the chart the ground covered is very little over, say, half an hour, and the tide may well have more influence on the yacht's position than anything else. The helmsman must be given a chance by the skipper, and if he is sailing

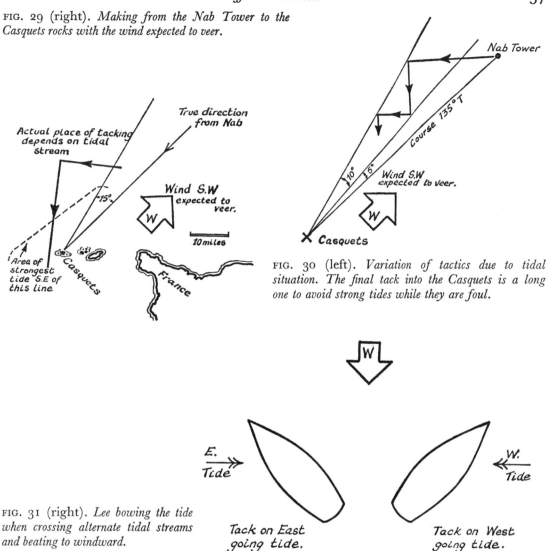

FIG. 29 (right). *Making from the Nab Tower to the Casquets rocks with the wind expected to veer.*

True direction from Nab

Actual place of tacking depends on tidal stream

Wind S.W expected to veer.

10 miles

Area of strongest tide S.E of this line

Casquets

France

Nab Tower

Course 135°T

Wind S.W expected to veer.

Casquets

FIG. 30 (left). *Variation of tactics due to tidal situation. The final tack into the Casquets is a long one to avoid strong tides while they are foul.*

E. Tide

W. Tide

FIG. 31 (right). *Lee bowing the tide when crossing alternate tidal streams and beating to windward.*

Tack on East going tide.

Tack on West going tide.

the wrong tack for a few minutes there is negligible diversion from the best course. It will be better to wait and see if the wind "has made up its mind". Tactics in this case may well revert to trying to find where the wind is and going there. This is something like the case of *Joran* mentioned earlier.

Tidal variations When beating to windward across the tide, the 10-degree rule should be modified in order to lee bow the tide (Fig. 31). The real result of this is to free the true wind, the velocity imparted to the yacht by the stream having the effect of a more favourable resultant wind. This was the reason that the majority of yachts in the *Joran* case went about when the tide turned to the east. Very often, however, the tide is directly with or against the wind, or very nearly so, and it is not to be considered in the decision as to when to tack. It may be simpler to think in terms of the yacht being "pushed up to windward" when the tide is anywhere on the lee bow. On the other hand this is no reason for pinching up to get the tide from the weather to the lee bow, in the hope that there will be an advantage in "push to windward". In fact the resultant wind is the same and the yacht is more likely to sail slower because she is being pinched. If the course with the yacht sailing well close-hauled is found to result in the tide fine on the lee bow, this is a good sign but it is not something that can be forced.

Tidal streams have the most effect on tactics when considered in relation to the configuration of the coast. Many offshore races have legs along or approaching coasts and the tide usually varies in strength both with its distance from the shore and its position along it. The general rules that the tide is slacker close to the shore and in bights rather than at headlands are well known. How are these to be used in tactics? When beating to windward along the shore, use can be made of the fact that the tide turns earlier along it. The last of a foul tide can be taken by standing out to sea where it turns last of all: this has to be weighed up against the possibility of being able to cheat it by going in really close. Which tactics are adopted will depend on the topography of the coast and the local streams as shown on chart and tidal atlas.

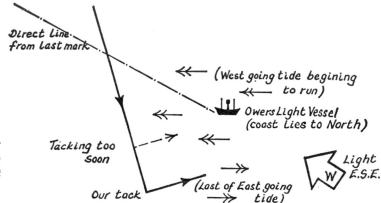

FIG. 32. *Tactics adopted near the Owers Lightship. How* Chieftain *made use of the last of the fair tide.*

In a JOG race in which the Owers Lightship was a turning mark, the fleet was beating down towards this mark in a light east-south-east breeze (Fig. 32). The tide was turning against the yachts. In the 21 ft. *Chieftain* we were laying down on the port tack in company with several other boats. In the haze the lightvessel seemed to be so far away, that the urge to go about became strong. Surely we had gone far enough out on this tack? The other yachts went about, but we held on out to sea to get the benefit of the very last trickle of the fair stream offshore. On the face of it we overstood and then finally went about on the starboard tack. As we neared the Owers, the west-going tide began to force us further to leeward, but we had enough in hand and rounded it. The other boats had reached this foul stream much earlier and were making frustrating tacks a mile or more from the mark.

The discussion about "just laying the mark" becomes more realistic when tidal streams are considered as well. This is more a matter of navigation but with a stream across the course one way or the other, the yacht will either have to remain hard on the wind to lay

it or will be freeing off to counteract the stream. However, with the navigational adjustment made, there will still be the tactical decision—if the final results is just close-hauled
—to be taken as already discussed for this case. In the realm of tactics, tides do sometimes
receive overriding consideration regardless of wind and this is wrong. In the case of neap
tides, or where they are weak in the area anyway, it may be necessary to go into a stronger
foul tide to find enough breeze. In the English Channel light east winds can often die at
night near the coast due to inversion effects and it would be better in such a case to go
out into a foul tide rather than hug the shore and lose the wind completely.

At the other end of the spectrum, in heavy weather the speed of yachts enables slightly
less emphasis on the tactical side of tides. In strong winds, the question of tide races and
areas of smoother water and thus faster speeds will intrude. Going to windward the
strongest areas of fair tide will create the most confused conditions of sea. With an ocean
racer which is good in rough weather every advantage can be taken of such conditions, a
factor to remember later in considering design.

Other than finding the best tack in windward work, tidal streams are more related
to the shore from the tactical viewpoint. Once well out at sea they can have little bearing
on the immediate move. It is in fact a mistake to throw away considered tactics for the

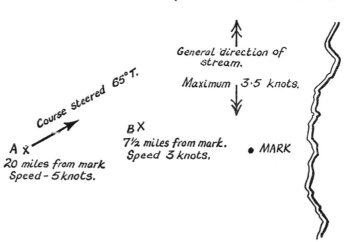

FIG. 33. *Calculations when approaching a mark with tides across the course. With the yacht at A, the average tidal stream over the next four hours (the estimated time to reach the mark) is 2 knots due S. and a course is set accordingly. Then at B the wind drops and yacht's speed becomes 3 knots, which means it will now take a further 2 hours 10 minutes to fetch the mark. A fresh tidal calculation has to be made. The total time from A will in fact be 4 hours 40 minutes. So ETA at the mark needs to be kept under review in these circumstances.*

purpose of finding a slightly favourable tidal situation many miles away. So though a
factor always in mind, there is often little that can be done about the stream in the open
sea. As the destination or a mark near the shore is approached the tidal phases have to be
watched closely. At some stage an alteration of course has to be made and the less this is
the smaller the distance sailed. Under sail the ETA at the mark is less and less accurate
the further from it, so with a cross-tide ahead this is a recurring problem (Fig. 33). The
problem is eased in fresh winds but becomes acute in light winds and strong tides.

With a fair wind With the wind anywhere from abeam to the quarter, the direct
course will be steered and there is less scope for tactics rather than navigation. A watch
should be kept in case the wind starts to creep round ahead, because if the tendency
continues it may pay to harden up a little, with a view to carrying the spinnaker on a
freer course before being forced to lower it and thus reduce speed. Generally, though, the
agreed course should be steered. If headed, you should lower the spinnaker and keep up

on the mark. How often one has seen yachts hanging on to their spinnakers and slowly edging to leeward of the fleet as a result.

When the wind is dead aft steering is a strain in fresh winds and sailing is slow in light winds. It seems unlikely that the helmsman will make good exactly on the mean course when this brings the wind dead aft. Different helmsmen will vary, but this is another case, in addition to close-hauled, where the navigator will want to know the actual course made good and on a suitable compass there will be no trouble about giving this. The skipper should be aware which side of the ideal the yacht is being taken and should gybe in good time. It often happens that there is a wind shift, which will decide this moment for him. On the same principle as in close-hauled work, do not get carried too far out one way. When the mark is about 10 degrees to leeward, it will be time to gybe.

With winds that are light, the question of tacking downwind arises. It is undoubtedly sound tactics because it increases the apparent wind, but also unfortunately the distance sailed. Tactics therefore depend on the amount which profits the yacht and this the navigator can be asked to plot, especially if a speedometer is carried. For instance, diverging from the correct course by 15 degrees the yacht sails four per cent more in distance. Each occasion has to be worked out for the particular yacht, wind, and courses attempted. Offshore conditions in winds under 8 knots can make it worth steering off as much as 35 degrees in some circumstances. This is when there is a sloppy sea, knocking what wind there is out of the sails. Modern spinnaker designs can alleviate the necessity of tacking downwind and this, coupled with the selection of the correct sail, makes this practice which, after all, means sailing more mileage, a little less frequent. Such a line of thought on sail design is worth pursuing. One should not accept certain well proved tactics as inevitable, if new ideas can enable a different sailing technique to be profitable.

Kedge anchor Used more of necessity than by tactical plan, the kedge is a way of sailing the boat over the tide when there is no wind and should be used without hesitation. In the absence of shore transits, it is difficult offshore to decide when the boat is no longer moving over the ground. A log line may be lowered if the depth is not too great, but usually it is a matter of the navigator calculating that the yacht's speed is less than the expected tide, and then checking this after the kedge has bitten. Enough kedge warp should be carried to anchor in any part of the tidal waters in which the yacht sails: even one inch (circ) is practicable, if used for kedging in calms for a 25 ft. ocean racer and some 40 fathoms of this can be kept on a reel. My experience is that a CQR anchor will hold with very little scope in calm conditions: obviously the strength of the tide and the nature of the sea bed are arbiters in how little scope can be given (Fig. 34). It is interesting to realize that a rather staid technique like kedging in deep water is the prerogative of the ocean racer, cruising boats invariably motoring or preferring to drift when out at sea.

Covering other yachts In handicap racing covering other yachts in the inshore racing manner is usually a mistake. Remember we are racing against the clock and the boat to beat is that which is just ahead of us on corrected time; a bigger boat out ahead or a smaller boat over the horizon astern. Such a boat may not be seen, but it is certainly not the boat alongside, unless her rating is very close. Then, yet there *still* may be another yacht out of sight who is more of a menace. So race against the clock. At the finish there will be even more of a desire to beat the next yacht on elapsed time and if battling for a prize for "first home" there may be something in this. The expression "line honours" is used outside England, but frankly seems to me less appropriate than the more prosaic "first to finish". One of the biggest yachts will be first home and the "honour" even amongst the several largest yachts in the race should surely still be to the best corrected time in that class. If a small yacht is first home then she is likely to win on corrected time anyway. Awards for first home tend to encourage size for its own sake, which seems the wrong avenue of development for offshore racers.

At the finish of a passage race on the west coast of Scotland at the port of Campbeltown, I was in a Folkboat (20 ft.) doing well enough to have a Pioneer (24 ft.) class yacht just astern of her. The finish was between the Davars Island lighthouse and the Otterad Rock buoy, and so intent were we on beating the larger yacht across the line that we at first failed to notice that one end of the line was closer to the course on which we were approaching. Tacking towards the line and covering our opponent was interesting sailing but we had been sailing all night and for all we knew a yacht with a closer rating was already tucked into Campbeltown Harbour. As it happened we were able to cross the line at the correct place and before our rival, whom we were bound to have beaten on corrected time.

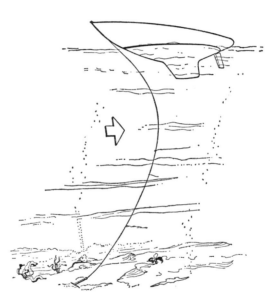

FIG. 34. *Kedging: a racing technique. Depending on the sea bed and strength of tidal stream, little scope is needed to hold a modern yacht in a calm.*

· 5 ·

NAVIGATION

SOUND tactics depend on accurate navigation which is attained by perseverance and experience in the peculiar conditions of navigating a sailing yacht offshore. Inshore yachtsmen do not realize what an important part navigation plays in the winning of ocean races and are surprised at the space in the ship given over to the navigator. Cruising yachts have to be properly navigated but it is more a question of safety than speed. They can arrange wider margins, for instance arriving up tide of the destination "just to be sure" and then conveniently sail down to it. The little extra time does not matter and the passage has been made in a seamanlike way. Ocean racing navigators, in their attempt to arrive spot on, can end up in a tight position. The winning yacht cannot afford to be other than exactly accurate: in practice there is often a small error, but the aim is to make it minimal.

Navigating offshore is a practical matter. No amount of working at charts on shore can be a substitute for experience at sea. Working conditions are often far from ideal and the whole plan for the navigational facilities on a small ocean racer must seek to alleviate the angle of heel, the inevitable dampness brought below and the restricted working space. Remember the race is for pleasure and it is certainly satisfying to sail across the open sea and watch the results of little pencil marks on a sheet of paper. But it is profoundly irritating if the same pencil disappears whenever the yacht heels, charts cannot be found from among others, books have to be moved on a particular tack—such things happen on some boats for want of planning for navigational needs. So when thinking of the facilities needed, imagine the scene in the early hours of the morning, pitch dark, only the red and green sidelights picking up streaks of white foam in their respective colours. An expected light has not appeared, but this could be due to bad visibility or some other factor. In any case the position must be plotted and checked and the navigator, in oilskins wet from a few minutes earlier on deck, works on the chart. Now the light available must be adequate, the necessary data to hand, the ability to work unhindered by the necessity to hang on or hold fast to the tools of the job.

Who is navigator?   With five in the crew, the combination of skipper and navigator is a good arrangement. With less than this number, the skipper will be taking a watch and it may be advisable for the mate of the other watch to take a share of the navigation, though one man must be responsible for co-ordinating it. With seven or more it will be possible to have a separate navigator, though this depends on personalities and if there is any question of other than close agreement on the way in which the race should be conducted between skipper and navigator, then the jobs are best combined. The asset of splitting the tasks lies in the fact that so often in a race "everything happens at once". For instance, the yacht rounds a mark and sail changes are needed at the same time as a reassessment of the course and a tactical decision. Especially on shorter races, the conduct of events appears as steady sailing interspersed with bouts of activity: for short periods there is more than enough to occupy everyone. So probably the skipper is the best person to do the navigation, with ideally one person in the crew backing him up for the odd check on work and a discussion of navigational problems which may occur. This person will be a suitable personality in the crew due to his experience at sea or temperament and such a system is preferable to a "free for all" discussion. More on the allocation of crew duties is given in the following chapter. Here we refer to the "navigator", whatever other duties he combines.

Navigator's duties   For a clear understanding of the facilities in the yachts which should be made available to the navigator, it is useful to be reminded of his duties. These are:

1. Knowing at any time where the yacht is by
   (a) keeping the dead reckoning from log, compass and reports of course steered and (b) fixing the position by various methods.
2. Piloting, when near the shore or in close waters, by eye and navigational aids, by day or night.
3. Obtaining weather forecasts, and other information to mariners, by radio receiver or from shore before the race.
4. Checking and maintaining all instruments on board both electronic and the more commonplace including clock, barometer and stopwatch.
5. Providing data for tactics including the start with its obstacles, currents, whether the line is angled etc.

Preparation   All these functions can be aided by as much preparation as possible before the start of the race. Books are heavy and, in the smaller boats, no more than are strictly required should be carried, but for a race of any length a proportion of the books held must be taken. The navigator will have to judge which of these to carry on any particular event.

Pilot Books. These are issued by the government authority; in Britain they are known as the Admiralty Pilots. There is useful information in them among much that is of less use. However, the relevant "pilot" must be on board for ultimate reference.

Yachtsmen's Pilots. There are an increasing number of these produced for all parts of the world where yachting is becoming popular. Their usual function is for cruising men and they are concerned primarily with entering harbours. However, there is very often information about local weather conditions, currents and coastal features of value to the ocean racer. In addition, if the coast is unknown to the navigator, they serve their intended purpose of assisting to enter harbour after the finish or in the event of being forced in elsewhere. Sometimes there are more than one published guide to an area and these contain conflicting information. Yachtsmen's guides get out of date and there is seldom any amendment system such as is found in government publications which employ full-time staff for this purpose.

Tide tables.   In tidal waters these are vital information and Admiralty tables are published for the world. They are comprehensive and include the Mediterranean tides, for instance, though most people would consider those negligible. In that region the prevailing currents are more important and changes in sea level are more likely to be due to other factors.

Lists of lights and radio signals. These are published by the governments concerned and for the whole world by the principal maritime nations. Obviously the only point in having these is if they are right up to date. Lights are given on Admiralty charts, the amount of detail depending on the scale. A list of radio stations for weather bulletins and beacons for radio navigation is a necessity. In Europe weather bulletins from various countries can be received in certain waters and navigators may develop a preference for the guesses of one or another! The sea areas used by different countries vary for the same place: for instance, whereas the British Meteorological office gives "Biscay" as one complete area, the Météorologie Nationale of France has it usefully divided into three, "Ouest Bretagne", "Nord Gasgogne" and "Sud Gasgogne". In contrast, the French have two English Channel areas and the British have three.

Nautical Almanacs. These refer to data on the heavenly bodies for celestial navigation and are essential if a sextant is being carried and used. Which are carried will depend on the method to be employed. When the race is out of sight of land for more than twenty-four hours and radio aids are not well placed then celestial methods can be valuable. However, as a practical point the books tend to be large and difficult to stow on a small ocean racer and the sextant itself is quite bulky when in its box and as a precision instrument has to be found proper stowage. The other type of nautical almanac is the coastal type such as Reeds for British and adjacent waters. This contains a mass of information, including that just mentioned, and the use of it can obviate having to carry several other volumes. Books of this type should be studied on shore before the season starts, not only to obtain general information and knowledge, but to see exactly what the book contains and therefore how it can help at sea.

Charts. There are charts of the world published by the Hydrographic offices of USA and Britain, but it is often useful to have the charts of the country in whose waters you are sailing, which give additional detail. Before the season or individual races a selection can be made with the aid of a chart index and lists of foreign charts obtained as necessary. Generally, the largest scale available should be taken for each area as well as those covering distances between marks of the course. When the scale is over one inch to the mile the chart becomes rather unwieldy in a small yacht and such big ones should be taken sparingly for special situations near marks or the finish of a race. I know this is contrary to standard advice but the practical navigator knows that too many charts can be a disadvantage when racing.

Charts vary in the amount of information they give, but it is the easiest way to obtain data rather than thumbing through books in a small yacht. The amount of tidal data, details of characteristics of lights and actual coastal details vary with the scale.

There are special charts in addition to the coastal type which can be useful. There are tidal charts for every hour of tide, notably the Admiralty Pocket Tidal Stream atlases. Such tidal information is more easily assimilated than the written word. A few charts provide the same kind of tidal reproduction as insets. There are charts of radio beacons and these are the best way of picking out those beacons which will be of most use to tune to, a glance at their position being made before obtaining more detail in the appropriate book (if not wholly given on the chart). There are charts of co-tidal lines from which it is possible to calculate height of tide in the open sea, which assists in using the depth sounder for navigation. Latticed charts for radio aids such as consol are obtainable and make work swifter than the use of non-graphic means.

R.O.R.C. CHANNEL RACE

START: FRI 1 AUGUST 1969 - SOUTHSEA

START - OWERS L.V.	120°	20 miles
OWERS - BASSURELLE L.V.	100°	64
BASURELLE - LE HAVRE L.V.	220°	77
LE HAVRE - NAB TOWER	342°	74
NAB - FINISH	320°	7
		242 miles

TIME OF START FOR CLASS III 1900 BST

			RANGE.
FRIDAY	HW PORTSMOUTH	1452	20·2
	HW DOVER	1423	
SAT		0250	19·3
		1506	
		0334	17·7
		1548	

TIDE AT START - EBB 2 KNOTS

TIDE TURNS	W. IN CHANNEL	0220	SAT.
" "	E. AT BASSURELLE	1000	
" "	W. OFF C. D'ANTIFER	1600	
" "	E. NORTH OF LE HAVRE	2200	
" "	W. IN CHANNEL	0330	SUN.
" "	E. IN CHANNEL	1000	

PRINCIPAL LIGHTS AND RADIO SIGNALS ON COURSE

OWERS L.V.	3 ev 20		
BEACHY HEAD	2 ev 20		
BASSURELLE L.V.	4 ev 15	· · — · — · ·	294.2
CAP D'ANTIFER	1 ev 20	— · ·	305.7
LE HAVRE L.V. (SUMMER BUOY)	2 ev 10	— · · · — [10 MILES ONLY]	296.5
ST CATHERINES PT.	1 ev 5	· — · · — —	291.9
NAB TOWER	1 ev 10	WHITE/RED · — · — · · · [FOG ONLY]	298.8
HORSE SAND FORT (FINISH)	2 ev 10		

When the particular publications needed on board have been sifted the information can be made even more readily available to extracting it and making notes for chart table use. A sheet with the data on it can be kept on the chart table. When the race is over about 200 miles the amount of information becomes large and it is better then to confine it to the start, but in shorter races a table can be made out with the following information:

1. Courses and distances between marks.
2. Time of start, state of tide or current at start.
3. Times of high water for likely duration of race at standard port or port of tidal atlas or chart reference.
4. Time tide turns at most likely places where yacht will be at the time of that change.
5. Description and lights of the turning marks.
6. Similar data for nearby important features and lights and for radio DF beacons.

An example of the way this is tabulated is shown in Fig. 35. The last two items are better not broadcast to the crew. It is sound practice when a light is sighted to ask the crew its characteristic. "What does the XYZ lightship show?" should be answered with "Just tell me the characteristic of the light you can see", otherwise there is a real risk identifying the light as the desired

FIG. 35. *Navigator's summary of data for a race.*

one by genuine wishful thinking. Confirmation should be made by the navigator with his stop-watch.

Basic equipment   In addition to the books and charts put aboard for the race, certain cards should be pinned round the chart table, for ready reference. If these are not already made of waterproof material they can be enclosed in transparent plastic. Waterproof paper is now available and is used by at least one printer who specializes in yachting programmes. It will stand continuous immersion and is a soft material not to be confused with paper that has been coated with a lacquer. Items suitable for displaying to the navigator are:

> Table of compass deviation;
> International code flags;
> Tide table of standard port;
> Chart of radio beacons (if available in small enough size).

Pencils, rubbers and dividers should be in a rack immediately to hand and arranged so they cannot fall out when the yacht heels. Three-sided pencils as sometimes issued by firms with their names along the side are the least likely to roll. Dividers should be of the single-handed variety and two sizes can well be carried. Rubbers should be soft. There should be spare rubbers and pencil sharpener available.

Charts are extremely accurate reproductions and often useful detail is difficult to see. A magnifying glass is needed for picking out items of detail on occasions. There are readily available chart magnifiers with a dry battery and illumination by torch bulb. These are the best sort to have and ensure that the chart can be read should the main lighting be dim. They also have the advantage that the instrument gives the correct magnification through its glass when it is placed flush on the chart, while an ordinary magnifier may be difficult to hold against the motion.

For plotting bearings, laying off a course and all chart work the parallel rule is the traditional instrument. The alternatives to this are the roller rule, chart protractor and set square or draughtsman's plotting arm. The latter is rather heavy and may be difficult to site in the chart area. Parallel and roller rules are difficult to use at an angle of heel and on a yacht's chart table and if they have slipped on transferring them across the chart from compass rose to track there is no means of checking except by repeating the process. It is to some extent a matter of personal preference but unless you have a lifelong familiarity with parallel rules, I would recommend the use of a chart protractor. Examples of these are the Brookes and Gatehouse "Hurst" and the Sestrel-Luard. The advantages of both these and similar types are:

1. The magnetic variation can be set into the protractor eliminating the need for mental arithmetic.
2. When the compass rose has been folded under the chart or is not available as on French charts.
3. The alignment of the bearing is checked simultaneously with the plot; no chance of undetected slipping.
4. The protractor arm enables straight lines to be drawn.
5. The instrument can be used quickly to see where a certain course (e.g. the alternative tack) would take you, without having to draw lines.

The Hurst has a grid which facilitates orientating it with a meridian or line of latitude. It also has a clamp to fix in the magnetic variation. The Sestrel shows the true and magnetic 360 degree scale and has a flexible arm which is useful to bend up, if the chart table is not quite large enough to accommodate its length. In both cases the first advantage above applies; the protractor is actually set up true with the chart but all readings are applied and taken off in magnetic.

The navigational set square has its adherents, though it has no more facilities than a protractor and has the disadvantage that only true bearings can be used. It is recommended for speed in laying off DF bearings. Using a meridian, the scale on the set square which is marked to 360 degrees is immediately orientated. It is then slid down the meridian until its hypotenuse cuts the DF beacon and the line of the hypotenuse drawn in. Obviously the set square must be large enough to cover the distance between available meridians and any DF beacon.

Other than chart work the basic instruments of navigation are the compass and log; elaborations of them will be dealt with later and in particular the electronic impeller log, which has less resistance than a towed log, combines as speedometer and can be read from the chart table. The mechanical log, usually Walkers, obviously has the slight advantage of reliability against any electrical device, but even in its modern form of the "Knotmaster" which has a waxed terylene line both thin and short, there will be slightly more resistance. To read a patent log of this type can be difficult in bad weather and I have known errors to occur when it is read in rain and spray by the light of a torch. Repeaters are available so that the reading can be made from a more protected position, but this involves the use of the ship's electric current. Streaming and handing the log is a job which the navigator can well do without. Having said this, it is often useful to carry a patent log when races are going to be over 250 miles. It can be streamed when a departure is made and used where dead reckoning becomes very important out of sight of land. A yacht under 24 ft. which does not normally enter races of this length, only needs a patent or electronic log, not both.

The compass on a small ocean racer deserves the most careful consideration right back to the design stage, when plans must be made to allow for its use when steering. Designers perhaps feel that owners have their own preferences while builders are too busy with the general construction, so enough thought is seldom devoted to this. Care on the installation of the compass will be appreciated whenever the yacht is sailed, if the following points are acted on:

1. Assuming in a small yacht that the standard compass and steering compass are the same thing, it should be found, as far as possible, a permanent site. It may be in yachts under 20 ft. that this is not possible. Then permanent mountings must be fixed and the compass kept in secure stowage below. For instance, there may be two mountings one on each side of the companionway, the use depending on which tack the yacht is sailing. However, it would really be better to have two permanent compasses in this case with horizontal viewing. The advantages of having the compass available in this way include the many instant checks that it can be used on: quick bearings of shore objects, tacking angle, wind direction for imminent tactics, pilotage checks when not actually sailing compass courses. A further advantage is its lighting system can be made more secure than if it is of portable type.

2. In siting the compass itself, obviously it must be clearly read by the helmsman in any possible steering position. Some common places to put the compass are:

(a) *In the bridge deck.* Here it will be vulnerable to crew moving in and out of the hatchway, but it should be secure under armoured glass. The trouble then is that the helmsman is looking downwards and not able to glance continually at sails, racing flag and sea.

(b) *In a pillar in the cockpit.* This is a central position but not possible on yachts under about 26 ft. The pillar is rather vulnerable and must be really strong with metal guards over the compass. It is likely to be more suitable for wheel steering, with which the structure may be combined.

(c) *In the bulkhead of the cabin.* Unless there are twin hatches which are seen on a few yachts allowing a solid member on the centreline, this means twin compasses. They will need to be of the horizontally read type. It is a secure position and lighting can be led from inside. They cannot be used for taking rough bearings but the real snag is that unless the cockpit has a crew position aft of the helmsman, the crew will block off the view of these during normal sailing.

(d) *The after part of the cockpit.* This may have to be resorted to in very small yachts, but has the same disadvantages as (a). In this case the compass will tend to be below the helmsman and to one side assuming that he steers from an offset position, be it windward or leeward.

(e) *On top of the coachroof.* How this is arranged depends on the height of the coachroof in relation to the eye of the helmsman. It may be possible to arrange a compass with a horizontal card and assuming a central hatch, a pair will again be needed. If this type cannot be seen from the helmsman's position then one with a horizontally viewed edge such as the Sestrel Moore will be needed. This can be on the box over the hatch and is very useful for taking bearings, being in fact fitted with a set of sighting wires. It is a little exposed and there must be protection for it. On steel yachts it may be essential in order to keep it clear of undue magnetic influence.

3. Only certain types of compass card are suitable for ocean racers. A number of excellent types are really for wheel houses and power craft and should be avoided. The grid type is easy to read, but on racing courses the occasions when the yacht remains on one course for a long period are less common than the times when small alterations are made. The important time for navigation is when beating to windward and unable to make the desired course. Then frequent "course steered" readings make the grid type undesirable. Even in the smallest boats the apparent card size should be $5\frac{1}{4}$ inches to get enough separation of the edge markings. A liquid filled bowl with spherical top is best so that it is unaffected by the angle of heel and there should be no limit to the roll and pitch angle which the compass will accept. Divisions on the card will depend on its size but should be in multiples of degrees, a 6 inch card would be in 5 degree divisions. The old point notation is superfluous. A black card with white lettering is the most comfortable for the eyes by day. By night this should be illuminated by a light sited *above* the card with red glass over the bulb, so the effect will be red lettering on a black background. The range of compasses made by Danforth White (USA) fulfils these requirements. Recommended specifications are in Fig. 36.

4. As the compass is the most important instrument in the yacht, it should be swung professionally. Once this has been done in a glass fibre or wooden yacht, it should then only be necessary to check from time to time against a known transit, when conveniently

FIG. 36. TABLE OF DANFORTH WHITE STEERING COMPASSES
FOR SMALL OCEAN RACERS
(Danforth, Portland, Maine, USA)

Under 20 ft. W.L.

Name	Card diam.	Mountings available
Lodestar	3¼ in.	Bracket
		Flush

Under 26 ft.

Corsair	4¼ in.	Bracket
		Flush
		Vertical
		Bridge Deck
		For steel yacht

Over 26 ft.

Constellation	5 in.	Bracket
		Double Bracket
		Flush vertical
		Flush
		Binnacles and for
		Wheel steering pedestals

FIG. 36. *All the above are spherical for unlimited roll and 40 degrees pitch. Black cards and white markings with red lighting above. Clear optical plastic domes. 5 degree markings. Temperature range – 50°F. to 150°F. (slightly less range for "Lodestar").*

available, for several headings of the yacht. In steel yachts such checks should be regular and recorded in a log kept for the purpose.

5. In siting lockers and stowage, care should be taken to obviate the possibility of metal objects being placed near the compass position. This may not be as plain as it seems if a small locker is situated on the opposite side of a bulkhead to the compass position. If there is a possibility of this due to existing design, a small notice on the edge of the shelf involved which states "Compass—no metal objects", can avoid an undetected deviation at a later date.

Compass repeaters are now available which can alleviate the siting problem: the repeaters themselves do not require the space insulation from other materials and instruments. They need some electrical current, with which there is always risk of failure and they can only be in addition to a visible steering compass. Some repeaters show the whole compass face, with a directional indicator revolving on it. This presentation can be mounted in a vertical plane and is uniquely useful in this way. Neco Marine Ltd., Cosham, England, specialize in this type of indicator for yachts. The Brookes and Gatehouse compass-course indicator shows a needle which is kept lined to a central point on the meter in a vertical plane. The course in this case is set on an electrically-linked master compass dial below decks. For steering when tired it is certainly simple, but is really a more elaborate application of the grid compass idea and has the usual disadvantages for sailing yachts. The equipment is not light or cheap. The cost of repeaters is rather better spent on one or more really high quality steering compasses and their mountings and protection.

Though it is useful to be able to take bearings with the steering compass, a hand-bearing compass is essential for coastal navigation and obtaining accurate bearings of shore objects. A really heavily damped compass is needed for this as the navigator will be attempting to keep the compass lined on the object despite the movement of the yacht. These have improved considerably in recent years with much steadier cards and the Sestrel handbearing compass with a Beta light is suitable on a small yacht. While a Beta light is not bright enough for a steering compass, it is preferable to a battery and bulb in a handbearing compass to which the eye is held close.

What should be carried as spares in the way of compasses? An ocean racer should always have at least two compasses on board. One of these can be the handbearing or may be on the DF set. For races over about 250 miles, a second steering compass that can be rigged in a reasonable position should be carried. An adaptor for steering by the handbearing compass should be considered. A proper tell-tale compass as used by ocean voyagers is too elaborate, but the spare compass or handbearing can be rigged near the chart table and properly lined up. The navigator can then check the course without going on deck and when the helmsman is not "trying specially hard".

Other instruments   Under the navigator's control come the barometer and clocks. A barograph will give the most useful indication for weather forecasting though a light-weight model is desirable. The barometer should be mounted near the chart table so that regular barometer readings will be recorded instead. A column of readings in the log book, ascending or descending, gives a vivid picture.

An eight-day clock visible from the hatch assists in changes of watches, log records and when working to a schedule in the few hours before a race starts. In these days most people carry waterproof watches but they are sometimes awkward to get at under oil-skins. An eight-day clock is mentioned so that there is no necessity to wind it up during a race of a few days. Small clocks run by dry batteries have the same advantage and are worth considering. The navigator should have an accurate waterproof watch checked against a radio time signal each day. For convenience, two stop-watches should be in the equipment, an ordinary one for timing lights and a yachting timer for the start of races. An ordinary sweep second-hand is not good enough for rapid reading in the heat of the starting manoeuvres.

Though not strictly a navigational instrument, some yachts carry clinometers to indicate the angle of heel. This is useful for decisions on sail changing. There are several other instruments in plastic of the moving graph type which may be carried. Some of these concern the height of tides, and others solve the standard problem of laying off for a known cross-current. Unless such instruments are found to save time in a race, they are better not collected. Most of the problems can be solved by reference to an almanac and some lines with the protractor which is already on the chart table. As a practical point, there is just not room for numerous items in front of the navigator.

A pair of binoculars should be under the control of the navigator and are best kept in a special shelf where they can be reached from the cockpit and then speedily transferred back into dry stowage after use. The seaman's favourite is the 7 × 50 glass which, with a 5 mm. object glass, gathers useful light at dusk or other conditions of poor light. Anything with a magnification of more than 7 will be too "jumpy" from the deck of a yacht. If a second pair of binoculars is carried, perhaps for the crew, reserving the others for the navigator, they can have a 30 mm. object glass which is ample on the sea for day use.

A signalling lamp can be bulky and it is worth looking round for something appropriate. Some years ago I managed to obtain an ex-RAF lightweight lamp, which was in thin aluminium. Probably it was not resistant to corrosion, but care was taken to keep it clear of sea water. Possibly still obtainable from Thomas Foulkes of London, it has a sight with twin grip and lever operated by finger. Power comes from the yacht's 12-volt circuit and it is ideal for signalling shore stations, other craft or even, with its 30-watt bulb, as an occasional steamer scarer.

The sextant comes under the category of an "other" instrument for small offshore yachts, again because of the difficulty of stowage and infrequency of use. These points really are valid: too easily the simple offshore racer can become cluttered with items which, however good individually, fill lockers and add weight and work. Whether a sextant is carried depends entirely on the nature of the course. For crossing the ocean it is essential and where races are out of sight of land for more than 150 miles it is desirable. In RORC courses, the Fastnet, Solent–Spain and Harwich to Baltic would come under this category. Some courses in parts of the world where there are a shortage of suitable radio beacons would be easier for the use of a sextant. It has uses in coastal navigation such as finding the distance off by a known height, but one feels that persons who recommend sextants in small yachts not in open water are rather like those army men who extol the advantages of barrack square drill; they are determined to have it and think out the arguments in its favour afterwards.

The problem of finding the distance off a single object without any other which will give a cross-bearing arises from time to time. The Davis Instrument Corporation of Oakland, California, makes a compact rangefinder which can be held inside the hand. To operate this the height of the object must be known, and this is given in pilot books and charts. By stacking the images in accordance with the instructions issued with the range finder, the actual distance off can be read on the dial. A secondary use is to focus the instrument on another yacht, which you are perhaps trying to overtake: set in it on the height of the top of her mast and it can be seen if she is pulling away or not.

Electronic Instruments   The development of easily read data produced from compact electronic instruments, has had a considerable influence on the precision of the sailing and navigation of yachts. There is no doubt that properly used they are of immense help, both in racing and generally navigating the yacht safely. But however useful, they will not win races for you and they remain *aids* to navigation only. For ocean racing it is possible to summarize the need for the electronic instruments in use today as follows:

RADIO RECEIVER	essential
RADIO TRANSMITTER	for emergency use only, inconvenient to carry
DEPTH SOUNDER	essential
SPEEDOMETER	essential

ELECTRONIC LOG	convenient in comparison with mechanical log
WIND DIRECTION AND SPEED	very useful, especially at night

Radio receiver. Apart from the requirement by some ocean race committees for the carrying of a receiver on board, these are now so compact in transistor versions that it would be disadvantageous not to be able at least to hear weather forecasts. However, with the receiver should be a DF aerial which is essential for successful navigation in ocean races. A set picking up the wave-bands of the forecasts available in the part of the world where the ocean race is held will be needed as well as the marine and aeronautical beacon band (160–415 kc/s). A great number of special receivers for yacht use are now available and continue to be introduced but the Homer receiver with Heron DF aerial is as good as any for a small ocean racer. It is manufactured by Brookes and Gatehouse Ltd., Lymington, England, whose other instruments I shall mention freely in this section. This is because they seem to be expressly designed for sailing yachts and have the following advantages over other types:

1 The presentation is suitable for yacht cockpits.
2 The instruments are of a shape which fits easily into the cramped conditions of a small yacht (e.g. no horizontal surface needed for mounting).
3 The external parts (aerials, transducers) appear to be most suitable for the needs of a racing yacht.
4 They are completely proof against bad weather.
5 They are of the very high quality needed for ocean racing.

Once the race has started, the navigator should use headphones for all reception so as not to disturb those off watch or to cut out the noise of others working when he is trying to listen. The Heron DF aerial has an integral compass and uses the directional property of a tuned ferrite rod. Except on steel yachts where the aerial has to be above deck, the compass and loop together can be used at the chart table. The old system of trying to orient the loop (or rod) to the ship's head and that in turn against the steering compass is not accurate.

The Heron is easily cradled in the hand and is read off looking down at the heavily damped compass. Alternatives are available, for instance, for mounting on the hand bearing compass and in small yachts—which perhaps are not often going far offshore, and will be taking visual bearings more than radio—this is more suitable. Larger yachts will carry both instruments. Like other forms of navigation, the key to success is to estimate the reliability of the radio bearing. This is done by the sharpness of the null point and checking on the nominal range of the DF station: near the maximum range reliability is affected. The navigator should be thinking ahead so that he does not suddenly want DF position lines at unfavourable times of day, such as dawn and dusk.

DF bearings are certainly not the answer to all the navigator's problems. Their performance varies immensely for reasons outside the control of the navigator. Sometimes these are because of the layout of the aerial at the DF station or the output of the station. An experiment conducted on a DF coastal station in Europe by a yachtsman found a slowly increasing error across a 100 degree sector. Remember that a yacht is low down on the water and my own experience is that even a little land close to the line of sight of a shore-based beacon or a beacon which is low on the water, such as a buoy, can give poor results, probably a vague null and a position line which is wrong. This is not always obvious and emphasizes the importance of all methods of navigation being used. Tiredness and ocean racing conditions generally are not conducive to accurate listening of an impersonal "whistle" and a visual meter which dips at the null point enables both hearing and vision senses to play their part. Even when the yacht is travelling fast there is nothing the navigator can do about the time taken for each DF station of a series to come up, he just has to wait. For this reason and when great accuracy is being worked, it is advisable to note the time that the station bearing was taken.

The Homer operates on dry hearing-aid batteries (mercury cells) as are most of the Brookes and Gatehouse instruments. This is advantageous keeping it clear of the electrical system of a small yacht, which is always vulnerable. The Model K Homer has the following wave-bands which are fully adequate for small ocean racers:

Long wave, 160–415 kc/s. This contains all the coastal radio beacons and consol and in Europe the 200 kc/s service of the BBC (Radio 2) which has regular shipping forecasts. In the Mediterranean Radio Monte-Carlo gives weather bulletins on 218 kc/s.

Medium wave, 600–1650 kc/s, which has the majority of the world's ordinary broadcast stations and therefore plenty of useful time signals as well as general broadcasting. Different countries will broadcast weather information on such frequencies, including a number of French regional stations with forecasts for certain stretches of the French coast. Bordeaux, for instance, on 1205 kc/s gives forecasts for the coast from the Loire to the Spanish frontier.

Marine R/T band, 1600–4150 kc/s, is of limited use on a receiver only, but there are coastal warnings and local forecasts broadcast on it. At least it completes the range of radio reception which is comprehensive despite such a physically compact set.

There are also numerous less expensive types of receiver with DF facilities and one of these sold at a much lower price than the Homer is the "Seafix" made by Electronic Laboratories Ltd., Ramsgate, England. The compass is similar to that on the Heron but in this instrument it is mounted on top of the receiver, the whole of which is held on a vertical grip on its base, in the hand. There are no other items except the wire terminating in the headset: power is again internal. Naturally the wave bands are limited; to long wave for the DF beacons and any long-wave broadcast stations available. Although the whole system is portable, a bracket is provided and the set can be chocked off near the chart table.

For ordinary broadcast reception, part of the rigging can be used as an aerial. The backstay is popular, but insulators need to be fitted and the lead in brought to above the lower insulator. Some thought may have to be given to this where the backstay is tensioned by a wheel or screw, but quite small nylon covered strong insulating links are available and there should be no problem about windage: the bulky type often seen on cruising yachts is not necessary. Where even this is not acceptable, the aerial can be taped up the backstay, being itself an insulated wire. There will be an electro-magnetic connection to the backstay, but even in wet weather the adverse effect of this will not worry the Homer. For less windage still, the aerial can be kept down to the hull, but it has to be accepted that reception will be inferior especially on the short wave-band and if there is a heavy swell causing screening. Obviously an internal aerial should be kept as high up in the boat as possible, for instance under the coachroof and laid in more than one direction. Even life-lines with suitable insulators have been pressed into service as an aerial in some yachts.

Depth sounder. This is an essential for racing as clearly the old lead and line (which should be carried as well) is too slow to use. Soundings are one of the basics of navigation and it is not necessary to enlarge on their use to the navigator in numerous different circumstances. The Hecta has a pointer and, as a repeater is available, there should be a dial at both the chart table and in the cockpit: both will be needed at various times. Two tranducers should be fitted so that the leeward one is effective when heeled and it is strongly recommended to fit a gravity type change-over switch for these so that the correct one is automatically brought into use. For a new boat, consult the manufacturers on the siting and type of transducer as various angles are available to suit the shape of the hull.

Speedometer. This too is essential for racing. The Brookes and Gatehouse one is the Hermes and the underwater unit can be removed from inside the hull if it becomes fouled with weed or damaged. It is quite easy to fit a spare impeller to this. The same underwater unit is used for the Harrier which is a log combined with the speedometer. Certainly this has the minimum drag and so is extremely popular, for this reason alone, in ocean racers. Even on short races it is highly useful navigationally to obtain a distance run and with Harrier this is always being clocked at the chart table. The reason that the impeller can be so small is that there are no mechanical connections under water. There is a small magnet in the impeller, which when it rotates induces a current in a coil in the part of the unit just inside the hull. Again, advice should be sought on siting and it may be necessary to have two units of which the leeward is used. However, if it can be got close to the centre line this will not be required: a position well forward is recommended. What is not always so easy is to obtain clearance inside for withdrawing the unit.

This is an instrument that requires preparation before the racing in the form of calibration over a measured mile and this is nearly as important as swinging the compass if the distance run depends on it. The flow of water past the point where the impeller is sited may not be the speed of the ship, for the flow may be retarded but it has been established that this is proportional for all speeds and a single adjustment is fully accurate. So the instrument has to be checked after it has been installed. The speedometer is certainly the instrument to watch in the cockpit when trimming sails, altering course or maintaining good helmsmanship. It is immediate evidence of the effect of any action by the crew.

Various settings can be put on the Harrier, including "calm" or "rough" and a scale differential. Normally it will be on "rough" and the 0–10 knot scale, but in quiet weather the sensitivity of "calm" and the enlargement to 0–5 knots may be used. Even more sensitivity can be obtained by inserting a Hound amplifier which magnifies a small part of the scale, but this will not often be used in offshore racing. It could be useful for very fine adjustments to sails and rig, but conditions are seldom constant enough to allow such readings to be taken.

Wind direction and speed. Though not strictly navigational, these instruments are uniform with those just described and, once installed, will be found to be in use much of the time. The Brookes and Gatehouse Hengist and Horsa are really on their own in this field, though there are some variations available, such as a circle of lights which show the wind angle. The wind speed is simply understood, being a straightforward reading: it will be

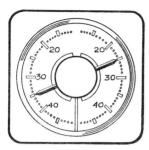 

Closehauled starboard tack, (25°
to apparent wind)

Pinching on port tack (18° to
apparent wind)

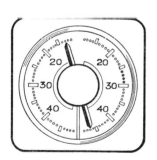 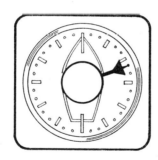

Reaching (70° to apparent wind).
Coarse scale only in use

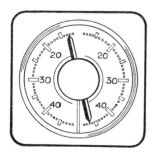 

Running, near a gybe starboard
tack. Coarse scale only in use

FIG. 37. *The fine and coarse dials of
the Brookes and Gatehouse wind direction indicator: what the helmsman
sees on various points of sailing.*

found extremely useful for deciding on sail changes, which are always difficult to judge. In time a wind of, say, 18 knots when close-hauled will scream for a different genoa. There will still be border line cases and exceptions, but this help to one's judgement will increase in value as the instrument becomes more familiar (Fig. 37).

The masthead unit is acceptable for racing, weighing $1\frac{1}{2}$ lb. and the mast cable is $\frac{1}{2}$ lb. for every ten feet. The unit is on a spar to clear the sails (which may have upward air currents) and the spinnaker block and head.

The displays which must be sited so that the helmsman can see them at all times, are the coarse and fine wind angle indicators, the wind speed and yacht's speed. When steering to windward, he can concentrate on the fine dial which can be read to one degree. Gradually he will get to know the angle of the apparent wind at which the boat is sailing best. At 50 degrees from the wind the fine dial comes against "stops" and the 360 degree scale is used. This is even easier to respond to, with an apparent wind "diagram" on the "boat" which always is heading to the top of the dial. It can be used close-hauled, when no fine dial is available, but apart from this it has the following uses:

1 When reaching, indication of wind shifts so that sails can be constantly trimmed.
2 Indication that wind has drawn far enough aft to be able to hoist spinnaker.
3 When running dead, a clear indication if there is any tendency to run by the lee—but be warned that the needle is damped and a masthead flag will give more instant warning.
4 When checking the wind before the start of a race, the head to wind position can be read in conjunction with the compass: this will later be an aid to tactics.

The Hengist and Horsa does not have its own batteries but relies on the yacht's supply—minimum 12 volts. It is also worth noting that the direction indicators are only available in a 4 in. diameter size which weighs $4\frac{1}{2}$ lb. In the smaller yachts, the complete array of instruments, if placed high up (e.g. above the main hatch) where they can be seen, is a significant weight. However, a lightweight model of only $\frac{3}{4}$ lb. has now been introduced and should be used wherever possible.

An effective non-electronic wind direction indicator is the Swedish Windex, a visual aid on the lines of Fig. 38. The fixed wires illuminated by Beta light can give a quick alignment of the close-hauled position when tacking or hauling up after rounding a mark.

Calculation of VMG.   Apart from the uses for instruments suggested above, it is possible to calculate VMG for a particular course being steered from the water speed, apparent wind direction and apparent wind speed: these can be read off, and the leeway angle, estimated, is also needed. A diagram as in Fig. 39 could be constructed to give VMG. The Hawk calculator can do the job fairly quickly, but even then the ocean racing navigator seldom has time to try out different points of sailing, even if this is practicable when racing. If various values of VMG are to be found in this way, trials should be arranged, which might prove quite revealing.

Pilotage   Offshore races may follow for the shore for considerable distance or near it by a turning mark. The start may well involve sailing close to the land before the open sea is reached. Some of the navigator's job can thus be termed pilotage: a mixture of compass and eye navigation. Once again, racing demands more work than cruising where the task is

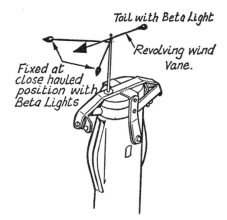

FIG. 38. *Inexpensive masthead wind indicator.*

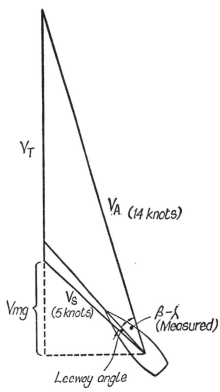

FIG. 39. *A diagram which will give VMG the speed made good to windward. VA (14 knots) and VS (5 knots), the apparent wind and water speed respectively are read off the instruments. So is the apparent wind angle. With the very small estimated leeway angle, the triangle formed by the solid lines can be drawn. The pecked lines follow, giving the value of VMG.*

usually one of keeping clear of dangers. Near the start or finish of a race, marks may be more frequent than the course as a whole and many minutes have been lost by failing to identify the correct mark. With the preparation already mentioned, the compass course to the next mark should be known and it is important to have this even if it is within visual distance. It is an essential check against wrong identification. Any compensation for current will have to be made and if there is a steady current whose velocity is known, a textbook solution can be applied using the velocity of the yacht. Sometimes, however, the marks used on ocean races, being navigational aids, are at critical points, for instance on the edge of a deep water channel. As the mark is approached, the current can increase and it will be found that the yacht is not after all laying the mark. Such variations must be foreseen.

Where tactics dictate that the yacht stays close the shore, a close check must be kept on position by bearings, distance off and soundings, with the instruments described above. On coasts where the depths are uneven and the dangers off-lying the chart can be made more easy to read by pencilling in the outline of the dangers to be avoided. The detail on the chart tends to be considerable and clarifying it in this way enables "tighter turns" to be taken (Fig. 40).

Tidal indications on charts and pocket tidal stream atlases are of limited help very near the shore. For thorough navigation on an ocean race, it is necessary to try to collect as much data about streams on possible shore legs from different sources. These can include the official and yachting pilot books mentioned above and also talking to yachtsmen who

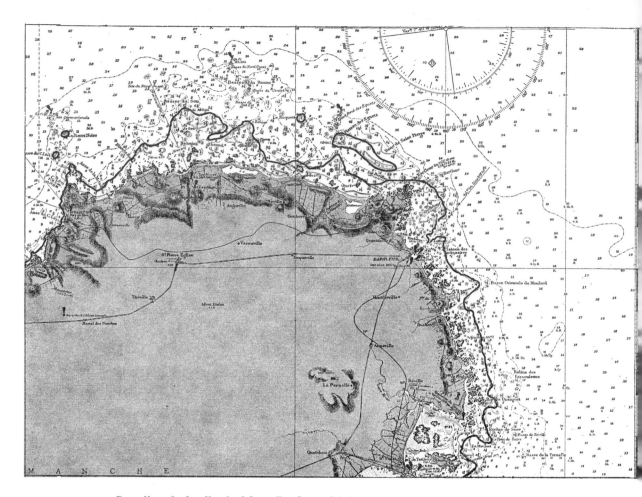

FIG. 40. *Rounding the headland of Cape Barfleur with its many associated rocks has been made easier by the navigator marking in a line at 9 ft. chart datum. The shape of the maze of shoals then becomes clearer and tide dodging and other tactics can be pursued. (Reproduced from British Admiralty Chart No. 1106 with the sanction of the Controller of H.M. Stationery Office and the Hydrographer of the Navy.)*

have sailed the same course. Outside racing circles, it is not easy to get information as cruising yachts just are not involved with the close subtleties of the stream. Failing reliable information, the rule that the stream turns earlier inshore applies and remember close to shore, an eddy may well start running two or even three hours before the turn of the main stream, the currents in fact being continually out of phase. A clue here is in the difference between high water at nearby ports and the turn of tide given on the chart.

No opportunity should be lost of checking tidal set when there is a fixed object in view. This may be a single object, such as a lobster pot, on which a compass bearing can be taken or if available, a transit. Here again racing practice demands that such checks be made frequently because early alteration of course will win the race (Fig. 41).

Dead reckoning in racing Dead reckoning remains the basis of sound navigation and when racing the emphasis should be on keeping the dead reckoning with as much accuracy as possible. This can be helped a great deal by ensuring that a careful record is kept of all data that can affect the navigator's calculation of his position. The person in charge of each watch is responsible to the navigator for seeing that he is informed and the way to do this is by an efficiently kept log. In bad weather, this is just one of the tasks on board that become a chore, but at such a time regular entries are even more vital than usual. To ensure that all the navigator needs to know is recorded, an effective log book should be provided. It should be on the chart table where it is readily accessible by a member of the crew coming

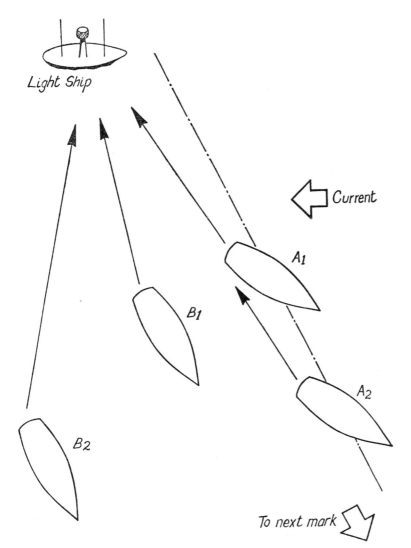

FIG. 41. *Maintaining the desired course after rounding a mark saves useful time. Bearings at A1 then A2 before lightship is out of sight show true track. Neglect of this at B1, B2 causes yacht to head right but move with uncertain current.*

below and where he can find it immediately. All this may sound simple, but too often someone will be trying to find the book amongst a littered chart table; when it is discovered, the entry may be found to be made in the wrong place or a pencil is not available or it is broken or something else is wrong. This just will not do and an efficient accessible chart area with ready log book will do much for the dead reckoning calculation.

Apart from emphasizing the importance of this to all watch masters or crew members, the navigator must provide a log book for the purpose. In it might well be inscribed the words of Chick Larkin, ace navigator of many American ocean racers: "I don't mind you writing your name on the ocean. I hope you don't go back and erase it. But if you do, please log it!" Few log books are suitable for ocean racing, though several people have produced printed sheets which can be obtained locally. Most yacht log books either have insufficient space for the important elements of dead reckoning or are sub-divided with items in which the ocean racer is not interested. Nor am I in favour of printed timings (e.g. every hour) as it is better to put the actual time the reading is made: a course is changed at twenty-three minutes past or the log reading was not taken on the hour as the spinnaker was being gybed, but it was taken at eleven minutes past—then put the information down and the navigator can use it. My suggestion for making your own log book is shown in Fig. 42. You may have other ideas. This is all to the good and you can adapt your own design.

Possible errors   With the data properly recorded, the navigator can cope with other factors in the dead reckoning which will tend to affect the accuracy of his plotted position. These are:

>   Helmsman's error
>   Variations in estimated current
>   Surface drift
>   Leeway
>   Compass error
>   Error in distance run instruments

The helmsman's error problem illustrates the difference between theoretical and practical navigation, as it essentially is a sailing yacht problem which is difficult to pin down. Ocean racing crews being optimists will, unless experienced, tend to report the course that they think they have maintained. The course is going to oscillate over, say, seven degrees (this varies immensely with conditions) and the most common mistake lies in steering so that this seven degrees limit ends up to one side of the course. The mean course is thus $3\frac{1}{2}$ degrees away from the desired track. By the same token, working to windward a helmsman might report a course which is closest to the wind rather than the mean. As this human failing can invalidate the most carefully calculated dead reckoning, these steps should be taken:

1   The navigator should check the course over short periods of time unknown to the helmsman, by tell tale below deck.
2   He should co-operate with the helmsman and find out if there are any special difficulties in maintaining the course ordered.
3   When going to windward, he will in the same way work very closely with the helmsman who has to record the mean course steered in sailing the yacht.

Date-time	Course to steer	Log	Course made good	APP WIND dir	speed	TRUE WIND dir	speed	Sea	Baro	Kedge Tack Motor	Remarks

FIG. 42. *Log book headings. "Date-time" left blank beforehand enables accurate times to be entered for the data and entries to continue through midnight without changing pages. "True wind" data can be calculated from "apparant wind" obtained from instruments and speed. Plenty of room should be left for "remarks", probably a right-hand page of a book. "Kedge, tack, motor" are to ensure the log is entered when tacking (change of course and log needed), lowering or weighing kedge (log reading) and for running motor when charging or before or after race, for engine hours record.*

4 The course should be logged every half-hour, one of the watch on deck coming down as near the end of the half-hour as possible and entering up the log.

5 The helmsman himself must note the amount by which the course deviates to one side of that ordered and compensate to the other. This does not mean he purposely steers off, but he steers by the compass to make the required course a mean. A man who can combine some technique of this sort with good helmsmanship (i.e. in relation to the sails) is a real asset offshore.

Variations in estimated current. There are currents in many parts of the world and many are unpredictable, by the year, by the season or by the hour. Heavy rains, an unusual wind blowing for days on end or the height of the barometer are just some of the natural reasons which cause pilotage information on currents to vary. The key here is for the navigator to realize this and look actively for anything that will tend to vary the predicted rate of current. In the case of tides, the height is greater when the barometer is low and sometimes this is accentuated as in the southern part of the North Sea: the phenomenon of storm surges in this area can be found in reference books and one can take it that the same effect on a much reduced scale will be caused by a shallow depression.

At least it is possible to apply the rate of tidal stream or current as carefully as possible together with its accurate direction to the dead reckoning plot. After that it is a question of estimating the maximum probable variation and allowing for it. Clues may be obtained from consulting persons who have been sailing in the waters that season (beware "bar talk!") and observation of the current on buoys, etc., against the prediction.

In the Mediterranean where the tide is negligible, there are numerous perpetual currents whose speed varies with the seasons because of the evaporation rate. Their weakness means that a wind in more than one direction for more than several days can alter the rate by 100 per cent. A current predicted at between one-half and one knot may become a two knot flow when a fresh breeze blows in the same direction. In the English Channel a high barometer which frequently goes with east winds will hold down the tidal level and weaker tides than usual can be expected: such tides can also be delayed on their predicted time of change by up to thirty minutes.

This brings us to the question of surface and leeway. The best plan for the navigator is to separate the various effects in his calculations even though they may be originally due to the same cause. There is variation in the tidal stream as just mentioned. Then there is leeway: the actual sideways drift of the yacht. Leeway can be considered as under one degree in the modern ocean racer on the wind in slight seas and nil with the wind anywhere abaft the beam—negligible altogether. In rough water going to windward the modern boat should be allowed between $1\frac{1}{2}$ and $2\frac{1}{2}$ degrees.

The third effect is wind induced current. Captain C. W. McMullen, R.N. (in the Royal Cruising Club annual) has summarized some findings based on his own observations and those of other authorities. A rule of thumb for small craft is that the wind induced current on the surface is 2 to 3 per cent of the wind speed. A yacht of 2 to 3 ft. draft should allow 3 per cent and one drawing 6 ft. calculate at $2\frac{1}{2}$ per cent. Due to the rotation of the earth the current direction is twenty to forty degrees to the right of the wind direction in the northern hemisphere and a similar amount to the left in the southern. Yet one more factor in heavy weather is the actual movement of the water due to the breaking of the tops of seas, so in such conditions even more drift must be allowed.

In fresh conditions all these effects are on the increase and it need hardly be pointed out that it is then that the navigator, who is aware of these and can make an attempt to estimate them and then allow for them, will not be in the position of wondering why he is *still* so far to leeward, a result that most yachtsmen have had at some time.

Compass error. The positioning and swinging of the compass have been mentioned and if carried out as recommended will eliminate compass error. The question of parallax, which arises because the helmsman is sitting to one side and sees the lubber line against the marking which is not then in the fore and aft line of the yachts, has to be remembered. This is largely avoided by a good installation but in extremes of weather he may be in an unusual steering posture and then it must be allowed for. There are enough variables in dead reckoning without having any doubts about the accuracy of the compass and its table of deviation. In an ocean racer it must be above suspicion. When the boat was first swung the adjuster should have been asked about heeling error which he would then have compensate, if necessary, by vertical magnets and no further action is required. Ordinary horizontal deviation, however, should be checked by the navigator when convenient transits present themselves.

Error in distance run. In a big following sea with a towed patent log, the instrument will over-read on distance and the rotator is towed up and down the seaway. Under-reading will be caused in the opposite conditions. When the speed is under half a knot the rotator will fail to respond and some miles will be piled up unknown. No doubt an unexpectedly early landfall will be welcomed in such conditions! The nylon impeller of the Harrier electronic log is much more sensitive and less affected by either extreme condition, though its accuracy is less certain under half a knot. In drifting conditions, treat log readings with caution, though in such weather there will be more time to take fixes and deliberate on probable inaccuracies. The navigator should brief the crew to watch for the rotator stopping and I can remember, as navigator, coming on deck and noticing immediately that the patent log was foul of weed. How long had it been like that? The crew did not know . . any time since the last log reading. By such small things is the dead reckoning put out. In the case of the latest electronic log, there is an audible signal when the impeller stops. It is so irritating, you will soon clear it.

Plotting. With the information in the log book in the necessary form and a full awareness of the factors leading to accuracy and otherwise, it only remains to plot on the chart. Though for pilotage the largest scale chart should always be used, it will often be more convenient to use a smaller scale sheet to keep the dead reckoning. This is because of the size of the chart table and the rapidity with which the track can move across a large-scale chart. It will obviate too frequent transfer of position between sheets. The more detailed sheets can be consulted at the same time. The manner of plotting is a question of personal preference, but I prefer to keep the chart clean. That is to say the minimum amount of pencilled workings appear on it. It is best not to draw in the intended track for a sailing yacht, but instead to note the course to be steered in the log. At any given moment, the problem is to get the yacht from its position to the next mark and the theoretical track is of no interest. DR plots when worked up can be shown and a circle or ellipse is a suitable

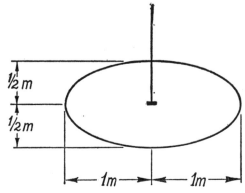

FIG. 43. *Area of DR position. Log reading along course from last fixed position is accurate to half mile, but error across course, in this case, could be up to one mile either side due to variations in current, steering error etc.*

mark. This can show the possible area of doubt on the DR position. For instance, sailing across a current whose speed is in doubt could result in a plot as in Fig. 43. Lines used to measure distance from the last position and to construct triangles of velocities for current etc. should be erased. The DR plots will then give an unconfusing picture of the yacht's journey. Fixes can be shown by small triangles, their construction having been erased as well. So about the only line to remain on the chart is an uncrossed position line (see next section).

Against the DR plot (and any fix) should be put the time and the log reading. Having taken over from a navigator who has only put the time, I have found it tedious to work up the next plot, the log reading in the log book being only recorded against the hour and not each time a plot was shown. There is no need to enter the log, if the reading is shown on the chart.

Position fixing Perhaps "aligning" would be a better heading to this section. Dead reckoning is the basis of navigation, but position lines are the confirmation of your work and the correctors of uncertainty. The ocean racing navigator will not waste any chance of checking his position: this does not mean it can only be done when a "fix" can be obtained. It is often just as telling to obtain a single reliable line and cross the dead reckoning track with it. In the example of a DR plot given earlier, a single good radio bearing crossing the DR area is very welcome (Fig. 44).

The standard methods and means of fixing the position will be known by navigators. These include radio bearings, visual bearing by shore mark or light, radio by consol or

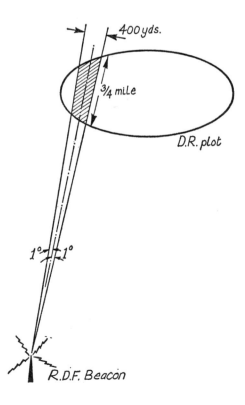

FIG. 44. *Same DR plot as Fig. 43 with the addition of a radio bearing, which the navigator estimates has up to 1 degree error each side. The position must now be in the shaded area.*

similar systems, lines of soundings and celestial observations. In all these the key to their use is reliability and this is where the experienced man once again scores. When the line is less reliable it should be disregarded in favour of the DR plot, while a good position line can correct a doubtful DR. Two good position lines which are near a right angle where they cross, it need hardly be added, will finally fix the yacht's position with certainty. Factors making for reliability in each case include:

Visual bearing
1 Certain identification of landmark or light.
2 Steadiness of hand-bearing compass.
3 No excessive distance from object of bearing.
4 A transit, if available, which obviates use of a compass.

Radio beacon
1 Narrow audio or visual null.
2 No chance of refraction due to bearing being along shore.
3 No local electro-magnetic effects (e.g. metal loop caused by lifelines or rigging).
4 Knowledge of which side of the beacon is probable (arises with lightships and sea marks).
5 Distance inside the nominal range given by almanac; the nearer you are the better.

Loran and Decca
These are radio systems which, like Consol, pick up distinctive signals which are then related to charts showing plotted lines. Whether in time equipment will be available which is acceptable to small yachts by reason of size and cost remains to be seen. In the future similar navigational systems will be produced, although in small ocean racers, by definition, there will also always be a "power" problem. In any case, these systems are not allowed in RORC races.

Consol
1 Confirmation of number of dots and dashes by counting on several cycles.
2 Use during hours recommended in the "accuracy charts" drawn in government publications.
3 Use of special charts published for the use of ships (the official charts are designed for aircraft and are less suitable).
4 That the stations used are those within the area of reliability shown on the special charts. (Consol is a prime example of where one line only may be of significance. This can still be of great value where it cuts the DR estimate).

Soundings
1 That the depth sounding instrument is accurately calibrated.
2 The bottom is shoaling regularly.
Soundings are the "vaguest" means of obtaining a position and often will be of a blanket safety criterion rather than an accurate alignment. The reading itself can be the most reliable (and reassuring) of all aids.

There is no reason why a celestial observation cannot be taken even within sight of the shore, assuming that it cannot be identified. However, with the number of modern navigational aids just described, it is unusual for small offshore yachts. Whether or not to carry a sextant was discussed before. The distance-off instrument mentioned is another method of fixing position in conjunction with a bearing of the object. By itself it will give a line which will be the circumference of a circle.

Transferring a position line is second best to a simultaneous fix and depends on being able to produce an accurate dead-reckoned course made good between the time of the two fixes. It is possible that this is less reliable than the DR position when the first position line was taken and so once again a theoretical exercise is not always the answer at sea. In fact the position lines and the dead reckoning will be kept going on the chart as a continuous plot. The value in remembering to use a transferred position lies in the navigator looking out for a second source of navigational data as soon as he has obtained one position line (Fig. 45).

Maintenance of navigational equipment   Most modern equipment requires minimal maintenance, but it is the navigator's responsibility to ensure that equipment does not fail at sea. Mostly this consists in ensuring that there are adequate spares and replacement batteries. Especially if he is also skipper there are small items of which the navigational

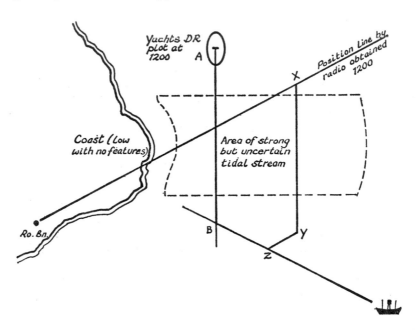

FIG. 45. *Obtaining various position lines. The yacht's reliable DR plot at 1200 hours was at A and the small ellipse shows the area in which she was thought to be. At the same time, 1200, a radio bearing was taken giving the position line shown: this did not pass through the DR plot. After sailing due south through the area of strong and uncertain tidal stream, a visual position line was obtained from the lightship at 1330. So XY was plotted, X being any point on the radio position line and Y being the result of course and estimated distance, allowing for tidal stream from 1200 to 1330. Z is the transferred position to give a fix, which has thus been obtained from the radio line, the visual bearing and the estimate of distance run. The latter is the weak link in the plotting and the navigator prefers to trust his earlier DR position, A, the course from there and the same visual position line from the lightship. He does not try to depend on the area of uncertain tide. This gives the best position at B in preference to Z.*

department consists which are liable to be overlooked among all the work on deck before the start of the race.

There must be spare batteries and bulbs for all equipment. Both can be changed before the race and night equipment should be *checked on the mooring* before leaving, where it is easy to make adjustments. After dark at sea the small components of, for instance, the lighting on a compass are far less easy to cope with. Pencils should be replaced and sharpened and old markings erased from charts. The patent log should be oiled and returned to zero ready for streaming.

A look should be kept for wiring on the electrics which has been forced in a tight radius or where insulation has frayed near sockets. Sealed units also have desiccators which turn pink when there is a certain level of humidity in the set. They should be taken ashore and dried slowly.

After a rough passage, the chart table area will have to be wiped clear of dried salt, any damage to charts noted, all equipment cleaned and defects put in hand well before the next race.

· 6 ·

CREW ROUTINE AND KNOWLEDGE

MUCH of this book is devoted to the detail and design of running a small ocean racer successfully. Fascinating hours can be spent on perfecting these wonderful seagoing boats, but rating advantages, clever equipment and even the abilities of good helmsmen can be thrown away by bad crewing. The top boats and top crews tend to go together so it is impossible to answer the frequent question as to whether boat or crew is primarily responsible for success. I have noticed that before yachts race the talk is of sails, gear and design, but after a race it is of faulty tactics and deficiencies in crewing.

There are just as many new designs which fail to place well as those which win and this is best demonstrated by a race in which several boats of the same design compete. After several successful seasons the Twister class was extremely popular and individual boats which raced were owned by a variety of people. As a result, boats of this class racing on both the south and east coasts were spread well around the list of results. The first ones to be designed were in the hands of skilled men and had placed consistently very well indeed. This is not to decry the design, which is indeed excellent. In fact, when the design appeared, experienced yachtsmen spotted its qualities immediately and thus the early boats were in the right hands.

Demands of design   There are easy and difficult boats to sail. This is really where design is related to crewing. It is dangerous to generalize, but an example might be the heavy displacement transom type such as *Contrail* designed by Illingworth and Primrose which can carry her canvas in a breeze, does not require frequent sail changes and is positive to steer. Lighter displacement boats which, to name one item, are sensitive to angle of heel, may require so much attention to sail area and trim of sails and hull that the demands on the crew are considerable. Neither boat is "better", for there are many other factors to affect the outcome of any one race.

Number of crew   It is frequently debated as to what is the right number of crew for any boat, but it is best to try out various numbers and then to decide, after making allowance for the weather and the length of the race. For the same boat the number can be the same inshore or offshore, though the jobs will be different. Inshore racing, the yacht will be rounding buoys at frequent intervals and therefore gives work for all the crew; offshore, there has to be a system of watches and thus the same number needed in a pool to allow for men off duty.

Inshore, each man can have the same job throughout, though it will be wise to change helmsman when the race is more than a couple of hours. A 21 ft. waterline boat with four on board could have on an inshore race:

Skipper/helmsman
Tactician/navigator
Cockpit hand
Foredeck hand

If the skipper prefers to act as tactician, then the helmsman is freer to concentrate on just sailing the boat, leaving the skipper to watch for other yachts, decide when to tack and generally "run the race". It is scarcely necessary to add that there must be a clear division of responsibility between these two. I can remember using this method in *Chieftain* when a small hard-driven yacht was approaching on the starboard tack. As skipper I warned the helmsman, but he thought I was going to tell him what to do. As he was an experienced man, I, on my part, gathered he had the situation well in hand. It was only by both yachts luffing up hard at the last moment that we avoided cutting this yacht down. So it is difficult for the man with his hand on the helm to avoid being responsible for avoiding other craft and obstructions.

Let us say in yachts under 21 ft. (and this is still inshore racing with crowded conditions assumed) that the skipper will combine as helmsman and sailing master, but, over this size, skipper, helmsman, tactician and navigator's duties should be split between two members of the crew. At the bigger end of the scale five, six or even seven men will be fully occupied in executing manœuvres, but there is still only one helm and the same number of sails, and more of the crew will be "extra". They must be placed where at least their weight is working: on the weather deck. If the weather is very bad, below decks on the weather side is the alternative and in the light stuff it will be a matter of minimum movement and the weight inclined to leeward to keep sails and boom in the right place. An aspect of athwartship trim recommended by the famous American keel boat sailor, Arthur Knapp, is to heel a yacht to windward on a dead run. There is no reason why experiments of this sort should not be tried in small ocean racers.

With a full crew on an inshore race, the number of people can be exploited to the full by techniques of this sort. One thing is definitely wrong: to allow the crew to cluster in the area of the cockpit whatever the weather. Fore and aft trim will without doubt be upset.

Offshore organization   Inshore races have been mentioned because most yachts will race in various types of event. When to put the yacht on to an offshore organization with watches should be decided. I would say any race that is liable to exceed 8 hours: a complete crew will just not remain at its optimum beyond this time. For small yachts, this is a race of 35 miles and for the larger 45 miles. Of course, if a short race starts to become drawn out and turns into an after-dark affair, a switch to offshore routine should be made.

The most common type of watch system is the standard "four on–four off", with dog watches to alternate the times daily. There are variations of this, incorporating, for instance, a five-hour watch from 0800 to 1300. The idea of this is to enable one watch to have breakfast, a good sleep and a lunch meal before coming on—a morning off, as it were, on alternate days.

Watches will be arranged in accordance with the number carried. The successful

French ocean racer *Pen-ar-Bed*, although a light displacement boat of 24 ft., carried seven on board. The system consisted of three watches of two men each and a skipper/navigator. This allowed six hours sleep to the watch below and only a two-hour stint on duty. It was reckoned that the result was a very fresh crew, then if there was any call for full manning the whole fresh strong crew of seven could come on deck and deal with the situation. The system will not appeal to everyone, the main snag to my mind being the fairly frequent situations where two are not quite adequate. It worked best in the longest races.

What is called the Swedish watch system has two six-hour watches during the day and three four-hour night watches. Being an odd number, no dog watches are required. The advantage is in the ability of each watch to get one long sleep during the day. It might be thought that four hours is enough but, in practice, with settling down after coming below, preparing for the next watch, and small jobs including washing up, the time available for sleep will be nearer three hours.

On *Summertime*, in the 1967 Fastnet race, we varied our usual total of five and took one extra hand. The system we used with six would not be suitable for short events. There was a skipper/navigator and the usual two on each watch. The sixth man was cook and extra hand in an emergency—for instance, getting in the spinnaker in a heavy squall on the run out to the rock in a south-easterly. With four on deck in this 24 ft. yacht it was never necessary to disturb the watch below. Each day the cook was rotated, and in this five-day race each member of the crew had a turn, which included a full night's sleep and a chance to try his own culinary skills. It worked out rather well.

Individual crew members   The necessity to work watches offshore means that everyone has to do almost every job at one time or another. This is not the same for larger yachts or in inshore racing. Nevertheless, it is still useful to note the particular abilities of individual members of the crew. It takes quite a few races before this becomes apparent, but if the same people are on board the yacht, it will be found that one is a good light-weather helmsman, another never really settles down at the helm but keeps a cool head on the foredeck, while there is often someone with such specialist skills as signalling or knowledge of diesel engines. At a critical period of the race, perhaps the beginning or end, or attempting to fetch a mark on the last of the fair tide, the ability of individuals on the helm, spinnaker trimming and so on can be brought into play, even though it cuts across the routine of watches.

Apart from this, watches should be strictly kept. An informal cheery disregard of time has few ill-effects for the first twelve hours of the race, but it then really tells. If the skipper is firm about watches, the crew will be glad in the long run. It will soon be found how much time it takes to change watches. At night one man of the oncoming watch should go up first and spend a few minutes with the offgoing watch to accustom his eyes to the dark and have lights and other shipping pointed out. He should also be told of recent sail changes and the most recent trend of the weather. By the time his companion(s) are with him he is familiar with his surroundings and the men going off have removed their weight from its undesirable position in the cockpit.

Sleep   Once offshore, food and sleep become the simple needs of the crew when not actually sailing the yacht. For a comfortable night passage the crew must be allowed to sleep soundly. This is often difficult after coming from a shore life, but the habit of sleeping well when off watch is most valuable.

Sound sleep for the crew on passage is assisted by:

(a) Narrow berths which mean the body does not move far when tacking.
(b) Comfortable sides to the berths, i.e. cushions carried up sides of yacht and deep leeboards of wood and/or terylene.
(c) No gear stowed that is likely to be needed so that sleepers have to be disturbed to obtain it.
(d) Correctly adjusted ventilation in vicinity of bunks.
(e) Lights used by other members of crew arranged not to shine on sleepers.
(f) No drips on bunks, whether due to small leaks or condensation.
(g) No more noise than is necessary, e.g. winches should be of the silent type and the men on watch should when possible keep voices low.

Sleeping bags are practical, but the very highly insulated type designed for camping are not advisable in a yacht, where, though conditions may be cold and damp, heat is not removed by convection. A medium-weight bag together with a pillow is snug enough.

There is one time when the crew will sleep soundly and that is after the race, but they should try and sleep well *before* it. A night passage from a home port to the start of a race some distance away is not advisable unless there are twelve hours to rest crew and adjust ship before the gun. Other yachts are going to start with fresher and more alert crews.

Food Apart from physical necessity, hot food at regular intervals has an encouraging effect on the spirits of the crew. Unless working some system with a separate cook such as mentioned above, it should be worked out in advance which watch is to cook each meal. Lunch can usually be a light affair and in the system which has a five-hour forenoon watch from 0800 to 1300 hours it can be prepared by the watch below who then eat their own meal leaving the watch coming off to have theirs without hurry. The same sort of division between the two watches can be worked at 1800 hours at the end of the dog watches. On several boats breakfast is the province of the skipper/navigator. He listens to the BBC shipping forecast at 0645, then gets up to date with his plotting. Between 0700 and 0800 breakfast is served to the watch below, the rest of the crew having it when they come down at 0800.

You will note I mention eating below. However small the yacht, meals taken in the cockpit only interfere with the sailing of the race. A mug of tea in one hand is just acceptable, but otherwise all meals must be consumed below, clear of members of the crew busy sailing the boat. Meals are undoubtedly a distraction and it is often difficult to keep a balance between the desirable relaxing atmosphere of meals and their interference with the concentration needed by all hands when racing.

An oven enables the menu to be expanded considerably but most small ocean racers will rely on a two-burner stove. This limits the type of food taken on board and the best plan is to have a standard list of items which are bought for every race. The quantity can be varied depending on its length. By having a set of these lists a check can be made at the end of each race and the boat restocked to scale at the beginning of the next. A suggested list of items for races not exceeding five days is shown in Fig. 46.

Cooking can be an unpleasant job when beating to windward or in heavy weather.

The cook will need more than an ordinary ventilator near him, and he is more likely to put his head out of the main hatch for fresh air. Later when we consider the siting of galleys, it follows that it must not be too far forward in the yacht. In any sea, oilskin trousers should be worn when handling hot foods to avoid scalding due to spillages.

Not everyone can be a first-class sea cook, but an offshore crew can show seamanlike thought in dealing with cooking "at an angle". For instance, a cup of coffee should have the hot liquid put in last just before being handed to the recipient and not poured in before milk and sugar. Spillage is bound to result if these are left until the mug is full of liquid.

Clothing   I must confess to seldom being able to take the right amount of clothing on an offshore race. Usually I take too much and come ashore with a quota of clean clothing, which means that unnecessary gear was carried round the course. With modern foul-weather garments, the clothing underneath remains dry in quite severe conditions, though a change should be taken as it may be soaked in certain conditions.

Shore-going clothes are not recommended unless there is a party at the end of the race or individual members of the crew must bring them to travel in for some reason. Boats over 21 ft. should have a hanging locker for these and shore-going shoes can be accommodated at the bottom of this. If a wooden hanging locker is not used a zip-up polythene curtain enclosure is most effective. This is the sort of facility which, though of no direct help in racing the boat, does give encouragement to the crew: they know that on this boat they will be able to go ashore after the race, with their good clothes in a reasonable state, and that there is no need to worry about them while sailing.

Quilted jackets and similar wind- and showerproof garments are of limited use in small boats offshore. When there is wind there is often spray as well and once wet with salt water they are difficult to cope with and to stow. Plenty of light clothing is generally preferable to a few heavy items. For instance, even early in the year in north-west European waters light cotton trousers are sufficient and foul-weather gear will usually be worn over them. Here is a clothing list for one man, on a race which is expected to last two nights at sea. It includes items already being worn as well as spares.

> Waterproof bag with heavy-duty zip or lacing.
> 2 Towels.
> 1 Narrow towel for neck.
> 2 Shirts with short sleeves.
> 2 String vests.
> 2 String pants.
> 2 Light cotton/terylene trousers (no turn ups).
> 1 pair socks.
> 1 pair seaboot stockings.
> Handkerchiefs.
> Toilet gear (including soap, razor, comb).
> 3 Sweaters with high necks (e.g. Guernsey or Jersey).
> Non-slip yachting shoes.
> Sperry Topsider knee length seaboots.
> Foul-weather jacket and trousers.

The reason short sleeves are mentioned on shirts is that shirt cuffs tend to slip through

FRESH SUPPLIES *(renew for each race)*

Fruit: apples, bananas, oranges,
 cherries, raisins.
Bread, ready sliced.
"Vita-wheat"
Biscuits, several types.
Butter
Cooking fat or oil
Sugar

Bacon
Cheese
Eggs
Sausages, preserved meat
Salad
Prepared stews, etc. } For first 24 hours
Cake.

JARS, PACKETS *(renew to make up quantities)*

Powdered milk
"Long-life" milk
Chocolate
Barley sugar (medicinal type)
Cereal (in individual packets)
Porridge
Jam and marmalade
Bovril
Salad cream
Coffee (instant)

Tea (bags)
Cocoa
Chips (ready to use)
Potato powder
Squash (orange, lemon)
Salt (sealed screw container)
Pepper
Mustard (tubes)
Soups

TINS *(limit quantity for race)*

Stewed steak, meats, sausages and
 variations
Potatoes
Ham
Vegetables various

Puddings, rice and variations
Fruit various
Beans, spaghetti and variations
Soups

FIG. 46. FOOD CHECK LIST
Food check list for races not exceeding five days. Quantities have to be estimated against the number on board and expected length of race. Suitable for use where there is no oven.

foul-weather jackets and soak up water. The boots must be knee length, the so-called calf-length boot is proved to be a sure method of getting wet feet.

Foul-weather gear, known in England as oilskins after the obsolete type of fabric that was used for it, is the key to comfort in anything other than light weather. The fabrics are steadily being improved with PVC on a variety of backings including nylon, cotton and a combination of both and in different forms of weave. Bright colours are popular offshore in case of falling overboard and air-sea-rescue orange is particularly practical. The very lightweight materials such as proofed nylon are not sufficiently waterproof offshore and whatever the backing there must be a layer of PVC which is impervious to to liquid. This results in the problem of condensation inside, but this is preferable rather than allow salt damp in.

Trousers should button at the bottoms, coming down outside the knee-length boots. A high chest is really waterproof with permanent braces and this is practical for foredeck hands, though for the navigator or anyone who normally works aft a drawstring waist will be less constricting. Helly-Hansen of Norway have a range of gear very suitable for offshore work and are one of the few manufacturers who produce a jacket with a hood. This is preferable to a smock-type garment which has to be pulled over the head, often a very difficult job below decks on a small yacht.

The Helly-Hansen jacket does not have "storm cuffs" but there is provision for tightening the wrist so that shirts and sweaters can be arranged not to push through and soak up water. A jacket can blow up at the back when, for instance, its wearer is bending down to some job on the foredeck and in bad weather a belt to prevent this is useful. If a knife is required it always seems to be in a trouser pocket and inaccessible when wearing foul-weather gear or stowed below in the PVC jacket at other times. The solution is two knives, one of which is left in the jacket.

Storage   Every item must have its own storage space and the crew needs to know what these are as soon as possible. On coming aboard they will be shown their own personal lockers or spaces or nets. But there is the storage of the working gear of the yacht to be learnt as well. If gear is divided up by types, each in its own part of the ship, matters will be simplified. Suitable headings are:

> Harbour gear—fenders, warps.
> Sheets—genoa, spinnaker cordage.
> Small tackles, outhauls, signal flag halyard (not used when racing).
> Emergency spares—winch handles, rigging screws.
> Bosun's stores—tools, twine, seizing wire.

A table of cordage held in the ship is advisable as shown in Fig. 47. Without these familiarization takes too long. A series of canvas bags of different colours with the particular gear they contain enables the crew to locate them without delay. Typical examples are:

> "*Reefing*" contains reefing handle, kicking-strap adaptor for reefing.
> "*Deck tools*" contains pliers, adjustable spanner, engineer's hammer, spike, shackler (a more comprehensive tool bag is kept below).
> "*Sail tyers*" contains tyers which are always untidy to stow and probably wanted in a hurry.

One stowage place that should be marked on the outside of the locker is the location of the first-aid kit. In an emergency this can be found by the sight of a simple red cross on the locker front.

For emergency equipment in general a stowage list is important, for this is just the time that the owner who knows where everything is may not be available. The listing of emergency equipment is shown in the chapter on maintenance. Thought put to the question of stowage undoubtedly is an important aid to good crewing and it is in the first instance up to the owner to spend a day working out the stowage system. At an even earlier stage, locker space has to be designed into the yacht to accommodate the ship's and crew's gear needed for a race.

14. *Left*: Designed for RORC racing under handicap by Dick Carter, the 24 ft. WL *Angel* owned by David Edwards.
15. Foul weather gear. This Helly-Hansen suit is lightweight and can be removed without pulling over the head. Woollen hat inside hood prevents head turning into it. Trousers are worn over knee-length Sperry Topsider yachting boots. Cuffs and trousers can be buttoned tight. Harness or separate belt prevents jacket blowing up in strong winds.

16. The start of the RORC Channel Race for some of Class III.

17. Typical One Tonners with high aspect ration mainsails and big foretriangles. British *Morningtown* and the Dutch *Belita VI*, designed by Stephens and Carter respectively. There is a difference of opinion on spinnaker staysails.

18. *Optimist*, designed by Dick Carter and twice winner of the One Ton Cup, in the final race for the trophy in 1968.

19 (*a*). Three Half Tonners, each 22 ft. LWL. A Super Challenger, *Morgaine IV*.

19 (b). A Swedish Arpege class. Very roomy below and built in France by Michel Dufour, these boats are now in use all over the world.
19 (c) (Right). Philippe Harlé designed Scotch class, with separate helmsman's cockpit and short coachroof (see plans on pages 118 and 119).

TABLE OF MAIN CORDAGE ON BOARD 24 FT. LWL YACHT

Purpose	Description	Circ. in	Stowage
Genoa sheets	16 plait terylene	1¼	Fo'c'sle
Spare genoa sheets	16 plait terylene	1¼	Below port quarter berth
Heavy weather (jib) sheets	3 strand matt terylene	1½	Fo'c'sle
Spinnaker sheets	3 strand terylene	1¼	Fo'c'sle, but leave rigged on deck when racing
Spinnaker guys	3 strand pre-stretched terylene (with black thread)	1¼	,,
Spinnaker foreguys	3 strand terylene	1	,,
Light weather spinnaker sheet	16 plait ulstron (green)	1	Fo'c'sle
Light weather genoa sheets	3 strand ulstron (green)	1¼	Fo'c'sle
Main boom foreguy	3 strand terylene with snap shackle	1¼	Bosun's locker
Genoa sheet outhaul (to main boom)	3 strand ulstron (green) with two blocks		Bosun's locker
Kedge warp	3 strand nylon	1¼	Fo'c'sle on kedge reel
Mooring warps	16 plait ulstron (white)	1½	After locker
Mooring springs	3 strand ulstron (green)	1¼	After locker
Spare sheet and warp material	3 strand matt terylene (in coil)	1¼	After locker
Cod line, hambro, marline	—	—	Bosun's locker

FIG. 47. *This should be tabulated and pinned up where the crew can see it. It is assumed that in this case roller reefing is used.*

Emergency equipment The crew should be shown the position of all emergency equipment and, what is more important, the mode of using this. This includes how to use the life-raft, flares and daylight signals, and the life-ring and its equipment in the event of a man overboard. Life-jackets are best for small yachts if of the inflatable type, but before each race they should be blown up and left for a short period to see they are in working order. New members of the crew should be made to put on their life-jackets so that if required later they can be donned without delay.

There should be a life-jacket for each member of the crew stowed away as part of the ship's equipment. If individual members wish to wear buoyancy aids and inflatable garments this is acceptable, but a set of life-jackets for use at a time ordered by the skipper should be available in addition to any individual equipment worn in the normal course of sailing.

Man overboard Briefing on the drill in the event of a man overboard should be thorough. It is the one thing that can happen without warning at any time. The equipment, which is considered fully later, should be checked and the lifebuoy light tested if it is of the dry-battery, mercury-switch type. Even with water-activated cells the bulb can be taken out and tested.

As soon as the cry "Man Overboard" is heard all the crew should come on deck. The life-ring, always ready for instant release and never lashed down, must be thrown: another one is ready. What happens next depends on the number of crew available, but one man should watch the man in the water. Assuming the yacht was close-hauled the yacht should bear away in order to gybe and return to the man head to wind. This is not easy to practise. If the yacht is running without a spinnaker, there is no need to gybe, instead it will be possible to round up. Unless very quick a tack or two will be needed. The most serious case is running with the spinnaker hoisted. It will be impossible to alter course instantly and the distance between the yacht and the man in the water increases rapidly. A false move could result in fouled spinnaker gear and an inability to return to windward in sufficient time. Therefore the first move is to lower the spinnaker and a method that has been tried successfully with a rope halyard is to cut it, allowing it to run through the block at the masthead. It can then be pulled in without having to let go from the end of the boom. Emergency lowering drills should be thought out for different types of gear.

Once the yacht is under control and able to beat to windward she will have to tack back along the reciprocal course to where the man in the water can be found. This will have been aided if it has been possible by throwing other objects such as cushions along the path the yacht has sailed. Further difficult actions follow, including laying alongside him and getting him on board, which is no easy matter. I am afraid that all this takes time and demands the highest seamanship and preparation. So (*a*) drills must be known and practised; (*b*) the equipment must be comprehensive and suitable.

Crew harnesses   The best way to avoid the possibility of the events described above is to keep the crew on deck. Handholds, lifelines, non-slip surfaces and cockpit layouts, especially the means of entering and leaving the main hatch, all help here. In general the greatest aid is personal safety harnesses. Now these are often a little awkward to put on and the wisest course is to have a rule about them—always worn on deck except in very light weather on sheltered waters. The attachment line has to be hooked on the life-line or rigging and this can often foul other gear. Some arrangement whereby wires run inboard along coachroof or deck can help here. The safety harness attachment can be snapped to these for ease of movement (Fig. 48). There is a British Standard Specification for safety harnesses, BS 4224 of 1967. This lays down that the line shall be a minimum of 5 ft. in length and 2000 lb. in breaking strain. It also contains design and material specifications for the hook, straps and assembly. The metal parts are required to have non-magnetic properties.

Risk of collision   The possibility of collision is a safety aspect which must concern all the crew as it can happen when cruising to the start as much as any other time. There seems to be frequent difficulty in determining whether risk of collision exists, especially with steamers and boats under power. Though it is known that a collision will only result if the bearing of the other vessel from the bow fails to alter, in fact this bearing will change only very slowly at first when the steamer is going to pass ahead.

Sometimes when racing, an approaching steamer is seen to alter course unpredictably when a mile or so off and this may be because she has seen other yachts in the race, but which are not in your own horizon. So when racing it should not be assumed that a ship will hold her course. All this can be distracting to concentration and one member of the crew can be detailed to watch any danger of collision, allowing the remainder to get on with racing the yacht.

The main danger is at night and a sharp look-out must be kept for the navigation lights of other yachts racing. Offshore clubs are increasingly conscious of the need for efficient lights and, with large fleets cross-tacking, they have to be effective. There should be no difficulty about giving way to other yachts when racing rules apply. At night, as it is not possible to distinguish a sailing craft in the race from one cruising in the area, it is necessary to abandon IYRU racing rules and revert to International Collision regulations. These cannot cope with racing manœuvres such as rounding marks, but, in practice offshore, no difficulties seem to be caused. In the 1967 Half Ton Cup races, the French yacht *Dame d'Iroise*, which had a good chance of winning the series, luffed an opposing yacht at night and was disqualified as racing rules did not apply during the hours of darkness.

By day or night, if a miscalculation is made in a port and starboard situation, on no account attempt to bear away under the stern of the other yacht. Both yachts involved should luff up, which will avoid serious damage. Except at very slow speeds, the crew should never attempt to fend off another craft with hands or feet. It is better to allow minor damage to rubbers and paintwork than risk possibility of personal injury in this way.

Deck scraping genoas make a proper lookout on the lee bow difficult and a man should be posted in the pulpit when using this sail when other yachts are about. Dinghies are fitted with transparent windows in headsails but this is not at the moment practicable in larger craft due to insufficient strength round the edge of the panel and the difficulty of stowing it without damage in a sail bag.

FIG. 48. *Use of personal safety harness. A wire running along the deck inside all tracks and life-lines enables the line of the harness to be attached while the crew is still in cockpit. He can then walk forward closely attached.*

7

THE RULE AND THE RULES

WHEREVER ocean racing men meet the conversation at some stage turns to "the rule" and how each yacht fares under it. For the ocean racing yacht, the most important single figure among all her data is the figure quoted in feet to one decimal place from which her handicap is obtained. So when "the rule" is mentioned it is the rule of measurement and rating that is meant and we look at it closely below. But there are other rules for the racing man, those of the customs of all racing and the right of way and what in inshore and dinghy racing would be known as class rules. The latter, concerned with size and type, are closely allied to the organizations which give particular races and are dealt with in the next chapter. Yet a further important set of rules are those on safety and seaworthiness.

IYRU rules   The notice of the race or the sailing instructions will state that the event is under the current racing rules of the International Yacht Racing Union and these are published in every country by the national authority, which usually adds its own prescriptions and modifications. In fact, several of the IYRU rules are so phrased as to intend amplification from the national authority. Each authority is concerned with yachting as a whole in its own country and in Britain it is the Royal Yachting Association (RYA), in the USA it is the North American Yacht Racing Union, and in France, the Fédération Française du Yachting à Voile. The IYRU can supply a complete list of these national authorities, which are its members. It is not necessary to explain the contents of the IYRU rules, but there are a few ocean racing aspects. A copy should be kept on board with the other reference books, in case of protests or doubts. It is worth reading the sections other than the right-of-way rules, because some of the rules are the basis of ocean racing regulations. The setting and sheeting of sails (IYRU rule 54) is important, and is likely to be further amplified and amended for ocean racing. There are basic rules about anchoring, accepting outside assistance, who can race yachts as an owner and who is an amateur. Rule 27 refers to flag usage, and in England it is necessary to fly a racing flag at or near the masthead, though this is not the practice in many countries. A more positive way of showing that the yacht is not racing or has retired from the race is to hoist the ensign at the stern.

Part IV (Sailing rules when yachts meet) is the centre of the IYRU rule book and these apply offshore as much as in races round the buoys. However, they do of course only operate between yachts racing (whether in the same race or not), and at night or in fog it may not be possible to be sure that a yacht approaching is racing. You may have a shrewd idea that the other vessel is in the fleet, but if there is uncertainty, or if you were acting under the racing rules, and the boat turned out to be a cruiser, collision could result. So IYRU rules cannot be used at night, except in waters where there is no possibility of any other sailing vessel, which is rare. Accordingly International Regulations for the

Prevention of Collision at sea are used at night and the sailing instructions should make it clear at what time the changeover occurs. The trouble is that the collision regulations do not allow for such situations as yachts converging on a mark or one yacht passing another to windward.

The organizing club will usually issue racing regulations which are permanent amendments to some of the IYRU rules. One of the most important for ocean racing is to make a breach of rules punishable other than by disqualification. In the RORC, five or ten per cent is added to the time correction factor when working out the corrected time. The relevant JOG rule reads as follows:

"If a yacht disobeys any of the following rules or JOG special regulations in circumstances which, in the opinion of the committee do not constitute a gross breach of the rules, she shall be penalised by having her elapsed time for the race increased by one hour."

What follows then is the IYRU rules Part IV, the international collision regulations, some of the rules about carrying certain equipment and IYRU rule 52. This rule states that a yacht which touches a mark shall retire immediately. The intention here is that the crew of a yacht which is expecting to race for a whole week-end and probably on passage to another port in the course of the race, can continue in it if an accidental offence is committed. It must be remembered that the IYRU rules are based on inshore racing. Other racing regulations of the RORC and JOG which affect IYRU rules concern the composition of a protest committee, the size of sail numbers, recalls, boarding and leaving the yacht while racing, use of the engine and the cancellation of races. There is a veiled suggestion in IYRU rule 12 that if a yacht's position is very good and she prejudices this by rendering assistance, the race can be cancelled. Offshore, the double reason of the necessity for always giving assistance at sea whatever the circumstances and the practical unlikelihood of re-sailing an offshore race, make it better to strike this idea out at an early stage. The nature of an ocean race is such that there should never be any time limits, and this is the case if there is no reference to it in any instructions. The IYRU rules are amended from time to time (though often frozen for a couple of years before each Olympic Games), so the ocean racing man should keep up with any changes. As far as racing regulations by the organization giving any race is concerned these are slightly different everywhere and should be studied carefully before the racing season or particular event.

Rating   The object of a rating rule is to enable yachts of different size and type to race together, but once the rule is established yachts will be designed to its formulae so it must not "produce" undesirable features in hull or rig. The management of rating rules in effect becomes a running battle between the rule authority, which tries to maintain a mathematical formula that reflects the racing potential of the yacht, and the designers' attempt to construct the fastest boat for the value of the rating, naturally exploiting any weaknesses that are detected in the formulae. Rating rules are thus in a continual state of evolution, partly because of gradual discovery in cheating the rule and partly because the development of new materials and techniques in construction and the sailing of the boat. This is no bad thing, if the process can be kept to a reasonably slow pace and so yachts given a racing life of a number of years. The influence of rating rules permeates the whole history of yacht design and is responsible for many features on cruising yachts which are never raced. To naval architects it is equivalent to the cargo capacity or tonnage of a commercial ship, which is also used to measure her; gross and net tonnage (by which yachts can also be measured for government purposes) being calculated from formulae concerned with size. It is significant that yacht measurement rules came from the same root, for in 1854 "Thames Tonnage" was used to handicap yachts. The formula for this is still well known in England, for curiously it has been retained to refer to a yacht's "tonnage". It is $\dfrac{(L-B) \times \frac{1}{2}B \times B,}{94}$ and really meaningless today,* depending as it does so much on beam. It is not surprising that it produced yachts that were extremely narrow and is a simple (and extreme) example of how a rating rule influences design. If this British rule was simple so was the Seawanhaka Yacht Club formula of about the same period. This was $\dfrac{L \times SA}{4000}$, thus leaving out beam altogether. So the creators of this rule got a beamy, light yacht with much initial stability to travel as fast as possible for its limited length and sail area (SA). But then you have heard of those "centre-board bugs" and "cutter cranks".

Restricted class rules   One way of gaining control of design for the purpose of fairer racing, is in addition to the measurement formula to specify maximum and minimum length, beam, height of mast and so on. This can only be done if one size of yacht is envisaged, so the designer's object becomes to arrange the factors in the measurement formula so that the rating comes to a predetermined figure. This was the way in which the "International Rule", first worked out in 1906, was constructed. It was for inshore racing yachts which were rated at various sizes such as 6-metres, 8-metres and 12-metres. The 12-metre, using basically the same formulae, is still with us today in use for America's Cup contests. The sixes and eights no longer race internationally, but can be found in a few scattered places in North America. The measurement rule brought in factors to regulate displacement and freeboard as well as the major components of length, beam and sail area. Its successor was the IYRU post-war "cruiser-racer" rule, which attempted to sponsor "metre boats", but with accommodation and therefore presumably suitable for offshore racing. For instance, the rule could be applied to build an 8-metre cruiser-racer and the LWL would have to be between 26·25 ft. (=8 metres) and 27·40. This is interesting in view of the development of the One Ton Cup dealt with in the next chapter. These metre cruiser-racers never became popular because yachtsmen preferred to sail offshore and on handicap under the rules of the CCA and RORC.

Ocean racing rules and time scales   Where the ocean racing rules succeeded and the IYRU ideas failed, was that the former could be applied to any yacht, giving a nucleus of yachts in any race, which over the years could grow in popularity. The measurement rule of the Cruising Club of America and the Royal Ocean Racing Club could be used to measure a yacht of any size who then had a rating in feet, which could be used for handicapping. The handicapping system should be understood as being separate from the rating rule. Once a yacht has a rating in a linear measure (i.e. a figure such as 25·52 ft.) a variety of handicap systems can be used with it. In most racing in Britain it is used to

---

* Where L is length between perpendiculars and B is beam.

obtain a time-correction factor by the formula $TCF = \dfrac{\sqrt{R \times 2 \cdot 6}}{10}$, where R is rating, which
is simply used to multiply the elapsed time to give a "corrected time". This is the time-on-time system. It does not depend on the length of the race, which may not be in fact the distance which the yacht has to sail owing to tidal streams. It can give an advantage to the smaller boat, if there is a period of prolonged calm and time is increased without any distance increasing between yachts of different size. There is no reason why any time-scale cannot be used with the yachts' ratings to suit local conditions and experience of racing.

A time-on-distance system gives a theoretical number of seconds per mile to each
yacht, derived from the rating by the formula BSF (basic speed figure) $= \dfrac{514 \cdot 3}{TCF}$
seconds per mile. By agreeing on the distance of the race, the boat with the smallest BSF becomes scratch with the others given so many seconds over the course, calculated from the difference of their BSFs multiplied by the number of miles. The advantage of this system is that the handicaps can be worked out before the race and only subtraction is required to find the corrected times at the end. Its disadvantage lies in the distance on which it is based not being correct, because of windward work and currents. The system is widely used in USA. The time in seconds obtained from the rating figure is known as an "allowance" and tables are published giving the seconds allowed for every rating figure. These are then used in the same way as the RORC BSF. It is common practice to vary the nominal distance of the race if it has been found to give unequitable results in the past. This is a quite legitimate method of varying a time-scale. The important point about time-scales is that they give clubs in different parts of the world ways of varying the handicapping of yachts, without touching more involved matters of measurement. The time-scales mentioned are only those in recent use and the principles are unaltered if any variation or a combination of both time-on-time and time-on-distance is used.

The CCA and RORC rules The CCA and the RORC rules were those under which most of the world's ocean racers developed since the 1930s. The CCA rule was of the form: Rating $= 0.95 \, (L \pm B \pm Draft \pm Displace \pm SA \pm Freebd \pm I) \times Bal\ Ratio \times Prop$ (I is rated length, B is beam, SA is sail area, I is iron keel allowance). The details of the rule, like all modern rating systems, are considerable, but the various factors were determined by their variation from an ideal or "base" boat for any length and the final rating figure was in effect the length of the yacht corrected by the influence of factors on the speed producing qualities. The tendency was to correct their value from year to year as yacht design progressed. The British accusation was that the rule was type-producing, but if this was so, it produced a fine type! It was also accused of unnecessary complication and expense. Note that displacement is in the rule and this was determined by weighing—logical but laborious.

The 1957 RORC rule was of the form:

$$\text{Rating} = \frac{\cdot 15L\sqrt{SA}}{\sqrt{BD}} + \cdot 2(L + \sqrt{SA} - \text{stability allowance} - \text{prop} - \text{draft penalty}. \quad (D \text{ here}$$

meaning "depth" as carried on into the IOR rule.) This is usually considered a freer rule than the CCA, the American view being that it was too easy to exploit and could produce freaks. But the really successful rule cheaters have been fine sea boats. Each factor in the rule was the subject of many corrections and sub-formulae, but as the general concept is not unlike the international offshore rule, there is no point in detailing this. The similarity of the basic formulae should be noted as a step in the evolution of rating rules. There were and are other rating rules for handicap racing offshore. Among them are the SHR or Baltic Rule, used off the coast of Scandinavia, although the RORC rule came to be used for the more important races. In the USA the Storm Trysail Club rule and Off Soundings rule were also established. Because of the unsuitability of the CCA rule for small yachts, the Midget Ocean Racing Club with yachts under 30 ft. LOA drew up its own MORC rule, which was based on that of the CCA, but these bodies have since changed to the IOR rule.

The International Offshore Rule　　In 1960 a group of international yachtsmen met in Bremen, Germany, to see if it was possible to reconcile the CCA, RORC and other conflicting ocean racing rules. From this was formed the Offshore Rules Co-ordinating Committee (ORCC), which met at intervals and CCA and RORC details bringing them into line where acceptable to the two clubs. It took a spurt forward in 1966 when the IYRU took a hand. Thinking in terms of an offshore racing class for the Olympic Games, it asked the ORCC to take more active measures. Fortunately, there was a man of sufficient stature available who had designed and raced boats to both rules for more than thirty years. This was Olin J. Stephens Jr., of New York, whose reputation as a genius of yacht design was so established that he could speak with unsurpassed authority, without undue dispute from the designers of the world, on such a difficult issue. He became Chairman of a sub-committee of the ORCC known as the International Technical Committee (ITC), consisting of six men who worked on the new rule for two and a half years. They were Dick Carter (USA), winner, like Stephens, of a Fastnet race* and an admirer of the concept of the RORC rule, two British experts in the management of the international application of the RORC rule, David Fayle and Robin Glover, and from Europe, the noted yacht designers Gustav Plym (Sweden) and E. G. van de Stadt (Netherlands). The basic formula of the rule they produced is shown as:

$$\text{Rating} = MR \times EPF \times CGF$$

where

$$MR = \frac{\cdot 13L\sqrt{S}}{\sqrt{B \times D}} + \cdot 25L + \cdot 20\sqrt{S} + DC + FC$$

The meaning of the symbols is:

    MR is measured rating;
    EPF is engine and propeller factor;
    CGF is centre of gravity factor;
    L is length, B is beam, D is depth, S is sail area, DC is draft correction and FC is freeboard correction.

The rule is seen to be very similar in its basic formula to the 1957 RORC rule with freeboard and draft borrowed from the CCA rule also given above. EPF (engine and propeller factor) and CGF (centre of gravity factor) are present as they were in the RORC and

---

* In 1969 he won his second Fastnet race.

CCA formula, though they were not called that. What has disappeared is the direct measure of displacement (in the CCA rule) but in the detailed assessment of sail area many of the CCA methods are used as well as innovations.

Each of the factors above is quite complex and is derived from a whole set of subsidiary formulae, designed for use on a computer, and therefore cannot be set out here; the rule runs into many pages. An owner should always obtain the rule booklet and study these details as deeply as possible.

Conditions are laid down under which the measurements are obtained: the yacht must be in "measurement trim"; sails must be stowed in a specified position; water tanks must be empty; fuel tanks must be full; no men are allowed on board and there are rules about the position of anchors and chains and such things as bedding.

Length   Length and sail area can be seen to be the most important factors in obtaining a rating. Both are obtained from many ancillary measurements. Length is derived from length between girths (LBJ) by the formula:

$$L = LBG - FOC - AOCC$$

FOC is forward overhang component and AOCC is after overhang component corrected. Fig. 49 shows the various "girth stations" and these are found by passing a line around the hull equivalent to a proportion of the rated beam, B. For instance, AGS (after girth station) is where a chain of $\frac{3}{4}$B fits, FGS (forward girth station) is where $\frac{1}{2}$B fits. AIGS (after inner girth station) is $\frac{7}{8}$B, FIGS is $\frac{3}{4}$B. A system of checks and balances uses these positions to give FOC and AOCC so that the rule does not encourage chopped off, extra long, or any other distorted ends of a yacht to reduce L. Freeboard at various points, as shown in the diagram, is involved in these corrections such as FA and FF in the figure.

The freeboard correction in the basic formula, FC, increases the rating if the freeboard is very low and rather less if it is very high. There is a base freeboard (FB) based on L. If the measured freeboard (FM) is close to this, the freeboard correction will increase negligibly. The formulae for this are simple and typify the way a rating rule works.

$$FB = 0 \cdot 057L + 1 \cdot 20$$

$$FM = \frac{1 \cdot 2FF + 0 \cdot 8FA}{2}$$

These are combined to give FC, depending whether or not FB is bigger than FM.

$$FC = 0 \cdot 25(FB - FM)$$
$$or \quad FC = 0 \cdot 15(FM - FB)$$

Beam and depth   The point of maximum beam on the hull is found and this is called "BMAX". A distance of $\frac{1}{6}$BMAX (Fig. 50) is found below the covering board, or equivalent, and B is the maximum beam at or below this point. This prevents a yacht being designed with excessive flare just at deck level to obtain a high B measurement. In the basic formula, the more beam then the lower the rating, but B occurs in a number of places in the calculation of AOCC and FOC to check the tendency to gain by having a large B at only one point on the yacht.

Displacement is one of the most important single characteristics of the yacht and it is

H

measured indirectly by means of "depth". Depth is taken in two places, MDI (midships depth immersed) is one half of LBG abaft (FGS) (Fig. 49). Fig. 51 shows how it is measured, one-quarter of B out from the centre line. The result is the depth of the hull below the waterline, which reflects the fullness of the hull. A similar system is used one quarter of LBG abaft FGS and one-tenth of B out from the centre line to measure FDI. Depth is then obtained by putting them into this formula:

$$D = 1 \cdot 15 MDI + 0 \cdot 9 FDI + 0 \cdot 055$$
$$(3FOC - AOCC) + \frac{L + 10}{30}$$

Draft is dealt with in the same manner as freeboard with a base draft calculated from L. When the measured draft exceeds this by more than a given amount, the factor DC in the basic formula increases the yacht's rating.

Engine propeller and heeling   EPF in the basic formula is equal to

$$\frac{1 - EMF + DF}{100}$$

EMF is the engine moment factor which is based on the weight of the engine and its distance from MD with allowance for the size of the yacht. DF is the propeller drag factor based on the diameter and type of the propeller, again allowing for the size of the yacht. To avoid extra thin propellers for rating purposes, if the diameter is greater than four times the width of blade it is the latter which is used in calculation. Propeller type has a scale of constants, of which the following are examples:

Solid 2 blade in aperture	2·25
Solid 2 blade out of aperture	2.00
Feathering 2 blade with "exposed shaft" (as defined)	1·25
Folding propeller out of aperture	0·5

The CGF (centre of gravity factor) is a measure of the position of the centre of gravity, a higher ballast ratio resulting in a higher rating. As a multiplication factor in the basic formula, a very low centre of gravity (e.g. a 12-metre class yacht) might give 1·1, that is an increase in MR of 10 per cent. A tender sea-going yacht might have a factor of 0·96. To obtain CGF the yacht is heeled to between 2 and 4 degrees by means of cans of water of known volume. The heeling angle is measured with a plumb line. Calculations are then made for a "tenderness ratio" at 1 degree of heel, and CGF is obtained directly from this (Fig. 52).

Sail area   Sail area not only has a large impact on the basic formula, but often is the aspect of rating of most concern to the owner and which he can alter fairly simply. The rules take into account every possible rig and there tend to be amendments from year to year in this department as sails of new shape are developed, sometimes in order to "beat the rule". The rule can be examined, for example, for a yawl, where there are rules for the size of sails between the masts. The way sail area is measured can be shown most simply on a masthead sloop rig. The symbols used for the various lengths measured are in Fig. 53. The letter C with a symbol means "corrected" e.g. JC is J which has been corrected. In the sloop rig it is the mainsail (RSAM = rated sail area mainsail) and the foretriangle (RSAF) which are measured. These are the formulae:

$$RSAM = 0\cdot35EC \times PC + 0\cdot2E(PC - 2E)$$

$$RSAF = 0\cdot5IC \times JC\left(1 + 1\cdot1\frac{(LP - JC)}{LP}\right) + 0\cdot2JC(1C - 2JC)$$

Fig. 54 shows LP, which is the greatest of (LPG perpendicular from clew to luff of largest genoa) or LPIS or 1·5 J, J being the base of foretriangle regardless of what sails are on board. The biggest headsails can be cut high in the foot as long as their LPG measurement are the same.

The expressions after the plus sign in both RSAM and RSAF are means of rating the aspect ratio. There is minimum value, under this rule for the size of mainsail. It is 0·094 (IC)².

Reasons for which E, P, I and J might be corrected are as follows:

E. Distance aft of clew of a tang on a main boom to sheet a headsail; battens and headboards in the mainsail more than a certain size.
P. Gooseneck too high or top of P more than 0·04 I below top of I.
I. Height of spinnaker boom track; luff/leech of spinnaker too long.
J. Spinnaker too wide or spinnaker boom too long.

Sail restrictions Minor rules on sails, their sheeting and cut are made quite frequently. The minimum quantity for RSAM above, is to prevent all or nearly all the area being put in the foretriangle. A spacing rule for battens ensures that the top one is at least twenty per cent of the leech down from the head: this prevents the "gaff", which was used on RORC measured sails. The luff/leech measurement of a spinnaker is restricted to $0\cdot95\sqrt{I^2 + JC^2}$. Twice any excess is added to *I* to give *IC*.

There are rules to keep a clear distinction between headsails and spinnakers. A spinnaker must be symmetrical and the mid-girth must be at least seventy-five per cent of the foot length. A headsail mid-girth must not be more than forty per cent of the foot length. So a "genaker" with a mid-girth of between fifty and seventy-five per cent of the foot length can never be used under the IOR rule.

Safety rules Any club giving an ocean race is careful to make it clear that the responsibility for the safety of the yacht and the crew cannot be other than on the owner or person in charge. But the organizing body does feel a duty towards those that sail under its flag and there will be a list of safety requirements for the event. The danger to newcomers to the sport is that they may feel that if they carry all the special equipment required by the instructions then they are "safe". I am not keen on the term "safety" for these matters, as the material required for the handling of the yacht seems to be of two types: that needed on a day-to-day basis such as the compass or fog horn, which one would be unsafe without but is not exclusively thought of in terms of safety and emergency equipment; what I term "emergency equipment" is that which is not normally used unless an accident occurs. In this category come such things as life-jackets, distress flares, the first-aid box. However, all are usually included in safety regulations. As in all forms of modern life, there is a tendency for these rules to increase and I believe every attempt should be made by the organizations concerned to keep them minimal. On the other hand, owners welcome a limited number if they insist on matters which are good practice, for the reason that they ensure that the "next man" does not leave ashore equipment which ought to be carried at sea. So they give fairer racing.

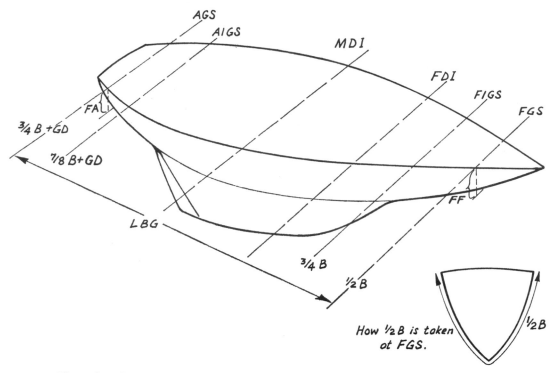

FIG. 49. *The various "stations" used on a yacht's hull in the determination of length and depth. By taking girths related to B length, between them as used in the various formulae, freeboards at certain places and depth at MDI and FDI are found.*

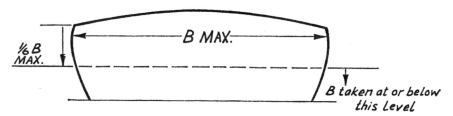

FIG. 50 (above). *The system of finding measured beam, B. B Max. is found at the point of maximum beam and then B taken of this below the covering board or at any point below if greater.*

FIG. 51 (right). *The meaning of depth measurement. MDI (midships depth immersed) is a factor reflecting displacement.*

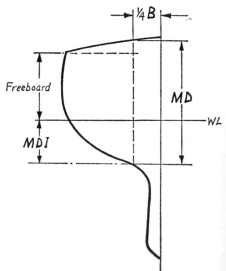

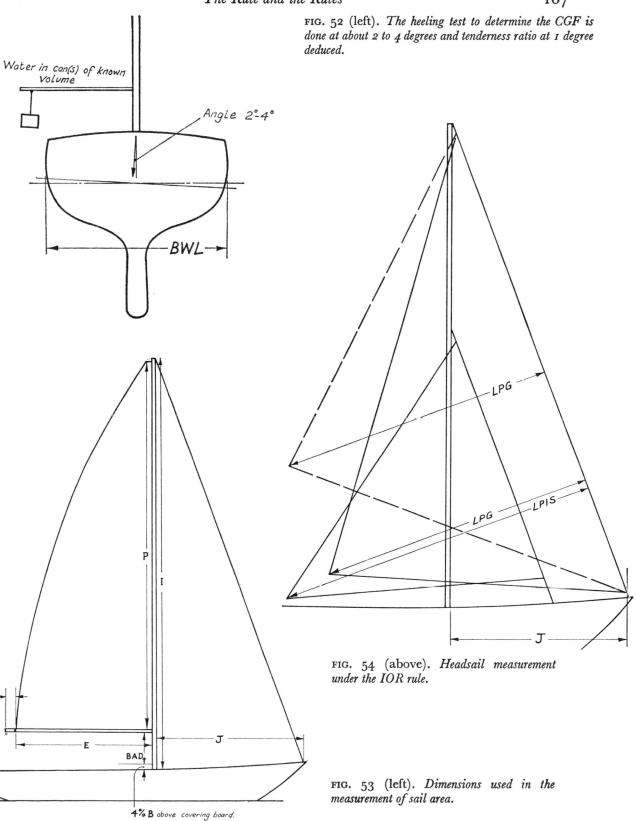

Water in can(s) of known volume

Angle 2°-4°

BWL

FIG. 52 (left). *The heeling test to determine the CGF is done at about 2 to 4 degrees and tenderness ratio at 1 degree deduced.*

LPG

LPG LPIS

J

P

I

J

E

BAD

4% B *above covering board.*

FIG. 54 (above). *Headsail measurement under the IOR rule.*

FIG. 53 (left). *Dimensions used in the measurement of sail area.*

Safety rules are now coming under the scrutiny of international interest that has in turn unified the yacht racing rules and the rating rules and as in these first two, the matters dealt with are mainly the same in different parts of the world. At the time of writing each organization issues its own so that when a yacht takes part in international events she must check that she complies, especially in structural matters such as the cockpit arrangement and the position of stanchion bases. If international agreement is reached on safety rules, there are still bound to be national and regional variations as in the manner of the prescriptions to the racing rules. For yachts over about 24-ft. waterline the safety rules of the North American Yacht Racing Union and the RORC are of wide interest, the first having established some uniform standard for the yachts in the USA whereas most of Europe and many other countries overseas have rules at least originally based on RORC practice. The various organizations giving races for yachts offshore which are under 24 ft. have almost all based their rules on those of the JOG. For instance, the Scandinavian Ocean Racing Committee have rules that are almost word for word the same as the JOG. While the GCL in France have expanded theirs, as have the American midget ocean racing clubs. New Zealand and Australia differ in few points from the JOG and naturally there are some variations in all countries, if only to suit local conditions. Special contests such as the Half and Quarter Ton Cup races have constructed their regulations from the existing rules. (*See* Appendices 5 and 6.)

NAYRU and RORC safety rules   The NAYRU Safety Rules are interesting in that they try to cover all types of offshore events categorizing them into:

1. Long races in open water for extended periods where yachts must be completely self-sufficient and capable of withstanding heavy storms.
2. Distance races of extended duration which require a high degree of self-sufficiency.
3. Medium distance races which are overnight and in relatively protected waters.
4. Short day races close to shore.

A comprehensive list of needs is then given and the category number or numbers placed against it. For instance, "radio transmitter—min power 35 watts, moisture proofed" is labelled 1, 2. "Water resistant flash lights and signalling light" is labelled 1, 2, 3. For sails, there is "Storm trysail and storm jib" as 1, 2 and "Heavy weather jib and reefing equipment" for 3, 4. All this is certainly an attempt to co-ordinate regulations, though I feel that category 4 is so different that it should really not be included at all. It is up to the organizing body to decide in which category its race comes, and the owner is helped by being able to equip his yacht correctly up to the most stringent category into which he intends to enter. The full rules are available from the NAYRU, 37 West 44th Street, New York.

The RORC is only faced with the necessity of formulating safety rules for its own races, though they have been used in many parts of the world with little alteration. Certainly they are excellent for the changeable weather of north-west European seaboards. The RORC tries to keep the requirements as simple as possible and they are briefer than any others issued by any offshore club. The club does, however, do random checks on its fleet to ensure compliance. It also helps owners by providing, if requested, a comprehensive list of the equipment an offshore yacht should have, without laboriously listing such things in its rules.

The RORC has its own rules for the equipment needed in emergency life-rafts, which is less than that for ships under government regulations. This standard for yachts has been useful for life-raft manufacturers, who make standard rafts with "RORC pack". The standard involves two separate buoyancy compartments, each automatically inflatable, an automatic inflating canopy and a valid annual certificate (this is given after a stringent test). The pack comprises:

1 Sea anchor or drogue
1 Bellows for hand inflation
1 Signalling torch
3 BOT approved hand flares
2 Parachute flares
1 Baler
1 Repair kit
1 Safety knife
2 Paddles
1 Rescue quoit and line

Safety rules for smaller yachts   The rules for smaller yachts need to be different, if only because the potential dangers are different in emphasis and some equipment needs

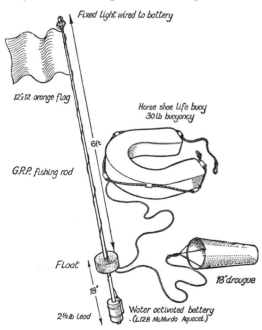

FIG. 55. *Man overboard gear with life-buoy and dan buoy. The light is "fixed" rather than flashing, as it will appear to flash as it dips in the seas. A lightweight GRP fishing rod is suitable and the drogue prevents drift.*

to be scaled down in bulk and to save expense. All safety rules are amended, usually in small details, from year to year, but in 1969 the JOG published new rules. While not radical in any way they received considerable thought and the opinions of a number of designers and of other offshore men were sought before they were finally agreed. The GCL rules are similar in most respects, but this French club specifies a radio receiver and a minimum crew of three. One omission from JOG and GCL—but which is insisted on by the JOG Association of Australia, and the Midget Ocean Racing Association of Northern California among others—is a dan buoy connected to a life-buoy for throwing to a man overboard. This is a useful piece of equipment in any circumstances and a suitable arrangement is shown in Fig. 55. The JOG safety rules are divided into two grades, mandatory and recommended. Some criticism has been levelled from time to time on the use of such as "suitable" and "adequate", but every yacht is inspected by the JOG before racing and these words can be given a standard meaning by the inspector. The rules begin by emphasizing the responsibility of the owner. Because they are of use to those who sail small ocean racers everywhere, I am giving them in full.

The holding of JOG Certificate of Inspection in no way relieves the OWNER of a yacht from THE SOLE RESPONSIBILITY that the yacht and her crew are fit and properly equipped for offshore racing. Owners and skippers are reminded that they must expect to spend longish periods at sea when there may be no harbour or refuge within easy reach and no means of obtaining assistance.

Apart from assuring themselves of the soundness of the yacht and its gear, they should look to such matters as rudder hangings, chainplates, deck fittings, etc. They should make sure that glass or perspex in deck openings, coachroof, etc., can be protected easily and secured if broken; that all openings in the hull have seacocks on the flange of the openings; that propeller shafts are properly secured and cannot withdraw; that pumps are adequate and in good condition, can be worked at sea and can be cleared in the event of choking.

PART I

Mandatory Rules

Rule I. The yacht must be self-righting (i.e. must possess an adequate range of stability) and, as a guide, the product of the following formula should exceed 1.10:

$$\frac{B+2F}{L}+\frac{DR}{2}$$

where B is maximum beam
F is freeboard at 50 per cent LWL
D is maximum draft excluding centreboard
L is length on waterline in measurement trim
R is ballast ratio, i.e.

$$\frac{\text{ballast lb.}}{\text{displacement in measurement trim, lb.}}$$

B, F, D and L are to be measured in feet to two places of decimals. In computing R, inside ballast will be reckoned at 50 per cent its actual weight. Metal centreplates, i.e. other than wood boards, will be reckoned as outside ballast but draft will be taken without reference to the plate.

To be acceptable, a yacht fitted with a centreboard or boards must be self-righting (*vide* self-righting test) with its plate or plates fully raised; and the Committee must be satisfied that, when the plate or plates are fully lowered or in any intermediate position, the boat is not likely to be strained in a seaway.

In cases where the inspecting officer is not satisfied with the safety of the boat, he may ask for a self-righting test to be carried out at owner's risk. During this, after closing hatches, scuttles and vents as necessary, the boat will be hove down on her beam ends, when a satisfactory righting moment must be developed.

It is emphasized that the above test and Rule (I) are designed to ensure that a yacht has the ability to recover from a severe knockdown in a seaway. This ability may be only distantly related to her ability to carry sail, and is a prime prerequisite in a boat intended to keep the seas.

Rule II. Hull, decks, and upperworks, mast, rigging and fittings must be sufficiently strong to withstand the weight of a heavy sea upon them or the stresses imposed by the vessel being rolled on her side.

Rule III. To be suitable for JOG racing a boat must possess sufficient windward ability to enable her to get off a lee shore in bad conditions and boats must have at least 60 per cent of RORC maximum draft without penalty. (RORC maximum draft without penalty is 16 per cent waterline length plus 2 ft. or 60 cm.)

Rule IV. The cockpit must be watertight to seat-level except that outboard drains are permitted. (As a guide, the overall volume must be limited by the following formula, the product of which must not exceed 7.00.

$$\frac{100V}{FB(LWL+LOA-LWL)}$$

where V is Volume of cockpit in cu. ft. up to deck level, i.e. excluding coamings

F is freeboard as in Rule (I)

B is beam as in Rule (I)

LOA is overall length in feet excluding bowsprit or bumpkin.

LWL is L as in Rule (I)

Locker space in the cockpit must have well fitting lids which are secured by clips or similar fittings or lashings when racing. It must be possible to secure the companion way (hatch) to the cabin in rough weather to prevent ingress of water in the event that the cockpit be flooded to the coamings.

PART I

Mandatory Equipment

Rule V. The following items of equipment must be carried:

(a) Two serviceable bunks not less than six ft. long. (1·8 m)

(b) Cooking stove capable of safe operation at sea.

(c) Adequate chart table or plotting board.

(d) W.C. or fitted bucket.

(e) One anchor and suitable cable. When an anchor warp is used, at least 2 fathoms (3·6 m) of chain must be fitted between the warp and anchor.

(f) An efficient compass, properly mounted.

(g) An efficient fire extinguisher.

(h) First-aid box, including material for treating burns, and instruction book.

(i) Suitable storm canvas. Alternatively, the working canvas must be suitable for reduction in area and withstanding storm conditions.

(j) Internationally recognized distress signals. The following must be carried as a minimum: 2 parachute rockets red, 2 five-star flares, 1 daylight smoke flare, 3 red hand flares.

(k) Port, starboard and stern lights so fitted that they are not masked by the sails. Two powerful electric torches and at least 3 white flares.

(*l*) An efficient lifejacket of a type approved by National Authority for each member of the crew. (In the United Kingdom lifejackets to British Standards Institute specifications are acceptable.)

(*m*) Efficient safety harnesses for each member on deck, with a line for properly securing to a strong point or lifeline.

N.B. *These are regarded as being the most valuable single items of safety equipment and should be worn whenever risk of falling overboard exists.*

(*n*) Adequate handholds about deck and cabin top.

(*o*) A pulpit at the bow, with taut and efficient guardrails or lifelines, properly supported at a height of NOT LESS THAN 12 in. (30 cm.) clear of the deck, from the pulpit to half way along the cockpit on each side of the vessel. Where the pulpit is positioned to the rear of the forestay the top of the pulpit must not be more than 15 in. (38 cm.) from the forestay. This guardrail must be capable of supporting the full weight of a man.

(*p*) A life-buoy with self-operating light or flare of approved type, carried on deck and able to be jettisoned readily.

(*q*) A suitable fog signal.

(*r*) A radar reflector of minimum size of 12 in. cube.

(*s*) Bilge pump (not fitted in a cockpit locker if only one carried).

(*t*) A suitable dinghy or life-raft: such dinghy may be of an inflatable type.

PART II

Recommended Equipment and other Recommendations

1 It is recommended that the following items should be carried in additon to the mandatory items set out in Part I.

(*a*) A self-inflating life raft fitted with canopy.

(*b*) A second fire extinguisher.

(*c*) A second bilge pump.

(*d*) A second anchor.

2 It is recommended, in yachts which do not carry life-rafts, that the yacht should carry sufficient positive buoyancy to support her, together with keel, stores, crew and a reserve of at least 250 lb. (1·125 kg.).

3 It is recommended that the area of the mainhatch or forehatch in plan should not exceed 3 sq. ft. (280 sq. cm.) in the smaller yachts or 4 sq. ft. (370 sq. cm.) in the larger and that hatch openings should be at least 3 in. (7·5 cm.) above deck level.

4 It is recommended that adequate ventilators should be fitted to cabins and should have efficient water traps.

5 In larger yachts, it is recommended that a properly supported guardrail or lifeline should be fitted on each side, at a minimum height of 17·5 in. (45 cm.) above the deck and that a stern pulpit ("pushpit") should be fitted to complete the encirclement of the deck. It is also recommended that the stanchions supporting the lifelines should not be spaced more than 58·5 in. (150 cm.) apart, and should be through bolted to the hull.

· 8 ·

THE CLUBS AND THEIR RACES

Rule 2. The objects of the Group shall be (a) *To encourage the racing of small offshore yachts of such a size as may be from time to time determined,* (b) *To study and encourage the design, building, navigation and sailing of such yachts*—from the constitution of the JUNIOR OFFSHORE GROUP

THE CLUBS and associations, which make it their main task to give ocean races, will be found on the whole to be directly managed by those that take an active part at sea. Inshore and local clubs have their older generation who as the years go by help mainly with the social side and act as officers of the day and other necessary tasks. With more time to devote to the club, they may well have a more considered view of how things should be run. This is not the case offshore where experience, over the horizon as it were, is everything. Offshore clubs are less involved with local interests and motives and all this adds up to organizations run by offshore men for themselves and growing on their own merits in many different parts of the world. In England and USA the national authorities have no direct control over ocean racing and the IYRU itself, until recently, has taken little interest. More recently it has done so because of a possibility of ocean racing in the Olympic Games. If this should occur, the size of boat will not be larger than those considered in this book, because of the need to have a yacht of reasonable price. So far the yachting section of the Olympics has been confined to inshore boats and any introduction of ocean racing will bring its own problems. However, it was interest in this matter that caused the IYRU to request the Offshore Rules Co-ordinating Committee to accelerate the unification of the CCA and RORC rules. With this task, as indicated in the previous chapter, fulfilled, the ORCC has remained in being as a unique body of international offshore men. It has formed the basis of an international Offshore Rating Council (ORC) to give offshore sailors their own world organization. There are growing tasks for such a body to undertake: the amendment and supervision of the operation of the International Offshore rule (the particular role of the ITC), gradual unification of safety rules and co-ordination of international events.

IASORY Because of the increasing internationalism of ocean racing, a number of clubs and associations giving races for the smaller yachts met in July 1967 and formed the International Association for Small Offshore Racing Yachts. At the time there was concern about uncontrolled proliferation of fixed rating classes (such as the Half Ton Cup dealt with below) and worry about the effect of the International Offshore rule on smaller boats. The author was appointed the Secretary and membership was open to clubs giving ocean races to yachts under about 24 ft. LWL or 30 ft. LOA, who then joined from every continent. There is no question of rivalry to ORC which was not yet established as an authority. Amalgamation will no doubt take place at a suitable stage. There is now international consultation on many of the matters affecting the smaller yachts.

Racing at fixed rating   The great mass of ocean racing is on handicap by the application of time allowance derived from a rating, but handicap racing in yachts of different size does lose something by comparison with one-design or restricted class racing where the first boat home is the winner. In 1965 the Cercle de la Voile de Paris in the guise of one of its leading members, Jean Peytel, decided to present a historic trophy for a new type of event. The Trophy was originally raced for at the turn of the century by the extinct One Ton class, an inshore keel-boat and it was then presented to the 6-metres, as a leading international racing class, which in turn faded out. Jean Peytel pointed out that the modern class that attracted the best international competition was the ocean racer under the RORC rule. He proposed a contest with several inshore races and a major event of 300 miles.

But the unique feature of the One Ton Cup was to be that the yachts would not race on handicap but level, the stipulation being that they must rate not higher than 22 ft. RORC.* By way of preventing "stripped-out" yachts, the rules of the IYRU 8-metre cruiser racer class were used for accommodation. The idea was received enthusiastically and a number of boats were specially designed and converted to take part at 22 ft. rating. The first series was won by the Danish yacht *Diana III*, a Sparkman and Stephens design, and as a result the second One Ton Cup was held off Copenhagen, where Dick Carter in *Tina* was victor. As he represented the USA the third set of races should have been there, but as the races used the RORC rule and the European nations were the main supporters, the event was at Le Havre and a development of *Tina*, *Optimist*, owned by G. Kohler of Germany, was winner (Fig. 56). This yacht won again in 1968 in her home waters of Heligoland. At that time there were boats from the following nations: Belgium 2, Germany 3, Great Britain 2, Finland 3, Holland 3, Italy 1, New Zealand 1, Austria 1, Sweden 3, Switzerland 1, USA 3. The entries per nation are limited to three and the winner is individual and not a team. The One Ton Cup attracts the top crews and designers and despite the European nature of the event American design dominates with the successful run of Dick Carter and an even larger number of Sparkman and Stephens yachts. In 1968 there were also designs by Britton Chance (including *Breyell II*, Fig. 77), Ted Hood, equally well known as a sail maker and William Tripp, leaving only four European designs in the races. In 1969 the New Zealand yacht *Rainbow* won the series.

The One Ton has come to mean the crack boats of the ocean racing world and the standard by which others are judged. Most One Ton boats return to their home waters to sweep the board. In the perfection and therefore the expense of these boats is the seeds of the destruction of the trophy series, for like other costly restricted classes they may discourage the majority of owners. Interest in England has become progressively less since 1965. The size of the boat is useful to many people and racing given by the series is excellent: it is to be hoped that some of the hot-house atmosphere of the One Ton Cup will in time wear off and that it will gain more general popularity.

The Half and Quarter Ton Cups   Similar trophies to the One Ton Cup have been introduced for yachts further down the scale—under the RORC rule the boats were 18 ft. and 15 ft. rating respectively. The Société des Régates Rochelaises initiated both these

* Under the IOR rule this has become 27·5 ft.

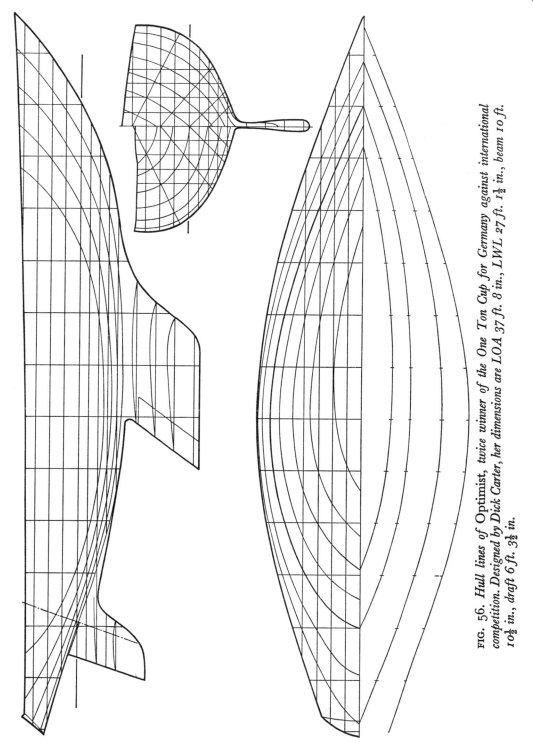

FIG. 56. *Hull lines of Optimist, twice winner of the One Ton Cup for Germany against international competition. Designed by Dick Carter, her dimensions are LOA 37 ft. 8 in., LWL 27 ft. 1½ in., beam 10 ft. 10½ in., draft 6 ft. 3½ in.*

and whatever their original names (the Half Ton is actually the Coupe Internationale Atlantique) they have become known as the Half Ton Cup and Quarter Ton Cup, confusing names which at least indicate the diminution from the One Ton Cup. Owing to their much more reasonable cost, the races have increased in popularity each year. The conditions are slightly different to the One Ton. In the Half Ton and Quarter Ton there is no limit to the number of entries and every boat sails as an individual, though in the Half Ton there is a team trophy for three boats per nation as well as the principal individual cup. The Quarter Ton accepts yachts which comply with the rules of the JOG or GCL, but the Half Ton has its own regulations, which include some on the size of the accommodation. They are interesting to show the requirements considered desirable in international racing in a modern ocean racer of about 22–24 ft. waterline, which is the Half Ton size and are reproduced in the Appendix. This is also a useful reference to owners who may only be able to obtain them in French.

The first three Half Ton cup races were at La Rochelle and were dominated by French yachts. After three wins by one nation, the rules require a change of venue, though it must be in Europe, and the fourth races in 1969 were at Sandhamn, Sweden. The French talent for the practical and strictly functional ocean racer of small size has had its reward in these races. Among the most successful designs were the Super Challenger, designed by Andre Mauric. *Dame d'Iroise* (Michel Perroud) which won the cup in 1968 was of this class, and the *Arpege* designed and built by Michel Dufour. There are now hundreds of these boats, but the early successful ones were *Safari*, owned by the designer and Andre Costa's *Chapparal*. Always to the fore in these races were boats of the Scotch class designed by Philippe Harlé. The lines of this boat, shown in Fig. 57, represent the finest in design for yachts of 22 ft. The sail plan and accommodation are in Fig. 58. Other yachts of note designed to the Half Ton rules are the S 31 (Sparkman and Stephens), the T 31 (Guy Thompson) (Fig. 80), *September* (designed by her Australian owner Douglas Gilling) (Fig. 78) and *Mistress* (Olle Enderlein). Many other designers have built to the Half Ton cup rule.

The Quarter Ton races have been sailed at La Rochelle and Breskens, Holland. Possibly there is no clear form so far, but the Van de Stadt designed *Spirit* was first and then second in the early couple of series (Fig. 59). Under the RORC rule the 15 ft. rating gave a boat of 19–20 ft., but the size may be sensitive to alteration under the International Offshore rule. The length of the offshore race is about 100 miles, which is about the minimum that should be considered for an international offshore race. Both Half and Quarter Ton inshore races include an Olympic type course. There has been some variation in the number and length of the inshore courses from year to year.

Ocean racing in Great Britain   There are a host of offshore races around the shores of the British Isles, mostly run independently by various clubs and regional associations. The Royal Ocean Racing Club confines itself to races over 200 miles, though it does have one shorter event every year, the Cowes–Dinard, of 180 miles, commonly known as the "Ladies race". Up to 1968, the minimum size of yacht allowed was 24 ft. LWL, but a new lower limit will be involved under the International Offshore rule. The main races are the Fastnet (605 miles) run on years alternating with the CCA's New York–Bermuda race, and races of much the same length to Spain and Scandinavia, usually on a non-Fastnet year. Regular races include Harwich to the Hook of Holland (220 miles), Morgan Cup and

Channel Race, the latter two being large triangles in the English Channel of about 220 miles (Fig. 62). It is the length of the races that maintain the pre-eminence of the RORC and in the British climate they can often be testing. Many other clubs give shorter races, but among those specializing in offshore events is the East Anglian Offshore Racing Association. The 24 ft. design in Fig. 60 by Holman and Pye of West Mersea, Essex, represents the all-round yacht which can be entered in such races.

The Junior Offshore Group gives races of the RORC type, ocean racing courses, which are for yachts not greater than 24 ft. (minimum size 16 ft.) and the courses are between 50 and 165 miles, the sort of thing that can be done in a week-end. Among their important ones are the Cowes–Dinard (154 miles, being a different route to the RORC), Southsea–Dartmouth (153 miles, going over to the French coast first) and Southsea—Le Havre (85 miles).

The JOG has classes divided by rating, which follow in sequence those of the RORC. In 1970 the RORC classes were arranged from I to V under the IOR rule and are generally followed in Europe.

The class divisions have been altered over the years mainly because of the trend to smaller boats, but in 1968 the size can be gauged in that the One Ton Cup yachts were in the top part of Class III. The JOG activities extend to Scotland with several races every year, including the Cultra–Clyde, a 90-mile run from Northern Ireland to a Scottish port. Some of the strength of the JOG lies in its insistence on the use of the current rule of measurement and the provision of racing and safety rules which have been adopted all over the world. It tends to attract the keenest offshore men, who are not content with the many day races run by local yacht clubs.

In 1968 the first international JOG series was held when the JOG Association of Australia presented the Captain James Cook Trophy for a series in the English Channel. This was for teams of three yachts per nation which came from England, France and Australia. The way it was run is interesting as it shows a real feeling for offshore racing in small yachts. There were no races "round the buoys". although the first race was a 25 mile canter down the Solent with a number of marks to round beginning at the Hamble River and finishing at Yarmouth, Isle of Wight. Though the shortest race of the series, it was a hard beat to windward causing more damage than the longer events! There followed races of 60 miles and 154 miles (the Cowes–Dinard), each finishing at a different port. The crews survived the entertainment at each centre. With the JOG upper limit at 24 ft. it was important to ensure that the national teams were not all "big" boats. The team yachts had to be one of 16·5 ft. rating or over, one of under 16·5 ft. rating and one of any rating. Any number of other yachts were allowed to compete and this did not appear to affect the chances of the team yachts: a trophy was presented to the best individual yacht of the series. Further Captain James Cook Trophy series are being held at intervals of a few years.

Europe   It was French boats under the flag of the Groupe des Croiseurs Legers that won the first Captain James Cook Trophy and this club, based originally on the JOG can be said to be the leading club for small offshore boats in Europe. Its races are held in the English Channel, Atlantic coast of France and the Mediterranean. Alain Maupas, who sails not only small yachts but the biggest racers as well, was President of the GCL for many years and instrumental in its expansion. The GCL organizes the longest race for small yachts in Europe, the Coupe d'Armen, a 240-mile course from St. Malo, round Brittany,

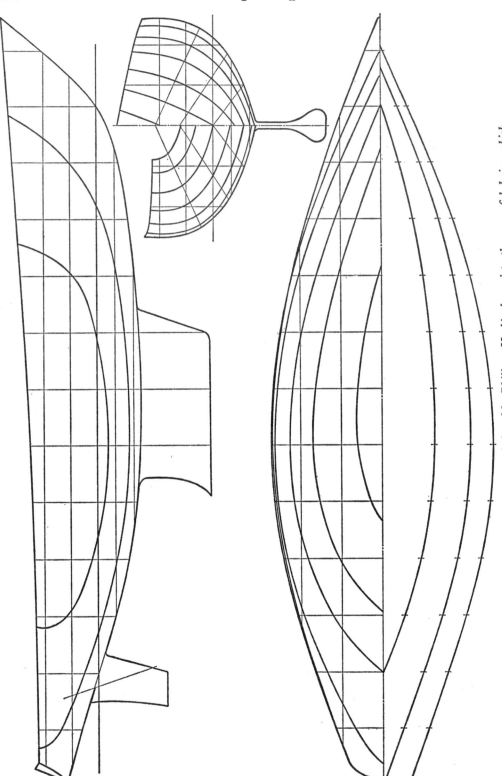

FIG. 57. *The hull lines of the Scotch class designed by Philippe Harlé. A consistently successful design which gives fast yacht speed as well as sailing to her rating of 18 ft. Dimensions are LOA 30 ft. 10 in., LWL 22 ft. 7 in., beam 9 ft. 1 in., draft 4 ft. 7 in., displacement 2·8 tons, ballast 1·38 tons, sail area 323 sq. ft.*

FIG. 58. *The Scotch class designed by Philippe Harlé. Several of these boats have been consistently good per-formers in the Half Ton Cup. The accommodation is well laid out for racing, as is the deck plan with separate cockpits for helmsman and crew. The lines are shown in Fig. 57. The mainsail area is 125 sq. ft. and fore-triangle is 183 sq. ft. The largest genoa shown is 165%.*

I

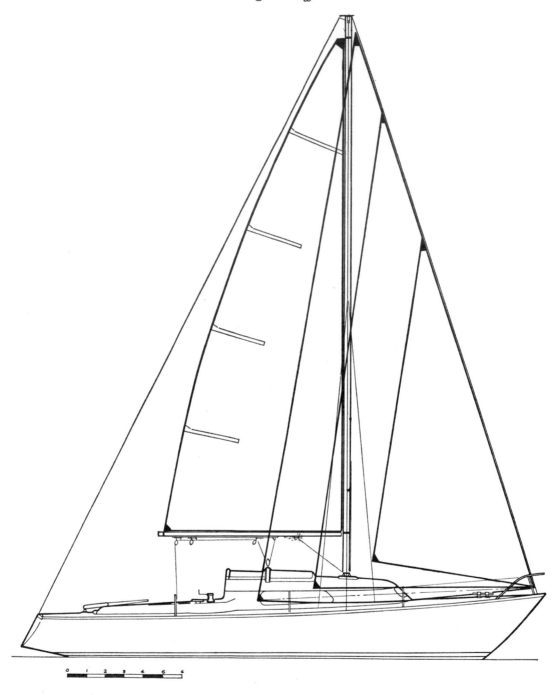

FIG. 59(a). *Sail plan of* Spirit. *The sheeting arrangement is for a track which divides the cockpit and for use with slab reefing. Sail areas. Mainsail 111 sq. ft., genoa 168 sq. ft., No. 1 jib 123 sq. ft., No. 2 jib 70 sq. ft.*

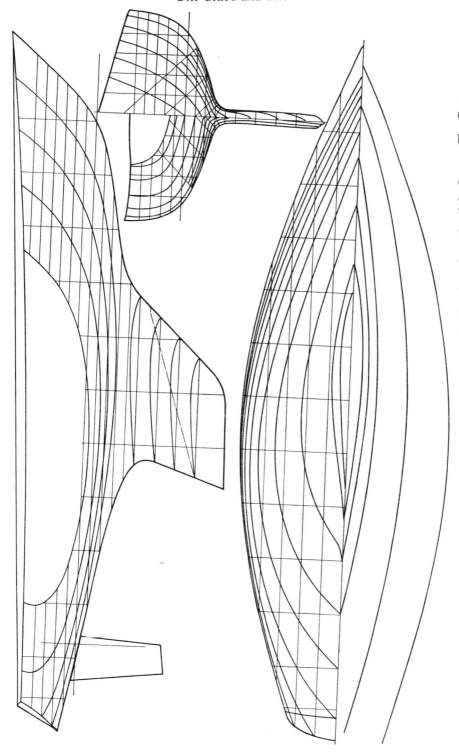

FIG. 59(b). *The hull lines of Spirit designed by E. G. van de Stadt, winner in 1967 of the Quarter Ton Cup and since then consistently successful. Dimensions LOA 24 ft. 3 in., LWL 18 ft. 9 in., beam 7 ft. 5 in., draft 4 ft. 11 in., displacement 1·35 tons, ballast keel 0·55 tons.*

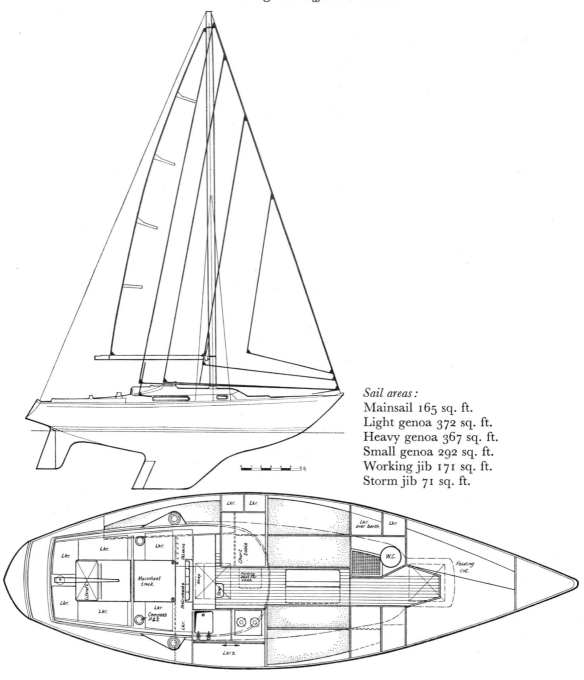

Sail areas:
Mainsail 165 sq. ft.
Light genoa 372 sq. ft.
Heavy genoa 367 sq. ft.
Small genoa 292 sq. ft.
Working jib 171 sq. ft.
Storm jib 71 sq. ft.

FIG. 60. *Typical of the modern boat which takes part in RORC and other offshore races in Europe: the* Centurion *designed by Holman and Pye in England and built in France. The profile is moderate with a trim tab if required. The accommodation gives a well placed galley and chart table, two pilot berths for the crew off watch, oilskin locker and W.C. forward but in its own compartment. Life-raft stowage is worked into the design. The dimensions are LOA 31 ft. 9 in., LWL 24 ft., beam 9 ft. 9 in., draft 5 ft. 10 in., displacement 4·8 tons, ballast keel 1·9 tons.*

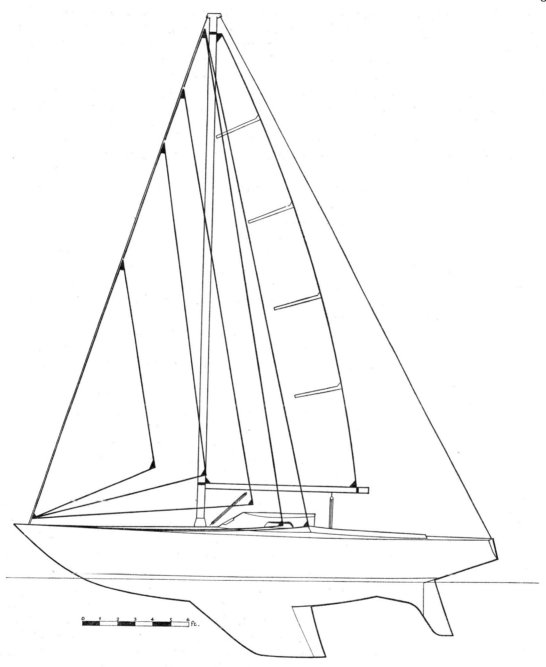

FIG. 61. Rafale, *an ocean racer of 19 ft. 5 in. LWL, in light alloy, designed by Dominique Presles. She has won the longest JOG/GCL race in Europe, the St. Malo–Lorient. Other dimensions are: LOA 27 ft. 4 in., beam 8 ft. 10 in., displacement 1·7 tons, ballast ·72 tons. Sail areas: Mainsail 111 sq. ft., 170% genoa 232 sq. ft., 152% genoa 221 sq. ft., small genoa 152 sq. ft., No. 1 jib 98 sq. ft., No. 2 jib 44 sq. ft.*

outside Ushant into the Atlantic and on to Lorient. Winner the first time this was held was the delightful light alloy Quarter Ton boat *Rafale*, a true midget ocean racer to look at as well as in practice (Fig. 61). The GCL gives a number of races over 100 miles, Le Havre–Hamble (100 miles), Le Havre–Ouistreham–Fécamp–Cherbourg (130 miles), La Rochelle –La Trinité (120 miles), to name but a few. The classes are divided in the same way as the JOG. One of the most important clubs on the Biscay coast is the Société des Régates Rochelaises. Besides originating the Half Ton Cup, it has for many years taken a leading part in offshore development. There are a number of races to other ports along the Atlantic coast of France which are normally open to RORC size classes and smaller, La Rochelle–Le Palais and La Rochelle–Santander, Spain (215 miles) are but two among many.

In the Mediterranean the Association Méditerranéene des Croiseurs Cotiers based on Marseille has the number of boats under its control expanding at a very high rate. It co-operates closely with offshore interests in Italy and Spain and this area of the world is in the process of becoming one of the most important for short ocean races. The Italian class C is based mainly on Genoa and races under RORC rating and to JOG standards. The most important race in the Mediterranean, held annually, is the 272 mile Giraglia event. This goes from St. Tropez on the south coast of France round the Giraglia rock at the Northern tip of Corsica, round a buoy to the westward and then to San Remo, Italy. The yachts below RORC size, go direct to San Remo, after rounding the Giraglia (Fig. 62). Newer Mediterranean events include those based on Malta and courses run by the Royal Yacht Club of Greece for all the sizes of ocean racer. The latter have a 95-mile course from Faliron to Andros, through the Doro Channel where there is often a hard beat to windward.

Returning further north, in Belgium with its very short coastline and Holland with her changing one, the national authorities are more closely concerned with ocean racing. Holland has a long tradition including the Hook–Harwich race and then the return with the RORC. There are wide areas of semi-sheltered water which make the development of the smaller yachts a little different from the open coasts of France and England.

Scandinavian waters consist of the Baltic Sea and the more open areas of the Skagerrak and Kattegat. The classes follow closely those of the RORC and JOG. Some races are open to all classes and some to the larger boats only. The complete offshore programme is co-ordinated by the ocean racing committees of the national authorities of Denmark, Finland, Norway and Sweden and then by the combined Scandinavian Ocean Racing Committee. The major race is the 300 mile Skaw race open to all classes, though those below RORC size have a shorter route before finishing at Skagen on the northern tip of Denmark. One of the hardest ocean races in recent years was over this route in 1966 when gale force winds prevailed nearly the whole race and one Norwegian JOG boat was lost. She suffered a knockdown so that the mast went under water. After righting the mast was seen to be broken, but the two men in the cockpit were still on board thanks to their safety harnesses. Being near the lee shore of the Swedish coast they let off distress flares and were rescued after a fine piece of seamanship by the Norwegian yacht *Istria* of the same class.

A popular race from Sandhamn and return is the 335-mile course round Gotland, the entry being mainly Swedish as Sandhamn is the base of the Royal Swedish Yacht Club outside Stockholm. Other typical races in this part of the world are Kiel–Marstrand (280

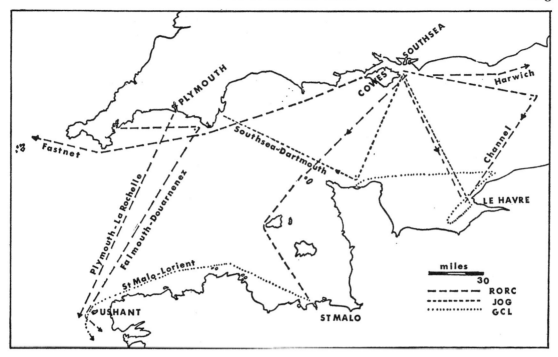

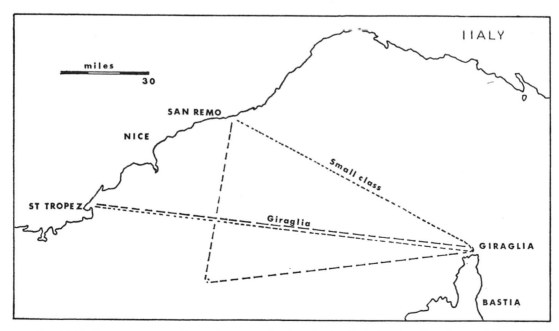

FIG. 62. *Typical ocean races run by offshore organizations in the English Channel and one of the principal Mediterranean courses, the Giraglia race.*

miles), Hangö, Finland, to Sandhamn (150 miles), Marstrand–Hanko, Norway (125 miles), but every year there is a very full programme in these fine sailing waters.

Southern Hemisphere and Far East   Not only would it be impossible to catalogue even the important offshore races of the world, but such is the rate of expansion that it would soon be out of date. Argentina is an important centre for ocean racing with the Buenos Aires–Rio race of 1,200 miles and smaller yachts are looked after by the JOG Argentino. Ocean racing courses in South Africa are centred on Cape Town and on Durban. In Japan there is a well developed series of courses on RORC and JOG lines, run by the Nippon Ocean Racing Club which caters for all classes. The same system is used by the Royal Akarana Yacht Club in New Zealand, the longest race being the 1,517 miles Hobart–Auckland race. Other races are of several hundred miles, with separate shorter courses, mostly under one hundred miles, for the JOG division. Northern hemisphere yachtsmen can always envy the Christmas holiday races.

Australia is a major ocean racing country and in 1945 the Cruising Yacht Club of Australia was formed, on the lines of the CCA and RORC with the assistance of John Illingworth, who proceeded to win the first Sydney–Hobart race. This is now an established classic being the same length as the Fastnet and Bermuda races. The CYCA runs many shorter races such as the 75-mile Bird Island and return event. Its racing and safety rules are close to those of the RORC, some being word for word the same, though radio transmitters are required in certain events. Many of the boats are kept in commission throughout the year because of the suitable climate. The southern circuit is run by the Cruising Yacht Club of Victoria along the coast from Sydney to Melbourne and Devonport on the north side of Tasmania and as far as Port Lincoln in the east. In Sydney is based the JOG Association of Australia, who presented the Captain James Cook Trophy, as mentioned above, for international racing by JOG yachts. Many of the members of this organization also belong to the Middle Harbour Yacht Club which takes a major interest in encouraging its members to sail in international events. In 1966, the Australian boat in the One Ton Cup races was under its flag.

North America   Most of the world's racing yachts are in North America! They are also big compared with the common size in Europe. Clubs and organizations all over the United States and in Canada run multitudinous races for all the sizes of yacht considered in these pages. The CCA which is basically a cruising club, but which runs the Bermuda race, has been mentioned chiefly for its rule of measurement and rating which is followed in close or loose forms, in most parts of North America. In the many established events, the successful boats are more often than not beyond the size dealt with here, though maximum and minimum class sizes have many variants. A typical boat at the top end of our scale that has been established as a design for a number of years and can count successes in all sorts of offshore events would be the Alberg 37. Her dimensions are 26 ft. 6 in. LWL, 10 ft. 2 in. beam and 5 ft. 6 in. draft. The displacement of 7·5 tons and sail area of 647 sq. ft. are high by European standards. The CCA rating would be about 29 ft.

To find a national pattern among the small ocean racers, it is necessary to turn to the yachts of the midget ocean racing groups. These were based at first on the JOG concept and now limit the overall length to 30 ft. The main organizations are the Midget Ocean Racing Club, the Midget Ocean Racing Fleet and the Midget Ocean Racing Association.

20. The light alloy quarter tonner *Rafale* with Alain Maupas at the helm (plan page 123).

21. *Below:* Quarter Ton cup races off Breskens, Holland. In the foreground one of the successful van de Stadt Spirit Class (plans page 120).

22. Near the bottom of the JOG limit, *Shakashe*, a Hurley 22 fitted for offshore races in the English Channel.

23. *Below*: Swedish Vega class yachts race on the Baltic. Freeboard and coachroof arrangement give them wide appeal as a standard cruiser racer.

24. The "Cal" boats designed by Bill Lapworth of California are sailing in North America in thousands. They have a high reputation in racing. This is a Cal 2-30 and features include the cockpit taken aft to the transom board, high freeboard, wide stern and large sail area. LOA 30 ft. 2 in., LWL 25 ft. Mainsail is 236 sq. ft. and foretriangle 228 sq. ft.

25. *Hot Foot* designed by Alan Gurney to the CCA rule (plans page 153). Further boats of the design, the Nantucket 33, are built in aluminium and GRP.

26. A successful MORC racer *Queen Daz* owned by Joseph Low of the Long Island Sound station. An Excalibur 26 of 21 ft. 8 in. LWL, she is designed by Bill Crealock.

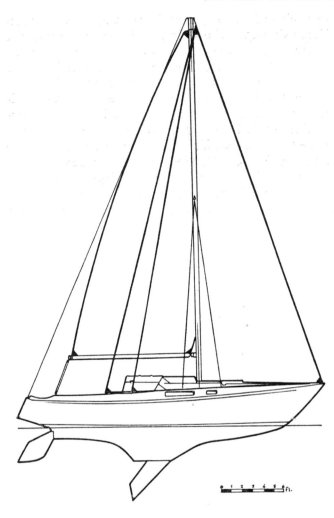

FIG. 63. *An MORC racing boat, the Northwind 29 class designed by Cuthbertson and Cassian of Canada. The efficient centre-plate is quite usual in MORC boats. The sail area is larger than on similar European yachts. The largest genoa shown is 180%. Mainsail area 162 sq. ft., foretriangle 198 sq. ft. Other dimensions are: LOA 28 ft. 10 in., beam 9 ft. 2 in., draft with plate down 6 ft. 9 in. (max.).*

The latter two are based on Southern and Northern California respectively and are independent of the MORC. They run the longest ocean race in the world for small yachts, the 400 miles San Francisco to Newport Beach event: that is the distance between their bases! The first race in 1966 was won by the Cal 28 *Sally Lightfoot* (Wayne Kocher) and the course has been repeated every year since. The MORC has its headquarters in New York where its first fleet was registered and there are stations at the following places: Narragansett Bay, South Florida, Boston, Tampa Bay, Detroit, South Jersey, East Long Island Sound, Lake Erie, Chesapeake Bay, Lower Chesapeake Bay, Milwaukee.

The type of yacht sailed in MORC events is rather different to that seen in the JOG or GCL. The influence of the MORC rule and the continental climate have produced a boat which, compared with its European counterparts, have large cockpits (the MORC safety rule on cockpits though constructed by the same type of formula has constants which allow a bigger volume), generous sail area especially in the mainsail and broad sterns. The stern might be said to be normal as against the pinched-in effect on RORC yachts. In the

American tradition there is often a centreboard. A design by the successful naval architects, Cuthbertson and Cassian, the Northwind 29, is shown in Fig. 63, and represents the most recent MORC thinking. The wide stern and sail area are at once noticeable; the profile with the centreboard down or up has low wetted surface. Another successful design is the Soverel 28, designed by Daniel J. McCarthy. This has a centreboard, short ends with a waterline of 23 ft. 2 in. and the cockpit is 9 ft. long, the main hatch being placed amidships. Since the Soverel boats are built at North Palm Beach, Florida, it can be understood that they are intended for a good climate. Their successes, however, have been gained in many parts of America, such as on the Chicago–Mackinac race (Great Lakes) and the Essex to Block Island race (East coast). In the MORC the battle is between standard designs, though sometimes the winners are in fact yachts which have been doctored by their owners to effect reduction in rating and better performance. A huge range of standard designs is available to MORC sailors; some of these are included among the boats listed in Appendix 1.

·9·

TYPES AND CLASSES

When we look at the different types designed to the rule we are astonished, for it is amazing that designers should arrive at such widely varying results—UFFA FOX in 1937

UP TO now we have considered the sailing and navigation of a yacht and the rules and organization under which she sails. The types of races available have been looked at and armed with this knowledge, it is now possible to attempt to decide on the yacht herself. The evolution of yacht design and construction is the experience of men on the sea combined with the advent of new concepts and materials and, to some extent, custom and fashion. Seldom is it possible to conceive a design from first principles or make a breakthrough. This has sometimes been done and the yachts become landmarks in design history. Even then they have been designed by very experienced people. There are numerous examples of "one-off" attempts at design, which have disappointed their owners and now remain laid up in yacht yards or perhaps happily but gently cruise.

Yachts in the breakthrough category are such vessels as the schooner *Nina*, the American schooner designed by Starling Burgess and the first yacht to be built to the RORC rule. In her first season of 1928 she won the transatlantic race and the Fastnet, and showed that an ocean racer was more than just a cruising yacht in competition and she came out of retirement to win the Bermuda race in 1962! *Dorade*, the yacht owned and designed by Rod and Olin Stephens, also remains for ever a name for ocean racing history. Designed specifically for ocean racing in the days when the ocean racing fleet was a group of heavily built and sparred cruisers, she also won the transatlantic race of 1931 and then went to take the Fastnet in 1931 and 1933. In 1947 it was the turn of *Myth of Malham*, designed by Laurent Giles to the requirements of John Illingworth which broke convention and knocked a hole in the RORC rule. Of light displacement, after a number of seasons of hard racing she was laid up and the rumour went round that she was unable through structural faults to sail again. Nothing could be further from the truth and she started a second series of races in 1961 and was one of the yachts of the Irish Admiral's Cup team. It is significant that both *Nina* and *Myth* were able to sail successfully as oldish yachts and under revised rating rules to which they were not designed. Whether Dick Carter's *Rabbit* comes into the category of these three, will be clearer as the years pass, but she put the seal of approval on the beamy, moderate draft large foretriangle boat of the sixties and showed that contrary to popular belief windward ability was not the only criterion by which a yacht could be judged. She won the Fastnet of 1965. There are other historic yachts which have influenced the evolution of design but these four stand out in the ocean racing world. It should be noted that in each case they made an advance under the current rating rule as well as being outstanding yachts in general performance at sea.

Finding your own winner   Recalling for a moment Chapter 6, the crew are equally, if not more, important than the yacht and there is a tendency, which I have seen on several occasions, for the owner of a new vessel to become so absorbed in detail as to leave the question of crew to resolve itself. This is especially the case where the boat is not ready at the beginning of the season: crews go off and sail in other yachts while the owner is busy trying to get the boat ready in time. When she comes to her races, the crew are a long way from being a team and there is more delay until the yacht begins to show promise. So in the chapters which follow, while the emphasis is on the yacht and making her as right as possible, this important crew factor must run throughout the planning period of the yacht. If the crew can be brought into assisting with plans for the layout and other details, the whole team will be closer, the crew as well as the owner understanding the "history" of the yacht.

The size of yacht   The abstract quality of size is nowhere so contrasting as in the realm of ships. That giant tankers and single-seat canoes can share the same stretch of a waterway is part of its delight, but yachts among all ships are but a narrow band, and ocean racing yachts even narrower. For almost everyone, the size is limited by the capital and running costs of the boat and certainly the cost of running a large yacht appears to increase in a roughly cubic measure, making even trifling professional work on yachts of a certain tonnage very costly. Here are the advantages and otherwise of increasing the size of a yacht.

Advantages

1. Distance is covered quicker and more interesting courses can be sailed.
2. Galley and chart table can be more adequately spacious.
3. Easier to keep certain parts of yacht dry in all weather.
4. Easier to lay out cockpit, steering position etc. for maximum convenience.
5. Less affected by blanketing of smaller boats in handicap racing.
6. More personal comfort.

Disadvantages

1. Heavier gear and more work on deck. Operations such as rounding marks and entering harbour take longer.
2. More draft, and so occasional further detours in shoal waters.
3. More persons in crew and so more chance of having to take less experienced hands. Necessity of recruiting numerous good crew.
4. The real limiting factor—the time and cost of keeping a larger yacht in racing trim.

     No mention is made above of seaworthiness and weatherliness. Our theme is the great ability of the modern small ocean racer to cope with any weather. However, in any handicap system which must be based on average weather as it evolves, the advantage lies with the larger boats in a hard thrash to windward in dirty weather. That is other things being equal, but they are not, and crew and design variations can often bring a small yacht out top in these conditions. The larger boat will be less sensitive to the weather and be less obliged to reduce sail in a breeze, but the smaller boat will round marks quicker and

EXAMPLES OF SPEEDS OF YACHTS IN RORC RACES

ace	Distance (miles)	*ANDORRAN 24 ft. 0 in.*				*CLARIONET 26 ft. 8½ in.*			
		1966		*1967*		*1966*		*1967*	
		Time	*Speed (knots)*	*Time*	*Speed (knots)*	*Time*	*Speed (knots)*	*Time*	*Speed (knots)*
		h. m.		h. m.		h. m.		h. m.	
orth Sea	220	43 49	5·2	44 48	4·8				
forgan Cup	235	56 7	4·2	(retired due to calms)		46 56	5·0	56 54	4·1
hannel	225	37 19	6·0	43 22	5·3			39 23	5·7
owes/St. Malo	215	33 57	6·2			30 38	7·0		
astnet	605			136 34	4·4			123 8	4·8
AVERAGES			5·4		4·8		6·0		4·9

FIG. 64.

spend less time in tacking. However, these are marginal factors, because we are concerned with ensuring that the yacht within a given range of size is fully efficient at sea. Ability to race at sea does become questionable when the smallest sizes of yacht are reached, from 18 ft. LWL downwards, and these are considered in Chapter 18.

Speed on races   After a season or so of racing in regular events it will soon be realized that the time spent on a race is an important matter in planning for crews and if considered early enough should affect the type of yacht owned. Many people enter a series over a season with vague ideas about the time involved with subsequent disruption to plans. Fig. 64 shows speeds and certain times of yachts in several races in two RORC seasons. Rather smaller, the Half Tonner *Shewolf*, an S31, of 22 ft. LWL launched in mid-season 1968 had on her programme only two races of about 150 miles. These were:

Cowes–Dinard:
>   154 miles: elapsed time 38 hours 21 minutes.
>   Conditions: Close-hauled in moderate breeze followed by three hours near calm
>   and very light following air.
>   SPEED: *3·99 knots.*

La Rochelle–Gironde–SE Rochebonne–La Rochelle (Half Ton course):

>   147 miles: elapsed time 27 hours 23 minutes.
>   Conditions: Moderate winds fresh at the end, one leg of 50 miles beating.
>   SPEED: *5·39 knots.*

These figures are interesting for planning the capabilities of such a boat, though she was one of the fastest for her size and rating at the time. But such is the spread even in the JOG range that the last boats (a couple of Folkboats of only 2 ft. less waterline) came into Dinard 15 hours after *Shewolf*. Admittedly this was due to the wind becoming even lighter after the leaders were in, but all ocean racing men know that this is a frequent hazard in any part of the world. Even in the Half Ton course mentioned, with stiff following winds increasing, the later yachts arrived $4\frac{1}{2}$ hours after the yacht mentioned and these were yachts of similar design and the same rating. In this case the $4\frac{1}{2}$ hours though huge for boats of equal rating, has little significance in planning events. Incidentally it does show the contrast in performance in boats of the same hull under different ownership. Returning from races which end at a distant port has to be considered and here the speed under power can contribute its part. When the engine can be used, calms are then less of a hold-up than head winds. In these circumstances probably the most irritating conditions consist of a light head wind, which for most ocean racers would be awkward to motor against, but is not strong enough to enable the boat to put up a reasonable speed to windward. The question of actual speed should be remembered when sailing some distance to a start: it should always be calculated. Hazy ideas about the time to reach the start line have resulted in the disappointment of being late on the line, not an encouraging way to start a race of 50 or 250 miles.

In all such planning the times to work on will be the probable slowest and possible fastest. The sustained maximum speed of the yacht will become known after she has been sailed for part of a season. As for the probable slowest, it is the light headwinds mentioned above which kill the averages. Throw in a few unfavourable headers and speeds as low as one and a half to two knots cannot be discounted. Mediterranean conditions can often produce a twice daily calm near the coast, when land and sea breeze are exchanging duty. For arriving at the start line, ample time should be left (taking into account available engine power and currents) and then relaxed shortly before departure is due, if the wind is favourable, giving a quick passage.

Which is the ocean racer?   The American magazine *One Design and Offshore Yachtsman* faced with the problem of listing racing yachts without having to include the hundreds of fast cruisers which are available in the USA was forced to this definition: "We define an offshore racer as a sail boat with cruising accommodation for at least two, provisions for a head and galley, a self bailing cockpit which meets the requirements of either the CCA or MORC rules for maximum volume; also it must be capable of racing with some reasonable expectation of winning." The punch line at the end of this definition is our problem in the selection of a yacht. Looking at the many seagoing yachts in any anchorage, they can be divided in this manner:

Yachts for cruising only. These are either evidently old, of the motor sailer type with large centre cockpits and under cover steering positions or with large bulwarks and deck gear and equipment so elaborate that they are not intended for racing.

Yachts with some aspiration towards racing. These include the great mass of modern cruisers, though not all. They need to be divided into two kinds, those with "some expectation" of winning and those designs which have no excuse for not winning. It is assumed that the pure cruiser is evident, but the selection of an ocean racer can lie in discarding the cruiser-racers which are not really going to give you a chance and, even more difficult, deciding about those border line cases between the latter and the genuine flyer.

Yachts come in so many shapes and sizes that there are bound to be exceptions to these generalizations. This especially applies to the old yacht, with an experienced crew and, re-rigged perhaps, proceeds to clean up in a series of races. But most people will put themselves at an initial disadvantage in such a craft and our problem here is to pick out the racing yacht. Even among yachtsmen, who have owned a number of boats, and sailed in many others, this is very difficult. I can think of several cases, which of course cannot be instanced where it has been said, "Why on earth did he buy a so-and-so?" And one wonders why a misjudgement was made.

The latest design   There is a dilemma in attempting to be armed with the very latest design. If a very successful yacht is adopted, say for the season following her winning streak, there is the possibility that a newer boat will have arrived on the scene by the time the second season owners begin to race. On the other hand, if a new yacht is planned to beat these successful ones, there is always the nagging fear that she may in fact not have this extra fraction of a knot which will put her at an advantage. She could even be fractionally slower. You might have been safer with the proved design. You do not know! Yes, there are tank tests and there are fine designers and there are assurances that this yacht is an improvement. But the proving is in the racing and no amount of talk before sailing—and there is plenty of it—can make it otherwise. An example away from the ocean racing scene makes the point. The America's Cup challenger *Sovereign* was evolved from her predecessor *Sceptre* who had suffered a heavy defeat in 1958. The changes were definite and planned. Yet in 1963 and in the months before the challenge in 1964 the new boat failed to make the impression she should have on the older one. Frequently the defeated *Sceptre* finished ahead of her and the classic uncertainty of yacht design was demonstrated. *Sovereign* was, of course, eventually defeated by even larger margins than *Sceptre*.

In the world of small ocean racers the individual design is becoming rare and often the nearest thing to it is a prototype of an intended series production boat. Fortunately there are a few people who will continue to have single boats designed for them: "one-off" boats, an expression used more in recent years, now that almost every boat has a class label.

"One-off" yachts   The owner deciding on the first boat of a production class is in many ways in the same position as the one-off owner. However, he does not have to approve the design, only to accept it. The key to adopting a one-off is the choice of designer. It is essential to go to a man who specializes in ocean racers of the size contemplated. Such designers will usually be found to have tentative designs sketched as an improvement of their current racing boats, so that as soon as the potential owner appears and wants an advance on a certain recent design, the architect is ready with at least concrete ideas for discussion.

Names of some designers are shown in the list of standard yachts in Appendix 1, but not all of them are specialists in ocean racers. In the case of motor yachts there is little necessity for the designer to go aboard the yacht after acceptance trials. Particularly if he has supervised the construction, he has a perfectly good idea of how the vessel is shaping up and what she will be like to live aboard at sea. But I am sure that the designers of ocean racers should put in a reasonable number of hours every season of racing at sea. Without this they cannot gauge the intensity of the competition and the many handling characteristics that are demanded. It will be found nowadays that this is the norm and that not only do the leading designers sail in their yachts but they frequently take a major part in campaigning their latest creations.

In selecting a designer, choose one whose latest boat is nearly in the style required and so that the new design is but a moderate step in evolution of the same idea. It is a mistake to admire the work of designer "A" and then to go to designer "B" and ask him for a similar craft. It is frequently done, especially if "A" resides outside the owner's country and is not convenient for consultation, but it is an unsound approach. Designer "B" will no doubt do his best to meet the needs set out, but the result of such a departure from his normal line of thought cannot be very certain.

The fees for a commissioned design in England are usually from 7 to 11 per cent of the contract price, so a 26 ft. yacht costing £9,000 is going to have a designer's fee of around £900. An immense amount of discussion and planning as well as drawings at all stages of the construction is involved for the designer. The potential owner should realize that he will be caught up in all this and it will take a considerable amount of his time.

If this expense and programming is to be embarked on then it is only sensible to take advantage of it in relation to timing. It is a question of being advanced enough to have the boat launched in good time for the season, but not having begun planning so early that advantage cannot be taken of the latest developments which have become apparent in the previous season. If it can be achieved, the ideal for a March launching would be to establish contact with the naval architect ten months or a year ahead, keep the design under review during the summer season and reserve building space. The design would be finalized in August, giving eight months for building. Such a scheme depends on the type of construction and size of yacht, but the point is that some such plan should be utilized for the one-off boat.

There is a lot of work to be done before the design is finalized but the sequence events for the owner is roughly this. After a detailed discussion of all the requirements, the designer submits preliminary drawings which are lacking in much detail but show the sail plan, accommodation and the all-important lines. With these approved, he can go ahead, with such consultation as the owner requires, prepare the specification and the drawings and it is these which are the basis of the contract with the builder. Sets are initialled and exchanged at the time the contract is signed. If amendments to this stage are kept to a minimum expense will be saved, for extras which creep in after the contract tend to be costly. Of course, various detail drawings continue from the design office during the building, but these should be close up amplification of items already included in the agreed specification.

Payment for single boats is usually done on a progress basis with 10 per cent deposited on signing the contract and one-quarter of the total price paid when the keel is laid. Further portions become due at certain stages; for instance when the yacht is fully planked up and when the engine has been fully installed. The final 10 per cent is reserved for payment on completion of "builders' trials". Some builders like to supply the sails from the sailmaker, for which they obtain some discount, but whatever financial provision is made, it is certainly essential in the case of an ocean racer for the owner to discuss the sails in detail with the sailmaker. There may well be more than one sailmaker and this can be preferable in these days of specialization. The mainsail and genoas could come from one sailmaker, the spinnakers from another and the working jibs from yet another who is less expensive.

Talking of cost, it will be one of the major factors in choice of sailmaker. It is not practicable to quote prices which vary over the years but the following are the *proportional* costs for some English sailmakers.

Firm using exclusively imported American cloth	£190
Same sail from a leading firm weaving own cloth	£134
Good firm using American cloth	£120
Same good firm using English cloth	£100
A less well-known firm	£100

One can shop around quite extensively, though a number of firms will be found to be somewhere near this lower price. Naturally there are cheaper firms, who are not experienced in racing sails, and these should be avoided for an ocean racer, where sails loom so large in the performance. The choice of sails is covered in Chapter 12.

Prototypes   The first of a class differs from the one-off boat, as it is the designer and builder who make all the decisions on the structure and main fittings. Usually it is the hull builders or finishing firm who sail the boat and it is advisable to race a single yacht before going into general production. If business reasons make it essential to plan a number of boats before starting on a mould (assuming the series is in GRP), it is still wise for the firm and the future customers to get a limited number on the water for the first season, in the hands of competent people. There is then a good chance of turning in satisfactory placings, and for constructive suggestions to be made rapidly on any modifications to the boat. If one of the users of a prototype, try to take delivery of a yacht which is rather bare inside. It will then be possible to add accommodation after some experience has been gained of the particular boat at sea. The best plan for the builders is to have the prototypes raced hard for the second half of a season with a view to have production craft readily available early the next season. The thinking behind this is the same as that of the timing of the arrival of a one-off mentioned above.

More likely you are standing on the side lines and watching the behaviour of several new designs during a season. A careful check can be kept on races results, noting the actual places gained and how many yachts were taking part. Frequent press mention is not sufficient: some firms have better public relations men than others. *Yachting World* in England and other magazines in USA and Europe organize One-of-a-Kind rallies for cruiser racers and the analysis which is published afterwards is valuable. Better still get down to the rally and see what the designs in which you are interested are doing. Observing a prototype's racing season there are several points to be wary of. Not infrequently the prototype scores several outstanding successes, but the owners of the series production yachts which follow are disappointed. This is because:

1. The prototype was sailed by a particularly good helmsman and crew for the sensible purpose of advertising the new boat.
2. She was likely to be unencumbered with the gear, which accumulates in a privately owned boat.
3. She may have been built in different materials.
4. The design may be altered for the worse when the plug is made for production.

It is not implied that there is any deception by the promoters of the boat in the latter two items, but a prototype is quite likely to be built in wood to be used as the plug of a GRP production series. Alternatively, after the prototype has been sailed, a fresh set of lines are used to construct the plug for the GRP mould. More likely smaller alterations are

K

made, the shape of the stern, the keel profile, iron instead of lead perhaps, or the position of the rudder. So, as a result, the class name covers boats which, though very similar, may *not be the same design*.

C.R. "Kim" Holman's Twister class has gone through a number of changes and the builders of the most recent yachts are meticulous in calling them a "Mark 2A", or whatever suffix is appropriate. The first Twister, built and sailed by the designer and later owned with outstanding success by Gerald Hume-Wright had a planked wooden hull. She was consistently more successful than the many Twisters in GRP which followed her. Later there were more changes in the design and these are shown in the Table (Fig. 65). In this case a few more wooden boats to the design were also built and in the right hands could usually better their plastic sisters.

An interesting sequence is Michael Henderson's Spinner design. The first yacht, *Moonspinner*, was built to the Half Ton rule in 1967. She was in fact a one-off yacht constructed by her owner Michael Tremlett and while still very new, she put up a good showing in Half Ton races. A few months later work began on a slightly modified yacht, *Starspinner*, of the same size in cold moulded plywood. Before she was launched, the hull was used as a plug for the GRP mould intended for series production of the boat. With advent of these boats in GRP, I supose they might be called "the prototype, the plug and production model". The point is that an intending owner needs to study the development of the design and the changes considered necessary (Figs. 66 and 67). The Spinners have been designed against competition in a way that ought to be encouraging to potential owners.

Compromise in choice of boat   The standard production yacht is intended to sell as widely as possible and the cruising and racing aspects will vary in their respective emphasis from boat to boat. We are concerned here with those which have the major emphasis on offshore racing, but it will be seldom that there is no compromise of any sort with other needs.

On *Summertime*, even though she was a one-off ocean racer, I have to confess to insisting on a small seamanlike fitting, which in theory was detrimental to sailing performance. This was a steaming light which needs to be shown when under power. Numerous sailing yachts when entering harbour with their engines are only able to show the red and green side lights and this is wrong and misleading. Our light was on the foreside of the mast at the minimum height allowed by the International Regulations for Prevention of Collision at Sea (9 feet above the side lights,) but it could be claimed that it was unnecessary weight and windage when racing.

Ocean racers designed with an eye to cruising appeal go much further than details of this sort and there comes a point when such a boat is no longer suitable for serious racing. We have remarked that an ocean racer makes a wonderful cruiser, for even with a family party, she can be sailed easily and fast without a press of canvas. The requirements for extended cruising, ocean crossing and single-handed work are not included in this definition of a cruiser, which is intended to apply to the average week-end and overnight passage maker. The qualities and amenities which label the yacht a doubtful possibility for ocean racing can include the following:

1. Designed without regard to rating.
2. Excessively heavy fittings and weight above waterline generally.

TWISTER DESIGN

	Twister herself		Standard glass fibre design		Mark IIA	
	ft.	in.	ft.	in.	ft.	in.
Length overall	27	8	28	3¼	28	3¼
Length waterline	21	0	21	6	21	6
Beam	8	1	8	1	8	1
Draft	5	3	5	0	5	0
R.O.R.C. Measured Area or actual main and No. 1 Genoa areas	sq. ft. MSA = 349 b = 11·5 p = 28·0 J = 10·9 I = 34·3		sq. ft. MSA = 357 b = 12·5 p = 28·75 J = 10·5 I = 34·0		sq. ft. MSA = 343 b = 11·0 p = 28·5 J = 11·0 I = 34·0	
R.O.R.C. Rating	16·6		16·95		16·76	

FIG. 65.

3. "Messy" rig (e.g. big spars, numerous external halyards, prominent mast fittings).
4. Hull unsmooth, large skin fittings and propeller mountings.
5. Small winches and cruising sails (e.g. cruising grade cloth, headsails not to maximum size).
6. Shape largely determined by accommodation with features like very narrow side decks, high coachroof and considerable freeboard.
7. Deck and cockpit layout arranged without handholds, ventilation and so that water drains into accommodation in rough conditions.

This list makes such a boat sound a real clumbungay, but it is a matter of degree and question of how far undesirable features are taken. In any case a number of modifications can be made even amongst the above items. Factors like hull shape obviously cannot be tampered with and if wrong, nullify the boat as a racer.

One difficulty today is that builders are less and less willing to alter standard designs, but they do frequently produce different versions. Ian Hannay's Galion class (Fig. 96), which can be used as a Quarter Ton boat, is available as a cruiser, cruiser-racer and off-shore racer. The layout and equipment will vary with each boat. However, if only the equipment and rig require attention, it is quite possible to take on the task of turning a standard fast cruiser into an offshore racer. An example of this is *Shakashe* a Hurley 22 (LWL 17 ft.) obtained from the builders by South Hants Marine Ltd., Chandlers Ford, Hampshire, England, and turned into a most reassuring JOG racing boat. Spars, sails, winches, lifelines, sail tracks and almost everything movable on the boat was replaced with non-standard gear and the obtaining of gear and its fitting spread over the winter months.

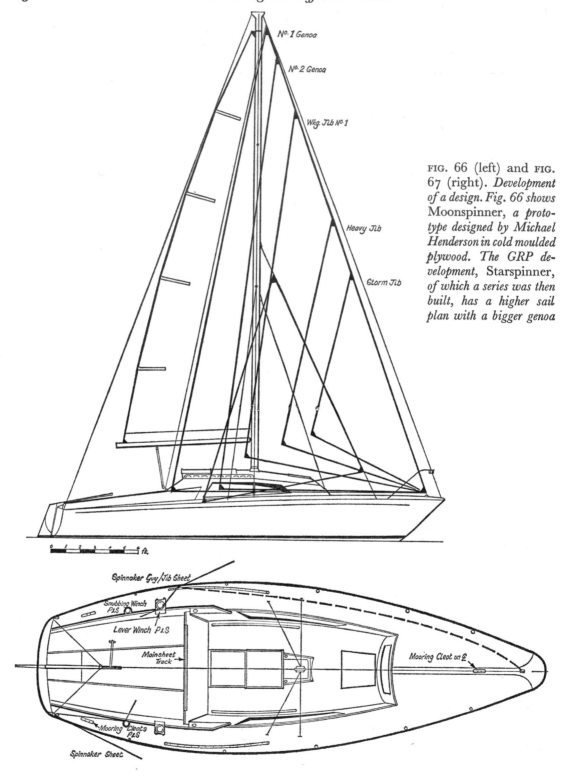

No. 1 Genoa

No. 2 Genoa

Wkg. Jib No. 1

Heavy Jib

Storm Jib

FIG. 66 (left) and FIG. 67 (right). *Development of a design. Fig. 66 shows Moonspinner, a prototype designed by Michael Henderson in cold moulded plywood. The GRP development, Starspinner, of which a series was then built, has a higher sail plan with a bigger genoa*

0 1 2 3 4 5 ft.

Spinnaker Guy/Jib Sheet

Snubbing Winch P&S

Lever Winch P&S

Mainsheet Track

Mooring Cleat on ₵

Mooring Cleats P&S

Spinnaker Sheet

and the mast position moved forward. The coach roof shape has slightly altered, but more important so have the shape of bow and stern. Both yachts are designed for the same purpose, Half Ton Cup racing, and have the same rating and a waterline of 24 ft.

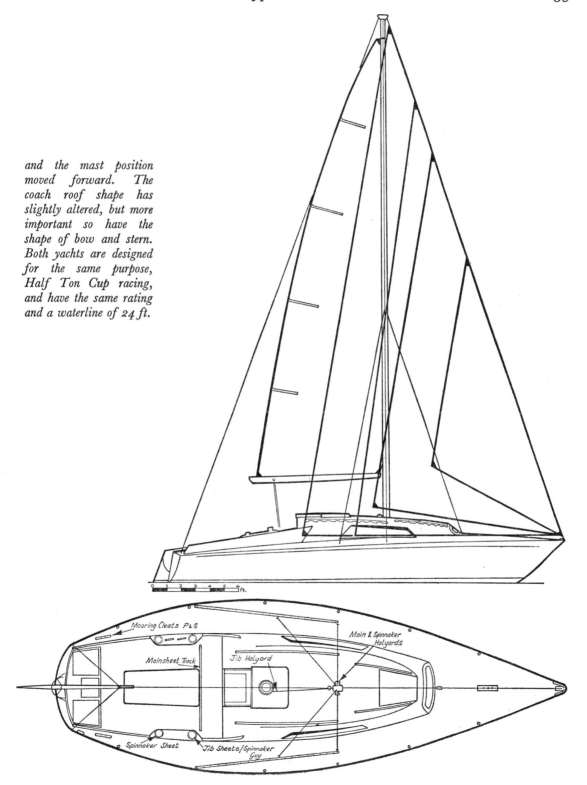

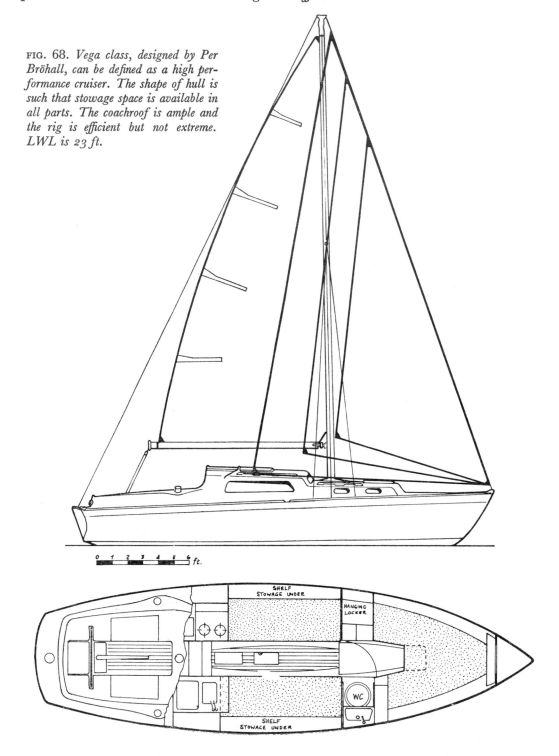

Cruiser-racers The attempt of designers and builders to appeal to many different owners does mean that progress is always being made towards yachts which can race and yet carry cruising comforts. One such yacht is the Vega class built in Sweden and designed by Captain Per Bröhall. Per Bröhall was an air force officer who designed small yachts as an amateur, but has since turned professional in view of the demand for his designs. Among Swedish designers, it is he who is the specialist in the less expensive and smaller family cruiser-racer. Vega, which has a waterline of 23 ft. 0 in., is fitted out on deck and cockpit in accordance with offshore practice. There are wide decks, well protected cockpit, proper arrangements for sheet leads, handholds, and lifelines and workmanlike narrow windows in the low profile coachroof and doghouse. Freeboard is a shade on the high side with a gently reverse sheer and the keel profile has a long straight bottom edge, which is favoured in Scandinavia. For this type of keel shape, the wetted surface is low. Down below the cruising emphasis is more marked with a forward cabin and no separate chart table, which could be arranged on top of the ice box. Standard items like fitted carpet and cabin table are other cruising items. Vega is a good example of a compromise to appeal widely which hovers on the useful borderline of cruising and racing. One word of warning when racing this type of boat. The locker and stowage space is ample and the temptation to fill it up with gear must be resisted. Any excessive weight added to the designed displacement of 2·3 tons is going to be very detrimental (Fig. 68).

Making comparisons Knowledge of the boats available apart from races and rallies comes from reviews in the yachting press, advertisements, the annual type of reference book which lists standard boats (these often have serious gaps in the ocean racing field), from writing to designers for the size in mind, hearing personal recommendations and seeing yachts in the yard or a boat show.

Most people will compile a list of possible craft within the size they have in mind. The word size is used because length and other dimensions and cost will vary with every yacht. Though everyone wants as much as possible for their money, the racing man presumably has an idea more of the size within the class limits and the type required for the racing conditions. So it is not just a matter of the "most for the least". The Table in Fig. 69 shows a list that an owner might use to compare yachts in this way. In the owner's list the common factor is the waterline length which in this case has been used to pick out the yachts for selection. The list is going to be narrowed down due to factors like the price being too high, the rating not being competitive, too much sail area for the waters in which it is intended to sail. There may be overseas yachts on the list it is decided will be too difficult to import specially. Then there will be personal preferences on the score of displacement, the type of stern and hull material, which are not essential one way or the other for ocean racers but have to be compared before a decision is reached.

Extremes in design A complaint often heard is that "all modern yachts look alike" and there is some substance in it. It would in fact be surprising if the yachts were very different, when racing under the same rule and bent on a similar purpose. But that each design has its own character is demonstrated by the ability of fairly experienced offshore men in being able to identify them at a distance by both the general appearance or some combination of distinctive features. The ocean racing rules are not intended to be type producing and the wonder is rather in the wide range of ideas which are seen in yachts which have equal chances of success.

Because design is a matter of evolution and the best designs are often modifications of earlier yachts which have succeeded, extreme features should be accepted with reserve. Very light displacement for instance brings its problems. It is liable to rate too high, despite less sail being required and even with modern forms of construction it will be difficult to ensure that the yacht is not heavier than designed. In this case there would not be enough sail, there would be more wetted surface than calculated and the concept will have fallen down. I am not here talking of light displacement ocean racers as normally understood, only of extreme examples. The Diamond (*Yachting World* keel-boat) class was designed by Jack Holt as an exciting racing keel boat. With plywood construction and, of course, none of the gear of a cruiser aboard, her designed displacement is 1 ton on a waterline of 24·3 ft. and she planes in the right conditions. With a displacement of this sort the section attained is shown in Fig. 70. With this displacement half the weight is in the ballast keel. The design was used to construct an offshore racer with cabin top and essential accommodation below. Apart from the hull not having been designed to any offshore rule, the excellent ballast ratio is lost and the disadvantageous factors mentioned above are combined to make what is a first-class boat for the purpose for which she was designed unsuitable for ocean racing.

Heavy displacement can equally well be an extreme factor, but is less obviously attractive than a tendency towards light weight for racing. Extremes in sail area may be more acceptable as the rig can be altered if the experiment is not satisfactory, but there is a limit to the amount of sail that can be cut to reduce rating. A good performance in the occasional hard blow that lasts for all of one race seldom makes up for continual sluggishness in moderate or light conditions. What was considered normal some years ago can be extreme today and this applies to beam. A 1956 design *Taeping* built by Alan Buchanan for his own use was quite usual in having a beam of 7 ft. 9 in. on a 24 ft. waterline. Dick Carter's *Rabbit* which won the Fastnet just nine years later in 1965 was 24 ft. 2 in. LWL and 10 ft. 1¼ in. beam, an increase of 30·5 per cent or three and a half inches a year! Naturally the older boat is truly narrow by current standards.

American yachts have traditionally had the greater beam which British and European yachts have since adopted. Though beamy American yachts habitually crossed the Atlantic and scored successes in British waters, especially in the Fastnet, the belief persisted that a narrow beam was necessary "to cut through the short chop of the Channel and North Sea". The persistence in lack of beam was not caused by differences in the then RORC and CCA rules which both favoured beam; it was national usage. The arrival of Carlton Mitchell's *Caribee* in Cowes in the fifties was according to her owner greeted by a prominent English yachtsman with the remark that her beam made her into "a bloody saucer". The "bloody saucer" then proceded to win three out of her first four Cowes Week starts. Why we were so slow in appreciating the advantages of greater beam in ocean racers is a puzzle. Some years later beam became fashionable: but would any designer then have been able to come up with an overall balanced design having increased the beam by the amounts mentioned above? As the whole notion of the design would thus be altered, it seems unlikely. So in general the circumspect approach is right, though fortunately for yachting, individuals will continue to experiment with refreshing ideas.

TYPICAL COMPARISON OF OCEAN RACERS OF NEARLY EQUAL LWL

Class of yacht and designer	LWL	LOA	Beam	Draft	Displacement (tons)	Ballast (tons)	Sail area (sq.ft.)	Ballast ratio (%)	$\dfrac{Displ.}{\left(\dfrac{LWL}{100}\right)^3}$	$\left(\dfrac{Sail\ area}{Displ.}\right)^{\frac{1}{3}}$	Remarks
	ft. in.	ft. in.	ft. in.	ft. in.							
Nicholson 32 (Nicholson)	24 0	32 0	9 3	5 6	6·2 (g.r.p.)	3	557	48·3	443	166	Cruiser-racer to RORC rule
Aquitaine 32 (Presles)	24 0	32 1	10 5	4 10	3·27 (light alloy)	1·18	370	37·5	233	177	French design to RORC rule
S. & S. 34 (Stephens)	24 2	34 0	10 1	5 11	4·1 (g.r.p.)	2	466	48·8	292	179	US design to RORC rule
Centurion (Holman)	24 0	32 10	9 6	5 5	4·8 (g.r.p.)	1·9	402	39·5	343	150*	British design French built
al 2–30 (Lapworth)	25 0	30 2	9 0	5 0	4·75 (g.r.p.)	2	480	42·2	297	170	US design CCA rule

* Based on sail plan giving particularly low rating.

FIG. 69.

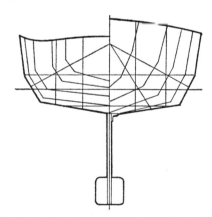

FIG. 70. *Very light displacement section of the Diamond class (Yachting World keel-boat). This is not a practical proposition for an ocean racer which needs ample construction and accommodation.*

· 10 ·

FEATURES FOR THE OFFSHORE HULL

Design of the hull   The only memorial to many fine yachts is the half model mounted in glistening varnish on its plaque on the yacht club wall. It is the hulls that are remembered of those yachts on which fine rigs were set and where crews worked with the considerable spreads of sail that were the rule in the first quarter of the century. Rightly, the hull is the central conception of the boat. The number of crew, the amount of canvas and class in which she will race, being determined by its design. An attraction of those half models is the wonder of their compound curves, such as are found, amongst the whole range of seagoing vessels, only on a racing yacht. Every designer may place emphasis on certain aspects of the hull, but the requirements of an ocean racer include the following.

Strength   Offshore the hull is subject to severe wracking and sudden shocks. The reaction of the body of water supporting the hull can change suddenly due to wave motion which is never strictly regular and sometimes violently irregular. With the hull at an angle of heel, when beating to windward it can leap out of one wave and on to the next, presenting the comparatively flat area of one bow, in contrast to the cleaving motion of an upright craft. In a 24 ft. waterline wooden yacht this was brought home to me when sailing in a short race out of the Needles Channel early one season. Near the South West Shingles buoy where the seas from the English Channel run on to this dangerous shoal, the yacht "fell off a sea" in the broken water. It sounded as though she had been dropped on concrete such was the crack, as the hull hit the water. Once clear of the worst of the seas we looked round for damage—and found it. A bronze tie bar joining deck and keelson had snapped; parts of plywood cabin joinery such as the hanging locker had split across or left the hull; quantities of caulking had spewed from the seams and the stopping between planks had shifted along much of the side which had hit the sea. This sort of thing is not exceptional. Porcelain bowls of lavatories sited forward have been shattered as ocean racers beat to windward; the Australian sloop *Balandra* even with close spaced timbers and double diagonal planking split several timbers and suffered damage to her deck when on trials in heavy weather.

Naturally the search is for strength with lightness. Partly due to rating rules which make allowances for heavy construction there has been no general tendency towards flimsy hulls for competitive offshore racing. Light displacement yachts are the ones in which the construction has to be carefully examined, but recent methods of construction, considered in this chapter, are already easing this problem. Although downwind sailing can seem more wild, it is the punch to windward that puts stresses on ocean racers which are not so common for other yachts. Better winches and stronger sail material means greater compression strains on the mast transmitted in turn to the hull. The tension forces on the forestay and hence the backstay mean the hull must have longitudinal strength, while up to half the yacht's weight being in the ballast keel means that it must withstand the local load of the fin keel.

Stiffness A fast hull when upright is no use if it cannot stand up to its canvas. Standard boats are sometimes advertised as "stable", which is really meaningless as any floating body must be stable to remain afloat in normal trim. No, what is required is stiffness and this is not always easy to retain in the smaller sizes. It can be achieved by a hard bilge which needs to be more pronounced the smaller the yacht, for a boat of the same proportions has less resistance to heeling as the size decreases. Initial stiffness is largely a matter of the yacht's section, a slack bilge having less resistance to heeling. It is a section of the centre part of the yacht that is usually first looked at on drawings, but where the ends are particularly fine, it must be realized that stiffness due to hull form is made dependent on a limited length of the yacht about amidships. These fine ends were a particular feature under the 1957 RORC rule where the vessel's measured length depended on girth stations. Another advantage of slackness is that other things being equal, it reduces the wetted surface.

Stiffness is also dependent on the position and weight of ballast and the main effect of this is felt at the greater angles of heel. It is important to remember that the ability to recover from a knockdown puff is not directly related to the power to carry sail in the normal range of sailing angles. The JOG have a clause in their safety rules to cover a test in which the yacht is hove over on her beam ends to see if she can recover from a knockdown (and also to test the arrangement of hatches and cockpit), but even if she passes this test it does not mean that she has the power to carry sail, to enable her, for instance, to claw off a lee shore in heavy weather. The extreme case of this is a multihull which has immense initial stability, but can capsize when knocked down.

Low resistance Low resistance to forward motion and therefore boat speed is attained in the hull shape by minimum wetted surface and minimum wave making. At low speeds the resistance is almost all frictional, but even in the fresh winds it forms a high proportion of the total drag, as the graph shows (Fig. 71). In recent years designers have become particularly conscious of this and have looked round for ways of reducing wetted surface. This has resulted in the universal adoption for racing yachts of the fin keel and separate rudder configuration, which is considered below. The reduction of profile in this way cannot be carried beyond the point where leeway becomes a factor. Apart from the obviously undesirable effect of a yacht having leeway, which on an ocean racer in smooth water should not exceed 1·5 degrees, the resistance of the hull will start to increase markedly if this type of side slip is present. Resistance due to wave formation becomes important at a speed of about $0·7\sqrt{LWL}$ and in the vicinity of $1·1\sqrt{LWL}$ the frictional and wave forces are equal. Beyond such a speed, shown in the table (Fig. 71), the wave resistance increases rapidly and is the cause of the yacht being unable to exceed a certain maximum. For a modern ocean racer this is close to $1·45\sqrt{LWL}$. A fine bow contributes to lessening wave making, but the stern has more effect at the higher speeds where the stern wave draws aft. A counter which leaves the waterline at the correct gradient can lengthen the effective LWL and therefore by the formula, the maximum speed. At some point the stern wave begins a down turn and there is no profit in extending the counter beyond it. In quiet weather there is a negligible stern wave and less water in contact with the surface (Fig. 72).

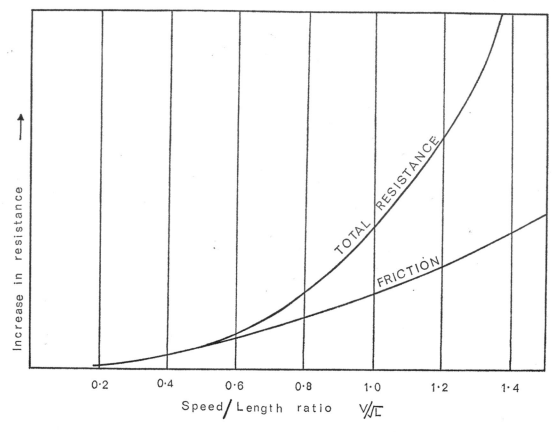

FIG. 71. *Comparison of frictional and total resistance on a yacht hull.*

A transom may have advantages under a rating rule, reducing measured length, but it must be a well designed transom, tapering to almost nothing at the waterline. The conspicuous sternboard should not be immersed.

Steering qualities   If the yacht is difficult to steer she not only tires the helmsman, but is likely to sail more distance through the water. The prime example of this is under spinnaker, when the extra speed which the sail gives in a fresh breeze is to some extent offset by the excessive yawing which is taking place. Up wind is equally important. Some yachts carry excessive weather helm and this is most pronounced when heeled. This is a matter of hull shape, for it means the immersed sections are tending to alter the balance of the boat. Bad effects follow. The rudder angle causes increased resistance and to counteract this and the strain of steering, sail is reduced earlier than necessary. For a yacht to put up a good performance in heavy weather, balance is one of the keys. She can then be pressed, which is so essential to get in the prize money. Usually the boats that are prone to trouble in this department are also brutes under spinnaker. When the yacht is heeling with a shy spinnaker and receives a puff which puts the rail in further, the effect is the same, as far as the hull is concerned, as sailing to windward. My experience shows that there is no direct relationship between the modern short keel and this behaviour. There are short keel boats which are unbalanced and difficult down wind and there are long keeled boats with transoms or counters which behave just as badly. Other short keeled yachts are very reassuring in these conditions and the positioning of the rudder far aft has an immense effect on steering. One quality which can alleviate the "you've got to keep her upright to keep her sailing" school is tumblehome. The absence of flare near deck level gives easier steering when the yacht is immersed up to the rail. The Sparkman and Stephens Half Tonner, the S31, has quite pronounced tumblehome and I am sure that this is one of the factors which makes this yacht so well balanced at almost all times. Any yacht will broach under spinnaker if conditions are severe enough, but the feeling in the S31 with her rudder right aft was that she was easily kept in "the groove" until the helmsman was careless, or a particularly strong or heading puff made her "jump the rails" and broach.

Low rating A hull is bound to show the effect of the rating rule under which she is designed. Rating rules take the blame for many features which are considered by some people to be undesirable. These features may be:

(*a*) not undesirable at all, e.g. convex sheer;
(*b*) not due to the formula of the rule, but a development to get faster speed whatever the rule, e.g. separate fin keels, which are seen on yachts designed under the quite different RORC and CCA formulae;

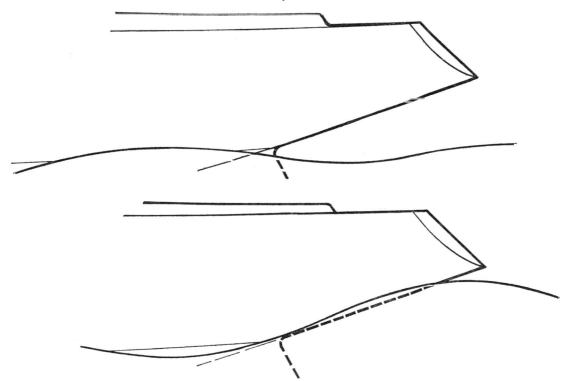

FIG. 72. *Observed action of the wave formation set up in a yacht with a short well designed counter. At low speeds the stern wave drops away near end of designed waterline. Then at near maximum speed the stern wave is carried to the end of the counter.*

(*c*) thought by the designer to be favoured by the rule, e.g. use of steel as a constructional material under the RORC rule. After Dick Carter's *Rabbit* had won the Fastnet and other races, there was an interest in steel which the rule was said to "favour", subsequent performance by various steel yachts cannot be said to have proved the proposition one way or the other;

(*d*) really due to the formula, e.g. a base draft is laid down as an expression based on the *L* measurement and it will be found that yachts tend to go to this. If the designer does favour shallow draft, he will reduce it enough to collect a bonus under the formula. Thus the rule pegs the draft and there is a lack of experimental variations.

Pitching   The problem of rolling does not affect the design of a sailing yacht unless a very long down wind passage is contemplated. One yacht may roll more than another even to the detriment of sailing qualities, but the tendency to roll or not is unlikely to be considered amongst the other factors when designing for ocean racing performance. Pitching, however, is a different matter. One of the marks of the modern ocean racer is her ability to keep going through the seaway, unlike the older cruisers that used to "go up and down in the same hole". Pitching is at its most serious on the windward leg where energy that would be used for driving the yacht forward is dissipated in the oscillations of the hull and the air flow over the sails is given an ever changing velocity. The alleviation of pitching depends on (*a*) the distribution of weight in the yacht, and (*b*) the shape of the ends. In general, weight extended out to the ends of the boat should be avoided, water cans in stern lockers, spare anchors pushed up in the bows and so on. Incidentally, these positions are also high in the hull above the waterline so they are doubly unsuitable for loading. Some yachts seem to benefit from weight inserted in the bow, the feeling of the helmsman being that the bows are kept "down to their work", but I suspect that any improvement in performance is due to correction of poor trim in the first place and some reduction of wetted surface by taking the wider stern sections a little out of the water. The shape of the ends has an effect on pitching in a seaway. A major fault is too much buoyancy in the bows and too little in the stern. The bow will then tend to rise easily. However, with moderate counter any depression by the stern will be resisted and the start of a pitching motion damped out. A fine entry seems desirable for this reason alone in windward sailing.

Overall effect   So much for the essential needs of an offshore racing hull design and it will be noticed that no mention has been made of accommodation, which has to fit in with the hull designed for racing. If extremes have been avoided and by planning a suitable deck and coachroof and with consideration of the shape available, this will follow. For a first judgement of a design the midship section should be sought and can perhaps be considered as the key to the design. At least from it can be seen at a glance whether the hull is light or heavy displacement has a hard or slack bilge, and what her characteristics are of beam, draft, freeboard and keel cross section. The displacement, which is the actual weight of the yacht, seems less critical than other factors, even though it is part of the conception of the basic design. Assuming that extremes of design are avoided, there is a range within which there is no indication that any particular displacement is desirable (Fig. 73). To compare the displacement of different hulls it is usual to take the length and consider the ratio: $\dfrac{Displacement}{(L/100)^3}$

DISPLACEMENT ON 24 FT. LWL

Tons	
1	
2	Y.W. keel boat design } Construction so light as to be unsuitable for offshore sailing.
3	*Coquelicot* (3·2) Pioneer (3·5) Cal 30 (3·65) Aquitaine 32 (3·7)
4	S & S. 34 (4·1) *Summertime* (4·25) Columbia 34 (4·45)
5	*Green Highlander* (5·3) *Zaleda* (5·5)
6	Nicholson 32 (6·0)
7	} Heavy shape of hull and large sail area, unsuitable for racing
8	

FIG. 73. *In a range of displacements for 24 ft. LWL ocean racing yachts, the* Y.W. *Keel-boat and* Summertime *are mentioned elsewhere in this book. Of the other yachts shown above,* Coquelicot *is a hard chine ply or alloy design by Harlé,* Aquitaine *is also a French RORC boat in light alloy.* Pioneer *is an early GRP boat by van de Stadt,* Nicholson 32 *a very popular GRP fast cruiser,* Green Highlander *an Illingworth and Primrose cold moulded transom stern boat.* S. & S. 34 *is a 1969 GRP RORC Stephens boat.* Cal 30 *and* Columbia 34 *are popular CCA rule boats in USA and* Zaleda *is designed to the 7-metre cruiser racer rule of the IYRU.*

Designers have quite different ideas, which they develop individually and by learning from the ultimate performance of each other's creations. This development is demonstrated in Fig. 74, where some of the ocean racing yacht shapes over the years are seen. Every year there are hulls which do not conform: sometimes these are ahead of their time and their true worth is masked by bad handling or, in the case of an advanced hull, a poor sail plan. A striking example of this is the adoption of the separate fin and rudder profile, now the norm for ocean racers. For many years individual boats appeared with this configuration, but as a design feature it did not sweep all before it. Some of the most successful JOG yachts were designed in this way and the Illingworth design *Dusty Miller* was winning races in the Solent area against a wide selection of ocean racing yachts in 1955 and 1956 yet there were no imitators. Illingworth himself returned to the old form in light displacement yachts typified by *Blue Charm*, where the rudder on the main keel would now be considered too near amidships and which required a dagger board through the counter to

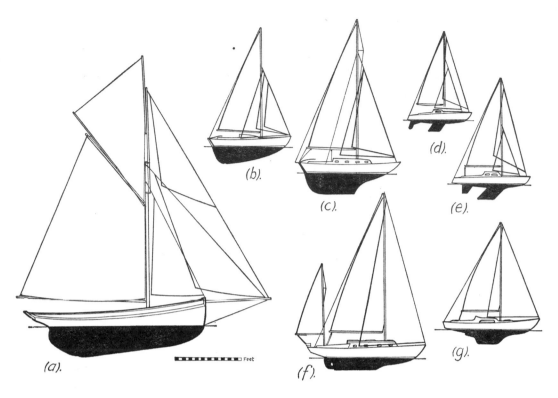

FIG. 74. *Some ocean racing hull shapes and sail plans.*

(a) Jolie Brise *which sailed in the early RORC races (1931) with such success. The working boat features of straight stem, low freeboard, heavily raked rudder post and sail area beyond the ends disappeared with purpose built offshore yachts. LWL 48 ft.*

(b) *Typical of a design presented for fast sailing in British waters in 1945. Morgan Giles' West of England One Design. She had a small foretriangle, deep narrow hull by later standards, 21 ft.*

(c) *An RNSA 24 designed by Laurent Giles and typical of the best type of offshore boat in 1948; still only 7 ft. 6 in. beam on the LWL of 24 ft. Alloy masts were just starting.*

(d) *and* (e). *Early JOG boats* Sopranino *(17 ft. 6 in.) and* Wista *(20 ft.) built in 1950 and 1954. Their fin keel profiles were not generally copied by larger boats for fifteen years. Both had RORC cutter rigs developed by John Illingworth. High freeboard and light displacement were used.*

(f) Finisterre *(27 ft. 6 in.) designed by Sparkman and Stephens in 1959 in U.S.A. had many imitators as a beamy, centre-board yawl which did very well under the CCA rule at that time.*

(g) *The Pioneer, 1960 design by E. G. van de Stadt, one of the first ocean racers (24 ft.) in GRP. Light displacement and separate rudder and fin (though not short) keel. The masthead sloop already established in the USA was starting to become normal for RORC yachts.*

aid the steering down wind. She was typical of the last of the old configuration for light displacement boats, though it is used in moderate displacement craft with an eye on cruising and where a transom has been decided on. Other early separate fin and rudder yachts were those designed by E. G. van de Stadt, usually with a spade rudder, whose designs still continue in this theme and Uffa Fox with his "Flying" series. From the small keel boat, the Flying Fifteen, ocean racing designs were developed such as the Flying Thirty Five, though they were probably not raced offshore enough to make any impact on the yachting scene. At the same time the amateur designer Guy Thompson, working for himself and using free sailing models, had altered the shape of hull of his own new yacht. Writing some years later in 1967, he said:

"Although I had never designed my yachts to the RORC rule, it seemed to me that the so-called rule cheaters were becoming too fine in the ends and the rudder was getting too far forward. So about ten years ago I went back to my boyhood days and designed a yacht with fin and skeg profile.

"When I sailed this model against the previous conventional one I found she sailed faster and steered straighter than her trial horse. The new yacht was built and we found she behaved just as the model had done.

"After this experience, I set out to develop the fin and skeg profile as I felt sure that this was the shape of things to come. I made several models before building another yacht and these showed that the actual shape of the fin and skeg was really more important than the amount of lateral area, so that with this type of profile the wetted surface could be cut down without loss of windward qualities. They also showed that the distance between the trailing edge of the fin and the leading edge of the skeg should be as large as possible. In order to increase this distance, I gave the rudder post a trailing rake, which added to the directional stability.

"The new yacht was built and proved that the work entailed in making several models was well worth while."

The modern profile   In the fin keel portion of a yacht's underbody, it is the forward part that performs the function of a symmetrical hydrofoil. Across this forward piece there is laminar flow, at any rate at low speeds, before the water stream breaks away from the hull. This is the reason that, if faced with undertaking a quick scrub or rub down of a yacht with a "long" keel, one should concentrate first on the forward part of the hull. But there is more to it than this, for complete removal of the after part of the keel has been found to cause no increase in leeway. There is, though, a significant reduction in wetted surface. The rudder, as we now know, in this concept leaves the main keel altogether and is hung aft. It may be completely independent—a spade type—or be mounted behind a skeg. This skeg is frequently enlarged into a "bustle" which has the effect of merging the skeg into the lines of the hull (Fig. 75). The arrangement was first seen on the America's Cup defender *Intrepid*, designed by Sparkman and Stephens, who then used it in their ocean racing designs. This is one of a number of cases of an America's Cup innovation benefitting yachts outside the 12-metre class.

For an example of a proved successful yacht which fits the general term "modern profile", I would choose the 25 ft. 10 in. *Hot Foot*. She is designed by Alan Gurney of New York to the CCA rule and in her first fifteen races took ten first, two thirds and a fourth. The design is deceptively simple and points to note are the moderate freeboard, overhangs

L

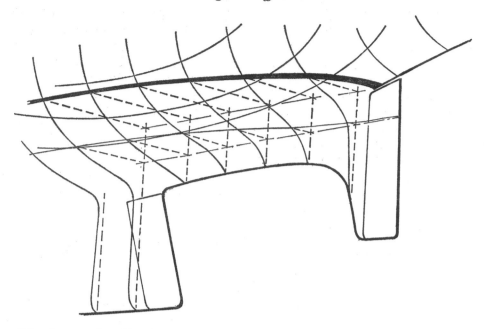

FIG. 75. *What is meant by a "bustle" in the separate keel and rudder configuration. Instead of a thin section skeg and rudder, the shape of the hull is brought aft and merged into the skeg.*

which are the norm for ocean racing and the spade rudder at the extreme end of the water-line. The accommodation is by no means sparse and shows what can be expected in a hull of 4·5 tons, which is moderately light for the length. *Hot Foot* was the prototype of the aluminium Nantucket 33 but her construction is double diagonal white cedar planking on Douglas fir stringers and no timbers, but GRP covered (Fig. 76).

Other hull design detail   One of the secrets of yacht design and construction is atten-tion to detail, so nothing can really be singled out as unimportant. But there are a few points still to be considered in the hull. Amongst them are the trim tab, the sheer line, freeboard and colour!

    Trim tab. It would be unfair to say that designers, having placed the rudder under the counter, could not then resist hanging something on the fin keel that was left, but such a comment could apply in a few cases. The fin keel of *Breyell II*, a Belgian One Ton yacht designed by Britton Chance, would hardly exist without the trim tab, which is just under half the width of the rest of the keel (Fig. 77). Skippers with trim tabs seem enthusiastic about them, their primary design function being to make the fin asymmetrical. This the trim tab cannot ideally do because the hydrofoil needed on one tack would be a smoothly curved section, whereas constructional limitations mean there is only a trailing blade. It can also be used to trim out weather helm and as an auxiliary rudder. If the rudder and trim tab can be coupled together, the effect of both blades is to give the yacht an extremely tight turning circle. With a wheel this can be achieved by having a second wheel of smaller diameter controlling the trim tab and on the same axis as the ship's wheel. Some form of clamp is used to lock both controls together for the double rudder effect. In some

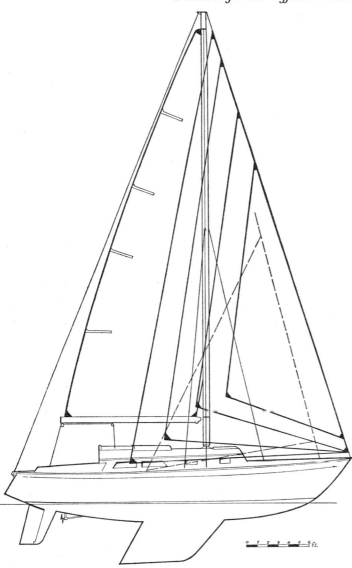

FIG. 76. *A successful sloop to the CCA rule.* Hot Foot *which became the Nantucket 33 design. Although there are differences between this and boats developed under the RORC rule they are not marked. The accommodation layout is simple in conception and practical. Dimensions are LOA 33 ft., LWL 26 ft., beam 10 ft. 2 in., draft 5 ft 6 in., displacement 4·7 tons, ballast 1·8 tons. The standard yacht is built in both aluminium and GRP Sail areas: mainsail 218 sq. ft., foretriangle 270 sq. ft.*

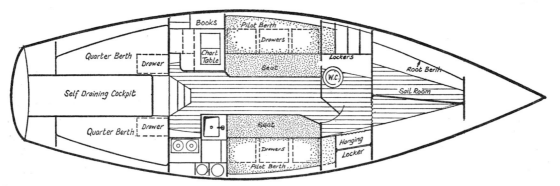

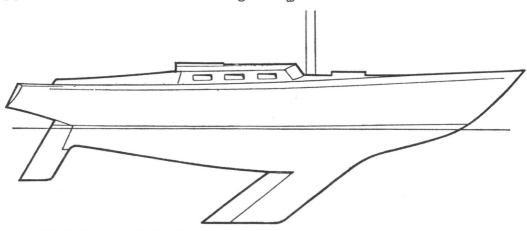

FIG. 77. *The hull shape of the One Tonner* Breyell II, *designed by Britton Chance Jnr., shows how the trim tab forms a large proportion of the fin keel.*

designs there is provision for a special tiller for the trim tab, which, again, can be clamped to the main tiller. The trim tab is available in the event of damage to the main rudder, but on the other hand, it is a piece of equipment which if itself is damaged is impossible to repair below the waterline at sea. There have been cases of yachts put out of races because of trim tab troubles.

Sheer line and freeboard. Too much freeboard means additional weight high up on the hull (topside height and deck position) and windage. Too little will make the accommodation cramped and, depending on the distribution of the hull shape near the deck, will mean immersion of the rail at an early stage in the angle of heel. The old 6-metres and similar yachts which raced inshore had low freeboard and cruising conversions of them, obviously further down in the water, and near relatives in the offshore scene in the late forties gave low freeboard a bad name. English yachts, as mentioned, were in addition narrow, which did not help matters. The reaction to this has been to say that a high freeboard is desirable offshore, but in the modern boat, this should be strictly limited. The actual appearance of freeboard on a yacht lying on her mooring is deceptive, owing to the sheer line, shape of the ends and colour scheme. The freeboard amidships of two yachts of the same LOA (31 ft.) when expressed as a ratio of the waterline shows the sort of figure found. The Liz 31 with a transom stern appears to have a much greater proportional freeboard than the S31, which might a few years ago have been thought to lack freeboard. In fact they are close:

Liz 31 (LWL 24·16 ft.)   Freeboard/wl   13%
S31 (LWL 22·0 ft.)   Freeboard/wl   11%

In the smallest yachts the sheer line is often dictated by minimal accommodation needs and a convex, or reverse, sheer is the result. It was a loop-hole in the RORC rule, long since closed, which first led to a convex sheer, as well as the reaction to low freeboard. The sheer line as such has little racing significance and can be said to be a result of the designer's ideas on the correct freeboard forward and amidships with the after part of the sheer line fairing in with these two. The sheer line may be false with the topsides carried forward in the form of bulwarks, while the deck remains straight or curves down in a hidden convex sheer. Among the reasons for the offshore classes being alone in these variations of sheer is the rule in inshore boats and the IYRU classes requiring their sheer lines to be "continuous concave curves". Sheer line and freeboard may have a bearing on hull colour with boot-topping and colour breaks in the topsides being used to relieve a high freeboard effect. An ocean racer with dark hull colours can be unpleasantly hot below in strong sunshine and pale colours are desirable whatever the material. Choice of colour will have to be made early where it is impregnated in the gel coat in GRP. Apart from these considerations, it is up to the owner's wife!

·11·

THE BUILDING OF HULL AND DECK

IF THE strength of the hull is one of the most important features that the designer considers as the drawings of a yacht take shape, it is also a known limitation that the design of any structure depends on the strength of the individual materials available to the builders. Perfect hydrofoil keels of variable geometry and rudders of changeable area are desirable but at present impracticable; planing ocean racers have occasionally been achieved, but the strength of the hulls which had to be used is not normally acceptable. But progress has been made in recent years with a variety of new materials enabling ocean racers to incorporate new ideas. Suitable types of steel mean that a keel with a particularly thin section where it joins the rest of the hull can be designed; epoxy resins and cellular foam productions have done much to make the use of metal hulls more practical, as has the development of new types of alloy. The rig has been transformed for some years now with man-made fibres in cordage and sails and metal masts and these features have in their turn put ever heavier stresses on the hulls of ocean racers. No other sailing craft upon the seas has as its primary function to be able to drive to windward in heavy weather at the maximum possible speed.

For this reason the hull of an ocean racer will always be more expensive to construct than its cruising counterpart. On the other hand, series production of ocean racing type yachts will often be found to be of an ocean racing standard and the cruising man benefits. If he does not wish to run to this expense, he may have to settle for a boat of inferior performance under sail which the builders know will not be hard driven. There are signs of a tendency for the pure cruising sailing yacht to disappear leaving the offshore racer or the motor-sailer as the choice.

The deck structure   The design of the hull only was looked at in the previous chapter, and although the entire deck arrangement is part of the conception, its design is more sensitive to the materials and constructional system used. A glance at the deck area of the yacht gives the clue to the material, but hulls in metal, GRP or wood are, if well built, not easy to distinguish even close up. This deck area, which term includes coach roof or dog-house, and cockpit, has three functions:

1. As a working platform for the crew.
2. As that part of the yacht that makes her suitable for the open sea by making her a watertight entity.
3. As an essential structure for the strength of the hull.

If a deck fails in one of these requirements, it makes the yacht unsuitable for offshore racing. Rating and safety rules also have an influence on deck arrangements. The One Ton and Half Ton cups specify a minimum area of coachroof under which there shall be a certain headroom. In the One Ton Cup this rule is borrowed from the IYRU 8-metre cruiser/racer class but the same regulating clause is achieved in the Half Ton boats by specifying the actual measurements (*see* Appendix 5). The Australian Half Ton yacht *September* designed by her owner, Douglas Gilling, has the size of her moulded dome type coachroof arranged to the minimum size (Fig. 78). Though the shape is unusual outside Australia, it is seen in yachts outside the Half Ton class and has not been forced into this style by the rule alone.

The RORC scantling allowance for decks has caused an undesirable trend in that one square foot of the deck weight was used in the rule without taking into account the total deck area. For this reason, some designers fitted coachroofs of large area surrounded by deck of the maximum possible thickness. Despite this the general trend has been to clear

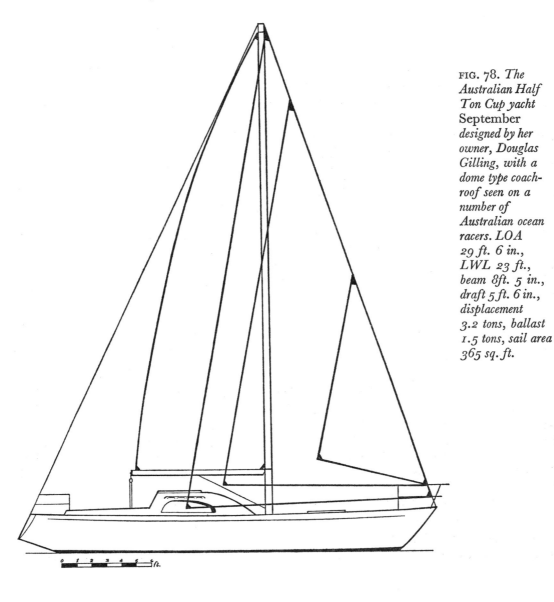

FIG. 78. *The Australian Half Ton Cup yacht* September *designed by her owner, Douglas Gilling, with a dome type coach-roof seen on a number of Australian ocean racers. LOA 29 ft. 6 in., LWL 23 ft., beam 8ft. 5 in., draft 5 ft. 6 in., displacement 3.2 tons, ballast 1.5 tons, sail area 365 sq. ft.*

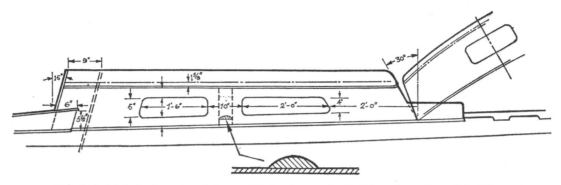

FIG. 79. *It is desirable to keep coachroofs low and their windows small. These dimensions of the ¾ in. mahogany coachroof of* Summertime *show a dorade ventilator box at the forward end and a fillet glued across the grain between the windows to check any possibility of splitting in extreme conditions.*

decks for rapid handling of the yacht by the crew and as the coachroof is a potential source of weakness in severe weather, its diminution adds to the seaworthiness of the vessel. The desire for room in the cabin can tend to produce coachroofs with sizeable coamings on small yachts. There are a number of recorded instances of yachts in very heavy seas being thrown on their beam ends and suffering damage to the coachroof by the splitting of the coamings and smashing of the windows. The smashing of windows, even in less extreme conditions, is not very uncommon and every yacht should carry boards which can be screwed over them in bad weather. Sometimes the method of letting the glass, however thick itself, into a GRP coachroof is not sound. There have been instances on ocean racers of the glass "popping out" of rubber mouldings. A more serious accident occurred in the 1964 RORC Santander to La Trinité race, when the French Class III yacht *Aloa,* lying a-hull in the Bay of Biscay in a severe gale was thrown on her beam ends. The lee side of the coachroof and the cockpit coaming were stove in. This was the beginning of a series of tragic incidents in which the owner was lost overboard, though the yacht was taken in tow twenty-four hours later. This race is one of the very few offshore events in which lives have been lost.

Also in the Bay of Biscay, the JOG racer *Tom Bowling,* designed by John Flewitt and of only 17 ft., was flung on her beam ends while lying under bare poles in a very severe gale. Although the mast was broken as it was forced below the horizontal, no damage was done to the hull. This was no doubt because she was a reverse sheer boat with no prominent coachroof. I would not, for choice, go to sea in some of the standard cruising designs that have large coachroof windows. The depth of coachroof and size of the windows as fitted to *Summertime* (Fig. 79), are quite large enough for a 24 ft. yacht. Even though in ¾ in. mahogany, we glued a wide fillet across the grain between the two windows.

The material of a deck and coachroof may not be the same as that of the hull. *September*'s GRP coachroof with its compound curves is in contrast to her planked hull. The RORC club yacht *Griffin III* has a moulded cockpit structure in GRP while her general structure is of conventional wood. Steel yachts may well have wooden decks set across various steel structures and the coachroof may be of wood. A combination which seems appropriate for small ocean racers is a wooden deck structure on a GRP hull. The advantages of the wooden upperworks instead of GRP which would logically seem to

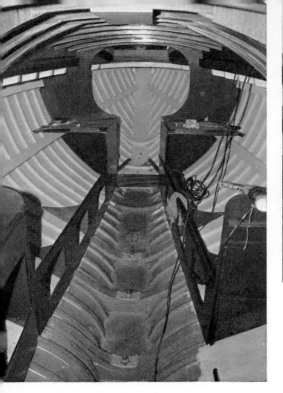

27 (*a*) *Left:* Traditional wood construction in progress on *Alacrity III* designed by Illingworth and Associates. Leaf floors, bilge stringers and basic cabin joinery are evident. (*b*) *Right:* Strength in coachroof and side deck is ensured by knees from roof to topsides and massive beam shelf.

28. Building a GRP yacht. Chopped strand matt is laid up with resin in the mould.

29. Completing the T31. GRP hull with wood construction.
(a) *Above:* Spacing pieces are laid across the empty shell.
(b) *Below:* The Utile shell has been bolted right round and spruce beams are in position.

(c) *Above:* Wooden deck laid on and some bulkheads in position.

(d) *Below:* Cabin furniture can be fixed with hull still open. Athwartships chart table is on the right.

(e) *Above:* Coachroof and coaming in position, also showing half beams and locker facings.

(f) *Below:* T31 nears completion. Patchwork effect is protective paper.

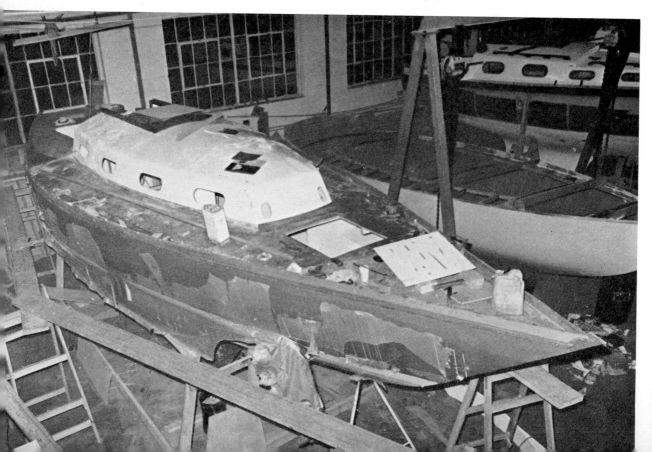

follow on a GRP hull are lightness, longitudinal stiffness, the ability to make minor alterations such as winch platforms and add or remove fittings (not always simple with GRP) and some aesthetic appeal. The only disadvantage, that has occurred with some yachts, are leaks appearing where the deck joins the hull. A method of joining which makes use of glassing over a basically sound system is used in the T31 (Fig. 80). This yacht is designed by Guy Thompson in collaboration with Dick Pitcher. A wooden deck or coachroof top on any racer is invariably made in marine plywood of suitable thickness. The only concession to the old teak laid deck is thin teak strips laid over the ply, but as this adds weight without much strength and is only for appearance, it has no place in the small racer. The plywood can be covered with canvas or nylon by the Cascover process (a method supplied by the Borden Chemical Co. Ltd., Southampton, England, using rescorcinol resin, nylon and vinyl paint), but since a non-slip surface must be applied to these, I prefer to use an epoxy or polyurethane paint mixed with fine sand direct on the ply after an undercoat. A further coat is applied with or without sand and the deck is thus sealed without the difficulties associated with fabrics. Joints near hatches and fittings should be treated with GRP tape and painted over like the rest of the deck.

Constructional materials   Prize winning boats continue to emerge built in all the materials used in yacht construction and long may this remain so. As a result there is interest by ocean racing men in the progress of each of the methods available. As far as building contributes to the performance of a yacht, it is the intelligent use of the chosen material that matters, not the material as such. Looking at each type of construction in general terms, Fig. 81 shows the advantages and disadvantages of each. The materials are those which are feasible for the building of offshore racers, though there are several other methods of constructing yachts, such as concrete, as well as combinations of different methods.

Wood planking   What is known in England as the traditional method of construction and in France as "classique" is seen less and less with the famous builders of wood ocean racers turning over to other systems. However, for a one-off yacht it has the advantages of being understood by many small yards for initial construction and repair. Many experienced yachtsmen have built up a fund of knowledge on traditional construction and so can check any difficulties which arise with the hull. In the same way although the planked hull has certain spots liable to weakness, these are well known.

Planking above the waterline will not be of teak in a small racer owing to the weight of 41 lb. per cu. ft., but it may be used below for durability. Honduras mahogany or Agba (32–34 lb. per cu. ft.) are more suitable above the waterline or for the whole hull and are easier to work in building. Planking can be caulked throughout, but the best plan is to spline above the waterline while caulking below to allow for minor movement of the wood, which can be faired completely in the boat's first season. Strip planking is an alternative to carvel with narrow planks glued with resorcinol and also pinned with nails driven in from one plank to the next perpendicular to the side of the boat. This makes repairs difficult but the effect of gluing every plank makes for a strong structure. The centreline structure of all forms of wood building now consists of laminated members probably in mahogany and this is stronger than the older methods of grown members scarfed with the resulting critical spot. The timbers or frames may also be laminated, but

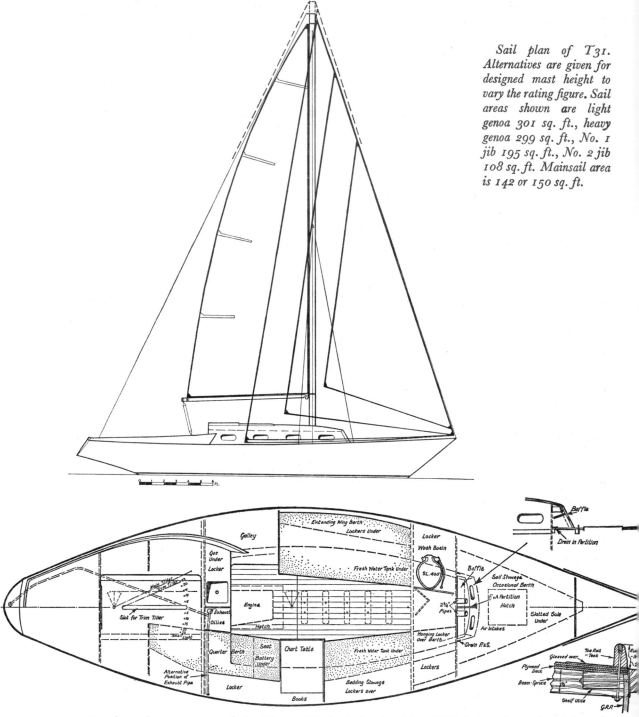

Sail plan of T31. Alternatives are given for designed mast height to vary the rating figure. Sail areas shown are light genoa 301 sq. ft., heavy genoa 299 sq. ft., No. 1 jib 195 sq. ft., No. 2 jib 108 sq. ft. Mainsail area is 142 or 150 sq. ft.

FIG. 80. *General arrangement of the T31 which is designed with a CRP hull and wooden deck and coachroof. The inset drawings show the ventilation arrangement in the forward edge of the coachroof and the method of fastening the wood deck to GRP hull.*

TABLE OF BUILDING MATERIALS

	Wood planking	Marine ply	Cold moulded	Steel	Light Alloy	GRP	Sandwich system
Strength	fair	good	v. good	v. good	v. good	good	good
Lightness	poor	fair	v. good	poor	v. good	fair	good
Stiffness	fair	fair	good	v. good	v. good	poor	v. good
Fairing and finishing	good	poor	v. good	fair	fair	good	fair
Insulation	fair	fair	fair	poor	poor	poor	v. good
Durability	fair	poor	good	poor	fair	v. good	fair
Cost	high	low	high	moderate	high	low	moderate
Remarks	Many variations in woods and exact methods of construction.	With sheet plywood limitations in shape must be accepted.	Only possible at a few yards.	Modern processes will prolong life. Electrolytic factor. Magnetic.	Limited yards with experience.	Quantity production lowers cost.	Limited yards with experience.

FIG. 81.

steamed Canadian Rock Elm is very satisfactory for this. Any timber with the slightest flaw, usually a crack along the grain after bending, must be rejected. Metal framing with its great strength is appealing for an ocean racer, but is less commonly seen in the smaller yachts. Light alloy suggests itself as the most suitable with perhaps several metal frames among regularly spaced laminated or steamed timbers.

Bilge stringers are of use in equalizing the strains on the hull in a longitudinal direction and two would be the rule in a yacht between 20 and 26 ft. They were allowed for in the RORC scantling allowance which encouraged their use in substantial sizes. The scantling allowance was such that there has been a tendency to specify larger bilge stringers than were necessary. The modern fin keel with the high ballast ratio and the punishment on the hull from modern rigs means that special attention must be paid to floors. A solid wood floor is suitable in the ends of the yacht, but laminated floors can be used over most of the length and have the advantage that they can be brought well up into the side of the hull and tapered off across the planking. In way of the shrouds they can even overlap with pads coming down which carry the chain plates.

The transverse rigidity of the hull should be further strengthened by the use of knees, which may be of metal or steamed or laminated wood and by bulkheads of a structural nature. Even if these are cut into, to suit the accommodation, they should be cut in such a way that where there are lockers or access for the crew, they become in effect extensive web frames.

Marine grade plywood has already been mentioned for the deck, which should be over spruce beams (28 lb. per cu. ft.) if lightness is required. For slightly greater strength it is as well to have the beams at each end of the coachroof and some of the coachroof beams in laminated African mahogany (35–44 lb. per cu. ft.). The cost of most of the woods just recommended is high: this includes Honduras Mahogany, Teak, Rock Elm and Spruce. Cheaper woods which may be substituted are Agba, Iroko, Utile and Sapele in the hard woods and European Redwood in the softwoods. But even these are only comparatively cheaper and if this is a consideration in the case of an ocean racer, it would be better to select a different method of construction.

Because planked construction is becoming rare, there is a natural desire to contrast it with the more common methods by varnishing the hull. This is beautiful and quite satisfactory except in a hot climate. The topsides will have to be splined and if taking the trouble to varnish, the planks should come from the same log. The alternative is contrasting colours of wood showing every seam and butt. In small yachts the use of a single log for each topside is feasible. This was done on *Alacrity III* an example of modern planked construction (Fig. 82). Designed by Illingworth and Associates, she was launched in 1968.

Electrolysis on wooden yachts   This appears in various forms on wooden yachts and is obviously of major concern on metal craft. Stray current can run through wet wood particularly mahogany, but there is really no need for any trouble with present knowledge. If phosphor bronze, yellow metals and copper fastenings are used throughout the construction, there is no need to introduce any iron and a major cause of electrolysis is avoided. Stray currents from electrical equipment can be stopped by meticulous installation of wiring and provision should be made to disconnect the battery by a main switch adjacent

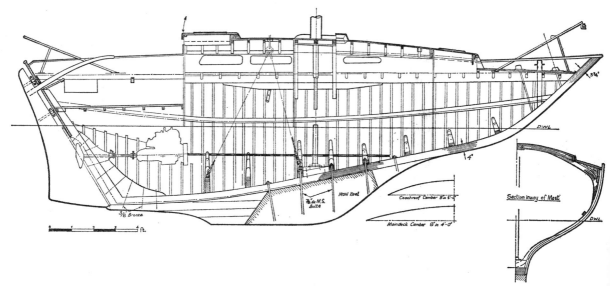

FIG. 82. *Traditional wood planked construction in* Alacrity III *designed by Illingworth and Associates and built in 1968. The timbers which show conspicuously as vertical lines are of Canadian rock elm at 5¼ in. apart. Planking is 3/16 in., bottom iroko and topsides mahogany. The bilge stringer can be seen and the laminated mahogany floors. There is further lamination in the section shown.*

to it when not in use. An iron keel may be specified and if this is so, it must be completely insulated by bedding compounds and plastic paints such as modern epoxies.

Cold moulded wood Before discussing cold moulded hulls, mention should be made of double diagonal planking which is a step in this direction. It was known before the days of synthetic adhesives because the two skins were clenched together on what was a conventional framing system. It is stronger and lighter than planking and allows different woods to be used on the inner and outer skin. It is not commonly seen on small yachts and is practised in only a limited number of yards.

Cold moulded construction depends on the use of resorcinol glues which, though demanding a little more care and temperature control than ureas, are completely resistant to any effect by sea water. They comply with a British specification which involves boiling a test joint in water over many hours. The resultant hull can be thought of as modern material mix of wood and synthetic resin, rather than layers of ply. The glue being stronger than the wood makes this so. The process is simple in conception but requires greater care in the execution. In the event of failure due to human error, it is expensive and difficult to repair. It is therefore essential to go to a first-class yard with experience of the technique. Chippendale Ltd., of Fareham, England, are experienced in the method though the name that stands out for moulded ply ocean racers is W. A. Souter & Son Ltd. of Cowes, England. They have perfected their ability starting years ago on dinghies and proceeding to Class I ocean racers. Part of their success stems from the feedback of experience from owners and designers of boats which have been sailed really hard. The lesson here is that an ocean racer is best constructed by a yard that knows the strains that are put on her—and perhaps has, on someone else's boat, seen the result of hard driving. One ocean racer built by them was *Green Highlander II*, completed in 1969 to the design of Angus Primrose (Fig. 83).

In the construction of cold moulded work, a soft wood male mould of closely spaced ribbands is first made. The centreline of the yacht, invariably a mahogany laminate, is set on this. The hull structure is then laid on, in the form of strips of veneer around 4 in. wide. For a hull $\frac{5}{8}$ in. thick, there might be four or five layers of about $\frac{1}{8}$ in. each. This is where experienced builders are essential, taking a stroke of the plane on the edge of the veneer, assuring that the spread of adhesive is correct and fastening each skin by plywood toggles and pins until the glue has been correctly cured. When all this is finished the result is a hull without strengthening which has been built upside down. The second stage is to turn it the right way up and fit the bulkheads. The floors and frames are best shaped and laminated inside the hull without at first being glued to it. They are then taken out, cleaned up and finally fastened and glued into position. It has been found that the best design is to have numerous light frames rather than a lesser number of heavy ones to obviate any "panting" by the hull or the possibility of "hard spots". A principal advantage of cold moulding is that by means of glued laminates the load of various members can be spread across the homogeneous hull. This applies to laminates bearing the chain plates and floors supporting a fin keel which can be carried up the hull in decreasing thickness. The whole method is so strong it has been necessary for designers working under the 1957 RORC rule to insert bilge stringers and similar members to get a reasonable rating under the scantling allowance, though these were not necessary for the soundness of the hull. It is also of interest to note that Souter's experience of ocean racers has led them into international favour for the construction of cold moulded racing power boats which are intended to be subjected to intense slamming at high speed in open water.

Sheet plywood   Sheets of plywood have been used on ocean racers from time to time and several light displacement yachts in this material have had a successful racing career. The popularity of this material even for cruisers has waned since GRP became the most widely used material and this is probably with good reason. But no one method of building is bad in itself and there is no basic reason why a sheet plywood boat cannot perform well. The advantages are cheapness, ease of construction and an easily obtained bottom surface. The chief racing disadvantage, outside any one-design class, is that the material restricts the choice of hull form since the designer has to incorporate corners in the shape of the section—the hard chine. The sheets of ply can only be bent in one plane and compound curves are not possible. Frederick Parker in his Half Ton *Mistri* design (Fig. 84) by clever geometry has managed to work in a flare forward turning into tumblehome aft using two sheets in the topsides. The design in section is also very close to a round bilge version of the same concept. But it is not the same and with the fine speed differences in ocean racing being decisive, a compromise of this nature is difficult to accept. Such recent developments as fairing the hull to meet the rudder skeg are not possible. In panelled construction of this type despite plentiful use of adhesives there is always the chance of hard spots. The ply sides of the yacht can be scarfed before the hull is attached to the frames: it is this speed in assembling the hull that brings the main saving in building costs.

On *Mistri*, $\frac{1}{2}$ in. ply is used and naturally only marine grade plywood to the official specification (e.g. British Standard 1088) can come near the building shed. For seagoing yachts all the veneers of the ply should be hardwood such as mahogany, not just the outer ones. These outer veneers should have sufficient thickness to allow for the cleaning off of joints without cutting down to the glue line. African mahogany is also usual for the frames in a ply yacht and with a 20–24 ft. waterline, 3 in.$\times\frac{7}{8}$ in. pieces spaced at around 2 ft. 6 in. would be appropriate.

Steel   Until recently steel, the most common ship-building material, has been out of favour for small sailing yachts. The problem has been, especially for racing yachts, that the alternatives were plating which was too heavy to achieve an acceptable ballast ratio, or if this was obtained the plating was so thin that it was easily dented or even deformed by a seaway when beating to windward. This unfairness of the hulls of steel yachts can frequently be seen on older cruising yachts in the material. For racing yachts, the material was not worth considering. However, a string of very successful racing yachts have been produced in steel including Dick Carter's 1965 Fastnet winner, *Rabbit*.

The secret lies in using the high tensile steel known as Corten which can be used in thicknesses as little as $\frac{5}{32}$ in. or 3 mm., which is of sufficient gauge to obtain the ballast ratios of wood or GRP. The nature of this steel and its resistance to corrosion means that no allowance has to be made for scaling, a factor which meant extra weight for the earlier types. Because small shipyards of a commercial nature work in steel, it is sometimes claimed that a steel yacht is less expensive than a wooden one of equivalent size. This is not certain, though Dutch yards which work on small yachts regularly in steel can quote very moderate prices. But steel is not an expensive constructional material.

Corrosion is the second big worry of steel yachts. There is the possibility of galvanic

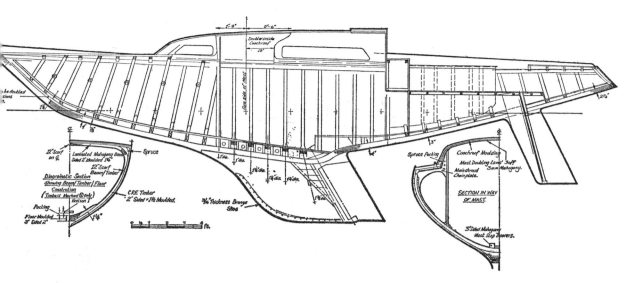

FIG. 83. *Cold moulded plywood construction of* Green Highlander II *designed by Angus Primrose and built by W. A. Souter & Son Ltd. of Cowes. LWL 27 ft. 10 in. The hull is six laminates of 3 mm. veneer. The coachroof is moulded with doubling for the distance as shown abreast of the mast. The main shroud chain plate is a light alloy web.*

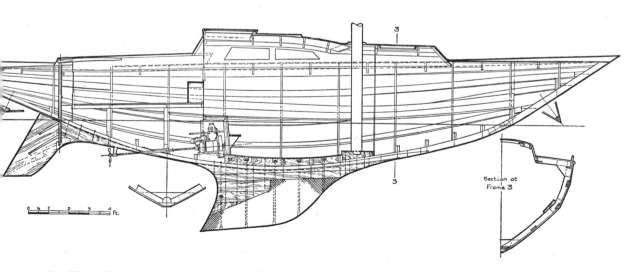

FIG. 84. *Hard chine plywood construction for offshore racing in* Mistri *built in 1969 to the design of Frederick Parker. The 22 ft. LWL yacht was built to rate at 18 ft. under RORC rule, so that bilge stringer scantlings are in excess of what is strictly required for construction. The skin is $\frac{1}{2}$ in with frames of 3 in. by $7\frac{7}{8}$ in. The deck thickness is $\frac{5}{8}$ in. and the keel is lead.*

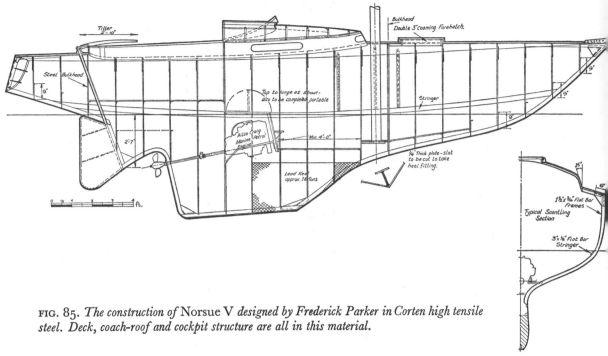

FIG. 85. *The construction of* Norsue V *designed by Frederick Parker in Corten high tensile steel. Deck, coach-roof and cockpit structure are all in this material.*

action, rust or electrolysis. Corten goes a long way to combat the first two and all surfaces of the steel must be meticulously painted. The inside of a hull can now be most efficiently treated with polyurethane foam: the weight of this material, which is applied so that it covers every irregular surface, is negligible and the bulk is slight. These are two qualities which suit the ocean racer. Electrolysis can hardly be prevented in the way recommended above for wooden yachts—the avoidance of iron! In this case, the opposite procedure is adopted and bronze and gunmetal fittings are avoided. If they have to be used, careful insulation with plastics is required and this goes for the aluminium mast and also for a lead keel, if such is used instead of iron to gain power for racing. The whole question of electro-chemical activity in steel hulls is well known and is no different for racing yachts than other craft. Suffice it to say here that all the usual precautions must be taken and these include extreme care in all electrical wiring and circuits, the provision of cut-off for batteries and the possibility of sacrificial anodes. Though each material mentioned in this chapter has its advantages, steel construction for yachts under 25 ft. waterline is one of the less suitable materials. Simplifying the conclusions it rather looks with steel that the bigger the yacht, the more it should be favoured. The logic of this is its lack of appeal for the smaller racers. A few Half Tonners have been built of steel including the Dutch *Hydra*, designed by Alan Buchanan and sailed by André Nelis in the 1968 races and Frederick Parker's *Norsue V*, built in 1967. The construction plan of the latter is shown in **Fig. 85**.

Light Alloy   The fact that only a few manufacturers can build an aluminium hull limits the output of this excellent method of construction. Large yachts are built of it in the USA, but more small craft are now being designed in the material. The production boats of the Hot Foot design are an example. Yards in Holland are practised in aluminium yachts, while in France the builders ACNAM of Suresnes have built a number of small alloy ocean racers including the Challenger class (17 ft. 10 in.), *Fabius* (24 ft. 10 in.) and *Casarca 4* (25 ft.). *Rafale* (19 ft.) is another example (Fig. 61). Because of the specialized men and equipment needed to build light alloy craft they are expensive and this is another reason why they will probably remain in the minority for some years. But for the strength and lightness required for offshore racing the material has no equal. Much larger but very successful yachts in aluminium are such household names as *Ondine* and *Pen-Duick III*. Aluminium can be thought of as one-half the strength of mild steel and one-third of the weight, but in comparison with wood and GRP not only has much higher tensile strength but has a quality known as toughness. Its ductility enables a hard object to be struck against it many times before rupture occurs. In fact, wood or GRP would be smashed at the stage where light alloy is heavily dented but still leak proof.

Metal fittings are essential in a wood or GRP hull for such items as chain plates and stanchion bases (I have seen the latter moulded in GRP but without success), but in the alloy boat these are integral, with all the advantages that accrues from using the same material for different components. In the case of chain plates the metal will be bulkier than steel but this can be worked neatly into the deck of the same material. Because of this homogeneity there is a fair choice of methods used to strengthen the hull both transversely and longitudinally. Floors can be carried across in way of the frames, while the material lends itself to web frames slotted in to suit the accommodation. Water tanks can be built direct on the hull.

The light alloys to be used for boat work are completely corrosion-proof and require painting on for appearance only. Their numbered specifications vary between countries. The aluminium will be that with a magnesium content and the latest types under British specification are NS5 for sheet, NP8 for plate and NE8 for sections. All this is of weldable quality, though as the thickness decreases extra care has to be taken with the security of jigs. Where a form of corrosion arises is in the threat of electrolysis with different metals used in fittings. Electro-chemical activity is high with copper and gunmetal and less so with lead, stainless steel, cast iron and mild steel, in that order. So below the waterline care must be taken with the type of anti-fouling (copper-based ones are common for racing finishes), the propeller and shaft and the ballast keel.

A method used to install the ballast keel on a recent Camper and Nicholson built yacht was to pour lead into the ready shaped fin; the lead was allowed to shrink and then epoxy tar poured into the surrounding space. A sealer plate in insulating material was bedded down over the top. The result was that the lead was hermetically sealed and there was no chance of elctrolytic action. This is one way of dealing with this problem, but it demonstrates the care that has to be taken with different metals on a light alloy hull. As many fittings as possible should be in aluminium to avoid any possibility of electro-chemical action, even above water, and this is easily done in the case of fairleads, cleats and so on. Where other metals have to be used they must be bedded in with an inert and permanently plastic compound. Even moorings must be remembered and synthetic warp rather than steel chain used. The increasing use of synthetic plastics and plastic-covered metal yacht fittings has simplified this problem immensely in recent years.

Sandwich The heading here is not a fugitive from the paragraphs on what to give the crew on night watches, but is the name given to a method of building applied to several

M

successful large yachts, including the winner of the 1968 single-handed transatlantic race, *Sir Thomas Lipton*. There is at the moment little data available on this system of construction over a period for ocean racers in general. Its immediate appeal lies in being able to build a one-off plastic yacht without the high cost of the plug and mould in ordinary GRP work. The mould is somewhat like that used for cold moulded construction, but the ribbands do not have to be closely spaced and it can be of very cheap wood. On this is laid sheets of PVC foam and a suitable type is "Plasticell" made by BTR Industries Ltd. This is thermoplastic, of between ¼ in. and 3 in. thick, and can be worked into a compound curve at temperatures of 160 degrees Fahrenheit. It is also easy to cut at any temperature with an ordinary saw or sharp cutting tool. Over the formed-up foam, the outer GRP layer of the hull is moulded and the materials have an affinity which makes the structure one. The "boat" is then taken off the mould and the inner GRP layer applied and at this stage the hull is basically finished and is stiff enough for some types of yacht to require no further stiffening. The resulting hull is a light one, but the layers of GRP are thin and, to obtain the necessary strength, woven rovings and not chopped strand mat glass fibres have to be used. Two applications of woven roving in each layer in the topside thickness is suitable for a 22 ft. yacht. This type of roving and the special foam both tend to increase the cost of the hull. Naturally, the yards who can undertake this are limited and the most experience in England has been built up by Derek Kelsall Ltd.; strangely, he works from the town of Sandwich, Kent. In Holland, Frans Maas of Breskens builds ocean racers with sandwich hulls: the 1969 Fastnet winner *Red Rooster* was from this yard.

The hull has the advantages of buoyancy and insulation, which are marginal for ocean racing, but the thin outer skin with foam below, although tough, may suffer minor imperfections due to the usual stresses and its fairness for racing could become suspect. As the outer surface of the hull is laid up and not out of a mould there is considerable work to be done to clean and smooth this, but the process is eased in that woven roving reinforcement gives a better initial surface than chopped strand mat. Whether sandwich hulls will be seen in large numbers depends on the building costs compared with other methods when quantity production comes into the picture. The system seems to have been used successfully by amateur builders.

Glass-reinforced plastics   All the advantages to yachts in general which have made glass-reinforced plastics the most widely used boat building material today, apply to ocean racing yachts, though there are several points to note when using this material for offshore boats. An increasing number of standard yachts suitable for ocean racing will be offered in GRP (Fig. 86) and this commercial reason will cause the number of such boats in the offshore fleets to rise. Once a long series of boats can be taken off the same mould they can be sold at a more economic price than cold moulded and light alloy, though a racing disadvantage in comparison with these two methods is the heavier weight of GRP yachts of equal size and strength. One way of alleviating this has already been mentioned, the wooden deck of the T31. It is the deck (and above) where weight is going to do most harm, but the T31 also reduces the thickness of the hull away from the keel. Near the keel the hull is 29 oz. per square foot, tapering higher up the bottom to 15 oz. The topsides then become 11 oz. and, as the plywood deck has beams of spruce, it will be seen that considerable thought has been given to the important matter of keeping the centre of gravity low.

The strength of **GRP** is no problem for racing yachts, but the low modulus of elasticity means that large panels of it are flexible. This is another argument in favour of the wooden deck, but the hull itself being of compound curves obtains extra rigidity from its shape. Substantial bulkheads and longitudinal strengthening are still essential. The need to keep a racing boat at a high standard of maintenance and the usual desire for appearance is made easier by GRP, certainly in comparison with wooden boats after a year or two of offshore work. Further advantages lie in the excellent initial surface presented by the bottom for applying under-water paint and the negligible absorption of water. This last undoubtedly affects the performance of wooden yachts, though modern synthetic coatings offer a possible, but time-consuming, solution. One advantage of **GRP** is its complete resistance to rot and corrosion, but this should not be taken as a signal by builders, as it has in some standard yachts, that ventilation need not be considered. Apart from keeping soft furnishings (bunks, clothing, blankets) fresh when the yacht is shut up, it has frequently been brought home to me on a beat to windward with hatches closed, how necessary ventilation is for the crew's physical comfort.

Lloyd's standards   While racing boats can be quite adequate without conforming to Lloyd's rules for wood, which are a shade on the heavy side, the "provisional" rules for the construction of GRP yachts laid down by *Lloyd's Register of Shipping* are an excellent safe-guard for ocean racers, because of the difficulty of gauging the state of the structure by an on-the-spot inspection when the boat is in use. Lloyd's lay down rulings on the materials to include the resin system, the glass reinforcement, fillers and colour pigment. They also inspect the plans of each class of yacht and suggest modifications in the method of

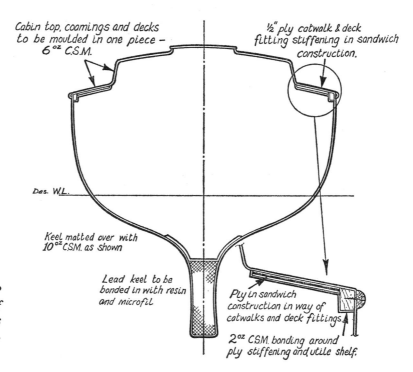

Cabin top, coomings and decks to be moulded in one piece — 6 oz C.S.M.

½" ply catwalk & deck fitting stiffening in sandwich construction.

Des. W.L.

Keel matted over with 10 oz C.S.M. as shown

Lead keel to be bonded in with resin and microfil

Ply in sandwich construction in way of catwalks and deck fittings.

2 oz C.S.M. bonding around ply stiffening and utile shelf.

FIG. 86. *A section of GRP construction forming part of the drawings of a designer's specification for a 20-ft. cruiser racer.*

construction to suit their standards. Here they will want to be satisfied about the laying up of the laminates, the hull framing for rigidity, and matters like bulkheads, fuel- and water-tanks and special parts of the structure such as the edges of a transom. The tables of some of Lloyd's standards in Fig. 87 are important in showing the spacing of framing and the

SCANTLING REQUIREMENTS FOR GRP YACHTS TO MEET LLOYD'S STANDARDS

Approx. LWL	Basic Stiffener spacing. Applies to framing and beams through-out hull and deck (*inches*)	Shell Bottom. Bottom thickness to be carried six inches above waterline (*ounces*)	Side (*ounces*)	Fin and Tuck (*ounces*)	Keel (*ounces*)	Deck Weight (*ounces*)
16	15	10	8	14	20	8
22	15·5	11·5	9	16	22	9
29	16	13	10	18	24	10

FIG. 87.

thickness of the hull at various points on yachts of different size. The laminate scantlings for GRP are quoted in the weight of glass reinforcement of chopped strand mat contained in an area of the laminate in ounces per square foot or grammes per square metre. The ratio of resin to glass by weight is in the region of 2·75 to 1.

Chopped strand mat is the most widely used reinforcement for ocean racer hulls. It is laid up on the mould in successive layers and as it is wetted out with the resin so each layer eventually cures as a cohesive structure with those on either side of it. Woven cloth is stronger, but is not quite so receptive to resin, its tightly constructed nature might in extreme conditions tend to delamination in the hull. Some builders, however, use one layer in the centre of the lay-up to add to the strength. A more usual use for woven material is where a particular line of strength is needed, such as along a line where fittings are to be attached and in awkward corners where it is difficult to work in the resin. When building a hull it is the gel coat that is first laid into the mould. This may be coloured and consists entirely of resin to give the smooth surface of the hull, the first layer of chop strand mat being laid on top of it after it has started to cure.

An ocean racer's bows with a fine entry require attention. The laminations should wrap round inside the bows so that they overlap giving high strength across the stem and it may be advisable to have slight extra thickness if the bow sections are flat, to obviate, in conjunction with framing, any "panting" of the hull at these areas. At the same time over the whole hull, as in the case of the T31 mentioned above, the weight of the glass can be tapered away from the keel. There should be no sudden changes of thickness: Lloyd's maximum allowance for change of weight is 4 ounces per inch.

GRP work in deck and interior Longitudinal strengthening can be obtained with wooden bilge stringers rather in the manner of wood yachts, but glassed in to the hull, or hollow GRP girders can be used especially to construct a multiple box of floors and

stringers for stiffening the lower part of the hull. The basic transverse stiffening will be
bulkheads invariably made of plywood, though sandwich GRP foam has been mentioned
above for the sandwich hull. However, wood really does help here as the bulkhead can be
a start point for much of the cabin joinery. In the Westerly 28 series built by Westerly
Marine Construction Ltd., much of the longitudinal stability comes from the interior
GRP moulding which is shaped up as cabin furniture. Being in very few pieces, it
"locks" around the inside of the hull and bilge stringers are not used. In this yacht the
wooden bulkheads are still retained, as in all the mass production sailing yachts of
Westerly. The support of the rig in the form of chain plates has to intrude somewhere into
the interior and when shrouds are brought inboard, this actually simplifies matters for
a GRP yacht enabling them to be fixed to a bulkhead. When they are near the gunwale,
a suitable method is to fix a trinagular wooden block of substantial dimensions which runs
out under the deck as well as being bolted to the topsides. The whole piece is glassed in
after an inverted U-type shroud anchorage has been bolted through it (Fig. 88). Techniques are now well developed for the fastening of all types of deck fittings to GRP and
the procedure is no different on ocean racers. However, a circular pad, or at least a curved
shape, is better practice than a rectangular one for taking the fastenings under the deck.

In racing boats the iron or lead keel should be on the outside of the moulding, not
glassed into it. When the ballast keel is set inside a moulding, as is quite common on
cruising boats, the exact distribution of metal cannot be guaranteed. The thickness of the
GRP under it has to be considerable to take the strains of the localized weight and this
has the effect of raising the centre of gravity of the keel. With a lead keel especially every

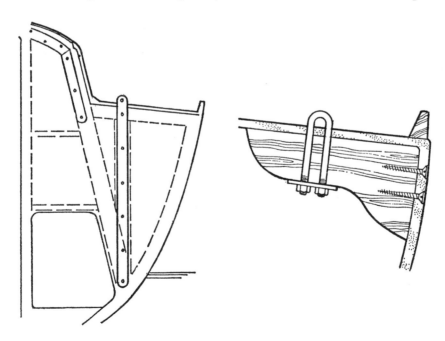

FIG. 88. *Two methods of fixing shroud plates in GRP where racing design requires shrouds set inboard. The
plate running the depth of a bulkhead transmits strains evenly over a wide section of the hull. A method less
demanding on design sites the shroud anchorage in glassed and bolted knee.*

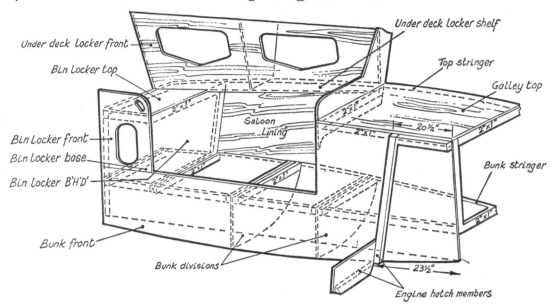

FIG. 89. *Construction from a kit. The components to assemble this part of the starboard side of the cabin would be supplied to fit a GRP hull. This example is from the 20 ft. LWL Cutlass class, supplied in kit form by an English yard.*

inch of variation in this is important. A further reason is that a sharp "V" to the bottom of the keel section is considered by many designers to be desirable for windward sailing. This does not lend itself to GRP.

The deck design of an ocean racer tends towards a small coachroof area with wide side deck and clear foredeck for crew work. Large areas without much curvature are the least suitable use for GRP, but there are methods of stiffening the deck without merely increasing the thickness and thus the weight. One of these is to use a sandwich of end-grain balsa. The proportions of the upper and lower GRP laminates should be 3 to 2 and the combined weight need not be greater than if they formed a solid deck. The balsa, cut very thin across the grain, is so light that its weight can be disregarded. The resin making up the laminates seeps into the grain and when cured, gives a minute "hinge" effect which aids in resisting sudden loads. The coachroof can be curved heavily to give stiffness, but this does not always suit the designer's concept. Contrary to popular belief, the edges of a GRP coachroof can be radiused small enough to appear with the proportions of a wooden structure, and vast bubble-type roofs need not be used unless the designer feels they are of racing benefit.

There has never been a racing boat, however carefully its deck plan was prepared, that did not require to have some fitting or other moved or added. There is no great difficulty with putting down fittings on a GRP deck, but trouble arises where a special moulding has been created for a genoa track or a winch. Handholds on the coachroof often have the flat pads to take the bases of the woodwork moulded in. Such embellishments should be viewed as a possible inconvenience in a standard boat. Winch mountings especially are best left out of the moulding and a metal bracket fitted to suit the selected winch.

Construction by kit A few builders offer yachts with racing potential in kit form for completion by the owner. The advantage of this lies in the saving on a substantial part of the price, cutting out as it does the labour consuming jobs involved in assembling work already done in the yard's joinery shop. Many more builders offer hulls in various stages of completion but I draw a distinction between these and supplied kits, which come with all parts, including fittings, almost ready to put in place and with an instruction book for assembly. Naturally, these are most popular in the small sizes: the saving on a 19-ft. yacht costing £2,400, ready from the yard in racing trim, would be about £450, money which can be well spent in obtaining extra sails and other racing equipment. So this is one way of obtaining a new racing yacht at cruising boat cost.

Building by kit is available for GRP hulls and the owner completion would be mainly in plywood with cappings as necessary. It is best for the hull to come with the deck in position, thus leaving to the builders the important fitting of deck edge to hull, which can give trouble if not expertly fitted. Other parts which the builders should be asked to supply are any special fastenings such as extra long bolts, perhaps to ensure the genoa track is linked to a structural member, self-tapping screws and the engine bearers ready glassed into position, for they are awkward to do later, and important pieces. Bulkheads will normally already be in, even if the deck has not been fixed, in order to preserve the shape of the hull moulding. Longitudinal stringers will also be in place for it is to these that the cabin joinery will first be linked. With standard boats coming from builders, who are increasingly reluctant (for good business reasons) to deviate from a standard cabin and deck layout, the possibility of obtaining a yacht for completion by the owner (or, of course, a local boat builder) should be seriously considered where a racing concept is envisaged. The smaller the yacht, the less the builder is likely to be persuaded to alter anything, yet the less possibility of compromising between cruising and racing (Fig. 89).

·12·

SAILS AND THE RIG

Efficiency   In any discussion on the rig of a yacht, the subject of its efficiency invariably arises and a new boat is often referred to as having an efficient rig. An efficient rig is desirable in any yacht but its criteria are different for dinghies, cruising yachts and ocean racers. For a small ocean racer the efficiency of the rig must be judged in how far it aids the yacht to win offshore races. The requirements for this are as follows:

1. To give maximum thrust in a forward direction to the hull on all points of sailing.
2. To achieve this over the whole range of wind strength.
3. To offer minimum resistance to forward motion.
4. To withstand the worst offshore conditions (e.g. knockdowns, sudden unfair loading).
5. To incur no unacceptable disadvantage under the rating rule.

It hardly needs to be added that the designer effects a compromise between these conflicting needs, and at the same time the whole rigging design must be in harmony with the hull. Their conception is parallel, the shape of the hull affecting the rig and the latest sail plan ideas altering hull design.

Even the first requirement above is impossible to achieve without sacrificing one point of sailing to another, and often boils down to the question: how far should windward efficiency be predominant? The answer may depend on the part of the world and the type of racing envisaged and the proportion of headwinds for the series of races. For the One Ton and Half Ton, Olympic courses are part of the programme and these contain three legs dead to windward (as long as there is no change in wind direction) (Fig. 90). For races in a fixed programme, especially those from port to port, windward work may in some cases be thought to be rare and the rig designed accordingly. Apart from special cases, I believe the rig should be designed for getting to windward and for using the spinnaker effectively. If the designer keeps these two pictures in mind, the boat strapped in and hard on the wind and the spinnaker set as effectively as possible, he will not go far wrong. On the remaining sailing, the close reach, equipment rather than initial design can take over; things like special sails, kicking-straps and sheet leads.

Rating effect on sail plans   The ocean racers sail plan is highly sensitive to rating requirements. Sail area is the largest single factor in the CCA, RORC and IOR rule, which is right, for it is the power plant of the yacht. A further aspect is that on a series of standard boats, or on a single yacht, the rating can be changed significantly by altering the sail area and its distribution. Experiments with rig are more practicable than attempting to regulate hull shape, ballast ratio and other major structural items. Regulators on the rig have been progressive as new materials have developed. The RORC until 1957 measured the foretriangle and counted only 85 per cent for area, but the resulting increase in "cheap" area made for bigger genoas, and 100 per cent was introduced. The ability to set big genoas of terylene and enable them to stand by wider sheeting bases and metal masts led to even bigger headsails in proportion to the mainsail. There may be nothing wrong in this, but the feeling that such area was not being rated correctly led to the **IOR** rule sail area measurements, based on those of the CCA.

This distinction, between "cheap" or "free" area and measured area, has a strong influence on rigs, for it obviously is wise to have as much free area as allowed; there are always limits of some sort. The roach of the mainsail is one, since the sail is measured as a right-angled triangle. The geometry of this system means that it does not pay for the boom to drop or lift. The overlap of the genoa is cheap, up to about 150 per cent and after that is paid for more heavily under the rule (Fig. 91). There is no mechanism for allowing for a non-overlapping jib.

Another regulator on the shape of the ocean racing rig is the aspect ratio tax. This prevents yachts supporting a mainsail of more than 3·33 to 1 in luff to foot ratio. The very

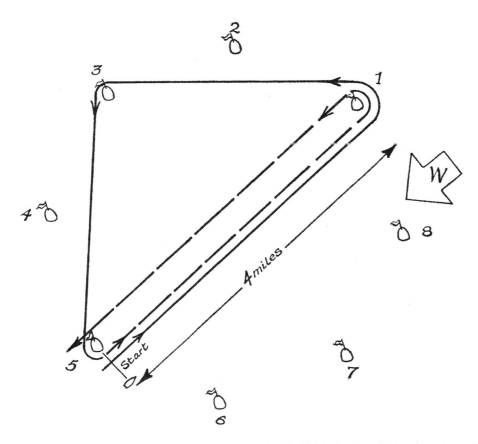

FIG. 90. *An Olympic type course as used in the inshore races for the Half Ton Cup. This shows the emphasis on windward work, the buoys in a particular race being selected for this purpose.*

small mainsails seen on some RORC boats, with a mast of normal height but a very short boom, were going even beyond this limit. These are just one or two of the salient influences of rating formulae, but the question of rating has to be considered when formulating any ideas for improved sails or sail plan, whether concerned with the shape, actual area, or proportions of one part of the sail plan to another.

Weight and windage   Let the yacht run downwind under bare poles in even a moderate breeze and it is at once apparent from her speed how much wind resistance is caused by the rig. Spars and rigging do no good except to hold the sails in position to drive the yacht. Rigs have been "cleaned" up considerably in recent years, but it is sometimes easy to miss an obvious cause of windage.

When Doug Gilling of Sydney, *September*'s owner, came aboard *Shewolf*, which had streamlined rigging and other means of reducing windage, he said, "You Poms are a crowd. You have this costly gear and then rig these", and he pointed to our thick spinnaker topping lifts, with their heavily whipped splices hanging from two blocks on the outside of the mast.

In mast and rig design this point about windage must be considered, and the following matters should be run through when thinking of windage.

1. Minimum mast and rigging scantlings, consistent with offshore sailing.
2. Internal running rigging and mast fittings.
3. Possibility of thin mast with thick walls (balanced against weight and strength).
4. No surplus halyards, e.g. masthead topping lift. A second spinnaker halyard might be used on downwind courses.
5. Weight of sails, as discussed below.
6. Winches and stowed halyards clear of mast.
7. Shape of mast section and taper.
8. Loose tackles, reefing gear etc. on boom and gooseneck.
9. Design and siting of all above deck fittings, as discussed later.

The weight of gear aloft has to be considered most carefully due to the vastly greater moment of forces. Michael Henderson gives the following figures for the proportion of weights and moments in a yacht of 5·02 tons displacement with 40 per cent ballast ratio:

	Per cent of total weight	*Moments in ft./lb.*
5 crew and gear	8·9	8,000
Accommodation, including electrics	7·0	5,200
Engine and its installation	4·5	2,750
Fuel, water, consumable stores	3·6	2,400
Mast rigging and set sails	3·1	9,800

A medium-size pair of blocks for the spinnaker topping lifts 15 ft. off the deck of a 30 ft. yacht and weighing 1 lb. give a moment of, say, 18 ft./lb. from the axis on the water-line about which the yacht can be assumed to rotate. Such small items should therefore

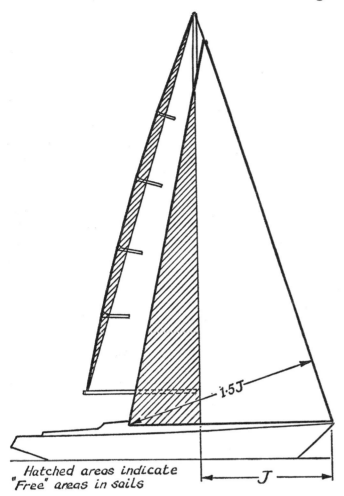

1·5J

Hatched areas indicate
"Free" areas in sails

J

FIG. 91. *A masthead sloop showing the areas of sail which are not directly measured under the rating rule.*

be queried as much as an 18 lb. cabin table, 1 ft. above the same axis, which would probably be thought to be too heavy. One consideration of the masthead rig is that much of the gear (genoa block, forestay tang and so on) is concentrated at the point of greatest moment. There are two aspects to weight in a boat; one is the mass which needs to be driven through the water, and the other is the positioning of all the weights, thus determining the centre of gravity. It is the latter which is so sensitive to every pound in the rig.

Geographical conditions The area in which the yacht is to race has a bearing on the sail plan. Where light weather is prevalent, as in the Mediterranean in summer, a larger sail area is needed than in north-west Europe with its higher percentage of fresh winds. Not that the Mediterranean is without plenty of wind at times. The only time I have been in a yacht where the mainsail blew to actual shreds was in a 21 ft. cruiser-racer off the coast of Cyprus. In the 1968 Two Ton cup races off the Italian coast the winning yacht *Meloria* was under bare poles in a reported 100-knot wind speed for several hours. But the

Italian Class "C" fleet, racing out of Genoa, normally expects some light weather during a race. Such a light patch in any race is often critical to the result and sufficient sail area, at the cost of rating, is necessary. With standard boats, the most satisfactory way is to increase the size of the largest genoa.

The boom arrangement will be influenced by local sailing conditions. Olin Stephens, when asked about the desirability of bending booms, with their system of blocks attached at a number of places, made the point that in some American waters where light weather prevailed they were useful. But, he argued that, in north-west Europe, yachts were often in winds where the question was ,"Do we reef or not?" and in such conditions booms more easily reefed were desirable. There is more on reefing later, but this emphasizes the geographical aspect.

Mainsail shapes   The Bermudian mainsail is still standard after some forty years and this triangular sail remains the basis of ocean racing rigs, much developed but to the same principle. Other types of mainsail appear from time to time, but have made little impact. Perhaps a completely new rig will be the next breakthrough following the universal change to separate rudder in hull forms. Some types that have been seen are:

Gaff rig. Unseen in ocean racing for thirty years, this rig was treated kindly in the 1957 RORC rule, but no one thought of it as more than a gesture. Some dinghy classes have a top batten so long that it is in effect a gaff and to some extent the top batten under the RORC rule could be made to do this when it extended from luff to leech. The Australian 21-ft. *Windjammer* tried a small gaff in 1968 to collect the rig allowance, but this was soon abandoned in favour of the normal mainsail (Fig. 92).

Wishbone sail. The value of this sail lies in filling the space between masts in a schooner rig and is usually seen only in the largest yachts.

Junk rig. This has been fitted on several yachts, for short-handed work, notably in the single-handed transatlantic races. The pioneer of this sail (Fig. 93) was Colonel H. G. "Blondie" Hasler with his Folkboat *Jester*. My experience of racing against this yacht was that she was far slower than normally rigged Folkboats, and in the 1968 transatlantic race she was last boat home by many days. Hasler's theme behind the creation of this rig was to try to get away from the modern ocean racer with her "complicated rig and numerous crew".

Wingsail. Designers know that if some form of semi-rigid aerofoil could be used, it would be far more efficient than the Bermudian rig. At the present time such an arrangement is nowhere near in view for sea-going rigs. When the next change in rigs does come it will be on these lines. Suitable materials will have to be found and the engineering problems overcome. Small ocean racers will be able to adopt such advanced rigs before their larger sisters, and so those developing such yachts should keep an eye on rig progress in the dinghy and racing catamaran field and not merely ape the bigger offshore boats.

Choice of rig for yachts under 30 ft. LWL.   Two-masted boats are rare in the range of size we are considering, though the yawl rig is seen on many larger ocean racers. Traditionally the yawl is more common in USA and its main asset is a means of splitting the sail area of a large yacht into manageable sizes. There is no argument that it is less efficient than a single-masted boat to windward, for the same total sail area, but off the wind the rating rule allows a mizzen staysail which is free area. There is a rig allowance for a yawl.

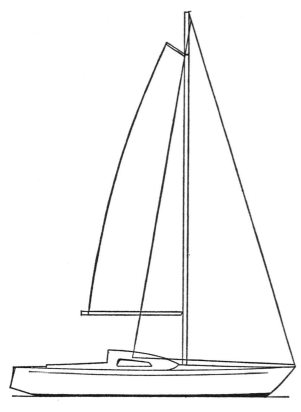

FIG. 92. *A "gaff rig" tried out for rating purposes on the Australian JOG yacht* Windjammer.

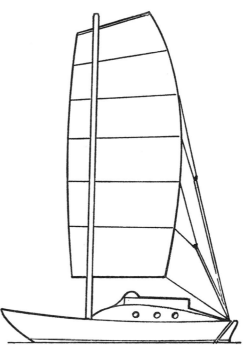

FIG. 93. *H. G. Hasler's "Junk rig" represents an attempt to find an alternative to the Bermudian rig, but the area that can be spread on one mast is limited.*

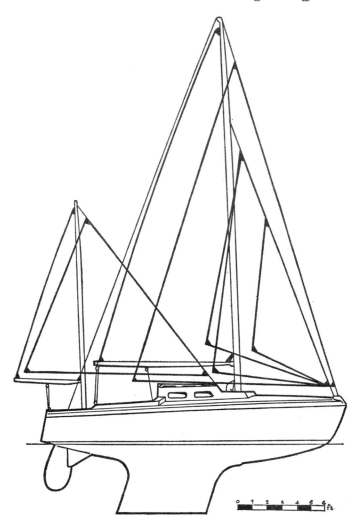

FIG. 94. *The yawl rig on a small yacht.* Trekka *designed by J. Laurent Giles for John Guzzwell was sailed by him round the world, and was therefore designed for offshore cruising. The LWL is 18 ft. 9 in.*

Under 30 ft., the weight and windage of the yawl rig is not acceptable for efficient racing; the smaller individual sails, difficulty of placing the mizzen mast and the extra expense conspire to rule it out. Two 20-ft. yawls designed by Stan Smith, who crossed the Atlantic in a similar boat some years previously, were racing in England and Scotland in JOG events in 1968. The 18 ft. 6 in. yawl *Trekka*, a Laurent Giles design, was a development of *Sopranino*, and was sailed round the world single-handed by John Guzzwell in 1958–59. But this was a trans-ocean cruiser and not a racing boat. *Trekka* was the smallest boat ever to sail round the world and the feat has never received the acclaim that it deserved (Fig. 94).

Modern masting, winches and the emphasis on spinnakers has made the yawl rig less popular even on the largest ocean racers, so practical racing considerations revolve around the single-stick rigs: cutter, masthead sloop and seven-eighths sloop. The cutter is really a variation of the masthead sloop, because all modern masthead cutters will set

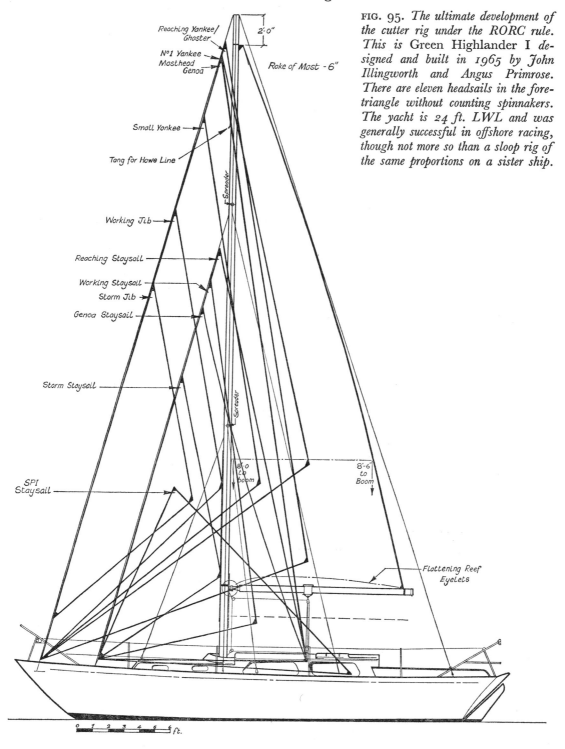

Reaching Yankee/Ghoster

2'·0"

N°1 Yankee
Masthead
Genoa

Rake of Mast - 6"

Small Yankee

Tang for Howe Line

Spreader

Working Jib

Reaching Staysail

Working Staysail

Storm Jib

Genoa Staysail

Spreader

Storm Staysail

8'·0
to
boom

8'·6
to
Boom

SPI
Staysail

Flattening Reef
Eyelets

0 1 2 3 4 5 6 ft.

FIG. 95. *The ultimate development of the cutter rig under the RORC rule. This is* Green Highlander I *designed and built in 1965 by John Illingworth and Angus Primrose. There are eleven headsails in the foretriangle without counting spinnakers. The yacht is 24 ft. LWL and was generally successful in offshore racing, though not more so than a sloop rig of the same proportions on a sister ship.*

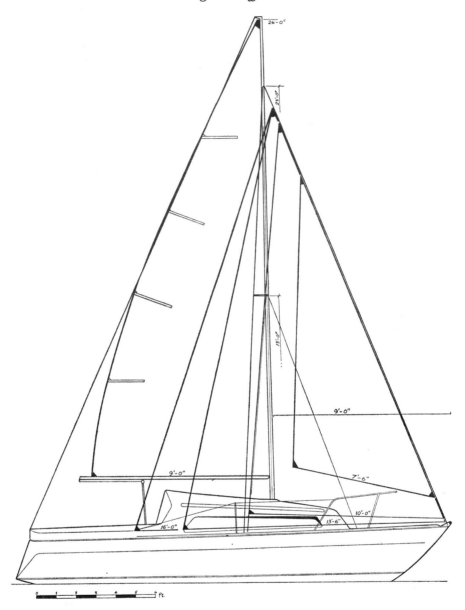

FIG. 96. *The non-masthead rig has advantages on smaller yachts, where sail area is reduced earlier in a breeze. The tapered mast also means less weight aloft. This lends itself to bending spars, which is done on the Galion class shown here. The biggest genoa shown here is 180%. The mainsail area is 104 sq. ft. and foretriangle 103 sq. ft. Note on this plan the pulpit position. The Galion, designed by Ian Hannay, is 18 ft. LWL.*

a single genoa in light weather. The question then arises whether it pays to set a jib and staysail in heavy going, instead of a single jib on the headstay. In the days before metal masts and synthetic sails and stiffer yachts carrying big headsails longer, this may have been the case. One argument is that the yacht is not left bareheaded when changing sails because the staysail is drawing when the jib is on deck. But with a well trained crew, how many seconds are lost in changing a headsail? Not many, and against this they will be longer on deck, while preparing two sails and their sheets and halyards. The cutter was a proposition when most sloops were seven-eighths rig, but the masthead sloop has overtaken it (Fig. 95). It is interesting to remember that in the USA cutters have never been favoured in ocean racing.

The practical rigs boil down to sloops, either masthead or seven-eighths. The RORC and CCA rating rules which gave free area to the headsail—which is, anyway, more efficient per square foot of area than the mainsail—have resulted in the prominence of the masthead sloop. It is also favoured because the spinnaker is large in proportion to the rig. It catches the wind at the maximum height and gets a better flow as the mainsail is narrow at the spinnaker halyard block, or more probably non-existent!

A non-masthead or seven-eighths sloop is without these advantages and in addition has to carry either running backstays or diamond stays. But the rig does have two aspects worth considering. In the smallest yachts, say below 19 ft., where stiffness is at a premium the lower foretriangle may be less pressing, while the extra rigging is not required (Fig. 96). Secondly, if bending masts can be further developed for offshore sailing then a fully bending system requires a lower forestay as part of the system in which of the top of the mast draws slightly aft as the centre bows forward to flatten the mainsail. Until recently this line of thought was inhibited by a wariness in bending masts offshore and because the headsail was the principal sail. In the smaller yachts, and with the reduction on emphasis of the foretriangle under the IOR rule, the seven-eighths rig could revive among the smaller end of the ocean racing scale.

The foretriangle The foretriangle of the masthead sloop is the power house of that rig, and its great flexibility lies in the different sails that can be set within it. The vast majority of racing is sailed in winds under 18 knots and boats of 18 ft. and upwards should be able to carry their full sail area (this does not mean their lightest sails) in such winds. Smaller yachts might prefer to change to a slightly smaller headsail at 14–15 knots.

Therefore the owner must decide what range of sails is needed for this band of wind strengths, in the light of the following:

1. Number of sail changes acceptable and the ability to change sail without loss of time.
2. Ability of light sailcloth to stand up to heavier wind.
3. Adjustment possible on each sail to adapt in to different strengths.
4. Expense.

The nomenclature of sails varies, but a selection of the following sails will be carried:

Ghoster or drifter
Light genoa
Intermediate genoa
Heavy genoa
Short hoist genoa

N

184 Ocean Racing and Offshore Yachts

Sometimes the sails are known as No. 1, No. 2, etc., or by the length of the foot. The last named for yachts over 22 ft. would probably not be carried in winds under 18 knots, but as one of the family of genoas it is listed here. Progress is fast at the moment in the field of light weight cloth for sails, the first stage in achieving this is in the weaving where the object is a high "cover factor". This means a tight weave making for stability, strength, non-porosity and smoothness. In the forefront of the development remains Hood Sailmakers, now with branches in many sailing countries besides the head office at Marblehead, USA. Owners were rightly slavish to certain weights of cloth for certain areas of sail, but now the properties of the synthetic materials (terylene, dacron, nylon) are under constant control for improvement and the resistance to strength depends on the fibre and the weave. Some of the very light terylene will resist the strength of wind, but is very easily torn when handling on an offshore boat; tearing may be the problem of the future as cloth becomes lighter. Hoods quote the following weights of cloth as a guide but owners should always enquire from their sailmaker, the properties of the latest cloth.

Cloth weight in oz. (US)	1·5 (nylon)	Size of Yachts (LWL) which use:				
		3	3·7	4·1	4·6	5·2
Drifter	All yachts					
Ghoster		Up to 28 ft.		Over 28 ft.		
Light genoa			Up to 23 ft.		23–29 ft.	29–35 ft.
Heavy genoa					Up to 23 ft.	23–29 ft.

(US weight is oz. per 1 yd. × 280 in., British weight is oz. per sq. yd., European weight is gm. per sq. metres, US 4·6 oz. = British 5·8 oz., 190 gm./sq. metre).

Jibs   Because of the strength of material the smaller jibs can be of the same weight as the heavy genoa, but the storm jib may be a size heavier to enable substantial fittings to be sewn into it. It should be possible to reduce canvas in severe conditions in proportions which remove the same area of headsail each time a sail is changed. Such sails will be cut high and flat in accordance with the designer's sail plan, but they should be tacked to the deck to keep the heeling moment down and should not be equipped with spans. As jibs are seldom used they must be checked at intervals for such things as jammed piston hanks and not left in the sail bag to mould. They may have quite different sheet leads to the genoas and this must be provided for on deck.

Shape and strength of genoas   A drifter and ghoster may be carried in yachts over 30 ft., but to carry both in smaller yachts is not necessary unless sailing habitually in very light weather. Carrying too many sails is not conducive to good sailing. There is seldom time to get to know them all well, and more chance of selecting the wrong sail change, besides it is expensive. If a large selection of sails is available for an important event which lies ahead, the minimum number should be selected for the races. A drifter usually has the clew cut high, which makes it useful for reaching and it may have no hanks, or just three or four. There are conditions—very light air and some swell—when it will do better than a spinnaker. A ghoster implies a sail used in winds not more than 4 to 5 knots and is shaped like the light genoa, but with several widely spaced hanks.

The light genoa is the sail which will get most use. It must be designed to fill the foretriangle, using every square inch of rated area and it will have an LP of 150 per cent, or greater if this is to be paid for in the sail area measurement. Under the CCA and IOR rules the biggest headsail overlap is measured by the perpendicular distance from clew to luff. So a high-cut sail has a shorter measurement than a low-cut one of the equivalent horizontal overlap. But it is better aerodynamically to close the gap between deck and sail and the foot can even be convex to seal this area. This may result in some folds in the foot, when sheeted home hard, but this need not affect the rest of the sail.

Wide options in sheet lead must be available for the genoas, and means of doing this are discussed later. Certain headsails may need to be sheeted in at an 8-degree angle, while others, or for different points of sailing will need to go out as far as possible, which will be the toe rail or outer edge of the deck. IYRU rules ban outriggers and leads outside the deck and rails.

The stretch luff genoa is made with a soft rope, tape or webbing luff and so cut by the sailmaker that by stretching the luff the sail is flattened as the wind increases. This stretch will be up to 5 per cent of the luff length. Tension can be taken up on the halyard, which is best brought aft so that it can be controlled from near the cockpit. A more refined system is to fit a Cunningham hole on which tension is taken by means of an adequate tackle. This means the genoa can be full size when not stretched, and will necessitate a different control arrangement.

Even if the light genoa can be flattened considerably and the cloth is fully stable in fresh winds, the sail will have to be changed for the heavy genoa as the wind freshens further. The reason for this is the shape of the leech, which will be cut hollow in the heavy sail. The leech is an important part of a genoa and the light one will close the slot in heavy going. In an offshore boat this is particularly bad in a seaway, when the yacht pitches forward. The acceleration of wind from the leech will backwind the mainsail heavily and only increase the heeling effect of the headsail.

The heavy genoa can also be a stretch luff sail although it will already be comparatively flat. Both sails should have leechlines which should be adjusted, by tightening no more than is necessary to stop flapping. Heavy curl caused by the leechline is not acceptable but a very slight local curl at the end of a leech section which falls away is acceptable. Some headsails in a masthead sloop are shown in Fig. 97.

Other headsails *The spinnaker staysail* or sneaker should be designed to set under and aft of the spinnaker. Its size and shape is limited under the IOR rule by LPIS (Fig. 54) but there is no limitation on athwartships position. One idea is to tack the sail to weather and then seal the gap to the deck as it curves round to leeward. A second line of thought is to tack the sail to weather, but make the foot high and the luff long and the effect is to increase the slot higher up the spinnaker. This type is on the sail plan in Fig. 97. The main

Spinnakers	Foot	Luff
Storm spinnaker	Rule max. (15% less area, reduction to be aloft)	95% rule max.
Heavy spinnaker	Rule max.	Rule max.
Light spinnaker	Rule max.	Rule max.

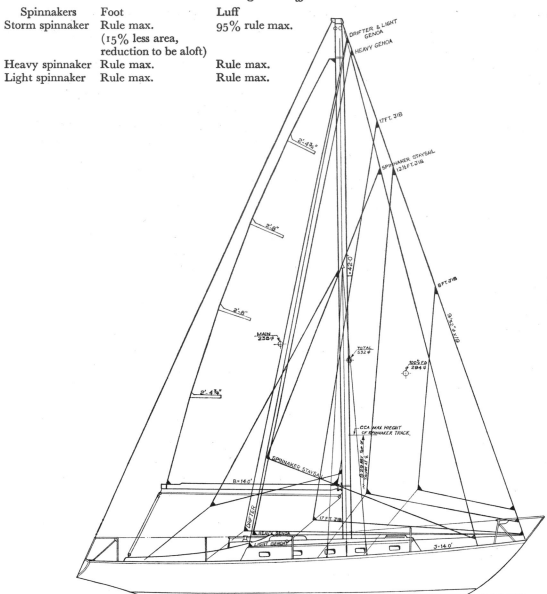

FIG. 97. *Sail plan for Design No. 1710, 25 ft. 6 in. sloop (Swan 36) designed by Sparkman and Stephens Inc., New York. If a particular rating class is desired, dimensions of the mainsail must be recalculated to suit measurement desired.*

DESIGNER'S GENERAL NOTES

1. Dacron leech line on all dacron rails; 2. All headsail hanks to be side pull type. Extra heavy seizings on all slides and hanks; 3. Batten pockets to be offset with light ties; 4. All sails to be marked with sail name, boat name and year; 5. All sail bags to be synthetic and marked in three places like sails; 6. Allowance to be made in leech dimensions of genoas so that clew height will be indicated when sail is properly trimmed; 7. Shape of leech to be the responsibility of the sailmaker; 8. All listed head and tack pennants to be furnished and shackled on by the sailmaker; 9. Check with mast maker regarding exact mainsail tack offset; 10. Headsail luff length is length of luff wire between centres of thimbles.

involvement of an owner with this sail is to decide on what halyard it should be hoisted, where it can be tacked down and sheeted. Usually it will have to be provided with its own tack eye-bolts and cleats, as when running with spinnaker and main boom guy rigged there is a shortage of cleats and leads.

Battened headsails. The RORC effectively banned the quadrilateral genoa by making the sail area gained by this shape very expensive and restricting the height above deck of sheet leads. If battens are carried in a genoa it can only be to project the roach of the sail, and then it will be counted as other than a "three cornered sail". Fig. 98 shows a headsail with battens used in Sweden for light weather sailing. Such a sail would not often be useful offshore in areas of generally moderate breezes.

Roller Jibs. These cannot be made flat enough when the sail area is reduced, and the whole load, once rolled, is on the forestay. With solid steel rigging, the problem has been looked at again. It was used in 1968 on the 35 ft. (LOA.) *Windborne III* in Long Island Sound racing with a 170 per cent genoa. Apart from reefing, such a sail is useful to reduce the genoa when the spinnaker is hoisted or when gybing at the start line. To have only one sail is an attractive idea and is an avenue for invention, the main problem being to shape the sail as it is reduced. However, do not expect much help from sailmakers on this one!

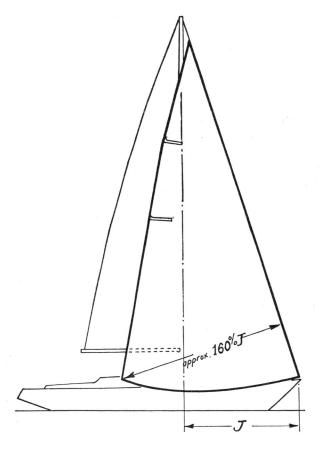

FIG. 98. *Genoa for very light weather with battens and pronounced droop in the foot designed by Per Bröhall. As the leech is projected aft by the battens, it could be liable to rating rules which legislate for quadrilateral headsails.*

Mainsail in the masthead sloop   These remarks on mainsails also apply to the cutter rig and the yawl, or other rigs where the modern Bermudian mainsail is in use. The problem with the mainsail is that it has to be used over the whole range of wind strengths, as light weather mainsails are not permitted under any ocean racing rules and "heavy weather" mainsails, if carried, are against the spirit of the rule and should be banned if found to be the practice. A spare mainsail (i.e. of the same weight of cloth as the one in use) is a different matter and may be seamanlike on a long race. Trysails are carried less and less, but are a genuine heavy-weather mainsail for storm conditions. A trysail can get you out of a nasty situation if the mainsail is lost. Many yachts can now beat to windward under a headsail alone, so owners may prefer to check the rules of the club under which they sail and then decide whether a trysail needs to be carried.

Many of the same principles on the shape and stretching of the headsails apply to the mainsail and the luff and foot can be taped for stretch properties, again up to 5 per cent of their unstretched lengths. A luff and a foot rope are used for the grooves in the spars, but these are put on the sail last of all and do not link up to the cloth which is controlled by the tape.

Two ways of cutting the mainsail are in general use; mitre or horizontal. Mitre cut is used for greater control of the cloth along the foot, but it is not such an easy sail to make and eyeing it along the leeward side may reveal an "arrowhead" section in the mitre, which is undesirable. Cloth development is making the mitre cut mainsail less sought after.

Cloth sizes as used by Hood Sailmakers on small ocean racers are as follows:

LWL	Weight in oz. (US)
16–21 ft.	4·8
21–26 ft.	5·8
26–32 ft.	7·75

Tension can be taken up on the mainsail by its halyard and on the Cunningham hole. The leech line should be led from the clew forward to where it can be controlled near the inner end of the boom. A soft jamb cleat sewn into the sail or a toggle system helps to control it. The leech should stand on its own in a 15-knot wind and then the line may have to be progressively tightened. If this results in a small curl along the leech, remember a yacht beating to windward in a seaway in over 15 knots has anything but laminar flow over the sail and the shape is more important than minor variations on the surface (i.e. the curl) in such conditions. The battens in a mainsail enable its leech to respond more sensitively to control than a headsail; there is little option about the number and length of battens, which are severely restricted under the IOR rule, as they were under the CCA.

Mainsail area distribution   The reason for having a high aspect ratio is to minimize induced drag. This is caused by the disturbance due to the difference in pressure on the windward and leeward sides. Its effect is across a certain vertical distance of the sail, top and bottom. Roughly speaking, the taller the sail the less the proportion of this effect. It is also reduced by "blocking" the end of the sail (in the case of the genoa, by "using" the deck). This is not possible with a mainsail, but even closeness to the deck or coachroof helps this. The rating rules tax aspect ratio as a factor, but the emphasis on genoa efficiency can largely dictate the height of the mast; then to keep the mainsail down to the required size the foot length is reduced. This is an additional reason for high aspect ratio which is limited by the amount in the rule mentioned earlier.

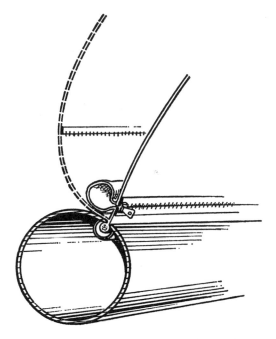

FIG. 99. *Mainsail zipper flattens foot rapidly and to prearranged shape.*

The main boom and reefing system   Although its influence over the sail is not great, it is worth having some means of flattening the lower part of the main apart from stretching the foot. This can be achieved by lacing, zip-fastener or bending the boom.

Here is what is claimed for each method:

Lacing	*Zipper (Fig. 99)*	*Bending Boom*
	ADVANTAGES	
(*a*) Cheap	(*a*) Simple	(*a*) Immediate and automatic control
(*b*) Foolproof	(*b*) Enough adjustment with two zippers	(*b*) Correct bend can be controlled
(*c*) Infinite adjustment	(*c*) Rolls into sail	(*c*) Big range from full to flat
(*d*) Rolls into the sail	(*d*) Quick	
	DISADVANTAGES	
(*a*) "Messy"	(*a*) Zippers can break or jam	(*a*) Expensive
(*b*) Claimed to be slow	(*b*) Only three positions (with two zips)	(*b*) Roller reefing not practicable
		(*c*) Mainsail cut important
		(*d*) Extra gear, blocks, tangs, etc.

Which of these methods is used may depend on the type of reefing required, and this in turn on the characteristics of the hull. For a comparatively tender hull roller-reefing is desirable so that reefs can be taken in and out quickly. It is not so much a matter of *speed* as of *decision*; with roller reefing a few rolls can be put in, then one or two out as a weather mark, perhaps, is reached. The disadvantages of roller reefing are that the boom has to be kept clear of gear, the kicking-strap has to be disconnected when reefing and the shape of the sail tends to become baggy. The large ocean racer *Ondine* gets over this by pushing pieces of foam rubber into the sail as it is rolled. It could be tried in other yachts. By using a claw ring of good design, it is not necessary to have the mainsheet at the boom end, if this is a bad lead.

Slab reefing can be used with any of the sail flattening methods in the above table. It means that fittings can be attached to the boom wherever required. There is no change over for the kicking-strap when reefing. Clew outhauls, leech lines, main boom foreguy, can all be rigged or have fittings arranged for them. In small yachts, no great tackles are required to pull down the luff pendant and clew pendant. If this is done before tacking, the bunt of sail lies to windward after the tack and the reef points or lacing can be secured round it and the boom. (Traditionally this is wrong and reef points should go above the boom round the sail. This is impossible with a foot groove but I have never known any difficulty on this score.) It is difficult to make a neat job in way of small yacht goosenecks, but the same applies to roller reefing. Certainly a better setting reefed mainsail is obtained, but the snag is the question of deciding when to reef, because it is a distinct step unlike the "gradual" process of taking in rolls.

To summarize: roller reefing is generally preferable offshore, particularly if the yacht lacks stiffness. However, with small yachts either system, if properly laid out, is easily handled. On the modern boat with all the equipment which is desirable in the area of the boom and gooseneck to trim, sheet and shape the mainsail, together with the ease of handling a modern short boom, slab reefing is well worth consideration.

Masting and rigging design   Only a handful of ocean racers are now equipped with masts in materials other than aluminium alloy. There may be a few individually made wooden masts of great expense for owners who have a personal preference or for reasons of rating under the RORC rule. Several firms in Europe make GRP spars, but they are heavier than alloy of equal strength. It is in light alloy masts that the development and refinement is taking place. At first this was mainly finding suitable sections and basic fittings, in recent years the emphasis has been on "cleaning-up" the mast to reduce weight and windage.

The common sections for masthead rigs are shown in Fig. 100. Pear-shaped sections in theory cause less windage, but an elliptical section gives more fore and aft stiffness to assist in keeping the forestay straight. Straight-sided sections are more flexible athwartships and stem from the pattern of wooden spars.

As the maximum length of extruded and drawn alloy (in England) is 30 ft., the masts of yachts over about 20 ft. will consist of joined sections. These are now satisfactorily welded as a scarfed joint, though many older masts will have a butt joint with an inner sleeve and riveting. The welding technique is also used to cut wedges out of the upper part of the mast and then join the exposed edges to give a taper. The taper possible on a masthead rig is limited, but worth having to save the ounces that are so important at the top.

The question arises whether a mast with shorter overall diameters of section, but greater wall thickness, would not give less windage for the equivalent weight. Such sections are more commonly seen in USA, but other properties, notably the fore and aft stiffness, also vary in the change of scantling.

Sparlight section	Depth. (in.)	Width (in.)	Thickness (in.)	lb./ft.
DQ6	$4\frac{3}{4}$	$3\frac{1}{8}$	·08	1·318
DQ6o	$4\frac{13}{16}$	3	·08	1·215
DQ7	$5\frac{3}{4}$	$4\frac{1}{4}$	·09	1·923
DQ7o	$5\frac{1}{2}$	$3\frac{1}{2}$	·08	1·398
DQ7t	$5\frac{7}{8}$	$4\frac{1}{4}$	·09	2·087
DQ8e	6	$4\frac{1}{4}$	·122	2·319
DQ8oa	6	$3\frac{7}{8}$	·104	1·969
DQ8ob	6	$3\frac{7}{8}$	·128	2·41
DQ9e	$6\frac{1}{2}$	$4\frac{3}{8}$	·122	2·54
DQ11ea	8	$4\frac{1}{2}$	·128	2·8
DQ13e	$8\frac{1}{4}$	5	·140	3·4
DQ15e	$8\frac{1}{2}$	5	·188	4·75
DQ15se	$8\frac{3}{4}$	$5\frac{1}{2}$	·134	3·58
DQ$3\frac{1}{2}$b	$3\frac{1}{2}$ dia.	—	·094	2·38
DQ4b	4 dia.	—	·094	2·38
A44	$\frac{1}{2}$ dia.	—	—	—
A51	$\frac{3}{4}$ dia.	—	—	—

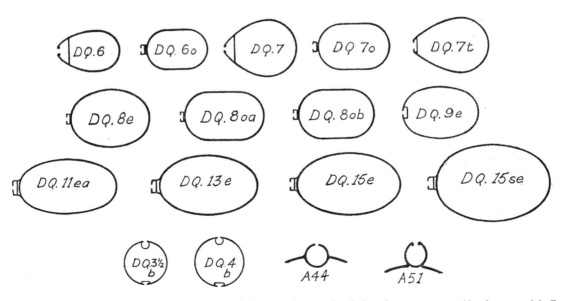

FIG. 100. *Typical mast sections used by Sparlight Ltd. for masthead rigged ocean racers. Also boom and luff rope track sections.*

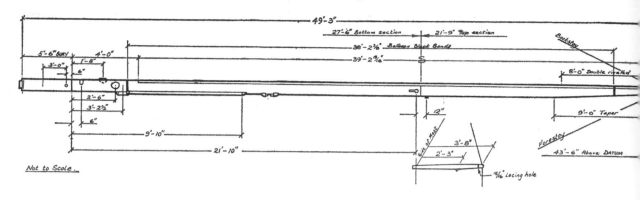

FIG. 101. *Light alloy mast and spreader for masthead rig. This mast for Tina is keel stepped, data are shown for positioning tracks, steaming light, black bands and winch pads.*

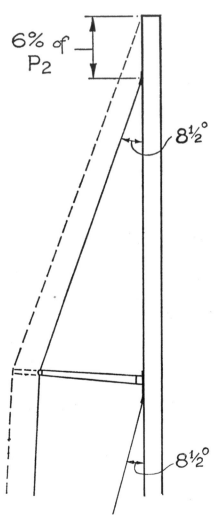

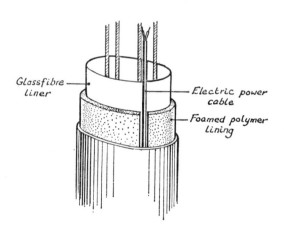

FIG. 102 (above). *Construction of a light alloy spar with foamed polymer for sound deadening, electric cable and GRP liner to stop halyards chafing these.*

FIG. 103 (left). *A method of reducing the length of the spreaders. The minimum shroud angle of 8½ degrees is possible with modern mast sections. P₂ refers to height of foretriangle.*

No comprehensive guide can be given for mast section against sail area or some other dimension, so the mast maker's recommendation should always be sought, so that he can select from his latest patterns. Factors that he will take into consideration apart from length of hull and the type of rig when finding the right section will be:

1. Displacement and beam of yacht.
2. Sail area, especially that part which is loading the forestay.
3. Ballast ratio, which affects stiffness.
4. Whether deck or keel stepped, since keel stepping aids the rigidity of the spar.
5. Offshore history of the sections which he has in mind. The soundest knowledge of the behaviour of types of spar at sea has been built on experience rather than calculation.

A typical ocean racing mast is that of *Tina*, designed by Dick Carter and built by Sparlight Ltd. (Fig. 101).

Basic mast fittings Numerous fittings are attached to masts, but the basic ones for any mast include the spreaders, mast track and halyard system. A single pair of spreaders is adequate for all mast sections up to 30 ft.-yachts and beyond. These may be circular or shaped in section, most likely to an aerofoil pattern. They should be given a downward aspect of 16 degrees to take the wind flow best at average angles of heel. The shape can be widened at the inner end to give a good fore and aft anchorage.

The history of the early Bermudian rig was one of finding a trouble-free mast track following the days of gaff rig and jackstays and mast hoops! Though many small yachts have standard alloy track and nylon slides, it has to be admitted that the sail is more efficient, if the gap between it and the mast is sealed. The mainsail should have a luff rope (this is not the bolt rope, taping normally being used to finish the shaping of the sail, but is a rope put on at the final stage of sailmaking) to run up the luff groove. The disadvantages offshore are having to feed the luff into the groove. This requires an extra hand and when lowered the sail falls on deck, instead of being held magazine fashion ready for instant rehoisting in the manner of a track.

Internal halyards are preferable for racing, cutting a significant amount of windage and the halyards are allowed to run together down the mast. This is quite satisfactory and mutual fouling is only likely to occur if one or more halyards are thinner than the others, when there is a tendency to wind round a thicker one. Electrical wiring must be kept clear of them and is inserted between the sound-deadening material and the mast wall (Fig. 102).

Shroud angle Modern materials in the rig enable the shroud angle to be reduced to 8·5 degrees. This is one of the reasons that a single spreader can be used and still not be too wide to prevent the genoa being sheeted home. Where the shrouds meet the deck they can be well inboard to clear the outer side decks for the genoa foot. A further reduction in the spread of the shrouds is effected by placing the terminals of the shroud on the mast below both the masthead and spreader bases respectively. The upper shrouds can be taken 6 per cent of P below the masthead (Fig. 103).

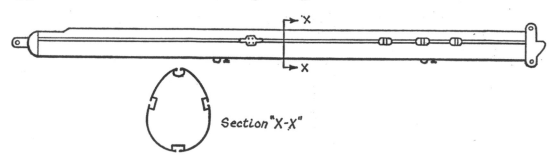

FIG. 104. *A boom section by Marco Polo for small yachts using slab reefing. The top groove and lower internal track are usual, but the side tracks can take a variety of fittings which are clamped tight by the crew. These can be adjusted for different sail fittings to cope with reef pendants, foreguys, outhauls, leech line and other mainsail gear.*

Boom sections The main boom section can be designed to take the foot rope which gives even loading and is always preferable to the extra weight of track and slides. Provision has to be made for a clew outhaul which must be controllable from somewhere near the tack. Systems which require a hand to work on the end of the main boom are awkward, even dangerous, and result in the foot tension not being adjusted so often or as accurately as it should. For roller reefing the boom section is usually circular and a lower groove can be used for kicking-strap slider. The clew outhaul can run externally. Such sections are often the mast sections of smaller craft. One interesting section made by Marco Polo of Paris is for booms of yachts up to about 20 ft. This is an irregular ellipse with a smaller diameter on top where there is a foot groove. There are internal track-shaped grooves along the bottom and on each side. The bottom one takes a slider for kicking-strap attachment, but the side ones are for easily fixed plastic cleats and fairleads which can be arranged to suit any slab reefing system and to take clew outhauls or other equipment as needed (Fig. 104).

The spinnaker boom section is circular and some manufacturers taper the boom along its length to give the maximum diameter at the centre. This gives least weight, while at the same time withstanding the sudden compression loads that come on the spinnaker boom. However, most spinnaker boom breakages are as a result of it being allowed to slam against the forestay and a cylindrical spar tapering only at its extremities is effective in withstanding this, and cheaper.

Bending spars offshore Dinghies and inshore keel boats have been equipped with bending spars for many years. Such equipment is not widely seen in ocean racing yachts because the loading problems are difficult in the larger sizes, the safety factor offshore precludes scantlings in proportion to the size of yacht and the rating rules have placed the emphasis on the genoa, while bending spars are a mainsail adjustment. There is also the fatigue factor in a seaway which, together with control of bend, are problems which do not arise in smooth water. An indication has been given above that in the future seven-eighths rigs may be developed to exploit bending spars. With the masthead rig, spars may be adjusted, though this is not a true "bendy rig". Tension on the backstay relieves hardness in the leech of the mainsail and slightly flattens the main by bowing the centre of the mast. Meanwhile, it counteracts the increased tension put on the fore-stay as the genoa is sheeted in to a freshening breeze. If there is an inner forestay this can be tightened to accentuate the effect. The deep elliptical section helps the mast to stand up to this sort of treatment and the maximum depth of the bow would be 8 inches in a 45-ft. mast. Methods of tightening the stays include wheels, tackles, winches and tweakers as well as rigging screws with permanent folding handles on them (Fig. 105).

Bending the main boom is quite a different problem as it does not have the compression strains of the mast with its need to support the genoa luff and blocks can be attached

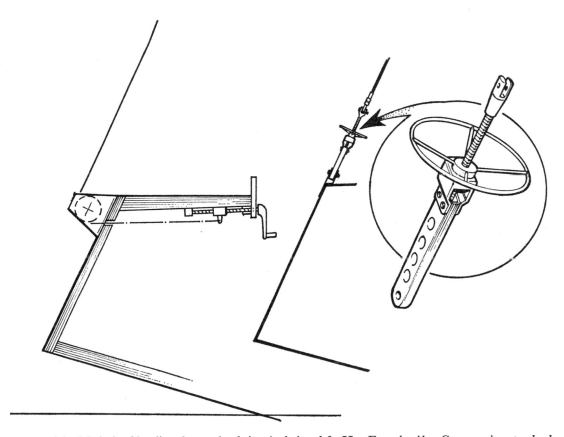

FIG. 105(a). *Methods of bending the masthead rig. As designed for* Hot Foot *by Alan Gurney using standard Merriman fittings, a handle in the cockpit permits quick backstay adjustment. The large sheave block is mounted outside the transom. On the right is an example of a backstay adjuster wheel made in a number of sizes by Sea Sure Ltd. It is made so that the backstay itself cannot turn.*

to any points on the boom to obtain the required curve. The alternatives of zippers and lacing have already been mentioned. Special boom sections (elliptical with major axis horizontal) can be obtained.

Future development   Methods of rapid adjustment to the yacht seem the most likely avenue of development, because unlike a mechanically propelled means of transport which is designed to accept a certain driving force the yacht has to cope with the continually changing wind. Apart from the search for aerodynamic perfection, lighter, stronger bending spars will be seen in the medium future. New materials, including titanium in metal masts or a switch to plastics, are possible. Plastic spars reinforced by carbon filaments, which are many times lighter than glass fibres, are the sort of thing which can be expected.

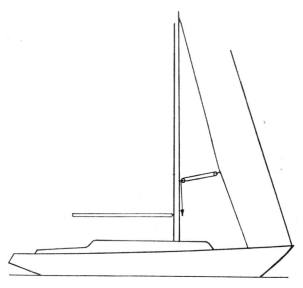

FIG. 105(b). *With an inner forestay, a simple tackle can put bend on the mast without going on the foredeck. An alternative is wheel or screw at the base of the inner forestay.*

SPINNAKERS, RIGGING AND
RACING EQUIPMENT

Spinnaker design The spinnaker is the largest sail on board and with its increasing influence on the design of the rig, many of the fittings and detailed layout of sailing equipment are concerned with this sail. In Chapter 3 various methods of handling the spinnaker offshore were reviewed and it remains to look at the design of sail and gear. As with fore and aft sails cloth development is making actual weight less meaningful. In winds under 6 knots light weight is at a premium, so that the sail can be made to stand and coated nylon of o·6 oz. (English) is available. Fittings on it must also be very light with dinghy-type clew rings and the sheet tied to it. If carrying such a sail the crew must not be afraid of changing spinnakers as soon as the wind comes in firm. The cut of a sail for light airs needs to be flat and it will seldom be used near a dead run because the yacht will be tacking downwind in such conditions. When conditions are such that the sea-way is shaking all wind out of the spinnaker, it often pays to hoist a drifter instead and it could also be made from the same lightweight nylon.

For spinnakers in winds from 5 to 20 knots, cloth weights ranging from 1 oz. to 2·75 oz. (English) or o·75 to 2·2 oz. (American) will be used on boats ranging from 16 to 28 ft. The question arises whether to carry separate reaching and running spinnakers in this range of "working" wind strengths. There is now far more emphasis on reaching with spinnakers and so the sail can be regarded as equally required for this point of sailing as for running. The needs for reaching are a full head to fly high away from the mainsail and a cut that will keep open the slot further down on both sails. The result is, in general terms, the big shouldered sail with the luff and leech cut to let the wind clear. Such a shape turns out to be very suitable for running in moderate winds. Sailmakers are working on ways of improving the cut of sails within the present general framework of horizontal panels. (Fig. 106). One specially good sail for offshore work is the Bruce Banks double mitre cut spinnaker (Fig. 107). This seems to stand when others break along the luff. The forward mitre on a reach will tend to fold in while the luff is still working. It enables the sheet to remain eased, and in a seaway the effect is sometimes that of the sail "pumping" along with the mitre going in and out, but the sail correctly sheeted and pulling.

The actual dimensions of the spinnaker are governed closely by the IOR rule. A foretriangle with an aspect ratio of 1 to 3 gives a spinnaker foot to leech ratio of 3 to 5, and this is ideal. The rule ensures by its provision that a spinnaker is symmetrical, and cannot be in reality a genoa of a size that cheats the rule. From time to time designs are worked out to do this in some way, but it is a field where the legislators are right in closing loopholes.

Heavy weather spinnaker On yachts under 20 ft., it will be better to resort to genoa, boomed out if necessary, when the wind no longer allows the working spinnaker

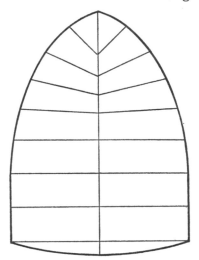

FIG. 106. *Typical appearance of seams on a horizontal cut spinnaker.*

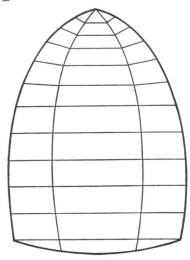

FIG. 107. *The double mitre cut spinnaker developed by Bruce Banks Sails. It has advantages in most conditions over the horizontal cut.*

to be carried. On boats over this size a heavy weather spinnaker is extremely useful. Experience in using such a sail tends to be limited outside trans-ocean contests. Sail designer Ken Rose of Bruce Banks Sails, Southampton, England, recommends a sail with a short hoist, because a tall one tends to accentuate rolling and to be unstable. The proportion of foot to leech suggested is 2 to 3. The sail will be cut flat and the cloth will be one size heavier than the main spinnaker. What is more important is that the tabling at the corners should be considerable, with the load spread well out from a secure clew fitting, such as a heavy stainless steel ring.

Colour of spinnakers is less important than obtaining the cloth from a good batch. If possible, inspect several examples of the weight before ordering a spinnaker as there are minor variations. One helpful colour scheme is several widths of panel to be white against a coloured background: on a night which is not too dark this shows up the set of the luff. Like other headsails a few good spinnakers are preferable to a great selection; in time the characteristics of each sail owned will become apparent and the right combination carried on board. Offshore use tends to be hard on spinnakers and one will normally carry at least two of full size.

Spinnaker gear   Various aids to spinnaker handling have been mentioned in Chapter 3, but the more basic gear affects design of the mast and deck arrangement. Internal halyards are preferable, and one possible design for the spinnaker halyard is for it to emerge through a forward facing "nozzle" at the masthead. Such an arrangement has proved to be prone to chafe, especially with the spinnaker set shy, and some designers have reverted to the ordinary forward crane with block and an external halyard. Sparlight masts have suggested the system in Fig. 108 which has an internal halyard emerging just below the masthead to a free ranging block—the advantages of both internal and external halyards. Spinnaker halyards in rope should be double ended, if external, and any system should have a parrel bead between the splice and the block to prevent jamming. Snap shackles on the clews should be of the extremity-hinged type for release under load, but this does not include the snap shackle at the head. I have known this open completely after not being fully closed by the crew, and brought down with spinnaker swivel hooked through it. Unnecessary weight should be kept out of the spinnaker clews. In light weather, a sheet will be tied on and snap shackles and heavy gear removed and this is not assisted if heavy fittings are already incorporated into the clew. Either a stainless steel ring sewn in or a cringle based on stainless steel is enough.

The height of the spinnaker boom track on the mast is limited by the rating rule and should be taken to the maximum allowed. Whatever system of gybing is used it is wise to carry two spinnaker booms and there will be two bell-type fittings on sliders. There may be a track for each, but if there is only one, on twin pole gybes, always use the upper slider first. Then when the time comes to rig the second pole before a gybe, the bell fitting will be accessible and not out of reach above the one in use. In view of the heavy strains on the spinnaker pole offshore, it is advisable to use bell fittings down to yachts of 22 ft. waterline: after that it may be possible to use a heavy eye on a slider. Movement of the sliders on the mast track is difficult when the pole is rigged and in use owing to the heavy sideways thrust, and positioning of the plunger used on many of these is impossible. Even if it is level with a recess hole the slide will be forced off centre and the plunger will not engage. So for all yachts except the smallest, the sliders are best without a plunger and can be controlled by up-and-down hauls. Light line can be used with jam cleats. Some yachts under 24 ft. use three or four suitably positioned heavy eyes rather than any track.

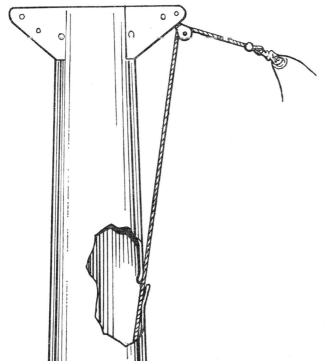

FIG. 108. *Internal-external spinnaker halyard. It has the usual advantages associated with internal halyards, but obviates the chafe experienced when a spinnaker halyard leaves the mast directly through a forward opening.*

o

Against the simplicity of this is the lack of critical adjustment and the difficulty of moving the heel of the pole under load.

The spinnaker foreguy (also known as downhaul or kicker) leads from the pole end to a block in the eyes of the boat. From there it should be led aft to the cockpit for control. There will be a pair for twin pole gybe systems. A Gibb clam-cleat is very useful for this and permits hauling in and instant cleating. The only thing to watch for with this fitting is the control on a heavy load when taking the line out of the cleat. As it is jerked out it exerts a sudden load held only by your own hands. For this reason when used in yachts over 21 ft. there should also be an ordinary cleat for use in heavy conditions. The foreguy can then be controlled by a turn in the usual way. If the topping lift is also brought aft, it becomes possible to control the end of the pole from the cockpit. In light weather, as mentioned earlier, playing the topping lift is a method of getting a reluctant spinnaker to fill.

Fittings on the spinnaker pole depend on the method of gybing. Basically, there are three types of end, though there are many different details in design available. There is the "opening and plunger", traditional, designed to clip into a ring, clew, etc. There is a fitting with similar action, but faired out so that lines pass through the end freely: the plunger also acts as a roller for this purpose. Thirdly, there are poles with trumpet ends through which the outhaul emerges or two in the case of a single pole gybe. The inner ends can be "opening and plunger" for mast ring, or designed to enter a bell fitting. For the latter there may still be an "opening and plunger" tapering to enter the bell, or a blind end which serves no other purpose than to secure in the bell.

One useful spinnaker end fitting is the Barient faired-out plunger type which shuts automatically as it closes over the guy (Fig. 109). The Barient Company manufactures some of the finest yacht equipment in the world and was founded in the 1950s by two Californian yachtsmen, owners of the big ocean racers *Baruna* and *Orient*, who being unable to obtain the right sort of winches first had them custom-made. Since then Barients have turned to all sizes of yacht, but concentrate still on deck sailing gear. Against the gybing systems the Table (Fig. 110) gives the options for fittings on spinnaker poles. No doubt variations will be found from these as crews seek more efficient ways of spinnaker handling.

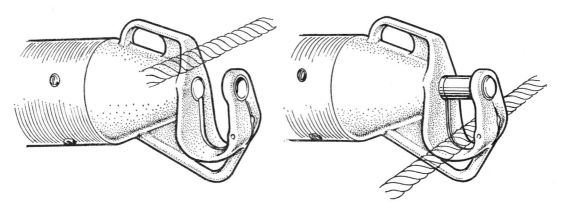

FIG. 109. *Barient spinnaker end. This threads on to the guy. As the guy enters, it pushes against the thin trigger which releases the plunger. The plunger has a roller to assist the run of the pole to its position at the end of the guy.*

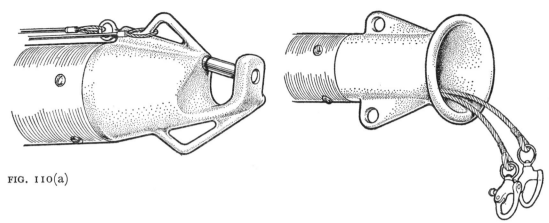

FIG. 110(a)

FIG. 110(b)

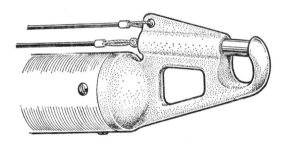

FIG. 110(c)

FIG. 110(a). *A plunger/roller end fitting with a flared jaw to facilitate the guy passing through it. The same fitting can snap on to a ring on the mast if required.*

FIG. 110(b). *Open spinnaker end with two lines which run to the corners of the spinnaker, when using a single pole. The eyes on the fitting are for the topping lift and foreguy.*

FIG. 110(c). *A plain snap-on end fitting, shaped to save weight. It will also ride easily on a heavy mast ring.*

SPINNAKER POLE FITTINGS

Basic method	Twin or dip pole gybe	End fitting	Inboard fitting on pole	Rigging connections
Guy and sheet on each clew	Twin* Dip	Plunger/roller Plunger/roller[a]	Blind End Blind End	Pole on to guy. Guy on to sheet ring.
Outhauls inside pole(s) connect to clews	Twin Dip	Trumpet with single line Trumpet with pair of lines[b]	Blind End with lead out for one or two lines. Cleats	Outhauls from pole snap to sheet/guy ring.
Manual attach- of poles	Twin Dip	Opening and plunger[c] Opening and plunger	Matching ends Matching ends	Pole snapped to sheet ring. Fore guy to second sheet ring.

(a) See Fig. 110 (a).   (b) See Fig. 110 (b).   (c) See Fig. 110 (c).

FIG. 110. *In all cases sheet is snapped to spinnaker clew. Topping lift is on pole. In cases marked * it is well inboard so that sheet not in use lies over pole and does not get fouled when pole is lowered.*

In yachts over 22 ft., a bearing out spar, or "jockey pole", for the spinnaker guy when set shy assists trimming, takes compression off the spinnaker pole and prevents the guy leaning heavily on the lifelines. The bearing out spar takes considerable compression in its own right. The inner end has an "opening and plunger" fitting on a heavy ring on the mast and the outer end has a sheave in a deep slot to bear on the guy. The length of the spar should be such that the sheave projects some 15 inches clear of the shrouds when it is rigged on the mast. The distance will need to be increased where the shrouds are well inboard to keep the guy clear of the after-lifelines.

Mast equipment The modern tendency to clean up the mast has been emphasized and sometimes this results in a simpler and even cheaper way of doing things and saves weight as well. One such example is the shroud attachments now standardized by Sparlight for stock yachts and custom-made spars. The shroud is capped with a ball fitting which is backed up by a stainless steel plate threaded loosely on the shroud. This assembly is literally inserted into a hole in the mast of suitable shape giving minimum weight, windage and ample strength. It is not necessary to add reinforcement to the wall of the aluminium mast (Fig. 111). It has already been explained that these are positioned down from the masthead or spreader fixture. The masthead rig spar will be flat at the truck and can then be fitted with a Brookes & Gatehouse wind indicator. The alignment of this has to be accurate. With one of these fitted, masthead lights serve no useful purpose; the RORC has banned the use of an all-round light for some years as they are against the collision regulations. Mast failures seldom arise from the breaking of wire rigging; it is usually a fitting that was not up to the job or even the mast itself. When a boat I owned was dismasted running under spinnaker through St. Catherine's tide race south of the Isle of Wight, the mast broke in two places, the basic cause being that the section used was just

not up to the job. A heavier mast was substituted and the yacht sailed better with a tighter forestay and firmer rig. An ancillary cause of this event was that several mast fittings had their fastenings in the same horizontal plane round the mast and the spar tore off like a postage stamp at that point. Another mast failure in which I have been involved was caused by a broken rigging screw, in this case a machined type which had sharp corners and varying thicknesses of metal: this is inevitable when it is shaped out of solid and I recommend using forged bronze such as are made by Lewmar in England and Merriman in USA. On another occasion the ball-type fitting let into the mast wall unscrewed from the thread of the bar rigging, to which it was attached and fell down inside the mast: a locking pin was all that was required. Split pins and similar very small items are so important on the masts of offshore boats that the person in charge should inspect the mast fittings and all rigging personally before every race.

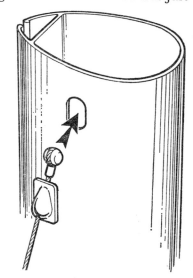

FIG. 111. *Internal shroud anchorage used by Sparlight is simple and has minimum windage.*

An enclosed worm roller reefing gear seldom suffers from trouble, except for the crew dropping handles over-

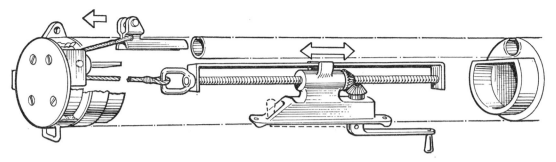

FIG. 112. *Clew outhaul by Nicro Marine; the adjustment handle is situated near the inboard end on the boom. It folds flush when not in use.*

board and several of these should be carried! Adjustable spanners are no substitute. Reefing is hard on the boom-end fitting on which are rigged the mainsheet blocks and the boom should turn smoothly inside this without its turning over and twisting the mainsheet. If a claw ring is in use the same principle applies. On small boats it is sometimes possible to make a more solid claw ring than can be found as standard. Ian Hannay on his Galion design had two Holt-Allen light alloy dinghy claw rings fastened parallel about 6 inches apart with stainless bolts. It is best not to have the kicking-strap on a claw ring because it will have to be slacked off when reefing anyway. A recessed keyhole is satisfactory and adequately strong in the same way as the shroud terminals mentioned above. If a slider on a lower track is used, it will have to be removed before starting to roll up the sail. A kicking-strap for use when reefed is possible by rolling in a strip of canvas with holes at intervals in it in which to snap the tackle. It is hard on the sail, but at least should not be necessary when on the wind as the mainsheet then gives enough downward purchase.

For adjusting the clew of the main a tackle or, for yachts over 21 ft., gearing inside the boom is desirable. A system devised by Nicro Marine of San Francisco is shown in Fig. 112.

Rigging wire Modern stainless steel rigging presents no special problems for ocean racers, the important detail being in the design and method of fitting various terminals as mentioned above. Thicker wire than necessary should not be used and swaged ends save windage and are now fully proved in certain types. 1 × 19 stainless wire is not easily spliced and swaging is usual. Two methods are roll swaging and rotary hammer swaging. Different machines are used, but in both the shaft of a terminal is squeezed into the lay of the wire. A neat job is therefore obtained, and on the ends of lifelines the wire can be swaged into a terminal which can be screwed direct into the barrel of the rigging screw. This method should not be used on the yacht's rigging, where an eye terminal should be on the end of the wire to be connected in turn by a clevis pin to the fork of the rigging screw. This is desirable to prevent any possibility of metal fatigue.

It is hardly necessary to mention how essential it is that all rigging screw connections must have universal action ensured by means of toggles. This applies to all yachts not just ocean racers, but many small standard cruiser-racers do arrive from their builders without this precaution. Almost always where there has been neglect of this, I have noticed on close inspection that the rigging screw has suffered slight damage which will later result in failure. Nowhere is this more important than on the bottom of the forestay in the masthead rig, where there is athwartships angle to the stay, varying perhaps over a total of 15 degrees between tacks, as well as after tension by the genoa. Several ocean racers whose owners should know better have lost their forestays for this reason. There is a British Standard for the quality of wire used for yacht rigging, in BSS 3972.

Rod rigging For racing with the modern masthead sloop there are advantages in using solid drawn stainless steel rod rigging. Performance is undoubtedly improved if a forestay can be kept as straight as possible and the lack of stretch in rod rigging is about one-third of that of 1 × 19 wire when loaded at 50 per cent breaking load. Ordinary wire rigging has even more stretch when it is new and if going straight out to sea with 1 × 19 rigging the process of hardening it up goes on for some time. Twist is absent in rod rigging. Other advantages are less windage due to not using rigging screws. On the shrouds the rod rigging can be obtained in an aerofoil section which again reduces wind resistance. The disadvantages are the danger of failure due to fatigue, difficulty in handling ashore or transporting overland, as the rods must not be allowed to bend sharply, the increased cost and the method of adjustment which involves turning the whole rod. This means that a man must usually go aloft to release a lock nut and then assist by turning the rod from above while a second hand works at deck level. Against this the negligible stretch makes this a much rarer event in comparison with ordinary wire.

South Coast Rod Rigging of Emsworth are suppliers of rod rigging in England and their method for terminals is to screw an eye or fork terminal on to the end of the rod, the threaded part of which has the same strength as the centre of the rod which has a slightly smaller cross-sectional area. This threading to the terminal is used as the rigging adjustment and the rod will have a square section near the deck to enable it to be turned with a spanner. The rod is locked by a split pin passing through a slit in the terminal and a hole in the rod. It can therefore only be locked at successive 180 degree turns. The adjustment for a $\frac{1}{2}$-in. rod is 3 inches but as stretch is $\frac{1}{8}$ in. in 30 ft. this is ample. Substantial alterations to the rake and position of mast would pose problems. An aerofoil or lenticular section can be used for shrouds and is said to have two-thirds less wind resistance than the corresponding circular rod. This is, however, a very small fraction of the total windage of the yacht and the lenticular section tends to be hard on sheets and very uncomfortable to hang on to owing to the fine edges. When setting it up the longer axis should be in line with the apparent wind on the windward side as it would be when the yacht is close-hauled. The fact that it then points out on the side which is leeward at any moment is acceptable, because the flow of air off the genoa turns inward.

A ball and plate fitting can be used at the top of the shrouds to enter the mast, the ball being screwed on the end of the rod in the same way as a fork terminal. It should be permanently locked in position as adjustment is carried out from the deck and the ball merely turns with the rod. As the backstay is going to be adjusting while sailing, it does not need to be turned and will be fixed by an eye or fork end to whatever is used for adjustment. As it is in the lenticular sections that the disadvantages are most acute, some owners may like to consider using rod rigging on the forestay and backstay, which are the rigging components where stretch needs to be avoided, and ordinary wire on all shrouds. It is the shrouds that are most likely to be damaged in general use, but if rod shrouds are installed

Rod rigging with terminals. The rod itself is turned by means of a spanner applied to the flat sides just above lower thread. The toggle connects to a shroud plate at the deck in the usual way.

BREAKING STRAINS AND SIZES OF STANDING RIGGING COMPONENTS

Rod Rigging

Size dia. (in.)	Pin size (in.)	Diameter of rod (in.)	Breaking load (lb.)	W.T. (lb./ft.)
2 BA	3/16		2165	·066
1/4 BSF	5/16	·170	4256	·083
5/16	5/16	·230	6750	·133
3/8	3/8	·280	10700	·200
7/16	7/16	·350	13800	·277
1/2	1/2	·400	19400	·367

1 × 19 Wire

Size dia. (in.)	Breaking load (lb.)	W.T. (lb./ft.)
5/32	3060	·049
3/16	4650	·076
1/4	6700	·111
9/32	9150	·151
5/16	11950	·220
3/8	14140	·275

Levmar forged rigging screw Steel/Bronze Alloy

Pin size and thread size (in.)	Breaking load (lb.)	W.T.
5/16	5511	6½ oz.
3/8	9347	10 oz.
7/16	15321	15 oz.
1/2	16093	1 lb. 6 oz.
5/8	22927	2 lb. 12 oz.

FIG. 113

metal fatigue must be guarded against by easing of the backstay and consequently slacking the whole rig when the yacht is on her mooring. Fig. 113 shows the construction of a length of rod rigging and a table of data of rod rigging, wire rigging and forged rigging screws.

Running rigging materials The manufacturers of synthetic ropes offer a wide variety of cordage for different purposes on the yacht. Advantage should be taken of this primarily so that the type of line is the most suitable for the job, but it also helps over identification. On some yachts spinnaker gear in particular is dyed in different colours. The system is referred to under the question of storage of gear in Chapter 6 and the table in Fig. 47 indicates different materials. Rope manufacturers are continually introducing variations in their synthetics. In addition to the running rigging in the Table, the kedge warp can be three-strand nylon and mooring warps, since they have to be carried when racing, for when the time comes to enter harbour, can be of lightweight polypropylene.

Sheets With a mainsheet wholly at the boom end, the track needs to be vertically below it when amidships and as wide as possible; to the sides of the yacht is ideal. Only a roller bearing mainsheet track will ensure smooth movement and the slider should be controlled with lines which are held at each side to limit its travel. How to hold these is a bit of a problem because quick adjustment is needed, for if the slider slams across unintentionally it can be dangerous. On an offshore yacht, with men moving around the cockpit area in a far from gentle manner, even the best type of jamming cleat can get released. For the same reason it is important to ensure that before tacking, the leeward control line is made up, or the slider will crash down the full length to its new leeward side. The advantages of lines for adjustment of track position is that they can be "played" when sailing instead of the mainsheet, especially on the smaller yachts. Yachts under 24 ft. can secure the mainsheet on a jamb cleat attached to the moving block on the track and the same system applies where the mainsheet is secured to the boom somewhere along its length by claw ring or tang. *Dame d'Iroise*, winner of the 1968 Half Ton Cup, borrowed a tip from the dinghy classes by having her mainsheet purchase connected to the boom by a single wire. When the sheet is hardened right in, the purchase is "two-blocks", the distance to the boom being taken up by the wire. Less length of tackle then needs to be overhauled or adjusted.

Once a bending boom or slab reefing with tangs on the boom for blocks are used a variety of mainsheet arrangements can be employed. Taking the sheet forward to the heel of the mast helps the downward component and it can then be led to a winch at the after-end of the coachroof, where it is easily controlled by the crew sitting forward of the helmsman. This avoids the common scramble across the helmsman to reach the mainsheet. With the number of blocks used on a centre mainsheet of this type it is important that friction is minimal, especially for playing the mainsheet in light weather. Lewmar make blocks with a diameter of $3\frac{3}{4}$ in. for rope up to $1\frac{1}{2}$ in. circumference which are very light running. On a modern yacht with its winches, worm gears and wire, the present main sheet systems available stand out as being in need of development. It would pay to give this department thought in making it effective for the various weights of wind and points of sailing.

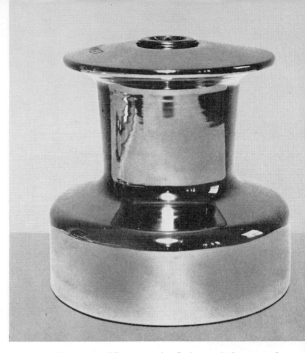

31. Lewmar No. 40 winch in stainless steel and bronze. Maximum load 2,500 lb. It can be dismantled without tools. Note slight taper of drum.

30. Sunken shroud terminal on alloy mast to give minimum windage. This is in use here with rod rigging.

32. *Below :* Halyard winches on the coach-roof of *Al Na'Ir*, an Italian One Tonner.

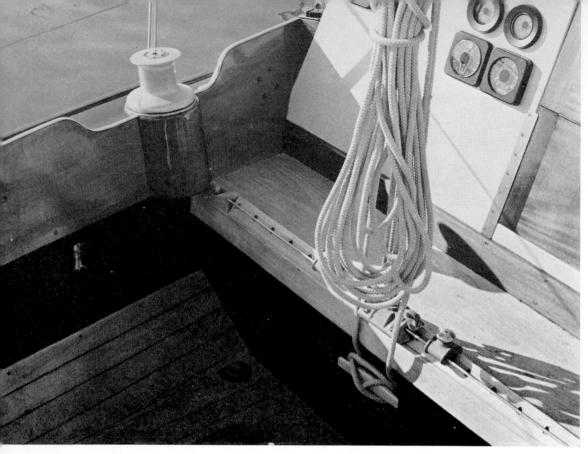

33. A good site for a sheet winch on *Yeoman XIII*. With no seat or high coaming in the way, crew can exert maximum strength.

34. Halyard box combined with ventilators and winch handle boxes on *Sootica* is extremely practical.

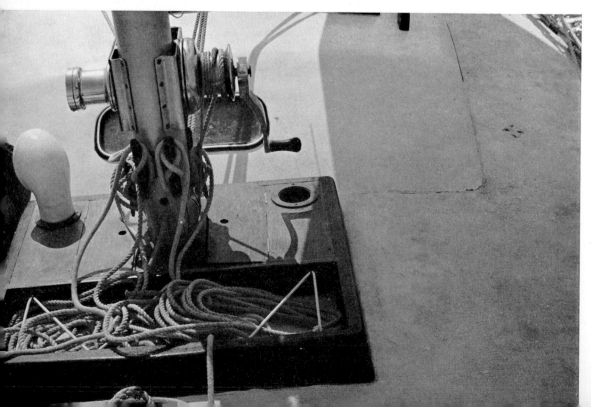

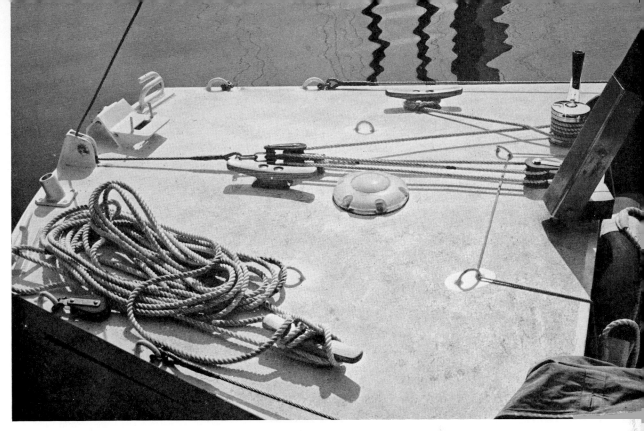

35. Stern deck of *Rafale* with easily operated adjustable backstay.

36 (*a*). Heavy mainsheet track on roller bearings for yachts over 24 ft. WL.

36 (b). Double genoa track on *Angel* eases close-hauled reaching sheeting drills.

36 (c). *Below:* The secret of the apparently very light track on *September* is the close spacing of fastenings.

Genoa sheets Synthetic rope and winches have long ago eliminated the horrors of wire and free blocks at the clew, ready to cut the flesh and crack skulls respectively. To get the best of a single genoa sheet to a winch in the cockpit, the lead must be right and this means canting the winch out to an appropriate angle and if necessary backing up the lead block with a snatch lead before the sheet arrives at the winch. Positioning of tracks is all important and they must be bolted along their length; unfortunately this necessity is not appreciated by all builders and once the yacht is complete it may be difficult to substitute bolts for screws because of the nature of construction or internal furniture. Whatever the beam it pays to have one track along the outer edge of the deck, if only for reaching, but probably also for high cut headsails. In beamy yachts another track inboard may be used for the working genoa and almost certainly for jibs. Sparkman and Stephens designs usually have this track angled towards the forestay and nearing the location of the outer track at its after end. On the Dick Carter designed *Angel* there are two parallel tracks, the second being about 8 in. inboard. Where the beam is not great all genoas will need to be sheeted as far outboard as permitted and one long track is enough. Tracks should be long, for the yacht's sail wardrobe is changed over the years and leads which may not be needed immediately may be useful later.

The genoa is normally sheeted inside the lifelines and even if the track in use is outside them, the lead of the sheet brings the clew down to just about the same vertical plane as the lifeline. The problem which arises as the sheet is eased off for reaching has been mentioned in Chapter 3. Figure 10 indicated a solution, which can be elaborated with the use of two tracks. Two winches are obviously helpful for this system on the larger yachts. At least two sliders with blocks will be in use, whether on one or two tracks. One of these can be of the roller type fairlead with wide mouth to take splicing, etc., near the clew. These have built-in stops to prevent them tumbling and remain aligned fore and aft. The lead is not therefore always exactly correct, though this is compensated by the wide sheave. I prefer a wide sheave block which can rotate, but with the lead of the sheet close to the track. Tumbling is prevented by a strong stainless spring (Fig. 114).

FIG. 114. *Suggested genoa sheet slider which is made non-tumbling by spring, can swivel to take up lead and is also light weight with large diameter block.*

After trying various ways of making fast the genoa sheets to its sail, including ordinary D-shackles, snap shackles moused with leather thongs or tape and special sister hooks, I cannot find anything better than tying in each sheet with a bowline. It is light, secure, non-jamming, enables one sheet to be removed while the other remains and it is easy on the clew—and on the crew if it is flailing about. It does not depend on splices, seizings or thimbles. The only snag is that sometimes if trying to remove one sheet while the sail is sheeted to the other one, it will be found to be jammed hard under the bight of the bowline in the clew cringle.

Small tackles　　Running rigging has been so cleaned up on modern ocean racers that there are few tackles in use. The kicking-strap is essential and methods of attaching it to booms have been mentioned. The dinghy type, that is one that swings at a prearranged length with the boom, is far preferable to any tackles pulling down the boom to the rail. A really powerful purchase is needed with an ordinary cleat or camb type on its lower block, that is a cleat which allows release under load. When the yacht is designed both the boom height and deck structure must take into account the kicking-strap. In the USA it is known as a boom vang.

Main boom foreguy or preventer　　This is an essential aid to downwind sailing offshore and even with a slight sea, if the yacht is rolling under spinnaker, it will prevent a gybe by the main boom. Methods of attaching it were given in Chapter 3. Ocean racing rules permit sheeting of headsails to the end of the main boom; under the IOR rule, if the sheeting position is more than 6 inches aft of the black band the excess is added to E (Fig. 53). Advantage can be taken of this when reaching and a snatch block rigged on the boom for the purpose (Fig. 9). However, with modern rigs the practice is less prevalent, high short booms, low-cut genoas and initially ample beam for sheeting making it less urgent to get the sheet outboard.

Tack downhaul and uphaul　　Unless the main boom gooseneck is fixed it should be possible to move it above and below the black band (measured limit) on a piece of track heavier than the fitted mast track. This extra size enables it to take more sideways thrust than a sail slide extrusion would. A small tackle will quite easily pull down the gooseneck after hoisting the main. A boom uphaul is not so common, but it saves time and the crew's temper as there are a number of occasions chiefly concerned with hoisting the main and reefing when the gooseneck needs to be supported and this can be difficult in a seaway. The uphaul is also used to relieve tension on the luff of the mainsail when the kicking-strap is tightened. A small block and tackle and jamb cleat will serve for an uphaul, which starts to be useful on yachts of 22 ft. and upwards.

Winches　　*Halyard winches.* The siting of halyard winches on the coachroof aft of the mast has several advantages; keeping weight as low as possible, security for the crew offshore when working them, reducing windage on the mast, not only of the winch but the rope, cleat and halyard exit that goes with it, and when the yacht is laid up the winches are more easily maintained on the hull than the mast. Halyard winches seldom lack enough power to do the job, but they should be provided on all sizes of racer down to the smallest. Small, light winches are available and they are far preferable to any form of tackle when racing. It is a bad policy to try to cut down on the number of essential winches either to save weight or cost. Main, genoa and spinnaker winches are needed. Apart from the obvious loading in larger yachts, in small yachts they are required in the mainsail to overcome the friction of the luff groove especially when there is weight in the wind; in the genoa, to obtain a tight luff and a stretch luff (if a Cunningham hole is not in use); and the spinnaker, because, if it fills with wind half hoisted, a winch will be needed to control it and get it the rest of the way. Top action winches are really essential for halyards owing to the length of line to be brought in. Reel-type winches are neat and useful for handling wire, but lose their point when the winch is on the coachroof. Riding turns on a halyard winch with wire are serious; at least with a sheet it is usually possible to slack off the working end. The angling of winches towards the halyard exit at the mast must be right. This is achieved by mounting the winches on suitably angled wooden blocks.

Siting of sheet winches A man needs the same space to exert his power on a winch whatever the size of a yacht, but in boats under 20 ft. he will seldom need to use his full strength, so the space problem is alleviated. In these small boats a bottom action winch is acceptable. Most of the sheet will be brought in by hand and only a few pumps on the handle required finally to trim it. The advantage of a bottom action winch is that the turns can be thrown on it with the handle in position and a by-product of this is that the handle requires less space to operate. Such winches are available in Tufnol, which saves weight, though on *Shakashe*, Ian Walker, when turning a standard boat into a JOG racer, preferred to fit small top action winches, normally used for halyards (no gearing) in larger boats rather than bottom action types which were readily available. It must be accepted that winches of Tufnol and bronze, as fitted on standard cruisers, will have a limited life under racing conditions and the owner should be prepared to replace or rebuild before they fail during a race.

Over 20 ft., when short tacking, two men can well be employed on a winch and this needs space. "The trick is in the tailing," said Don MacNamara, the controversial US 12-metre and Olympic helmsman, and this still applies whatever the size of yacht. For really effective tailing a second man must be ready to clamp on the top action handle and wind as soon as the tailing pace slackens. Then the siting problem becomes acute in small yachts as positions have to be found for these men. We will look at cockpit layout a little later as this has a large bearing on effective sheet winching, but among factors which make winching slow and difficult (always resulting in important loss of time in a race) are:

1. Winch too far outside coamings so that it is near water when yacht is heeled over and crew cannot get "over" it to wind.
2. Cockpit seat having same effect. Crew is either cramped, unable to exert force of body, or too far away.
3. Helmsman's position forward in cockpit interfering with the winching crew.
4. Mainsheet track doing the same thing.

Immediate measures suggesting themselves are therefore clear separation of crew and helmsman, winch position in or across the coaming rather than outside it and possibly no cockpit seat, or at least a narrow one in way of the sheet winch.

If a second pair of winches is carried intended for spinnaker work, remember that these are more usually operated at less of an angle of heel nor is the loading as great as those last few inches on the genoa. As the yacht becomes larger the problem eases for siting, although greater loads have to be coped with, and since in the small boats the sheets are at far less tension, which alleviates the space problem, I feel that most difficulty with crew work on winches arises in yachts between 22 and 25 ft. LWL. It is here that layout needs especially careful planning. Sometimes yachts have a single genoa winch amidships, probably on the bridge deck, the crew standing in the hatch to work it. This saves weight and gives a firm base to the winch man, but can interfere with access to the cabin and obstruct the cockpit. Several yachts have sheet winches on the coachroof. On larger yachts this keeps men out of the cockpit, but is insecure for them in bad weather. Then there have to be alternative winches in the cockpit for offshore use, while the others are used inshore. On the T24 design by Guy Thompson and some yachts of this size (20 ft.), coachroof winches can be operated from the cockpit which keeps the crew at its forward end and eases congestion. Coaming mounted winches must have clear waterways past them and this particularly applies to GRP yachts. When a GRP yacht is standardized with a winch base as part of the cockpit moulding, remember that you may wish to install a non-standard type for racing or when a new type appears on the market. So there should either be a liberal sized base, or a separate structure, which can be in metal. Do not forget the stowage of winch handles; rubber or plastic hose is cheap, silent, does not collect water, and can be put so that the winch man's hand goes straight for the handle, drawing, so to speak, the sword from its scabbard. One day he will throw it in the sea instead of back in its stowage, so there must be spares down below.

Winch design Ocean racing winches have gradually assumed a common pattern, based on operating experiences forced by the large foretriangles and hard driving of the modern yacht. Except in the smallest yachts where, as already explained, laminated plastic and bronze are acceptable for non-geared winches, the materials employed are manganese bronze for the casting and stainless steel for machined parts. PTFE, a synthetic substance of very low friction has been employed in some bearings. Aluminium alloy is sometimes available as an alternative for the castings and Goiot of France have their standard range in light alloy. The appearance of alloy winch has to be a little bulky, but the Goiot winches are widely used on French offshore boats.

A winch must freewheel, which shows minimal friction and ensures unimpeded tailing before the load is taken. For ocean racing, silence is another requirement; not only does a ringing winch tell other yachts that you are tacking, but it seriously disturbs the crew off watch, even when small adjustments are made, say to a genoa when reaching in moderate weather. Anyone who has had to winch in wire or natural fibre sheets will appreciate plaited terylene, which is fine for winching. This has resulted in a consensus among foremost winch manufacturers, in a drum either parallel sided or very slightly wider at the top, to stretch the sheet as it moves up the barrel. The lower part of the barrel leaves the straight edge at about 110 degrees and curves gently down the extent of the base diameter; this part accepts the sheet from a level slightly lower than the winch and ensures smooth arrival on the drum without a riding turn. The longer the handle the better mechanical advantage, but the more awkward to wind. Eight inches is a comfortable length on a small yacht, 10 in. acceptable on larger. The Goiot handle spigots are permanently offset from the centre of the drum, which can sometimes make siting simpler.

TABLE OF SHEET WINCHES FOR MASTHEAD SLOOPS

(Details are given in this order: name; mechanical advantage; high gear ratio, low or only gear ratio; base diameter, weight.)

Genoa sheet winch LWL (ft.)	*Second or main sheet winch LWL (ft.)*	*Barient (USA)*	*Barlow (Aus.)*	*Goiot (Fr.)*	*Lewmar (Eng.)*	*Barton (Eng.)*
16–19	19–21		No. 14 4·6 —, 1:1 $3\frac{1}{2}$ in., 3 lb.	No. 50 5·4 —, 1:1 $5\frac{1}{8}$ in., 3 lb.	No. 843 5·6 —, 1:1 $3\frac{5}{8}$ in., $4\frac{3}{4}$ lb. No. 7 (alloy) 6 —, 1:1 $4\frac{1}{4}$ in., 3 lb. No. 8 7·6 —, 1:1 $4\frac{1}{4}$ in., 6 lb.	No. 311 5·5 —, 1:1 $3\frac{3}{4}$ in., 4 lb. (Bottom action)
19–21	21–23	No. 10 7·6 —, 1:1 4 in., 5 lb.	No. 16 5·7 —, 1:1 4 in., 7 lb.	No. 55 Luxe 15·6 —, 3·9:1 $5\frac{1}{8}$ in., 6 lb.	No. 25 25 1:1, 3·5:1 $4\frac{3}{16}$ in., 9 lb.	No. 312 6 —, 1:1 $4\frac{1}{2}$ in., 7 lb. (Tufnol and bronze)
21–23	23–26	No. 20 14·4 —, 2·3:1 $5\frac{3}{4}$ in., $14\frac{3}{4}$ lb.	No. 24 34 1:1, 5·5:1 $5\frac{3}{4}$ in., 14 lb.		No. 1022 19 —, 3·3:1 $6\frac{5}{8}$ in., 17 lb. No. 40 40 1:1, 6:1 $5\frac{1}{2}$ in., $5\frac{1}{2}$ lb.	*Yacht Tests (Eng.)*
23–26	26–28	No. 26 34·6 1:1, 7:1 7 in., 22 lb.	No. 28 35 25:1, 7:1 8 in., 33 lb.	No. 60 Luxe 22 —, 5:1 $6\frac{3}{4}$ in., 13 lb.	No. 922 30 —, 6:1 $7\frac{3}{4}$ in., 17 lb.	No. MS 1 2·5 1:1, 5:1 $7\frac{3}{8}$ in., 17 lb.
over 26	over 28			No. 65 Luxe 25·6 —, 6:1 $8\frac{5}{8}$ in., 22 lb. (All light drums)	No. 923 38 2:1, 7·6:1 $8\frac{1}{2}$ in., 29 lb.	No. MS 2 48 (17 in. handle) 4:1, 10:1 $8\frac{3}{4}$ in., 27 lb. (Alloy castings)

FIG. 115

Female connection on the winch is essential for quick insertion of handle and safety; some old winches have an ugly spigot projecting from their centre. The recessed connection can be so shaped that the handle can be inserted from six or eight directions. Whatever the design for maximum effectiveness, the winch must be easily dismantled at sea with a minimum of tiny parts to lose. A good winch will only have thin oil as a lubricant; anything else will combine with sea water and increase friction.

The question arises whether to have single- or two-speed winches. The present fashion in the better winches is to have them two-speed, but for yachts under 24 ft. it is worth investigating whether a suitable single-speed winch is available. On boats of this size, if the sheet cannot be pulled in by hand round the winch, then it is unlikely to work with a handle in high gear and the low gear has to be used anyway. A further disadvantage of two-speed winches is that they cannot be ratcheted, without a special handle with the ratchet in it. However, on yachts over 24 ft., they are of service, for if the gear is low enough it will not be necessary to ratchet and the high gear enables the sheet to be brought in fast. Reversing the handle direction changes gear.

The table (Fig. 115) shows some winches suitable for small ocean racers. Sail area or size is not normally enough to specify when choosing a winch, because of different boats and the purpose for which they are used. However, here we can take a yacht which is raced inshore and offshore and which has the biggest masthead genoa carried to windward up to around 20 knots at times.

The mechanical advantage or "power" of a winch is given by:

$$\frac{\text{Radius of handle}}{\text{Radius of drum and sheet}} \times \text{gear ratio}$$

The gear ratio is given by:

$$\frac{\text{Number of handle revolutions}}{\text{Number of drum revolutions}}$$

It follows that merely increasing the length of handle increases the power and that gearless winches are entirely dependent on the length of handle for mechanical advantage. The makes of winch shown have been developed particularly for offshore racing: Barient in USA, Barlow in Australia, Goiot in France and Lewmar and Yacht Tests in England. My recommendations here are sometimes for larger sizes than the manufacturers would show.

·14·

THE WORKING PLATFORM

THOSE aspects of gear on deck closely concerned with the rig demand our first attention, but the deck area of an ocean racer is all part of the working platform so there are a number of items which should be given close consideration. A really efficient deck lay-out is a joy to see as well as satisfactory to sail on and, like a comfortable cabin, it recruits good crews for the yacht. The area given over to cockpit and coachroof determines the amount of deck proper and present tendencies are to have this as large as possible. Moderate freeboard and large beam contribute, the freeboard allowing enough room below without unduly extending the coachroof. "Flush deck" is a rather vague term given to the arrangement on yachts at the beginning of the century, where there was no coachroof, only a skylight in the deck, and the same term seems to be applied now where the coachroof has been reduced to a small size or a blister. By the early 1950s the coachroof had gone through various stages and for yachts of all sizes the dog-house was the rule. This gives extra headroom just forward of the cockpit, but it is not a very strong structure and invariably has a moderate area of glass. Now dog-houses are out of fashion again. Modern mainsheet systems and GRP coachroofs which can rise gently in the after-end have made such structure less desirable. There was also a feeling that they lacked seaworthiness, the most celebrated case in the 1950s being the Vertue class, *Vertue XXXV*, which was flung on her dog-house in the Atlantic and nearly foundered as a result.

In yachts over 21 ft., a coachroof ending short of the mast is smart and practical giving more deck space and better provision for strength in way of the mast. Under this size adequate headroom will still be required below, but convex sheer or camber to the deck can contribute to this. With an ocean racing lay-out below the headroom should not be needed forward of the mast. In very small racers the flush deck may be achieved by taking the whole coachroof out to the side, but this has to be done cleverly to avoid a slab appearance. A curve or flat slope between deck and topsides can be fairly easily introduced in a GRP moulding and it can still be used for shrouds and genoa fairleads.

The cockpit Experienced yachtsmen get heated in discussions on cockpits so perhaps it is unwise to be dogmatic. Everyone agrees that the shape he dislikes is uncomfortable and impracticable or even dangerous and he has probably spent unpleasant hours in the sort which has earned his disapproval. Some of the trouble is that cockpits are designed for different things, but for a small ocean racer, at least we can say what is required for it:

1. Comfortable steering at all angles of heel for the helmsman.
2. Reasonable view forward for the helmsman (it is accepted that owing to low-cut genoas that this may have to be supplemented by other members of the crew).
3. Places for instruments and compass (see Chapter 5).

4. Room for crew to work the headsail winches and other gear (e.g. trim tab, halyards brought aft, bilge pump).
5. Room for the watch on deck to sit in security in bad weather. (While crew weight should be distributed along the boat, the off watch men will achieve this in correctly sited bunks below.)
6. It is helpful if it can give some measure of protection against weather.
7. It will need to conform with the relevant safety regulations.

Requirement 7 covers the proviso that the cockpit should not hold a dangerous amount of water.

Cockpit designs can be broadly classified into what I call the American type, the Scottish type and others. The American type is characterized by seats level with the deck and low coamings; it is "large and flat". The Scottish is deep with seats well into it, but the sole is so far down that self-draining or even watertight features are not possible. Each has been developed by the local conditions: the American for fine weather, where it is fun to sit and see what is happening around; the Scottish is useful where the climate is often harsh, but the size of seas in the lee of the islands is unlikely to involve pooping. For offshore work the sea can be as nasty to a small boat in one ocean as in another. However, it is conceded that in climates that are warmer than north-west Europe a bigger—that is longer—cockpit is desirable, but to keep the volume within safe limits it must not be deep: the result is the American type, but how far it is ideal offshore has to be judged by those using it.

For offshore racing in small yachts there is no question that a vessel must be able to be sealed, so that with hatchways closed no water can enter. Doors opening into the cockpit are not acceptable and it should be possible to fill the cockpit with water, so that it then proceeds to drain over the deck and through the drains connected to the cockpit sole. It should not be forcing its way into the accommodation at this stage, so a bridge deck or bulkhead up to the water level which the cockpit holds is needed. A large wave filling the cockpit is one possible reason for these precautions but a more common one is that continual spray soon accumulates and it must drain away and not into the yacht. Cockpit lockers are a problem, for as fitted to standard boats they are seldom watertight and it is best not to have any at all. For deck gear which you do not mind getting soaked, a locker which is sealed on sides and bottoms and drains back into the cockpit does no harm, but for any volume calculation it should be counted as part of the cockpit. If the yacht has to have cockpit lockers, then there must be some method of clamping down the lid. A bilge pump should not be sited in such a locker: several yachts have been in difficult conditions and found that the open locker through which the pump was being operated was letting in quantities of water. In the JOG committee, we wrestled with this question for some time and consulted many experienced yachtsmen and designers and for 1969 came up with the following rule:

> The cockpit must be watertight to seat level except that outboard drains are permitted. The overall volume shall be limited by the following formula, the product of which must not exceed 7

$$\frac{100V}{FB(LWL+\dfrac{LOA-LWL)}{3}}$$

where *V* is volume of cockpit in cu. ft. up to deck level, i.e. excluding coamings;
F is freeboard at 50% *LWL*;
B is maximum beam.

Locker space in the cockpit must have well fitting lids which are secured by clips or similar fittings or lashings when racing. It must be possible to secure the companion way (hatch) to the cabin in rough weather to prevent ingress of water in the event that the cockpit be flooded to the coamings.

Elsewhere there is a rule about bilge pumps which states, "not be fitted in a cockpit locker if only one is carried".

Drains, coamings, seats   The cockpit drains should be at least 1-in. diameter in yachts over 20 ft. and not less than $\frac{1}{2}$-in. diameter in smaller boats. Generally they cross over below the cockpit and then go to skin fittings which must have seacocks. Naturally the cockpit sole needs to be above the waterline, when the yacht is upright or heeled, though in small yachts it may have to be accepted that a little water collects on the lee side. In the Contessa class, a Folkboat type designed by David Sadler, the cockpit sole is a few inches below waterline. In this case the watertight cockpit has to be manually bailed or pumped out as drains cannot be fitted. To save the racing surface of the hull some designers fit drains, through the stern just above the waterline, but this can lead to a "self-filling" cockpit, especially when running! Drains must be easily stripped down and a suitably shaped brush on very stiff wire should be carried as blockage of cockpit drains is commonplace.

Seats may be formed out of the lockers which we have just discussed, or be moulded as part of the deck structure. Probably the quarter berths will be below them. However, on yachts over about 25 ft. separate seats are worth considering (Fig. 116). The type that Raymond Wall designed for *Summertime* were close slatted, so that they were comfortable yet held no water. It was possible to put one's feet under the seat opposite and brace them on a bar which ran across, an excellent arrangement for helmsman and others when sitting to windward with the yacht heeled.

Coamings will ideally be at least 9 inches high and slope outwards; if they are less and also vertical to the seats, they merely constitute a nasty ridge sticking into your back. The actual depth is dependent on the size of yacht, but if the seats are sunk below deck level, it becomes possible to achieve the depth: the sloping out will be very much appreciated in use by any human body. The object of coamings as well as keeping water out of the cockpit and the crew and gear in it, is to provide some protection from the weather and even one of minimum height breaks wind and sea, and keeps the worst off the crew in their foul weather gear. A good system is for the coamings to be designed in conjunction with a breakwater running up on to the coachroof. On the Swan 36 and several other Sparkman and Stephens boats the coaming and breakwater is one continuous moulding and quite a massive affair but it does keep the water out. On the T24 the coamings extend almost to the side of the yacht and then sweep forward level with the coachroof coaming which they join. The breakwater is separate and further forward.

P

Deck and deck surface The deck surface on any ocean racer must be non-slip. In many standard boats, as offered, this is not so and the owner must take steps to correct this in the interests of efficient crew work and safety. GRP, however moulded, is always too slippery. Patterns in it, whether of diamond shape or imitation leather, do not provide sufficient grip. This is one point where the builder or supplier of the boat will not agree, but anyone with offshore experience will appreciate that some form of sanded effect is positively essential. GRP decks can be treated with an epoxy finish with fine sand mixed in it and a subsequent coat put on to seal it. Wooden decks can receive much the same treatment with a polyurethane paint and sand, these synthetic coatings additionally giving a completely watertight seal to the plywood.

There are other horizontal surfaces such as hatches and cockpit seats that will be stood on. The seats may be hard on clothing if sanded, so, here, bare teak, although adding a little weight, is ideal. Bare teak is a good non-slip surface for such places and perhaps a cockpit grating. Indeed, in the larger yachts the deck itself may be teak, the current system being to lay plywood and then thin strips of teak to give the impression of a laid deck. One thing not to use on horizontal surfaces is varnish, but if appearance dictates it, or if sailing a yacht where this is already found, the answer is strips of "Safety walk", a wonderful self-adhesive, non-slip material made by Minnesota, Mining and Manufacturing Co. Ltd., London, put over the existing surface. I have tested "Safety Walk" by using it in the bottom of a dinghy exposed to all the elements for a season and habitually under several inches of water, and it remained unaffected.

Additional deck aids should be provided in the form of handrails or toerails or the two combined. On the foredeck toerails running fore and aft should also have hand grips in them. On a number of yachts the handrails along the coachroof stop inexplicably at some point, leaving perhaps a gap before the crew reaches the shrouds. Check right along from aft to forward that a man can crawl along with a firm handhold throughout the length of the yacht. Toerails in way of the gunwale are essential otherwise there is nothing to bring the foot to when on the leeward deck. I was amazed to see a new One Tonner launched with no toerails recently and I regard this as a false economy when trying to save weight. On the other hand they must have adequate scuppers and there is a tendency by boatyards to drill these so that the deck drains on the mooring. The drain should be at the lowest point of the toerail when heeled. Apart from being irritating, you do not want to increase weight by carrying sea around on deck!

A useful item is a halyard box. Assuming it is not acceptable to stow the halyards on the mast because of windage, or with winches on deck, the ends need to be put somewhere; a low coaming round the mast or just aft of it may be the answer. This is also useful for winch handles and other deck tools thrown down when work is in progress. On *Sootica*, a 24 ft. Holman and Pye design in steel, part of this box has a lid for permanent stowage of handles. The coamings must be provided with small scuppers, but which will not let such things as marline-spikes slide out.

Hatches In wooden yachts the forehatch should be made with watertight double coamings and the advantage of this is that it is leak proof as soon as it is slammed shut. Increasing use of GRP means that a more common type on small yachts is the simple moulding which relies on clamps to hold it tight and it can only be finally sealed from below. Whatever the arrangement the forehatch should be on strong hinges. Securing with

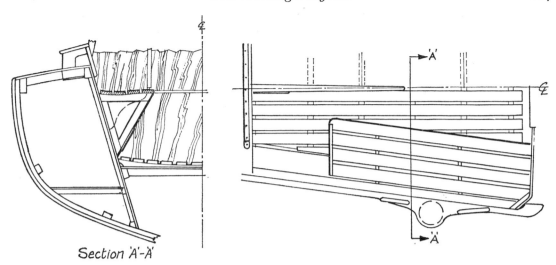

Section 'A'-'A'

FIG. 116. *Cockpit ideas in* Summertime. *The slatted seats of scrubbed teak are comfortably below the sloping out coaming, and they can hold no water. The teak grating raised above the cockpit sole is slightly dished. A stringer under each seat gives a foothold for a person sitting opposite. There are no cockpit lockers, but there is room below abreast of the cockpit for the feet of a quarter berth or stowage.*

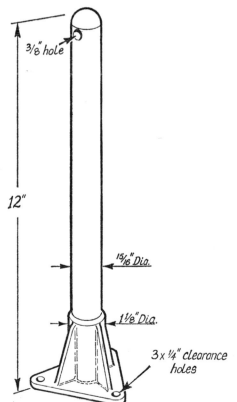

FIG. 117. *Stanchion 12 in. high to meet JOG rules, designed by George Stead. The alloy casting is grey plastic coated.*

shock cord is not satisfactory and on some standard boats the hatch arrives loose. On one such yacht I tried out, the GRP forehatch blew away! These remarks apply to other hatches for access to counter lockers (lazarette). A popular type of hatch is the Goiot in cast alloy and smoked glass. It is strong and tight-fitting. For the main hatch there is really only one satisfactory method and that is sliding into a box. The breakwater mentioned above may join to this box, or if a pram hood is carried it can go over it. A hinging hatch can also be made waterproof, but it is awkward for continual use. If the hatch does not adjoin the cockpit as on the Stephens One Tonner *Al Na'ir IV* from Italy, where it is in the centre of the short coachroof, then hinges may be convenient.

Lifelines and pulpit RORC special regulations and North American Yacht Racing Union offshore regulations specify double lifelines of 24 in. in height and this is ideal for crew safety. Such a height starts to get awkward on yachts of 22 ft. and below and JOG and other organizations have various rules to cope with this. It is therefore only necessary to comply with the regulations under which the yacht is sailed, but for offshore work I recommend for yachts 19–22 ft. WL double lifelines all round (i.e. pulpit and pushpit aft) to a height of 18 in. and, for yachts 16–19 ft., a single 12 in. lifeline with an 18 in. pulpit and not necessarily any pushpit. While 24 in. and 18 in. stanchions are often available as standard, 12 in. ones are not so easy to find. An excellent one is made by George Stead of Poole, England, in grey nylon dipped cast aluminium alloy, details of which are shown in Fig. 117. Stanchion bases must be designed to withstand an outward load and even an inward one. I remember *Shewolf*'s stanchion bases being forced out of the deck by the pressure inwards of the spinnaker guy, while we were waiting for a reaching strut to come from the manufacturers. Holes for lifelines must be bushed. The only time I have fallen overboard from a yacht when racing was when a lifeline parted. It had rusted through where the stanchion (unbushed) had cut through the plastic coating. Away from the immediate area of the stanchion, the wire was excellent beneath the plastic. Plastic coated line is always preferable, being easier on hands and sails, but if there is a section the sheets pull across each time the genoa is sheeted in, a lightweight shroud roller is worth fitting. With the ends of lifelines swaged direct to a screw end of a rigging screw, this can then be threaded through the stanchions when installing or removing.

Nylon insulators, now standard, must be fitted to break the loop of the lines round the yacht and obviate interference with RDF work. When lifelines have been set up they should be tested by jumping on them! It is up to the designer to space the stanchions where they will give support to the lifelines and at the same time not interfere with other fittings such as the swing of a winch handle. Most offshore regulations specify an interval: in the RORC this is 7 ft. and in the Half Ton Cup 1·5 metres (5 ft.). This latter spacing is a good one for yachts under 24 ft. Some yachts have stanchions angled out to accommodate the genoa, when sheeted, but this is usually limited by rules, the RORC allowing no more than a 10-degree slope from the vertical. A way of getting round this is to have a step out in the stanchion so that it grows from a point further out than the stanchion base in an approximately vertical line. There seems no objection to this, if it is adequately strong, except on the grounds of expense. Naturally, where the stanchion is outside the width of the topsides at any point, handling in harbour has to be watched.

Pulpit and pushpit. In some ways the pushpit is more of a safety precaution than the pulpit. Without it the lifelines have to begin sloping down to a dead-end on deck at just the place a man could be tipped out of the cockpit. In small yachts it is really a continuation of the lifeline and keeps everyone snugly in the after-part of the yacht. In larger craft, the stern deck seems very bare without one and anyway they are compulsory and general practice. Mount the stern light on the pushpit to give it better height than the deck can provide. One arrangement of which I am not in favour is the backstay linking to a centre strut of the pushpit, however firmly this strut is anchored to the hull to take a big tension. If the pushpit is damaged, an event in which I have been involved at a crowded start, the mast would be endangered. In our case the backstay was quite independent and we tightened up on the lifelines and continued the race complete with battered pushpit.

Pulpit designs come in all varieties: some are more useful than others. Here is a list of points to look for:

1. The feet must be just as secure as those of stanchions.
2. Except in the smallest yachts there should be room for one man ahead of the forestay for sail handling.
3. But it must hold him snugly. Two rails are more secure in pulpits over 18 in. high. If this interferes with bringing in the mooring, a detachable wire can be used for the lower rail.
4. Pulpit rests for the spinnaker booms are useful where a twin-pole gybe is used. Beckets welded to the pulpit, assist as places to snap halyard shackles and those of spinnaker sheets.
5. Navigation lights will have to be mounted on the pulpit in order not to be obscured by sails: they must be sited where they are not going to be damaged by other gear, especially in spinnaker work.
6. A spinnaker turtle should be made to fit the pulpit.

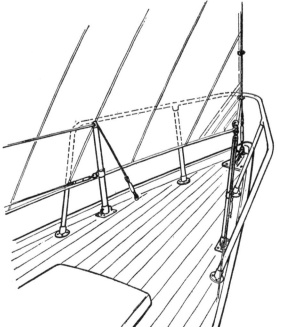

FIG. 118. *A method of sheeting the genoa close-hauled outside the lifelines. The lifelines supported by stanchions and the pulpit are separated but overlapping.*

The genoa when close-hauled will be sheeted inside the normal pulpit, but as the sheet is eased the foot of the sail begins to lift over it, as discussed in the chapter on sails. If the safety regulations permit there are several methods of allowing for this. The lifelines can be crossed over just aft of the pulpit. This is usually banned by rules which specify a minimum height throughout. On small yachts, and this is the system on the Galion design, the pulpit may end on the foredeck, the genoa and forestay being outside it. This is a good arrangement, permitting the hand to chock himself on a secure part of the yacht. Naturally, the distance from the forestay must be limited for easy working on it.

A further system on larger yachts involves ending the lifelines with a dead-end and the pulpit overlapping them at its after end (Fig. 118). This has its origin in the USA and means that the genoa can be slotted between the two structures and is always sheeted outside the lifelines.

Stowage of life-raft and dinghy **(Fig. 119)**   These major items if carried pose a problem, but at least the days when the coachroof had to be designed for a solid dinghy are over. Inflatable neoprene dinghies made by Avon Rubber Company, or similar craft, are carried. Sometimes these are supplied with solid floorboards and a type should be chosen that does not need these, otherwise stowage is more difficult. The rubber dinghy should be stowed below in its bag, which enables it to be compressed. It is possible that the dinghy will be wanted in a hurry at some time, as for instance, to lay out a kedge anchor after running aground. This is where an inflatable is at a disadvantage, owing to the time taken to blow it up. The solution here is to equip it with a CO_2 bottle to be used in emergency only: normally the dinghy will be inflated by bellows. The life-raft must be readily accessible. Some organizations state that it must be on deck or immediately accessible to the deck. Rightly, they usually add that if it is in a compartment, then nothing else must be kept in there. The MORC in USA, recognizing the difficulties of small boats, allow the raft to be kept below, but it must be immediately accessible to the companion-way. The JOG have reviewed the problem over the years for yachts under 24 ft. but refuse to make life-rafts compulsory, though they recommend them for their larger boats. A common place for stowage is on top of the coachroof. Here it interferes with the kicking-strap, puts weight and windage in the wrong place, gets trodden on by the crew and is in a place to be swept away by a heavy sea in extreme conditions when it might be wanted. From this you will gather, I do not think much of such a site. If some special form of locker can be designed for the life-raft, then this is the answer. On *Summertime* it was on slats raised from the cockpit sole abaft the tiller. On many yachts, it may be possible to allot a complete cockpit locker, sealed from the rest of the yacht, of course, and draining back into the cockpit. The weight is in the wrong place aft, but there are few possibilities forward. The main point here is that if the yacht is in the design stage the life-raft should be considered. British life-rafts are sold with various scales of equipment included. The most common is the "RORC pack", which is mandatory when racing with that club and for most others. However, for smaller boats there are life-rafts with canopies, but without the extra bulk and weight of all the items of the RORC pack.

Miscellaneous matters on deck   *Use of shock cord.* Heavy duty shock cord has various uses, including holding down halyards, spinnaker poles, and holding up blocks. Ocean

TABLE OF SIZES FOR LIFERAFT AND DINGHY STOWAGE

Dinghies

Avon Neoprene (no floorboards)

LOA when inflated (ft.)	Capacity (persons)	Length by dia. (cylindrical kitbag stowage) (in.)	Weight (lb.)
8	2–3	33 × 18	33
9	4–5	40 × 18	40
10	5–6	43 × 20	45
12	6–7	43 × 20	52

Oars, bellows and CO_2 Bottle (if used) not included in these dimensions.

Life-rafts

Type	Container	Dimensions (in.)	Weight with RORC pack (lb.)
Avon 4-man	Valise	23 × 13	42
Avon 6-man	Valise	25 × 13	55
Avon 8-man	Valise	28 × 15	80
Beaufort 4-man	Valise	28 × 12	66
Beaufort 6-man	Valise	29 × 12	74
RFD Tern 4-man	Plastic container	25 × 18 × 7	48 (RORC pack not complete)
RFD Teal 8-man	Plastic container	30 × 20 × 13	86

FIG. 119.

racing strains tend to ask a lot of it and it does perish. It should usually be backed up by some other means, such as a lashing.

Spinnaker boom stowage. This is an example where shock cord is often used in various ways. However, the ideal stowage muzzles the forward end of the spinnaker booms; then they cannot be lifted by a big sea or be fouled by a stray line. The after-end can push down on to snug chocks. Whatever the system, it must be a matter of "fit and forget" once on a beat to windward.

Leads. Not only sheets need fairleads. The foreguy coming aft to the cockpit can well come through a simple bull's-eye to limit its freedom over the deck. The same applies to other lines such as spinnaker topping lifts or the stretch luff genoa tackle.

Electrical connections on deck. So-called watertight plugs and sockets are often seen on deck joining, for instance, the lead from the navigation light on the pulpit to the power supply below. Another place is at the foot of a deck stepped mast for the spreader or steaming lights or for connecting a compass. Such fittings with tiny screws and components are just not appropriate on the deck of an ocean racer and will fail you sooner or later. The best method is to lead the wire from the mast or pulpit direct through the deck, which can be sealed by a tight gland. The hole for the wiring need only be very small. The necessary connections can be made once the wire is below, by means of a junction box.

Cleats and fairleads. Older cruising yachts always seem to be covered with many cleats of different shapes and sizes, while some modern racing yachts have so few that one wonders how they ever moor up. Perhaps they are hauled straight out of the water at the end of each race! It seems a pity to have to press genoa cleats into use for making fast the yacht herself. Modern cleats can be obtained in very light weight, and designs like those of the Lewmar Marine nylon-coated cast hollow aluminium are excellent. They seem to have got the shape just right and there are four well spaced fixing holes. With nylon-coated cleats and synthetic warp there is minimal friction, so it is advisable to take a few extra turns. The usual bow and stern fairleads must be provided. From the racing point of view it is a bad policy to try to save weight by an insufficient bow fairlead for the anchor cable. If the kedge is to be brought in smartly as soon as the wind returns after a calm, then a good lead is required. On smaller yachts there need not be a roller if there is a soft mouth which will enable a kedge warp to be hauled in, even if it is at a wide angle or tending to run under the yacht. What is not acceptable is to try to bring in a kedge warp over a common port or starboard fairlead at the bow.

Anchors and cable. These are common to every ship that goes to sea. Most rules insist that two are carried and the main anchor, which is heavier, should be stowed as low in a small ocean racer as possible. One assumes that it will not be required except in an emergency. The kedge anchor should also be carried below where its weight will not do any harm, but it must be readily available at all times: the normal system will be to pass it up through the forehatch. The RORC no longer insists on chain being carried and most yachts will prefer to have synthetic warp. Nylon is usually recommended because of its elasticity, but for quick kedging this very property can make it difficult to break out. So for yachts without chain perhaps the answer is a nylon main cable, which should be preserved for this job only and a light terylene three-strand warp on a reel for kedging. It pays to carry an adequate length of kedge warp for the waters in which you sail. Three fathoms of chain for the smaller yachts and four for the larger is recommended between the anchor and the warp. If chain is carried, it should also be in the lowest part of the yacht. The hawse pipe on the deck of an ocean racer is best sealed right off when not in use: a metal flush-deck plate is adequate.

To save weight, CQR or Danforth anchors should be used. A modern ocean racer because of her comparatively low air and water resistance will not put a greater demand on the size of anchor and cable than is estimated for the standard recommendations for this size of equipment.

37. The working platform. Teamwork on deck of an Armagnac class yacht hoisting spinnaker calls for well laid out gear.

38. The foredeck of *Rafale* discloses combined grab and foot rail, threaded line to prevent headsail falling under rail, small but solid pulpit, light strong fairleads, tack wire to work stretch luff headsail.

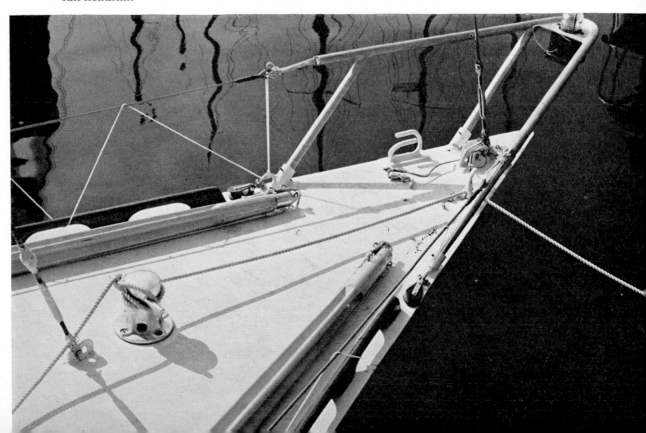

39. T24 class coachroof with halyard and sheet winches, grab rails, hatch box, breakwater. Note shrouds set well inboard to aid genoa sheeting.

40. Cockpits
   (a) Swan 36 (LWL 25 ft. 6 in.) with large breakwater and mainsheet winch at aft end of coachroof.

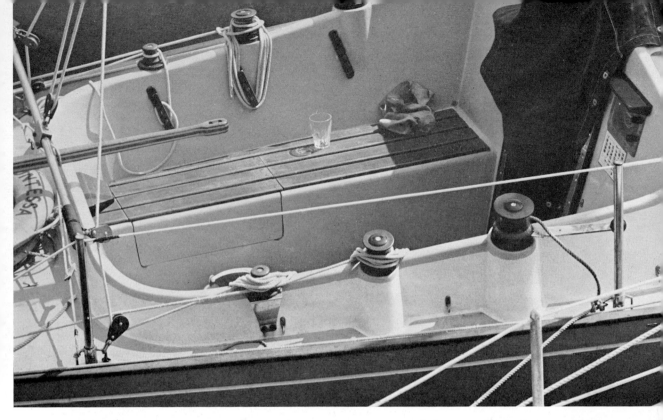

(b) *Contessa* (LWL 20 ft.). Plenty of protection to crew and three small winches per side for optimum sail handling.

(c) *Shakashe* (LWL 17 ft.). Even in this size there are top action winches, roller mainsheet traveller and adequate purchase on the kicking strap. There is room for the crew forward of helmsman.

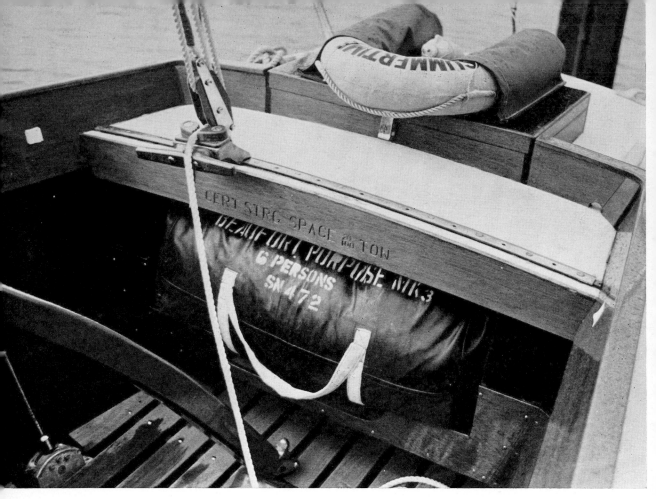

41. Life-raft stowage inside a protected position in the cockpit.

42. Ventilation box with low windage vent of soft plastic.

·15·

BELOW DECKS
(22 ft. LWL and over)

The best accommodation for an ocean racer is a hull empty but for a load of hay. It gives the best ballast ratio. The crew can sleep in it and eat it. At the end of a race it can be mucked out ready for a fresh lot next time—Traditional ocean racing answer to a question about the best type of cabin

As IT is the size of a man rather than the boat that determines the cabin fitments and accommodation, ingenuity in arranging matters below decks becomes more necessary the smaller the yacht. If it is possible to draw a line below which a rather specialized attitude is required towards the cabin, if the yacht is to remain a genuine offshore racer, that limit is in the region of 22 ft. LWL. So this chapter looks at yachts above that size: while many of the points discussed apply to all yachts, matters which apply particularly to yachts under 22 ft. are dealt with in the following chapter. If there are still exceptions to these suggestions when thinking of the smallest boats (14–18 ft.), then their particular circumstances are considered in Chapter 18. It is well known that the amount of room inside a yacht, in other words its volume, is a cubic measure and the difference between a yacht of 20 ft. and one of, say, 23 ft. is very striking. By the same token, once we are dealing with yachts less than about 18 ft., the lack of space for the essentials of racing becomes a real problem.

Few standard yachts are designed with an eye to the racing market only and it is in the accommodation that compromise becomes most difficult. Some builders offer two or three standard layouts, one of which is a "racing" one, but this seems to be less and less common as factory-type production becomes the rule. Here we will be looking only at racing layouts for offshore work or a combination of offshore and inshore work, the latter being a day affair having little influence on the arrangement below, except the requirement that there shall be as little of it as possible. The owner will have to decide for himself how much he is prepared to compromise with cruising facilities. What we really mean here is "harbour facilities", for once on passage the interior of the cruising yacht has the same needs as a racer. So if I do not mention the cabin table or pressurized water system, it means that such equipment is of little help in winning races.

This does not mean that accommodation should not be suitable for harbour use, where this is an aid to racing. For instance, the crew join late and the yacht sails down to near the start line, where she will be ready for the race which begins next morning. I did this recently in a yacht which left West Mersea and sailed through the Ray Sand Channel to anchor at the mouth of the River Crouch for one of the East Anglian ORA races. It obviously paid us to have room to sleep the crew in comfort, so that they would be rested for the 90-mile race on the morrow.

Rules about accommodation   While our thoughts are running on how far you can "strip out" a yacht's interior, there are rules as to minimum accommodation laid down by a number of clubs and organizations. The JOG rules give two bunks as a minimum and mention a stove capable of safe operation at sea. They also stipulate a W.C. or fitted bucket. The RORC has little to say in its regulations about the cabin, feeling no doubt that as most of its races are of 200 miles or more, owners will not find it pays to opt out of providing proper facilities for the crew below. This is the best way of preventing the ultimate "load of hay" approach. If the courses are of an offshore nature, that is where the crew without proper sleep and food will lose efficiency; and where navigation demands proper facilities, the design of accommodation will develop along lines that must be right for an ocean racing crew at sea. The NAYRU offshore equipment lists mention bunk cushions and permanently installed water tanks, which would be much better left to the discretion of the owner. On this business of equipment, Ian Cameron, who had been on the JOG committee for a number of years, said that every time a new piece of equipment was introduced into the rules, the committee should find an existing one that could be crossed off!

The One Ton and Half Ton Cup regulations are more explicit on accommodation. Presumably this is because of the high incidence of inshore races and the international pressure of competition. They are alone in specifying headroom. The One Ton Cup uses the rules of International 8-metre cruiser-racer class and the Half Ton lays down actual figures. The Half Ton rules also require a fresh-water pump, a sink which drains to the sea, a hanging locker "for at least four coat hangers", W.C. and other items. More of the Half Ton rules are given in the Appendix 5. Rule making is a thankless task, but what appears reasonable to one person does not to another. Swedish boats entering for the Half Ton Cup have pointed out that in the Baltic, where there is no tide, chemical lavatories are the rule in the interest of hygiene, but for the Half Ton Cup they have to make holes in the side of the hull for a discharge type W.C. An addition to a yacht in order to comply with the letter of the rules was made by Adlard Coles in *Cohoe III* in the first One Ton races of 1965: this was a draining sink which was actually installed under a quarter berth and used for carrying the ship's papers and cash. The crew then continued to wash up in a separate plastic bowl as always.

Cabin Essentials   Anyone who visits boat shows knows that the quality of yachts most widely advertised is the number of bunks that can be fitted in. The winner in this respect must be a 35 ft. trimaran, which boasts of ten permanent bunks—what does everyone do when she is sailing and how many trips in the dinghy are needed to take them ashore? I am afraid that the number of bunks also has to figure first when thinking of the living area of an ocean racer, though from a different viewpoint. The crew of a racing boat is large and it must be possible to sleep them all in harbour, but what affects the design below is the number who must be slept off watch. Remember, this may include skipper, navigator and cook. These people must sleep where they can do so in comfort in all conditions and where their weight is not detrimental to the performance. We will look at bunks further, but meanwhile the other essentials in the cabin of an ocean racer are:

1. That gear stays in its stowage however bad the weather and therefore the motion and angle of heel.
2. The minimum of water can come down below whether through hatches, with

members of the crew coming in and out or from bilge accumulation running up the sides of the yacht.

3. That some form of hot food can be made in bad weather.
4. That gear can be fetched from below without disturbing men in their bunks or the navigator at work.
5. That people sleeping, navigating or cooking do not conflict with each other.

Note that much of the reference above is to bad weather, because any cabin gets by when there is no angle of heel and when water is not trying to force its way below.

General arrangements   For ocean racing most of the men sleeping must be in the centre part of the yacht and the galley cannot be forward of them if it is to be usable at sea. This

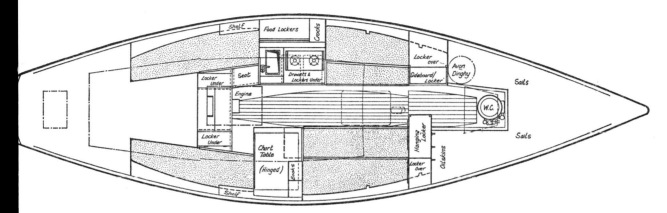

FIG. 120. *The accommodation plan of* Summertime *designed by Raymond Wall for the author and found to be highly practical at sea. Weight is kept out of the ends. Two men sleep off watch in pilot berths, and all the other berths are usable at sea. There is locker space under berths. Ideal sizes for chart table, galley and lockers have been attained by offsetting the saloon sole to port. Ample handholds are provided everywhere below. LOA 32 ft. 8 in., LWL 24 ft., beam 9 ft. 6 in.*

immediately limits the possible arrangements, though a number of variations on it are feasible. Over 24 ft. we can put a pilot berth each side and assuming the maximum beam is 9 ft. 6 in. or over a saloon berth can be on the inner edge of one of these. This is the arrangement in *Summertime*, where three people can be slept amidships as a result. One of the pilot berths merely has a short narrow seat (Fig. 120), but when there is 11 ft. 1¼ in. beam as in *Optimist* it is possible to have a saloon berth inside each pilot berth. *Optimist* could be said to represent an excellent example of a popular arrangement (Fig. 121). The chart table is just aft of the port pilot and saloon berth and the navigator sits on the head of his quarter berth to use it, while the galley is opposite. Such a galley can have a quarter berth aft of it, but the L-type galley can make use of stowage going aft a little way, while without a quarter berth on one side, a special cockpit lockerseat can act as life-raft stowage as suggested in the previous chapter.

Coming down to 22 ft. and attempting the same theme reduces the number of pilot berths possible to one, if any berth or seating is to be considered in the saloon. However the T31 (Fig. 80) has a pair of saloon berths in the right place with an extending berth on the port side. Aft of these we have the chart table, single quarter berth and L-shaped galley. In all of these boats and in this type of layout the lavatory is forward and the fo'c'sle used for sail stowage. If the lavatory is to one side it can be in its own compartment, or at least the fo'c'sle can be shut off from the saloon while it is in use, and this is desirable for crew comfort. One or two temporary bunks, such as pipe cots, can be rigged in the fo'c'sle for harbour sleeping, but because of the shape of the yacht in this area permanent bunks have to be higher than those in the cabin and therefore limit room available for sails.

Saloon berths with lockers   The second general arrangement for yachts of the size 22–28 ft. is to forgo pilot berths in favour of a spacious forward cabin. This may be a double or treble berth, or two singles, but brought into the boat enough to give standing head-room. Aft of this large fo'c'sle area would come the lavatory and probably hanging locker and washbasin. The saloon berths have lockers between them and the side of the yacht, with shelves on top. The galley and chart table are right aft on each side or with a yacht over 26 ft. there would be quarter berths, giving six bunks in all. This is an acceptable cruising arrangement and at sea the two in the saloon have their weight in the right place, with room for more in the quarter berths, if any. The snags in this arrangement are the fairly extensive lockers behind men who are asleep, with the likelihood of needing to disturb them to get at gear during the night and the forecabin which is of no use at sea, where there will be conflict between stowage of personal effects and so on in cabin lockers and the necessity to find somewhere for sails as well as warps, anchors, etc. This layout is usable at sea and really quite common on standard yachts where the builders think that pilot berths will scare off the cruising customer.

One way of achieving a separate double cabin without impairing the racing efficiency was seen on *Al Na'ir IV*, mentioned earlier. With the main hatch in the centre of the coach-roof the companion-way led down to the centre of the yacht. The after cabin was able to be on its own across the ship astern of this, with the chart table and navigator's seat between two single berths. The navigator was in touch with the cockpit through a special hatch in the after coachroof bulkhead. With some weight aft the engine box came up just abaft

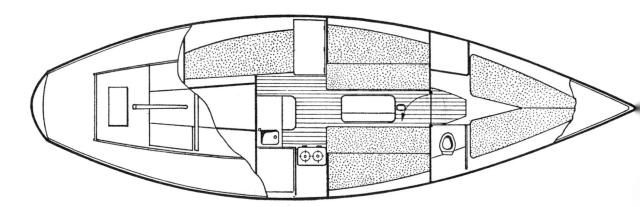

FIG. 121. *Layout of* Optimist *designed by Dick Carter and winner of the One Ton Cup in 1966. With 11 ft. 1¼ in. beam, the entire off watch crew can be slept abreast and just aft of the mast in two pilot and two saloon berths. At sea the fo'c'sle would only be used for sail stowage.*

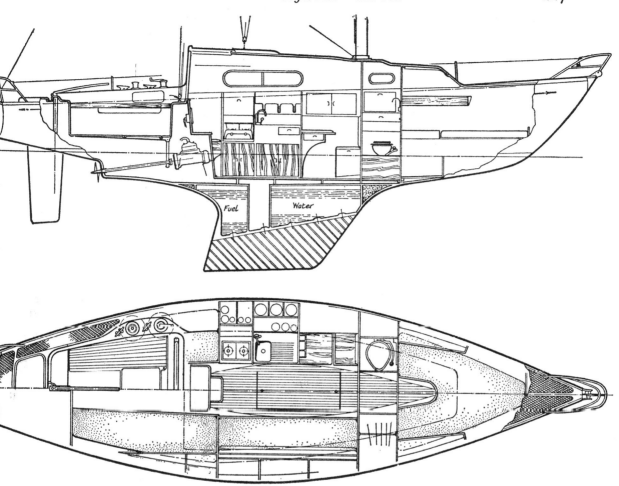

FIG. 122. *The Legend class layout designed by E. G. van de Stadt is a brave attempt to break away from the conventional arrangement. Both the galley and chart table on the same side of the yacht are each practical. It will not be possible to sleep two men off watch amidships. The Legend class is 22 ft. LWL and of GRP construction. Other points of interest in the layout of the yacht are the water and fuel tank positions, the cockpit moulding and the convenient position of the tiller within it.*

the mast in the centre of the saloon. The arrangement is ingenious, but probably not of wide appeal.

Dinette More and more yachts are seen with a dinette arrangement. I believe this started in caravans and went from there to motor cruisers and then to sailing yachts. In the dinette layout, the galley is on one side of the saloon with athwartships settees on the other and a cabin table between them. The main purpose of this is pleasant meal arrangements with the crew sitting at opposite sides of a table and food served from the galley a few feet away. Naturally, this applies in harbour or quiet weather. The table and settees are devised to convert into a double berth. The Swan 36 (sail plan in Fig. 97) had such a layout as standard and it did not seem to stop boats in the class winning races. But it really is only for yachts over 25 ft. where ocean racing is involved. This is because yachts of this size can find other bunks for the men off watch and the weight of individuals is not so important. On smaller yachts the dinette system causes a lack of ideal sea-going berths, though the galley can be made very practical. The arrangement on the Van de Stadt Legend class (Fig. 122) is unusual in that there is a settee berth opposite the galley, a very comfortable chart table being just forward of the latter. It represents a brave attempt to get away from the conventional. Assuming an offshore crew of five, the quarter berths will both have to be occupied at times, which means too much weight aft, with two men in the cockpit on watch and their companions immediately below them. The drawing shows the way in which the forward berths have to be lifted towards the deckhead, as mentioned above, with the resulting lack of room for sails.

Bunks Enough has been said to show that bunks must be sited in the right place and must be comfortable to sleep in. After all, they are where the men off watch (hope to) spend most of their time. To achieve comfort at sea the bunk should not be too wide, 22 inches is about right. Where a yacht is acclaimed as having "wide bunks", these are fine until she heels over, then a deep and comparatively narrow bunk is appreciated (Fig. 123). Even with a wooden side, as on a pilot berth, terylene leeboards should be provided for full security. If the bottom of the berth can be made of terylene or neoprene mesh this will save weight and because of its resilience, a bunk cushion of only $1\frac{1}{2}$ inches will be required. If the bunk bottom for structural reasons or to form a locker is solid, then the bunk cushion should be 2 inches. Bunk cushions should be in a completely water-tight material such as vinyl and a wide variety of surfaces and colours are now available. The colour of bunk cushions can do a lot to make an ocean racing layout, which to some eyes is rather too functional, congenial to be in. Blue and grey make the saloon look cool. Red colours and primrose are cheerful. The same coloured material can be used for associated cabin fabric such as splash prevention curtains, which are necessary in the mouths of quarter berths. In *Summertime* these rolled down from a stowed position to "poppers" along the edge of the bunk: they performed another function in keeping the bunk dark and aiding sleep in daylight. Generally, when on the wind the windward quarter berth has its terylene leeboard up and the leeward one has the splash curtain in position. In designing an accommodation full advantage should be taken of the foot area of bunks, where lockers can be built over, at the same time making a convenient stowage for bedding at the foot of the berth.

Galley Much ingenuity is now expended on galleys and modern materials again come to the rescue here to help keep things clean—a continual struggle when offshore and pre-paration of food is nearly impossible without some spillage. Formica surfaces, GRP mouldings, stainless steel and such things as disposable paper towels all help. The minimum of locker doors and the maximum of visible stowage by the use of deep fiddles is the ideal. One of the biggest differences immediately apparent from cooking at home is the lack of suffcient horizontal surface on which to prepare food. With the yacht heeled-over the preparations for a meal could not be spread around, anyway, while in harbour a horizontal chart table will earn its keep by being used for this job and is the answer to builders of standard boats who are worried that a chart table wastes space on a cruising yacht. An

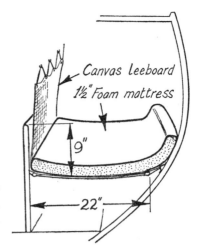

FIG. 123. *Pilot berth. The foam mattress is on terylene, which is laced to a batten inside the hull. In addition to the coaming, there is a terylene leeboard for acute angles of heel. The mattress runs up the side of the hull for comfort.*

L-shaped galley can be fitted with more horizontal area than one forward of a quarter berth: one possibility is a wood and formica cover fitting closely as a lid to the sink. Once offshore, adequate fiddles are more important than flat surfaces; everything has to be put against a fiddle—tins, knives, pieces of bread or anything else. These should be at least $\frac{3}{4}$ in. high with vertical sides. If one side slopes it should be the outer one. This applies to fiddles throughout the boat. A flat surface in the galley should even be broken up by fore and aft fiddles so that everything does not slide down to one side. These can be made removable by simple interlocking joinery work, which makes cleaning easy and gives more space when the yacht is on an even keel. Before leaving fiddles, which make for so much order and comfort at sea, it is worth mentioning that they should also be sited inside lockers immediately behind the doors and further in: then when the locker is on the windward side and the doors are opened, the contents do not fall out on top of you.

Another useful tip inside lockers is to criss-cross shock cord about 2 in. above the surface, and this will be found amazingly effective for keeping tins and jars in place. It is best to divide food stowage into:

1. *"Ready-use" stores.* These are things such as tea, milk, butter and bread which are in an easily reached locker and can be picked out individually as required.
2. *The Larder.* This is a mixture of tins, packets and so on which will be used for the meals due in the next twenty-four hours or so. A large locker in the area of the galley will be used and the food extricated from it when the meal is due.
3. *Stored food.* These are the supplies not required until the above two are exhausted and their extent depends on the length of the race. In a short race they are not needed, especially as it is these extra tins that are responsible for most of the weight associated with food. In a long race they must be stored in different parts of the yacht, the plan being to keep the weight low and out of the ends of the boat.

Hinged locker fronts are acceptable where the door does not swing out obstructively, but over the top of the stove, for instance, it is sounder to have sliding doors. Drawers should be kept to a minimum as they are heavy for the amount of stowage they offer. One or two for specific purposes may be useful, cutlery stowage for instance. They must lock in by lifting them in over a ledge and the back of each drawer must be high enough so that small items do not ride over it and fall into the bilge. Nylon catches are not sufficient to hold a drawer in against the heel of the yacht.

Plates and mugs need their own secure stowage, mugs probably behind deep fiddles and plates inside shaped locker fronts that only allow one plate in at a time, each one dropping down on the other so that they are all chocked in. Soup plate type are useful for serving up stew and so on at sea. Watch them if stowed as they tend to ride up over each other and release themselves from stowage. They should either be stowed upside down or the stowage redesigned. Plates and mugs are best made of melaware. China and glass may be slightly more pleasant to eat off, but invariably get broken, and this can be dangerous.

Stoves   In yachts over 22 ft., the stove should have two burners and possibly a grill. An oven is more than is required for ocean races of under a week, but would be a great help on a longer voyage. The stove must have a rail right round of about $2\frac{1}{2}$ in. high and further methods of holding on pots and pans in a seaway, such as cross bars which clamp tightly to the outer rails or shock cord which can be stretched across the lids of saucepans. When this gets singed, it can be replaced. The stove must swing athwartships and it is surprising how often this arrangement is non-standard on stock boats. A good stove position in the galley is on a low level so that the heat cannot hurt the deck-head or hot liquids spill dangerously. I like to have a tray swinging with the stove and under it to catch spillage and this can also be used to place a little lead to damp the motion, though if the weight is unacceptable the hinges should have washers that can be tightened to slow it. A number of standard swinging frames are now available for the commonly used types of stove.

Opinions differ as to the best fuel for cooking. Three sorts are in general use: gas; paraffin and methylated spirit, known as alcohol in USA. Gas is clean to use, can be regulated to a slow heat and lights immediately. In bad weather offshore, it is an advantage to be able to brew up quickly. Gas is the most dangerous of the three fuels, if there is negligence and it is allowed to leak into the yacht, causing a potentially explosive mixture. This is less likely with an ocean racing crew, but is another check for the skipper to have to make. Paraffin used in a pressure stove of the Primus type is the cheapest of the three and obtainable anywhere. It gives a hot flame which will cook quickly, but is difficult to use for simmering. The main objection is priming and this is sensitive to draughts, so it is necessary to ensure that the forehatch is not open and to take other similar measures. If it is understood, there is no need for a "flare-up" on a Primus, but sometimes it does need to be primed (with methylated spirit) twice. The modern type of pressure stove can be left pumped up and it is only necessary to turn a valve to switch on the paraffin. The same valve operates a pricker which cleans the jet. My own experience of the methylated spirit stove, which is popular in USA, from where most of the models come, is that action when cooking is much like the Primus. It needs priming, but of course uses only one fuel against the Primus' two. It is cleaner than a paraffin stove in the event of a "flare-up", but seems to have a high consumption rate of methylated, which is also quite expensive. It is more inflammable than paraffin in the event of spillage in the galley offshore. My main objection to this type of stove is that to reprime, if it has failed to get hot enough, involves letting a certain amount of fuel out which either makes too much flame or evaporates on the hot components making it impossible to relight until it has cooled off for a time. This experience was with only one make, but a common and by no means cheap one. Those that require less priming are slow to cook. In Europe spares are not always easy for these US alcohol stoves. Gas bottles and gas stove spares give no trouble, unless certain rare types are used, but Primus suppliers always appear to be well stocked with spare parts and a spare burner for one should always be carried on board

Sinks In recent yachts of over 22 ft. the sink can drain through an outlet in the hull and, as mentioned, this is a requirement of the One Ton Cup and Half Ton Cup rules. The sink on an ocean racer is of use in washing up dishes, a sump for the outlet of the fresh (and salt) water pump and a safe receptacle for dirty dishes and implements. On *Chieftain* I had a stainless steel sink, 7 in. deep with a drain hole at each end, so that it emptied on either tack, and met all requirements. A reasonable area of sink is desirable but depth is essential and an area as small as $4\frac{1}{2}$ in. × 10 in. is worth having: too often one sees shallow little things with a central plug-hole, only installed by the builders to make the "little woman" feel that the cabin could be a home from home! A seacock must be on the waste-pipe which is easily turned by the cook. I have been on boats where this has not been turned off and looked down into the saloon to see water gushing over the galley area. Fig. 124 shows a suitable arrangement. On the Arpege design there are two narrow, deep sinks, which are a help to the cook who wants to be really organized.

The best equipped galley is no use if the cook cannot comfortably operate in bad weather and some form of seat is often used, either a piano stool type or a narrow bench fixed to the cabin sole that can be passed by members of the crew moving in and out. Even a metal bar which comes off an engine box or from a vertical pillar in the centre of the cabin keeps the cook at his work. Whatever it is, it should be combined with a web belt which he can clip round himself, especially when the galley is to windward. A freshwater pump is useful, as tipping water out of cans is not easy at sea, even if such a procedure saves weight. A particularly good range of freshwater pumps are made by Munster Simms Engineering Ltd., of Northern Ireland. Their Whale angled pump weighs 16 ozs. and appears to have an action which stops any drips. The geometry of the pump makes it useful when heeled over and it strips down easily in the unlikely event of failure. The modern yacht, with less width in the depth of the bilge, does not lend itself to the conventional water tank in galvanized steel. An excellent tank can be moulded into a GRP hull complete with baffles; and in order to keep the weight of the water as low as possible it can be split up into several odd shapes without difficulty. Care must be taken to remove any taste of resin before use. Soft, lightweight plastic containers with screw-in tops which take the pump connection can be used and also fitted into odd places. There is a limit, however, to the lightness of the gauge of polythene that can be used, if only to avoid damage when taking in and out of stowage.

More water should not be carried than is necessary for the race, in temperate climates half a gallon per man per day is adequate, and it helps if this is supplemented by some tins of fruit juice and beer. If all the water is in tanks, there should be some reserve in cans independently stowed for emergencies, such as a miscalculation of the amount loaded at the start or total pump failure. This is a rule in some offshore regulations; though such measures should be taken by any responsible owner. An ice-box is a necessity in hot climates, where it should be part of the galley layout. In north-west Europe, I do not think an ice-box essential for ocean racing; butter and similar perishables will keep very cool if

Q

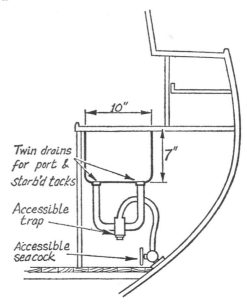

10"

Twin drains
for port &
starb'd tacks

7"

Accessible
trap

Accessible
seacock

FIG. 124. *Efficient deep sink for ocean racing.*

stowed right against the ship's side under the waterline. There should be a chock arranged for this somewhere under the galley furniture. In contrast, remember the place that will become quite hot when the sun is shining is a locker shelf sited immediately under the side deck.

Chart table   The various instruments and equipment which the navigator has to use were detailed in Chapter 4, and it remains to make sure that there is a chart area which will meet the needs which were indicated there. In the size of yacht under review in this chapter, it should be possible to arrange an athwartships chart table. This has the advantage of tucking the navigator into one side of the boat uninterrupted by the comings and goings of the crew. If the chart table is ahead of the navigator's quarter berth, he sits on the end of it and, like the cook, there can be a web strap to keep him in when it is the weather side. Of course, there must be enough headroom for this arrangement but it does not have to run the whole width of the chart table. Contrary to some authorities, I do not think there are critical dimensions for the chart table, connected in some way with the size of a government chart, because for easy use it will be folded. By using a chart protractor, it does not matter if the compass rose gets folded under, the scale may have to be marked off again down a meridian. Apart from a suitable seat to suit the human body, navigators being as human as the rest of the crew, the following will make for a chart table that is a pleasure to use.

   1. While a horizontal surface is best, a sloping desk type, as used on the Arpege is acceptable in giving extra working space for the area taken up in the cabin. I have seen on an otherwise crack boat a sloping chart table, not athwartships: this is pointless and takes on a hopeless angle when it is on the windward side. There should be a moulding or simple flat hinge along the near edge to retain the chart and a high fiddle or partial bulkhead along the inboard edge to keep everything back from the cabin.

   2. The top can lift to disclose the chart stowage but this means charts and instruments

in use are disturbed; better to have a slide-in compartment with all charts labelled on the edge nearest the navigator. If this is not standard to the type of chart inscribe them in this way.

3. The instruments mentioned in Chapter 4 should be mounted on the bulkhead in front of the navigator. Other essentials should be mounted in permanent stowage around the chart table so that the navigator can instantly put his hand on them or see them. These include combined pencil, rubber, dividers rack, tide at area standard port, and compass deviation table.

4. An athwartships book case—just a small one, say 10 in. long—to take the essential volumes can be worked in above the athwartships chart table and the contents will not tip out when the yacht heels (a fiddle should still be fitted). If the weight is thought too high site it under and alongside the table, but the high position will keep the books dry. The heavier volumes—big pilot books and tables—can be wrapped in polythene if not immediately needed and put somewhere lower down.

5. Transparent plastic folders as used in offices are useful waterproof holders for sailing instructions and other temporary papers. For more permanent use, put the paper inside and pin up with the top as one of the sealed edges leaving the bottom for condensation to clear from. If charts or pieces of paper have to be held by clips to the chart table the clips must be heavy ones and strongly fitted.

6. A flexible light over the chart table seems to be common practice but two lights are a good idea. One of these should be white and the other red for normal use to avoid disturbing the crew and temporarily blinding the navigator. The white one may have to be used on a difficult chart or in twilight and is useful as a standby for these conditions.

7. The ideal location of the chart table is far enough aft to lessen the motion and where the navigator can easily speak a few words to the person in charge on deck and then return to work, yet not so immediately adjacent to the main hatch that water is spread in the area by spray or drips from crew's clothing as they come below. How this can be fitted into the general plan of accommodation depends on the general layout already discussed.

Fo'c'sle A method must be worked out of keeping some order in the fo'c'sle, assuming this is used for sail stowage and bosun's gear. Sail bins either side can be used to retain the sail bags. If these have wooden frames, there are sometimes also vertical wooden battens to hold in the sails but these are rather heavy for such a job in the forward part of the yacht. Netting is better, being of negligible weight, but will need renewing after a season or so. Spinnakers can be kept in their turtles ready for bringing on deck and owing to the time needed to pack them, it is essential that there is a turtle for each spinnaker. If they are to one side, the most commonly used genoas could be on the other, with other sails like the trysail in odd corners and perhaps other running and reaching sails, such as the spinnaker staysail, with the spinnakers. Sails should be replaced in sail bags as soon as possible, and these should have numbers which are the key to each sail on their sides and bottom. Sails will not tumble out of the bags if the necks are secured correctly—that is the drawstring wound round and finished off with a clove hitch: it should not be knotted on itself. Anchors, even though below, should be lashed, as they can do as much damage adrift there as on deck. Warps in the fo'c'sle can be secured to the ship's side behind the sails with lashings that double back on an eye.

Position of engine Engines have now come forward from under the cockpit where they were inaccessible, to the centre of the yacht where they can be said to obtrude on the accommodation. However, it is possible to get an engine lower down in such a position and if housed in an engine box it is usually possible to make it part of the step down into the saloon or conceal it under a table or dinette structure! Certainly by removing the panels it is then easy to work on the motor.

Ventilation On some standard boats there is a prevalent idea that the introduction of GRP means that effective ventilation is no longer required. This is wrong, if only to keep a yacht fresh on her mooring, but proper ventilation is essential for crew comfort offshore. There are some good low windage vents to be had in light-weight plastic, which yields if you fall on the vents or a sheet pulls across. A pair of these should be fitted at the forward end of the living part of the accommodation, which will be somewhere in way of the mast. Further ventilators should be considered over the lavatory and galley. The vent pipes should be fitted to water trap boxes. Ready-made water trap ventilators in GRP are made by Souter of Cowes in two sizes and as these are a low box type with rounded edges they could well be suitable for use even further forward in the yacht (Fig. 125). The very shallow all-round vent seen on many standard boats is not adequate by itself and serves little purpose if proper ventilators are already installed. Large pieces of cork cut from fisherman's floats serve as emergency bungs which should be available for all ventilator orifices for fitting from below. Sometimes it is useful to seal the windward vent in bad weather; if it is cold, the draught of fresh air becomes too much for the man below. For minimum windage it is possible to work a water trap vent into the forward edge of the coachroof as on the T31 (Fig. 80). With this type it is not possible to turn the mouth to face astern, which can be useful when the spray is flying.

Miscellaneous items offshore Handholds below are vital for safe movement around the saloon. The siting of strong handles becomes obvious to anyone in a seaway, who then only has to put out a hand to where he would like something to hold to. Too often this is missing in stock GRP boats. Somewhere high up, probably along the lower part of the coachroof coamings, is a natural place to hang on the weather side. Partial bulkheads are a help but only if holes have been cut to allow the hand to grip the edge of them. As on deck

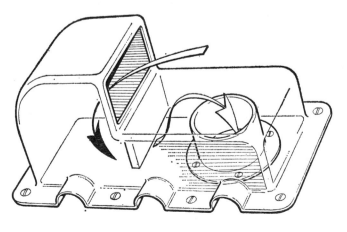

FIG. 125. *The Souter GRP ventilator is ready made up to fit on any deck or coachroof. It has the necessary qualities of non-fouling shape and quick draining of water.*

there should be a secure hold all the length of the boat. The cabin sole needs to be non-slip and down here the weight of teak is acceptable. Another possibility is teak-faced ply, though it is going to be damp for much of the time. Cabin sole boards should be quite loose when first fitted as they seem gradually to swell over a period and then try to raise. "Safety walk" is useful below at strategic points such as where the crew step down.

One way of lowering weight might be to bring halyard winches below into the cabin. Having experienced this, I would not recommend it owing to the time lost in moving up and down and the practical difficulty of communicating with the men on the winch, who are "working blind" and have to be told every move. The same applies to inner forestay and backstay adjustment, where the saving in windage, such as it is, does not compensate for the difficulty of control and the resulting time wasted: these tasks are better operated on deck.

·16·

BELOW DECKS
(Under 22 ft. LWL)

General arrangement   It is not so much a question of what is essential in the smaller yachts as what can be left out without impairing performance offshore. This is less room for compromise, so we see in this range yachts with high coachroofs, freeboard and big windows which are only suitable for estuary cruising. The weight of the crew has a considerable effect and anyone off watch should be in the correct position fore and aft and up to windward. Whether you move a sleeping hand over to the weather bunk when you tack depends on your dedication. This is where we start to approach bucket lavatories and folding chart tables, which are among the sort of fittings that people from the larger boats might regard as crude. An athwartships chart table is not possible but down to 19 ft. W.L. a fo'c'sle clear for sails is still possible by the simple arrangement of saloon berths and quarter berths, with the galley and chart table each side between them. The W.C. can be in the fo'c'sle with a curtain across. Forward berths are common in this size of cruiser, but I do not see it as a racing arrangement. The reasons already given apply with greater force in these smaller yachts.

Below 19 ft. we may have to accept forward berths, because the length of the yacht is such that any berth forward of the chart table and galley is forward. The quarter berths in effect have their feet in the quarters and their head in the saloon. On a drawing of the layout, the galley looks rather far forward, but remember that it is really only a couple of feet from the hatch. There is not going to be standing headroom anyway and yachts of this size are going to be wonderful passage makers with no pretensions to family amenities. Once again the yachts can have extra furniture which some people might think desirable for cruising, but that is not our concern here. The layouts of five quarter-tonners are shown in Fig. 126, and only in the heavy displacement Merle design have forward bunks been avoided.

Berths   The crew of a yacht over 19 ft. is probably four and in a smaller boat it will be three. This is the minimum number allowed under GCL and Quarter Ton rules. It is necessary to be able to sleep two men off watch and these will be in the saloon berths or quarter berths where these are combined with the saloon. Spray curtains are more necessary than ever and weight saving by the use of terylene berth bottoms. Locker space for the crew's personal effects is difficult to find and nets against the ship's side and under the side decks are very useful; the crew should provide themselves with some of the excellent small bags available in PVC, such as those made by Helly-Hansen. When there are forward berths these must be covered in totally waterproof material as damp sails and gear will have to be put on them at sea. The saloon berths will suffer almost as much, because whereas in the larger boats it is possible to come below and take foul-weather gear off, perhaps sitting on the engine box below the hatch, on the smaller yacht one comes straight down on to the berths. There is little one can do about this except to have wet outer clothing ready to strip off as you come below and get the worst of it on the cabin sole.

Oilskin locker   Now that synthetic materials are used, there is not the same necessity to hang foul-weather gear to preserve it. Wet oilskins still need to be put somewhere and even a narrow oilskin locker between two-ply bulkheads or some hooks in the fo'c'sle gives the crew somewhere to put them. In *Demeter* (18 ft. 6 in.), which had no quarter berths, we fitted a hanging space abaft the galley and they drained into the bilge. An opening of 7 inches is enough for a crew of three with lightweight short coats. As it happened on *Demeter*, which we raced successfully in the JOG in 1956, our total crew was normally two and anyway there were only two permanent bunks: this would be unusual nowadays. On larger yachts oilskin lockers, if given thought at the design stage, pose no special problem: sometimes individual caves may be provided for each member of the crew.

Chart table   If a permanent table cannot be fitted, then a folding one is best rigged over the foot of a berth. Even if it is temporary, it should be able to be left in position all the time when racing and not have to be removed to get into the bunk, to cook, etc. For this reason it is better to have a folding table rather than try to navigate on the covered top of the galley. JOG rules call for a chart table and plotting board and a flat space in the galley cannot count as a chart table. With a folding table the instruments can be mounted on the side of the yacht just above its level and on a bulkhead adjoining. It is possible to make the table double to take charts within it, but this is rather bulky and it may be better to stow them in a waterproof envelope under a bunk. For the reasons given in the last chapter a sloping table should be avoided. A portable seat which is really a board which just spans the cabin sole is useful for the navigator who can sit astride or to one side as he wishes and this is seen in the layout of the *Emeraude* (Fig. 126), where the chart table is rigged over the lavatory—a practical idea which could only originate in France.

Galley   The double-burner Primus stove is $22\frac{1}{2}$ inches long and would be large in any boat under 19 ft. The Sievert propane double-burner is 19 inches long and there are few stoves shorter than this which can give two rings. Radius make a neat single burner paraffin pressure stove with a rail, but if gas is to be used a satisfactory arrangement is one of the small "Camping Gas" cylinders fixed immediately underneath a burner, the whole thing swinging athwartships. Such cylinders, which originate in France, are widely used in Europe for camping and are available in 3 lb. and 6 lb. sizes. The advantage of this arrangement is that there are no fuel lines or a multiplicity of taps. If two rings are used they have independent fuel supplies. The code of practice for boat builders in England stipulates that gas cylinders should always be in a locker outside the accommodation (cockpit) which drains over the side or on deck. However, the absence of connections and the simplicity of the cylinder under the ring commends itself. A draining sink should not be necessary on these small yachts, but a deep one is still useful which can then be tipped over the side; it acts as a receptacle for plates and so on. Plastic water containers can be stowed in any convenient corners with a fixed stowage for the one in use. This one should have a top through which runs a pipe connected to the freshwater pump, still necessary to prevent spillage. Apart from these points remarks about galleys already made apply to all sizes of boat, with the obvious proviso that less can be installed, but then the crew is smaller. On some yachts the galley is seen split on either side of the saloon, perhaps one side with the stove and the other the sink, but if this can be avoided for offshore work, it should be. One also sees galleys which fold in various ways. Most of these are intended for cruising yachts and the idea is that the galley remains stowed and unfolds in harbour. In one such design, the stove was upside down over the sink and then unfolded to land beside it. The stove could not be made to swing when rigged and this was no use to the offshore racers. Sometimes sinks slide out from under the stove base and this is acceptable, if the arrangement is staunch. The arrangement where the L-shaped galley curls round under the bridge deck is more sensible; it should be tucked well under with a step clear outside it. The cook can use the same movable seat as the navigator mentioned above, depending on the actual galley position.

Bilge pumps   The bilge pump has been left until considering these smaller yachts, as one of the main difficulties with it is to find a place to install it. Larger yachts should be equipped with at least two hand pumps, but in the smaller, one permanently installed bilge pump is sufficient. If there is room in the cockpit it is the best place, where the watch on deck can work on it in security and permitting a loose flexible outlet which can merely be hung over the side, obviating another hole in the topsides. If there are the slatted seats previously described the lever of a diaphragm pump can be let through an enlarged slit. it is not satisfactory to have to open a locker top to pump. Even if it is self-draining into the cockpit, it is an awkward place. Down below is suitable, but there will invariably be some small leakage at connections and the outlet hose has either to be passed out into the cock-pit, perhaps necessitating a hatch left open in bad weather, or there must be a hull outlet with a seacock even if it is above the waterline. A diaphragm pump might be mounted near the companion-way where a man can face aft and work it or a bulkhead fitting plunger pump can be mounted on the engine-casing or the edge of a partial bulkhead. The inlet for the pump in modern designs with fin keels and a shallow bilge is a problem. When the boat is heeled a pipe of the centreline will leave water in the lee bilge. This is just where you do not want it because it will enter lockers and stowage. Some solution such as a two-way cock controlling pipes to port and starboard bilge seems desirable.

On a GRP boat there can be mouldings to retain a certain level of water and pre-

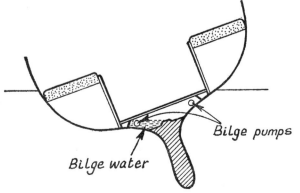

FIG. 126. *In a yacht with shallow bilge a GRP moulding which prevents bilge water from running up into the accommodation is useful. In this case there must be provision for pumping out on both tacks.*

Bilge pumps

Bilge water

43. Cooking in light weather for an ocean racing crew. Note deep fiddles all over galley and even deeper locker behind stove. There are hand holds right round galley. Stove is a double burner Primus.

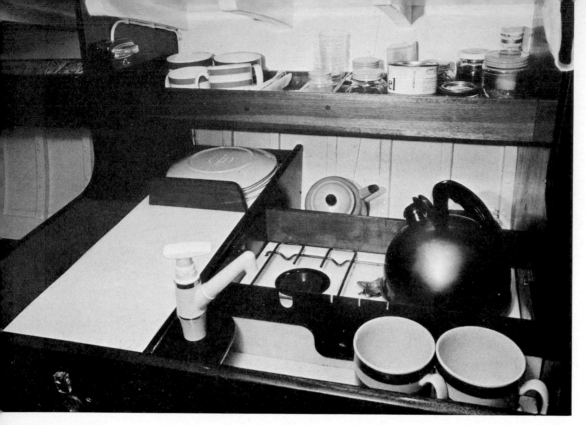

44. Galley of *Alacrity III* with swinging gas stove, cylinder clamped with it.

45. Arpege galley in GRP, also with swinging gas stove, but deep double sinks and mouldings for stowage.

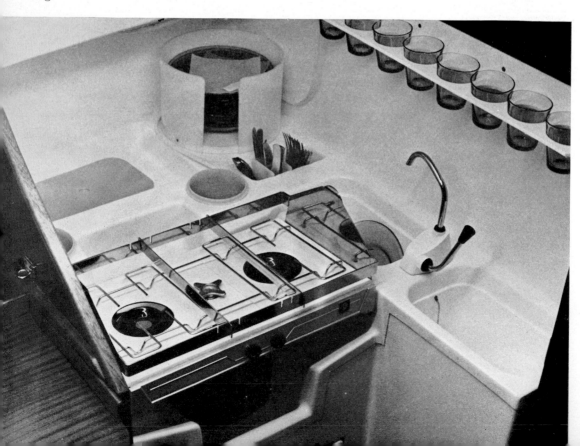

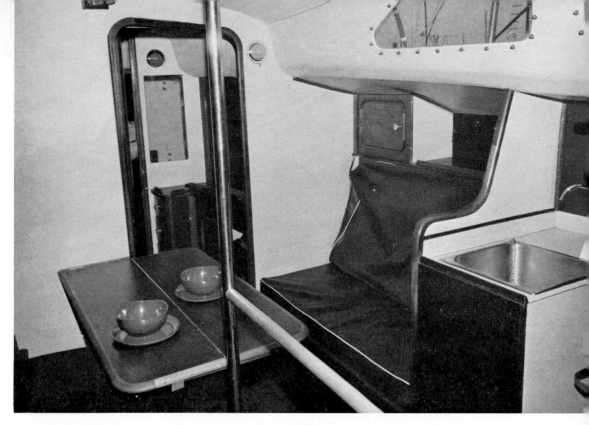

46. Saloon of the S31 with useful pillar for strength and hand hold.

47. *Alacrity III* though a much smaller hull cannot afford a much smaller chart table for racing. The fiddle is required as the table cannot be athwartships, but the book case still is!

48. Henderson bilge pump sited in an inconspicuous corner, but still easily operated. Front can be released for inspection.

49. *Left:* Athwartships table on *Al Na'Ir* faces aft. Weight of books is kept low. Everything will operate when the yacht heels.

W.C.S FOR SMALL YACHTS

Type	Handles	Pan material	Weight (lb.)	Overall Dimensions		
				Height (in.)	Width (in.)	Depth (to packs) (in.)
SL 400	One lever	Vitreous china	$21\frac{1}{2}$	10	$16\frac{1}{2}$	$19\frac{1}{2}$
Groco "UCC"	One vertical	Porcelain	$26\frac{1}{2}$	$12\frac{7}{8}$	$16\frac{3}{4}$	$16\frac{1}{2}$
Blake Baby Lightweight	One lever, one vertical handle	Porcelain	29	13	20	16
Blake Baby Light-weight with tilting base	27 degrees tilt each way and raises height when level by $4\frac{1}{4}$ in. The special base is of stainless steel and weighs $11\frac{1}{2}$ lb. There are seven positions and flexible pipes must be used.					
S.W. Marine Waterloo compact	One vertical	Porcelain	$25\frac{1}{2}$	13	18	17
				(narrower at base, if pump is mounted at slight angle)		

FIG. 127.

vent it running up the side of the yacht (Fig. 127). At sea there must be no doubt about the bilge pump; for racing it must be easily cleared, simple to maintain and no great weight. The Henderson pumps are widely used in ocean racers and are of the diaphragm type with an instantly removal front for clearing. It is unlikely that you will need to do this as they will pass large impurities such as bits of cloth, splinters of wood and the other inevitable items from a yacht's bilge. The Mark III is in plastic and weighs $4\frac{1}{2}$ lb. with its handle. The geometry of the casing allows the pump to be mounted in a number of positions and the angle of inlet and outlet can be varied against the lever handle. The capacity is 10 gallons a minute through a hose between $1\frac{1}{4}$ and $1\frac{1}{2}$ in. A plunger type for small boats is the Whale $1\frac{1}{2}$ in. with a 6 in. stroke. The overall length is 15 in. and it weighs 2 lb. with a capacity of 4 gallons a minute.

Lavatories A pump-out W.C. is useful in the smallest yachts, being more pleasant than a bucket, however trouble-free the latter may be. If there is a bucket, JOG rules specify that it must be "fitted". A W.C. that fails to work or needs unblocking at sea is not popular with the crew and a balance must be struck between "toy" ones and heavy affairs of steel and porcelain. There are a number of lightweight W.C.s on the market now, but the only one I can vouch for in reliability is the lightweight Baby Blake. The table (Fig. 127), gives a selection of those suitable for small boats. For sailing yachts W.C.s must pump dry. Some have a level marked in them for water, but they must be emptied completely for racing. It must also be possible to evacuate the pan immediately after using it in rough weather to avoid any chance of the contents slopping, which will not improve conditions below. The Baby Blake with tilting base, shown in the table, assists in preventing this,

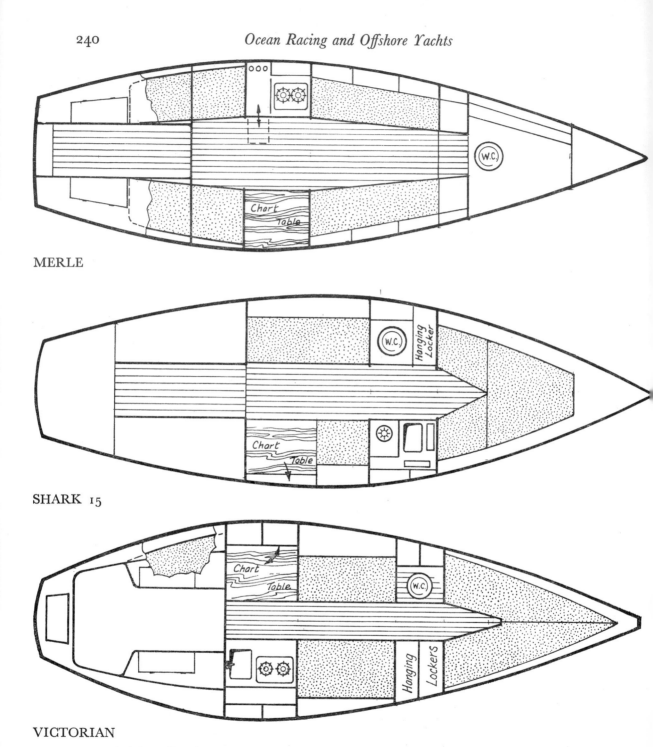

MERLE

SHARK 15

VICTORIAN

FIG. 128 (part of). *Ringing the changes in accommodation in Quarter Ton Cup yachts, mostly between 19 and 21 ft. LWL. Only* Merle *and* Cognac *manage to avoid two forward berths. The W.C. is always somewhere in the forward part of the yachts, but galleys vary from abreast the mast to level with the forward part*

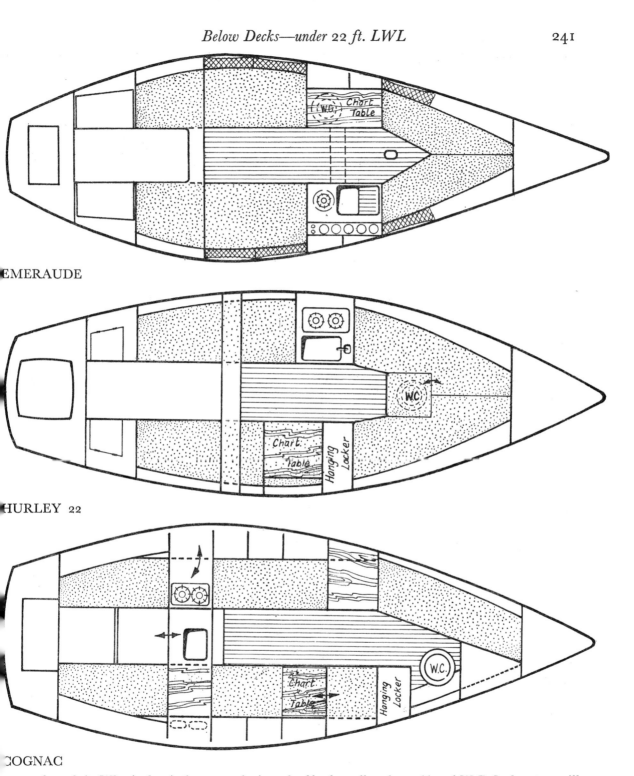

EMERAUDE

HURLEY 22

COGNAC

of a cockpit. What is clear is the common basic needs of bunks, galley, chart table and W.C. Locker space will vary with detailed ingenuity and access.

as well as serving its primary purpose of being more usable at an angle of heel. Porcelain bowls have been known to shatter when hammering to windward and some people recommend the use of rubber mountings. On the other hand light alloy bowls, no doubt since modified, have collapsed under the weight of a heavy crew member when the yacht hit a sea on the nose. Few lavatories enjoy a meal of the popular heavy absorbent type toilet paper in use today. Jeyes traditional thin khaki variety is best and if interleaved it can fit in a plastic holder on the side of the yacht, which at least protects it from stray water in the fo'c'sle. Care should be taken to avoid any objects in the lavatory which could block it. The Waterloo has a large drain plug for clearance of blockages. Harpic does not harm the Baby Blake and should be the only exception to the quite common notice, "Only put in the pan what has already been eaten".

Lockers   The use of GRP does offer the possibility of taking locker partitions right out to the ship's side. The same system can be applied to water tanks. One yacht which has a water tank across the hull just forward of the mast is able to regard this as a collision bulkhead, an idea that might be taken further. Few small yachts carry buoyancy material because of the difficulty of finding room for it, but if the yacht has no life-raft the owner might like to consider it. It would have to be in a portable form—something like sacks of buoyant foam packed behind bulkheads—so that deck fittings could be tightened and other repairs made in the buoyancy compartments. Air chambers alone are not practical. My own feeling is that the slow speed of the small yacht combined with the great strength that can be built into her makes loss at sea unlikely. Her main danger is on a lee shore when buoyancy is of little value. There are cases of small yachts being washed up on beaches clear of danger.

To return to the less dramatic topic of GRP lockers. These seem to gather a little water from the usual drips and then hold it, so drain holes should be made in these: this applies especially to yachts with interior GRP mouldings. Doors get very awkward in the small sizes and even cave fronts if made too small are difficult to put things in. So the best stowage in the smallest boats is deep fiddles with waterproof bags as necessary, leaving lockers for where they will be a useful size.

Handholds are just as important in the smaller yachts but the best plan is a few strong ones, which can be reached from different parts of the cabin. The grips need to be just as big as on larger yachts and there may be less strong points to fit them. The crew will not be standing except in the hatch as they descend and the emphasis for comfort will be on good sitting headroom and a bunk that offers a restful time off watch.

From some of my remarks the impression may have been given that living below in the smaller yachts is very rough. This is not the case and it is a delight to lie in your bunk, your feet and head not very far from bow and stern respectively as the water rushes past a few inches from your ear. My emphasis is on simplicity, in a new boat at any rate, and a small amount of reliable gear. The builders of the smaller boats have a variety of customers and if you intend to use the boat for much offshore work, it is best to add, in the light experience of racing the yacht, the interior extras that seem desirable.

THE ENGINE AND ELECTRICAL
EQUIPMENT ON BOARD

The engine of an ocean racer The purposes of the auxiliary engine in an ocean racer, where everything is directed to making the fastest offshore sailing craft, are:

1. To enable the yacht to reach the start line in calm weather.
2. As far as is allowed by the racing rules, to motor to a required position near the start line, prior to kedging or drifting in calm weather.
3. For emergency propulsion in "man overboard" or serious grounding situations.
4. To charge the battery for the yacht's lighting and electrical equipment used when racing.

The installation of machinery is considered by all rating rules to be a disadvantage and so allowances are given for the weight of a yacht's engine and the manner of the propeller arrangement. Apart from the fact that the engine will form part of the basic weight and lay-out design of a standard boat, the factors above mean that it is desirable to have a proper auxiliary installation in the racing yacht. Taking only the first purpose, I can recall a number of cases where yachts have been late at the start line of important races because their engines were not working. A tow out to the line may be all right for a 12-metre but remember she finds it necessary to have a permanent powered tender. The winners of the 1968 and 1969 Half Ton Cups had no engines or propellers.

Outboard motors are commonly used on multihulls and they have been used on displacement boats up to 24 ft. For an offshore racer, I would not recommend their use in boats over 18 ft., though under this size the design may not allow an inboard installation. There are several disadvantages in an outboard: the necessity on occasions to unship it just before the start of a race, the need to find safe sea-going stowage (apart from keeping petrol and oil from leaking with the engine on its side at sea, some outboards have powerful magnetos which can affect compasses) and that rating rules do not make any allowance for carrying the weight which is often difficult to keep away from the stern. In yachts which have to be equipped with outboard motors, they should, if possible, be dispensed with altogether when racing.

Engine problems An irritating problem for the keen racing man is the practical one that the mechanical (and electrical) components on board seem to require a high proportion of the time devoted to maintaining the yacht. The only solution to this is first-class initial installation and thorough out of season maintenance in the attempt to minimize work in this department during the racing season. The treatment given to the ocean racer's engine is lack of use rather than overwork. There is a high proportion of slow running if the engine is for charging and on occasions when under sail. If the engine is low down and near midships, to keep the weight in the correct place, the exhaust system will need to be effective even with a long uphill run. The motor will also be enclosed and air cooling is seldom practical without constructing air ducts, which cause more weight and complication. With a watertight cockpit the system of leading the controls also requires attention. It will not be advisable to install the ideal propeller as recommended by the engine manufacturers, who are generally not aware of the need to reduce the resistance of the stern gear when sailing. It may have to be accepted that the motor will not be able to deliver its full power through the stern gear, though the reduction gear to assist this as far as is possible should be used.

Selection of engine Despite the rating allowance and the less adverse effect on performance by a low down central siting of the motor, the weight of the diesel makes it less popular than petrol as an auxiliary. The Lister Blackstone 9 b.h.p., which is one of the smaller available, weighs 360 lb. Petters Ltd. make several lightweight diesels such as an 8·2 b.h.p. which weighs 600 lb. Usually with water-cooling diesel engines are slightly heavier than their nominal weights. In contrast the Swedish Albin o–21 (10 b.h.p.), which is a favoured engine for yachts from 19 to 24 ft., weighs 256 lb. and is water cooled. Where lighter weights are required it may be necessary to install a two-stroke and typical examples are the RCA Dolphin and the Vire, made in Finland, the manual start version weighing only 117 lb. A really lightweight four-stroke which I have found particularly reliable is the Coventry Victor MW2 (6 h.p.), weighing only 82 lb.; another advantage of this little motor is the horizontally opposed cylinders, which means the height is minimal, for fitting in a difficult space. It is fair to say that in Europe there are a limited number of engines both diesel and petrol suitable for sailing yachts, but among these are excellent ones whose characteristics are well known to designers to suit all types of ocean racer. Comprehensive lists of the data of all marine engines are always available in a number of reference books.

Installation details Two details which make for convenience at sea are not often installed as standard unless the owner or designer insists. One of these is the effectiveness of the stern tube greaser. If the stern tube is not packed with grease water may leak into the yacht. A remote injector will usually be needed and this should be a man-size gun with a proper handle which will really force the grease down the comparatively long thin pipe to the stern tube. The knurled knob of about one inch diameter often seen requires constant recharging and is difficult to turn at the pressure required. The second point arises from a number of boats where I notice the engine drip-tray is too shallow and cannot easily be withdrawn to clean. A deep drip-tray will hold its unpleasant contents when the yacht heels: as for removal, in some cases this has been impossible, so that it has to be cleaned out with rags and tissue paper—a ludicrous operation in a modern yacht. While on the subject of sump oil, it is probably necessary to have a pump for oil changing as there is unlikely to be room to drain the engine using the drain plug. Attention should be paid to other aspects of the installation which can be grouped under fuel, exhaust, stern gear and controls.

Fuel Gravity feed is satisfactory provided there is sufficient head of fuel in the tank, which which varies with the angle of heel. Designers will tend to keep the tank low which can mean poor flow when the supply is low and this may have to be accepted. Plastic fuel lines are acceptable, PVC-nylon combination is tough and flexible, provided there is no danger of touching a hot part of the engine, or of any chafe. The advantage is that the fuel flow can be seen. Copper pipe is slightly safer, but it must be coiled to give flexibility where there is any possibility of vibration or slight movement. Fuel trouble is well known as a prime reason for engine trouble at sea and the ocean racer gives her tank as good a churning as any vessel prior to starting the engine. So a big filter is essential. The "Auto-clean" filter for petrol will take a large quantity of sediment which is kept permanently clear of the flow by occasionally turning a small key. There should be ample taps in the fuel system in case it has to be dismantle, at least at the tank, filter and carburettor. Most yachts may get by with some simple form of air vent to the tank, but in a boat which will be hard driven under sail, the vent must be in the form of a small diameter pipe leading up the level of the coachroof. The end of this should have a shut off cap to eliminate any chance of leakage at a large angle of heel. This should be left open when circumstances permit.

Exhaust system This will be recommended by the engine manufacturer, though the problem for ocean racers has already been mentioned. The most common arrangement is to run it up into the counter in the form of a "swan neck" so that the final lead is downwards and prevents entry of water. For offshore work it should also be fitted with a seacock, so there is no chance of flooding the exhaust pipe, say in a heavy following sea. It will be difficult in a small yacht to keep the pipe clear of the structure and stowed gear and there should be heavy lagging with asbestos tape. Having suffered from a foul weather suit which has a burn hole, I can vouch for such precautions! Additionally, the cooling water in certain engines can be led out by a jacket over the exhaust pipe, entering it after the swan neck, which has an advantage of one less hole in the hull. An installation recommended for the Vire 6 h.p. and suitable for other motors of this size is shown in Fig. 129. In this case the cooling water is injected just above the silencer and the system is not jacketed.

Stern gear The marine gear-box which comes in a number of forms and at its simplest with a fixed propeller would provide ahead, neutral and astern. The main variations on this for sailing yachts are the centrifugal clutch, which provides ahead only when the engine reaches a certain number of revolutions, the propeller stopping again as the engine is slowed and the variable pitch propeller which provides gearing by having blade positions for ahead, neutral, astern and "sailing". At first sight the variable pitch propeller seems to have advantages as the "sailing" position has the blades in a fore-and-aft line. The snags in practice are several. It is difficult to achieve a perfect neutral with the blades with nil pitch as a little slack in the mechanism gives a slight pitch one way or the other; the mechanism involves a large boss to the propeller, adding resistance, and it needs to protrude an inch or two more from the stern post (if in this situation) than an ordinary screw; and the control systems are not always easy to fit in a watertight cockpit. As neutral involves the blades actually turning it is not possible to use the engine for charging the batteries when racing. It is not a helpful system, for instance, when becalmed in fog, where the

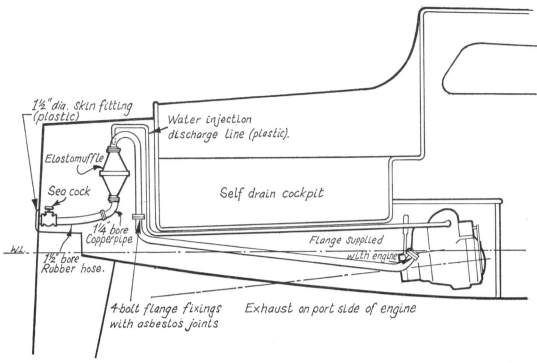

1½" dia. skin fitting
(plastic)

Water injection
discharge line (plastic).

Elastomuffle

Sea cock

Self drain cockpit

1¼" bore
Copper pipe

Flange supplied
with engine

W.L.

1½" bore
Rubber hose.

4-bolt flange fixings
with asbestos joints

Exhaust on port side of engine

FIG. 129. *Engine installation in sailing yacht 17 to 22 ft. LWL. Exhaust pipe has to run "uphill" and water discharge is injected into it for cooling and silence at a point where it cannot run back into the exhaust and engine. There should be a seacock in case of flooding in following seas.*

engine is kept ticking over in neutral as an emergency measure, because of risk of collision. Of course, a gear-box can be fitted in addition to the variable pitch mechanism but this is elaborate.

The simplest conception is the solid two-blade propeller on an ordinary marine gear box. This is a favoured pattern on transom sterned yachts, where the screw has to be in an aperture, as much of the resistance is caused by the aperture itself and a significant propeller factor is given for this design. It is twice that of the feathering (i.e. variable pitch), as shown in this extract from the rating rule.

Propeller factor

	Out of aperture No. strut	In aperture
Folding	0·50	1·5
Feathering 2-blade	0·75	2·0
Solid 2-blade	2·00	2·25
Solid 3-blade	2·50	3·00

The propeller drag factor is given by

$$4 \times \frac{\text{Factor} \times \text{size}}{\sqrt{BD}}$$

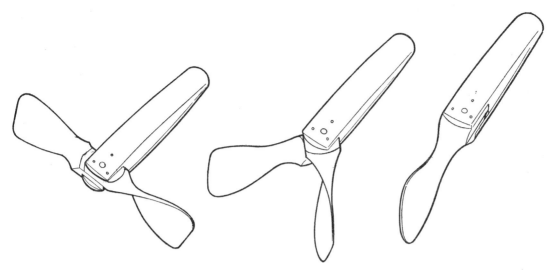

FIG. 130. *The Martec folding propeller which closes under the action of the water to give minimal resistance when sailing.*

The "size" is the diameter of the propeller or four times the greatest width of the blade whichever is less. This prevents the use of very narrow blades for rule purposes.

It will be seen that it is the folding propeller which has the least allowance under the rule and the question for the racer is whether less allowance compensates for the decrease in resistance. Whether this is so is influenced particularly by hull form and the modern configuration of fin keel and separate rudder seems sensitive to rudder drag, with the result that the folding propeller is widely used in such boats. My observations are that attempts to lower rating by using a solid propeller on this type of hull have not been successful. Much also depends on how well designed is the folding propeller. Walter Beck of Long Beach, California, sailed for two years in his ocean racer with a solid screw and then in a bid to improve the yacht's performance removed it, leaving only the strut and shaft. So striking was the increase in speed that he developed the Martec Low Drag folding propeller, which when folded gives a shape of very low resistance (Fig. 130). Walter Beck gives some drag comparisons, which are quoted here as given by his company for a speed of 1·96 knots. One would imagine that this is a speed at which propeller configuration is pronounced in its effect, the difference being less at higher speeds. There may also be different effects due to the depth of screw and one way of reducing resistance, with, say, a solid two-blade would be to site it near the waterline, the lack of efficiency under power being accepted. The Beck figures are:

Type	Drag calibration, prop. strut and shaft (lb.)	Prop. only (lb.)
Strut and shaft only	0·243	0
Martec folding	0·441	0·198
Other folding	0·662	0·419
Feathering	1·322	1·079
Solid 2-blade	4·415	4·172

R

The Martec is kept shut by the run of water past it, so it should be allowed to fold in a vertical plane (mark the shaft inside the yacht), otherwise at slow speeds one blade could fall open. It used to be considered desirable to put an elastic band round a folding propeller and I have bored small holes for a twist of fuse wire for the same reason. However, because the Martec is such a flush fit, blade to blade, I do not think that with it such measures are needed.

Care should be taken when operating the Martec not to open the throttle sharply: instead the blades should be allowed to open smoothly. When this precaution has not been taken, in modern fin keel yachts, damage has occurred to the area of fin close to where the stern gear emerges.

Controls The controls of petrol engine installation envisaged in the ocean racer will be simple, usually just a throttle and gear control. These will need to be in the cockpit, where the helmsman can use them without leaving the tiller and while still looking forward or abeam. Remaining instruments concerned with the engine such as ammeter, oil pressure gauge, ignition key and starting button are best mounted below where they are kept dry and do not clutter the cockpit for racing. It means some one going below to start the motor, but this is required in any case, to switch on the petrol, remove any shaft locks and so on.

Levers are not acceptable if the cockpit is to remain watertight, nor are controls in cockpit lockers satisfactory. The gear shift on the Stuart Turner engines has a vertical torque action. A useful arrangement with it is to have a deck plate in the cockpit sole or bridge deck which is opened when motoring to allow a shaft with a handle to project directly from the gear shift into the cockpit. However, this depends on engine position being far enough aft, and somewhere still has to be found for the throttle control. Hydraulic controls can be fitted in a watertight cockpit, but they demand accessibility for adjustment of the fluid which often causes siting problems. Though not originally designed for sailing boats, stainless steel sleeve controls, such as those made by Morse Controls Inc., Ohio, are ideal for nearly all installations. There are different core gauges in the Morse series, but in one of the smaller sizes, the No. 40, the cable will pull a load of 100 lb. and push a thrust of 80 lb. over a reach of 3 in. A minor limitation is the radius through which the cable can be led and for the 40 this is 8 in. There would be a larger radius for heavier duty cables, but these are not required for small marine engines. Morse controls are completely resistant to corrosion and have a huge variety of mountings for fitting to different motors: I feel they should be used even with the smallest engines where a Bowden cable used to be normal, as the latter would certainly have to be renewed at intervals. One of the main attractions of Morse is the cockpit control lever design, which enables watertight fitting to be made in a bulkhead or cockpit side. Only the boss and levers are exposed with the end of the cable actuated in dry conditions the other side of the bulkhead. In Morse model MS the levers can be unshipped when not in use, eliminating any chance of fouled lines when racing (Fig. 131).

Engine instructions As the use of an engine in an ocean racer is infrequent, but may be needed in an emergency, it is wise to fasten a notice close to it giving the step by step instructions for starting and for stopping. These may be simple but such information is of great assistance to anyone who has to go below and start up; all marine engines are slightly different, if only because of the location of such things as fuel taps. Fuller instructions for servicing should be carried with the rest of the yachts's documents.

Electric power   For racing at night an electric supply is needed for the navigation lights, compass light and chart light and occasional cabin lights, when cooking and at the change of watch. It may be needed at all times for the wind speed and direction indicator, the other electronic equipment mentioned in Chapter 5 using self-contained dry cells. Unless the engine has manual start the battery will also have the heavy duty of the starter motor. Starting the engine with the battery should be kept to a minimum before a race and for this reason the positioning of a convenient manual start is desirable: it is preferable to run the engine for a period after the starter motor has been used. On two yachts which I raced for several seasons, I had engines with only manual start and took the battery, which was one of high capacity, ashore for charging between races. This was in the interests of simplicity and weight saving and the battery was adequate for all races including the Fastnet of five and a half days. But this is not the ideal arrangement and an alternator on the engine will generate electricity at a high rate in comparison with its own weight (e.g 60 watts per lb.). It does not require a high engine speed to attain the required output, so the engine can be kept at low revolutions in neutral while sailing to charge the battery. Note that the RORC require separation of the propeller shaft and engine drive if the engine is run for charging purposes while sailing.

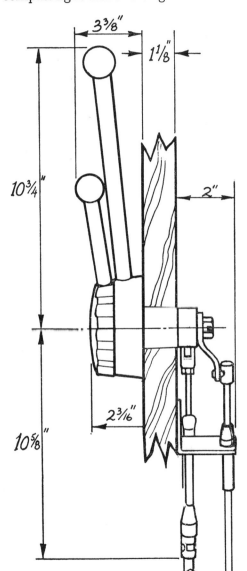

FIG. 131. *Morse control for cockpit use with linkages in watertight area behind bulkhead. In this model, the levers can be unscrewed from the central bosses, when under sail, to prevent the possibility of fouled lines.*

For yachts using outboards or where the engine has no electric start, the battery can be sited where its weight is most beneficial. A GRP box should enclose it to prevent acid spillage and bilge water coming into contact with it. On yachts under 20 ft. dry batteries are sometimes employed for navigation lights and the compass, but it will be found that a number have to be carried owing to the limited life. In the case of the port and starboard navigation lights in the bows, it is not advisable to have the batteries fitting directly into the light assembly as replacement when beating to windward in any breeze becomes impracticable. Instead, dry batteries should be fitted below with connections through the deck. My view is that any yacht over 16 ft. should carry a lead acid battery, even if it is a small one, for navigation and compass light only. When inspecting one yacht of 17 ft. for the JOG, the owner showed me his battery, which was of the alkaline variety. It was a truly massive affair which he said lasted the whole season, which I could well believe. Their bulk and weight make them unsuitable in general for small ocean racers, though they have advantages over the lead acid type in yachts where weight and space are not at a premium. The question arises how heavy a battery is required, in other words what capacity is needed.

Lights and other equipment The Brookes and Gatehouse Hengist Horsa wind direction and speed indicator takes a current of 0·1 amp and if a Hestia compass repeater is in use, it also uses 0·1 amp. If the wind direction indicator is used alone it is possible to run this off a 9-volt dry battery over a long period, making it independent of the main supply. The remaining equipment is only in use at night and ocean racing rules insist that the navigation and stern lights are used from sunset to sunrise. This time depends on the latitude and time of year, but assuming a nine-hour night, the load on the battery can be shown as follows:

Item	Current from 12-volt battery	Amp hours for 24 hour period—9-hour night
2 navigation lights each 6 watts	1 amp	9
Stern light 6 watts	·5 amp	4·5
Compass light	·2 amp	1·8
Chart and cabin lights, e.g. 2 ×6 watts for 1 hour	1 amp	1
Hengist Horsa 24 hours	0·1 amp	2·4
		17·7 amp hours

17·7 represents the capacity required of the battery for nine hours. In mid-summer on the Atlantic coast of France, where darkness would be for such a period an 80 amp hour battery would therefore last four nights. The same calculations should be made for any yacht, adding as necessary all the demands that will be made on electric supply.

Circuits The principles for ocean racers are no different to other marine installations, though if a fault develops it will not be possible to heave to, and work on wiring in an awkward place may have to be undertaken in unpleasant conditions. Careful layout of the wiring and fuses is needed. For instance, navigation, stern, compass and cabin lights should all be on their own fuses. A very well designed combined switch and fuse panel is made by the Crouch Engineering Co. Ltd. of Burnham-on-Crouch, England. It is in GRP, tends to drain drips away from the working parts, is easy to work on and available with internal layouts varying from 4 switches and 6 fuses to 8 switches and 8 fuses. It also has a socket for the searchlight. The weight is 3 lb. and the measurements are 11 in. ×9½ in. ×2¾ in. This may seem large for the smaller yachts, but the depth is very little and it should be possible to find a bulkhead or panelling position. In ocean racing conditions, switches can be accidentally pushed on and, to avoid waste of current, switches at the various appliances as well as the panel are advisable. There should be a main switch to isolate the battery completely when no electricity is required.

Siting and type of lights It is now a truism that sailing yacht navigation lights are inadequate and the 6-watt power mentioned above has a range of only three-quarters of a mile in normal conditions. The 6-watt stern light, because it is not shining through coloured glass, gives a satisfactory two miles' visibility. 12 watts in each side-light will increase the distance to $1\frac{1}{2}$ miles, but from the Table of battery use above, it will be seen to be a major drain on the power supply. One solution is to use a bi-colour lamp with a 12- or even 18 watt single bulb in it. A variation on this is to use one of the 21/6-watt twin filament motor rear-light bulbs: the 6 watt is used normally and the 21-watt filament brought into use when another craft is sighted. One of the difficulties is to find a bi-colour lamp to suit the modern yacht pulpit. I would go so far as to say that a really good set of side-lights for offshore use in small yachts still remains to be designed to cope with drenching by salt water, vibration from the headsails, knocks from crew and gear being used in the pulpit and easy bulb replacement in the sort of condition found right forward in a small yacht. Meanwhile, the owner with one of the existing types available should ensure that the alignment and screening is correct and avoid plugs and sockets above deck, however waterproof they are said to be. The only safe method is to lead an unbroken wire from the light, through the deck (the tiny hole can easily be sealed) and to a junction box below. It is hardly necessary to add that all the navigation lights must be clear of the yacht's sails and all her gear, so that high upon the pulpits, bow and stern are the places to put them.

The chart table light has been mentioned in an earlier chapter. The best plan with the rest of the cabin lights, in any size of boat, is to have plenty of them in all sorts of corners but only use the one or two that are required for the job in hand, be it getting into a bunk after coming off watch or finding a piece of equipment in the saloon. As far as possible, they should be on the forward side of bulkheads or partial bulkheads so that the direct light can never be in the eyes of the helmsman or someone coming below. Before starting a race, those lights most used at sea can have red bulbs substituted into them. If the cabin lights are arranged primarily for sea-going use, it is pleasant for the crew if there is one bright light which can be used on arrival in harbour. Fluorescent fittings are now available in light weight, give a refreshing light to a damp cabin after a tiring race and consume little current. They do not even need to be connected to the main supply, which may be an advantage on coming into harbour with weak batteries or wishing to conserve current before the start. There is one type known as the Calalite which uses the very small type of high powered battery (e.g. Every Ready HP1). The $9\frac{1}{4}$ in. tube is 6 watts and the $12\frac{1}{2}$ in. is 8 watts, but the light given is in excess of filament bulbs of the same power.

·18·

THE SMALLEST CRUISER RACERS

"What a curious feeling!" said Alice "I must be shutting up like a telescope." And so it was indeed: she was now only ten inches high—ALICE IN WONDERLAND.

BECAUSE yachts are so remarkably smaller in size than those that sailed the open sea, say, fifty years ago, there is a tendency to assume that this trend will continue, so that a class of yacht used for any purpose will be typified by smaller dimensions as the years go by. This process cannot go on for ever, outside Wonderland, and so we consider here the smallest size of yacht that could, in practice, be used offshore.

This size, to which the general remarks on design and equipment in the precedng chapters do not necessarily always apply, is where a yacht is less than about 17 ft. W.L. down to 14 ft. The word "cruiser" has crept into the head of this page, for the reasons that among these smallest boats the pure racing design is rare. When one reaches this sort of size the reason for choosing such dimensions is nearly always one of cost, and as racing is more expensive than cruising the market for the smallest boats is thought to be for the cruiser. If the yacht is built to racing standards it starts to become questionable whether any expense is saved compared with a larger yacht. The overheads of building and labour on the essentials of any sea-going yacht are going to be little reduced. The rigging will be shorter, saving a few shillings, but there will be the same number of terminals to be made up. The main hatch has still to be constructed and is dependent on the size of the human body. Much equipment cannot be reduced in size, for instance she can carry no shorter line for kedging than her slightly larger competitors: logically the only difference should be the few inches of the height of her stem, for the size of yacht does not affect the depth of water!

Limitations   But the smaller boat will be cheaper, if only in the estimates of the builder, who decides that this is the reason for her appeal to the public and so it only remains to assess how small we can go in offshore racing design. Racing organizations usually put lower limits on their events. The reason given nowadays, when small boats have such a reputation for seaworthiness, is to ensure the event finishes within a reasonable time or merely to limit the overall number of entries in some way. A more valid reason is to restrict the range of size or ratings to ensure that the yachts are not sailing in widely different conditions. The JOG lower limit has always been 16 ft. and the GCL has the same lower waterline. The East Anglian Offshore Racing Association has its lower limit at 18 ft. LWL, but unlike the JOG and GCL it takes in large RORC boats, so its logic in trying to limit the range of sizes is apparent.

There are natural limitations to the size of yacht that can be raced, or even seriously cruised offshore, and they fall into four categories.

1. The eventual limitation must be the *size of a man*; both the necessity to accommodate him and the effect of his weight on the yacht are final limits. But before this ultimate minuscule design is contemplated, it must be appreciated that even on a 16 ft. WL, a crew of two find it tiring to cook and navigate in the cramped conditions. The number of crew becomes limited by the need for minimal living conditions on board, and more than two will be tight for a race over 60 miles. But only one man on deck when racing means falling off in the speed with which matters like spinnaker work and navigation can be dealt with. Inevitably, both men are more tired than if they had been part of a larger crew in the same race, since there are frequent occasions when both (i.e. the whole crew) are needed. The GCL, in fact, rules that the minimum crew of a yacht in its races is three. Coupled with the factor of enough room for the crew comes the matter of installing all the equipment desirable for ocean racing and particularly that required by the safety regulations. More will be said about the effect of the weight of the crew later.

2. Whether *safety* of yachts upon the sea is limited by their minimum dimensions will be debated by committees who have to decide on lower limits. A practical point here is that, as so few yachts under 17 ft. are built for offshore work, it is not going to spoil the size of the entry list if they are not allowed to race. The distinction has to be drawn between racing offshore and other types of sailing and the real question on safety is whether yachts of a certain small size can be permitted to put themselves in the inevitable occasional circumstances of potential risk which are acceptable for their bigger sisters. The reasons that a very small yacht might be more liable to get into difficulties include:

> The possibility of the crew being washed out of the shallow cockpit, which it is bound to be, if self draining.
> Damage to gear which will be light.
> Being caught out in severe conditions, when larger and therefore faster yachts have reached shelter.
> Her inability to beat to windward in bad weather to escape dangers to leeward.

The first three of these possibilities can be faced up to and precautions taken to make them unlikely. The last one is more a basic problem of the size, if not *the* basic problem, at least for ocean racing.

3. *Speed and weatherliness*. The shorter waterline and sail area carried mean a slower speed on all points of sailing. First it is well to remember the likely maximum speeds for a given waterline assuming a very reasonable speed-length ratio of 1·4. These are 16 ft., 5·6 knots; 15 ft., 5·42 knots; 14 ft., 5·2 knots. Such speeds are achieved under ideal conditions, with little sea and full sail carried on a reach. Assuming the 14 ft. yacht can make two-thirds of the maximum speed on the wind, which is 3·49 knots in good conditions, it might be more like a little under 3 knots when there is a lumpy head sea. If she sails at 45 degrees to the true wind, which is about as close as such a boat will go in the conditions, it gives us a VMG of 2 knots. You can think of this in terms of a fifty-mile beat to windward taking 25 hours. With a foul tide of 2 knots, it can be seen that it is easy enough to be trapped into making no headway or actually losing in a wind of only 20 knots on the nose. Apart from the safety angle, when the speed of the yachts in a race is in the region of the speed of the currents, we are in a situation where the yacht's speed becomes critical in relation to, say, fetching a mark. One yacht manages it but the margin-

ally slower boat will fail to do so, resulting in huge differences in elapsed time. We know this happens in all racing in light weather where there are currents, but in the smallest yachts, it may happen on an unacceptable wide range of wind strengths. Applying the same calculations to a yacht of 17 ft. gives the speed to windward in ideal conditions as 4 knots with a VMG of 2·8 knots. This is a reasonable increase in terms of the speeds of tidal streams.

Apart from the actual speeds achieved, the smaller yacht has to reduce sail earlier and has not the power to carry sail to attain the theoretical speed attributed to her. All this may make it sound as though the smallest yacht is at a hopeless disadvantage, but this may only be until more demand for ocean racers of this size makes itself felt.

4. *Speed and manœuvre.* This is less a racing matter than one of handling generally. While there are places that a very small yacht can go by reason of her length and draft, if she is coming from offshore she may find it difficult to close with a harbour because of the same reasons as in paragraph 3 above. So often in offshore races a few of the smallest boats seem to come in many hours after the rest of the fleet. This is the counterpart of the point mentioned above in which the yacht is caught out in a gale, in this case the tail-enders catching the calm weather. Even when the race is over, the size of engine that can be carried in a yacht of 14 to 16 ft. which expects to race may not be enough to overcome the foul wind and tide to enter port with any speed.

Examples of the smallest sizes If the above appears depressing, it is only because it sets out the limitations as seen in the boats which might be used as the smallest ocean racers. If there are enthusiastic people who are prepared to develop such boats for off-shore use, then most of the apparent difficulties would be overcome. Naturally with the JOG and GCL limit as it is, there is little use in trying to develop an ocean racer of 15 ft. WL. If you are tempted to think in terms of getting out of the straitjacket of displacement, by constructing a dinghy sailing type craft with watertight hatches, remember that Patrick Ellam's offshore sliding seat canoe *Theta* was just this concept. It was after sailing in her that he decided to go over to a displacement yacht, though an easily driven one which even used a trapeze at times, *Sopranino*. She had a length of 17 ft. 9 in., though a beam of only 5 ft. 3 in. One of the reasons that many similar boats to her design did not follow, was that she rated very badly under the RORC rule of that time and would have done no better under the 1957 revision. This raises a side issue as to whether rating rules are necessarily suitable for the type of hull and rig which might be best in the smallest craft.

A different approach from the same sort of beginnings was made by the yachtsman and designer John Westell some ten years after *Sopranino*. Having sailed a 14 ft. International on a number of passages in open water, he designed a dinghy type hull, the Allegro class, which would plane. Roughly speaking, the forward half of the hull was cabin and the after half open, but self draining and watertight. The waterline was not too short, 18 ft. 6 in., and despite the harshness of the RORC rule on the type, she was second in the JOG section of the 1963 Round-the-Island Race, a 53-mile course. Presumably she was able to overcome the rating disadvantage by planing. I checked one of these boats for its self-righting ability at the time and with the mast hove down to the water, there was no tendency to flood. Several were built, but the idea did not really catch on. Of more immediate interest is a shorter yacht in the same theme, the Nimrod class designed in 1968, after a further interval of some years. Being in GRP and built by a mass producer, Westerly

50. The Midjet is one conception of the very small cruiser-racer (LWL 16 ft. 8 in.). Deck shape gives reasonable room below.

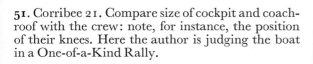

51. Corribee 21. Compare size of cockpit and coachroof with the crew: note, for instance, the position of their knees. Here the author is judging the boat in a One-of-a-Kind Rally.

52. Dismasted. Spinnaker boom has been rigged as jury mast set up with lines and a jib on its side is effective. Broken spar is being secured on deck.

53. *Top right:* Multihulls at the start of the Crystal Trophy.

54. *Bottom right:* S31 Half Tonner ready for the road!

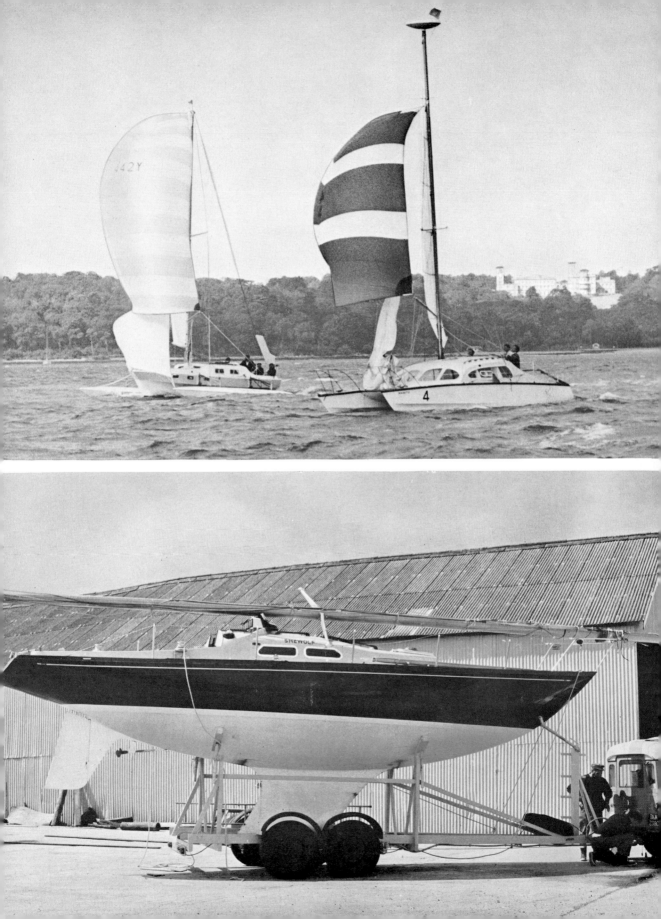

55. When the race is over and corrected times are awaited. JOG crews relax at Weymouth after a race.

Marine Construction Ltd., she may fall into the hands of people with ideas about offshore racing. Designed by the famous dinghy expert, Ian Proctor, there is no consideration of any rating rule in hull or rig. The waterline is 15 ft. 6 in. and the rig has a large mainsail (110 sq. ft.) and small genoa (56 sq. ft.) which goes to a point 3 ft. 9 in. below the level of the headboard of the mainsail (Fig. 132). Despite the appearance of the cabin top being only a cuddy, I have checked that there is room inside which includes two permanent berths, galley and space for a chart table. There is a W.C. between the berths. The side decks are large enough to move around on with ease and the hatch is a proper sliding structure.

Although the boat is self righting and has buoyancy to prevent disaster in the event of total flooding, she does not have the power to carry sail in a breeze without the crew sitting her out. I am not suggesting she is suitable for use offshore as she is, but changes in the rig and such matters as the security of the crew in the cockpit might make it feasible. The point is that this is a design concept which if developed can break the problem of the slow speeds of very small displacement yachts.

A yacht that has been successful offshore and was designed to the minimum sizes allowed was the Corsaire class. She has won both the JOG and GCL points championships, but is now too old a design to be competitive. She shows, however, that a boat of this size in a number of different hands has been able to make many offshore passages and win races. She was designed by J. J. Herbulot with a waterline of 16 ft., LOA 18 ft. 2 in. beam 6 ft. 4 in. and draft 2 ft. 9 in., again the minimum allowed. The yacht was constructed in hard chine marine ply, and the maximum crew at sea was three. When in harbour it was useful to have a hotel nearby!

A yacht only one inch shorter on the waterline which made two Atlantic crossings was *Nova Espero*, designed and sailed by Stanley Smith, with one companion on each occasion.

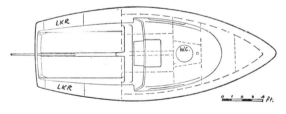

FIG. 132. *The Nimrod class designed by Ian Proctor is an example of an attempt to combine performance and ability in the open sea. The lifting keel gives 250 lb. ballast: there is 4 ft. draft with this keel down. The LOA is 17 ft. 9 in., LWL 15 ft. 6 in. and beam 6 ft. 5½ in. Mainsail 145 sq. ft., genoa 56 sq. ft.*

He has since built other and rather similar yachts inside the JOG limits, though they make no claim to racing ability. On *Nova Espero*'s second crossing, in 1951, from Dartmouth, England, to New York she went by a high trade wind route and took nearly four months to complete the voyage! The first voyage from Nova Scotia to Dartmouth by the northern route was only six weeks, which was just as well since the boat had no cabin top at that time and was virtually open, with a wooden dinghy inverted over her amidships.

It is useful to mention two other ocean crossings by very small sailing yachts. There was no question of racing, but the fact that such craft have made passages in all the weather a long voyage involves means that it would be feasible to develop a racing boat from their inspiration rather than the design itself. The American Robert Manry, in the 13 ft. 6 in. *Tinkerbelle*, crossed the Atlantic from Falmouth, Massachusetts, in 1965 to Falmouth, England in seventy-eight days. Once again note the appalling low speed. Probably the boat was being driven backwards at times. I was on the Fastnet race as reports of Manry's approach were being broadcast and we were experiencing easterly winds in the south-western waters of the British Isles. It was evident that his progress to windward was negligible. On several occasions during the voyage, he was swept out of the cockpit and overboard, though his lifeline kept him attached to the boat. In the same summer an Englishman, John Riding, was sailing the Atlantic in the opposite direction in an even shorter boat than *Tinkerbelle*. Called *Sea Egg*, which her high freeboard hull with tumble-home made very appropriate, she was only 12 ft. in overall length! From Plymouth, *Sea Egg* called at a number of ports before making Bermuda and then Newport, Rhode Island. It is interesting to note that the yacht was intended for racing in the 1964 single-handed transatlantic race, but her entry was refused, a decision which appears to be justified by the length of time on passage being longer than that of *Tinkerbelle*. Both these yachts were single-handers; it is difficult to imagine more than one person being able to live in them for any length of time.

After these minute sailing craft, which nevertheless were able to navigate to their destinations, two standard yachts should be mentioned. One is the British Leisure 17 designed by Arthur Howard. The other is the French Midjet designed by Georges Auzepy-Brenneur. The Leisure 17 has a waterline of 14 ft., beam 7 ft. and displaces 0·54 tons with a nominal 46 per cent ballast ratio. The GRP hull and deck structure with reverse sheer and a well-proportioned coachroof is extremely pleasing; without appearing unduly high, it gives sitting head room below (Fig. 133). If using the boat for serious offshore work, check through all the fittings and fastenings to ensure they have adequate strength. As in other yachts of this size, the fittings are light because the builder needs to keep to a low price and often only dinghy equipment is of suitable dimensions. This yacht seems to have a better turn of speed than the others mentioned above. Sailed by John Adams, one of them left Weymouth, England, in September 1967 to cross the Atlantic. She made the passage from the Canaries to Antigua in twenty-nine days. This particular voyage had a sequel when Adams drifted on to the coast of communist Cuba. As a result he spent five weeks in prison before being released and the boat was impounded.

The Midjet achieves room below by rolling the deck up from the rubbing strake, so there are no separate side decks. Her waterline is 16 ft. 10 in. so she is within the JOG and and GCL limits. The other dimensions are LOA 19 ft. 2 in., beam 7 ft. 6 in., draft 3 ft. She displaces 0·64 tons with a 46 per cent ballast ratio. The forestay comes just below the masthead: the rig generally is in accordance with offshore practice and this includes the

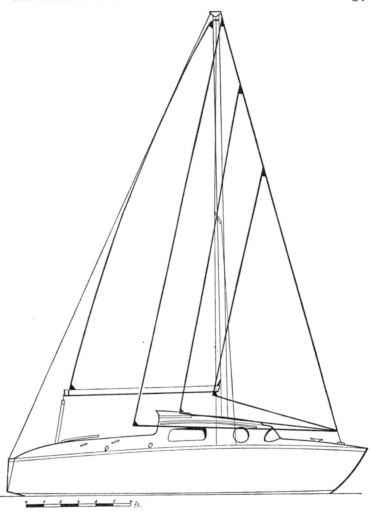

FIG. 133. *The Leisure 17 design with a waterline of 14 ft. The sheer line and coachroof ensure the necessary minimal volume below without undue boxiness.*

siting of main and genoa tracks. One piece of dinghy-type equipment used is a tiller extension to enable the helmsman to sit well to weather.

Weight and size Having decided on a certain short length, be it 14 or 15 ft. LWL, most designers with a standard boat in mind will want to include the maximum possible accommodation. The Leisure 17, for instance, has room to sleep four people. When they are in their bunks, there is room for little else in the boat! But size and space means displacement and weight in the hull rather than weight on the ballast keel. Since small yachts are inherently less stiff than large ones, this accentuates a potential fault. Fig. 134 shows two yachts of the same length and displacement, but one with more "room" in it. Because of the high structure and distribution of gear inside it, the centre of gravity of the yacht is higher. Putting it slightly differently, while the underwater shape in our two theoretical yachts is the same, there has to be less ballast in the keel of the roomy one, if she is to float to her marks; that is, her ballast ratio is less favourable.

The true position of the centre of gravity is the important factor and with a high overall coachroof, the effect of two members of the crew standing on it, struggling, for instance, with a fitting in the area of the gooseneck, is considerable. They weigh perhaps 330 lb., which may be half the weight of the ballast keel. Add to this the heeling moment of a 25-knot wind and the situation looks dubious. This is the worst case, but not unknown with several standard small cruisers, which are said to be suitable for offshore work (Fig. 135).

Distribution of weights must be made to ensure stiffness in such a boat. A reasonable proportion of the weight, say 30 to 40 per cent, should be in the ballast keel and a high structure should be avoided for the double reason given above. In the example in the Figure, the 40 per cent ballast ratio is reduced to 32 per cent with the crew of two and their gear (430 lb.) on board.

These are some of the problems for the designer of the smallest craft, which do not arise with ocean racers as they are known generally. The use of materials should not be forgotten, because very lightweight cabin tops and masting are of particular value to these boats. But even a lightweight structure must not be elevated, because of its own windage and the weight and windage of the crew and also fittings upon it.

Construction and accommodation   The tendency to put as many bunks as possible into standard yachts has already been mentioned. Both the Leisure 17 and the Midjet have room for four, though I would put the racing crew at two or three at the most. But since four bunks in a 14 or 16 ft. yacht will take up the whole cabin, they also become stowage areas by day. Deep lockers and dry covered and secured bags are more useful. Very little water is needed below to make the whole cabin wet and it must be possible to remove it quickly while sailing. Some ideas on clearing the bilge have been given previously.

Other sailing essentials will be a plotting board rather than a chart table, but it must be secured to prevent it falling into a wet area or on to one of the crew. The lavatory can be a bucket, though we have already noted the Nimrod has a W.C. A single-burner stove, such as a Camping Gaz cylinder with burner on top mounted to swing or a gimballed Primus, will be the essence of the galley. The bunk for the man (assuming a crew of two) off watch must be in the right place. That is as far against the side of the boat as possible so that he can lie down in it to windward and add significant power. The fore and aft position of this pair of bunks must be in the midships area for reasons of trim—an additional reason why trying to fit in four berths runs into difficulties.

One matter to receive attention in the construction should be the separation of the cockpit and cabin. This must be permanently watertight at least up to cockpit seat level. When cockpit coamings are taken out nearly to the topsides the first exit for the water if the cockpit ships a heavy sea, can be over the bridge deck into the cabin. Even with the wash boards sealing the hatching effectively there is a dangerous amount of water held in the cockpit. Such coamings should be designed with drains or gutters of large size which let the water flow out across the stern. This is in addition to drains in the cockpit sole, which should be no smaller than those on larger yachts (1 in. diameter) for the weight of water is more serious.

The tendency to put weak fittings on small boats has been mentioned and it must be emphasized that a man grabbing a handhold to save himself going overboard puts as much strain on it in a 14 ft. yacht as in a 44 ft. yacht. One vital item which should be given the

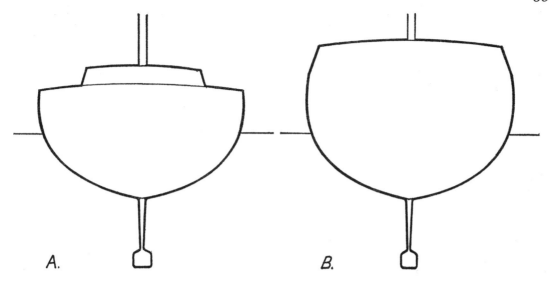

A.   B.

FIG. 134 (above). *Two yachts of equal displacement as typified by the area of section under water. There is more "room" in B than A, but the centre of gravity will be higher, even though the overall weight is the same.*

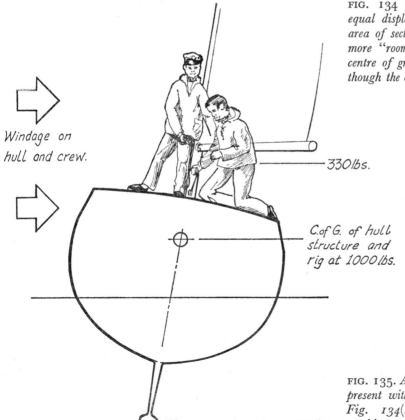

Windage on hull and crew.

— 330 lbs.

C. of G. of hull structure and rig at 1000 lbs.

670 lbs.

FIG. 135. *Additional heeling forces are present with the raised deck boat of Fig. 134(B) when the crew are working at, for instance, the foot of the mast.*

closest attention is the security of the rudder on a transom, though the Leisure 17 has managed to get it inboard of a counter. The transom mounting means that the rudder hangings cannot be spaced as widely apart as is desirable. They are then subjected to considerable moment by a deep blade due to the normal action of the water and in the event of striking an underwater or floating object. Apart from any design considerations, a skeg is desirable from which an additional hanging can be secured (Fig. 136).

Since it impossible for very small yachts to carry a life-raft, calculations should be made to find how much buoyancy material is required to float the yacht in the event of total flooding.

Engine An outboard motor is the most likely form of power under 17 ft.: yet for racing it would be better not to carry it at all. It may not be practical to leave it ashore, however, in the event of a calm before the start, to which the yacht had to motor to reach the line in time. Some form of completely sealed locker is preferable so that there is no chance of fuel escaping or giving any smell, when the engine is lying on its side and being shaken violently in a seaway. A side mounting bracket for the outboard will not be satisfactory, because of rolling. With a stern mounting, stowage for that becomes a problem. When racing, every effort must be made to unship anything except the most discreet structure. Ideally the whole thing should be left ashore and this includes spare cans of fuel, tins of oil, funnels and engine tools.

Rig All the points about efficiency and rating apply to the smallest craft as much as to the others, and the remarks above about weak standard fittings apply with particular force. I can recall several cases of small yachts being dismasted because the rig was built down to a price but the boat was driven in a racing fashion by her owner. The correct mast section for a masthead rig may not be available in very small sizes, but there is a Proctor section, though not especially deep, which is elliptical and measures 3·6 in. by 2·62 in. Tangs, rigging screws and other linkages must be in accordance with offshore practice. Small shackles and aircraft rigging screws should not be resorted to. Slab reefing is so easy to tie down on a small boat, that it may well be favoured in the interests of a well setting sail when reefed (Fig. 104), as this will be done more often than in larger yachts.

Despite the rating rule, some designers prefer not to have masthead rig in yachts under 16 ft. This is in the interests of reducing weight aloft and because of the stiffness demanded by a masthead genoa. Other reasons contributing to the case for a seven-eighths rig are the fact that the yacht reduces sail early, and so a smaller genoa can be held on to as the wind increases; it may be difficult to place the mast far enough aft to design an effective foretriangle; and in the size of boat, the rig does not need running backstays or jumper struts, so there is no extra windage.

Once out at sea, it is not acceptable to allow the weight of a man up the mast because of the danger to overall stability and possible damage to a rig of such light scantlings. All the more reason to examine everything aloft before leaving harbour—after all, it is only necessary to heave the yacht over alongside a quay or a larger vessel to inspect every fitting in comfort!

Crews Whatever is said about the rigours of life aboard small yachts at sea, applies to the smallest with greater force! In moderate or bad weather the motion will be violent;

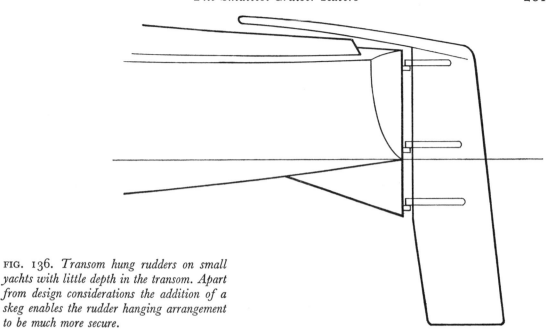

FIG. 136. *Transom hung rudders on small yachts with little depth in the transom. Apart from design considerations the addition of a skeg enables the rudder hanging arrangement to be much more secure.*

there will be little protection in the cockpit from wind, rain and spray; below decks a little damp, off foul weather clothing for instance, will spread quickly through the accommodation. On the other hand, the gear is child's play to handle. Life for a crew of two is simple in that the usual problem of teamwork, which has to be developed in bigger boats, does not arise. I can vouch that a real advantage lies in doing such light work and doing it all yourself or with one known companion.

The basic crew problem, though, is that as people get older and become more skilled at racing, they are usually able to afford larger boats. So the smaller yachts tend to contain the rather less experienced skippers and crews, and when their performance is not outstanding this tends to reflect on the yacht and her general type. For the same reasons, people owning such boats leave the class after a few years in favour of something larger instead of investing in an improved yacht of the same size. Thus the breed is left in the hands of builders and designers who must see what the market will accept, instead of there being a steady state of improvement through regular racing.

Only a handful of the yachts in the JOG which have engaged at any time in regular racing have been at the lower limit of 16 ft. or within one foot of it. This is in marked contrast, for obvious reasons, to the vast number of boats which were built and raced to the RORC lower limit which was 24 ft.

· 19 ·

MULTIHULLS OFFSHORE

Attraction of multihulls Racing is concerned with the relative speed between different boats and to some extent between boat and current. The length of course is set in accordance with the time available and the expected speed of the yachts. The possibilities of multihull craft offshore are in their increased speed, whose use lies in the increase in range that it gives the vessel. For example the distance from the Solent to Le Havre is about 80 miles, but such a race cannot in practice be run for conventional small yachts in a normal week-end, between Friday and Sunday night. Allowing an average of 4 knots for the fleet and just eight hours in harbour, which many skippers would consider insufficient, it is in theory possible to get back to the Solent before Monday, but few race committees would arrange such an event. With an expected speed of 10 knots, however, such a visit to a foreign port presents less problems of timing and such average speeds can be attained in multihull craft. Apart from the statistics of the matter, sailing a multihull is an exhilarating experience, with speeds like 15 or 16 knots commonplace in a moderate breeze in a yacht less than 30 ft. in overall length. All this is on a comparatively level platform making life often much easier than in a single-hulled yacht. Yet another attraction at the present time is that as the multihulls are in the minority there is a pioneering feel about them and room for experiment and innovation untrammelled by the many established ideas which hover about conventional yachts. So catamarans and trimarans attract the experimenters, the unconventional, and, as it happens, a number of newcomers who have no experience of other types of sailing. In passing it may be noted that any discussion on multihulls generates intense argument between their advocates and their antagonists. Sometimes this is because the parties are thinking in terms of different uses of the boats, though there are also those who are commercially actuated. Here we are concerned with craft suitable for offshore racing, and generally not those over 40 ft. LOA.

The multihull problem To listen to some of the strongest advocates of multihull craft, one would think that in some way they had broken away from the natural laws of naval architecture. The principles governing the multihull are the same as any yacht and resemble the behaviour of beamy yachts without ballast such as dinghies which depend for their stability on shape alone. The immense initial stability of a wide hull means that heeling is resisted and without the weight of ballast, the light hull can be driven very fast indeed. A simple raft would be the same except that its shape would involve unacceptable wetted surface and wave making.

   With a catamaran a semi-circular section can be adopted in each hull giving, by simple geometry, the minimum wetted surface for the volume of displacement. It is a fact that whether the unballasted craft is a dinghy, raft, catamaran or trimaran, when it is heeled to a certain angle the stability becomes negative, or, if you like, it continues to heel over by reason of its form until it reaches a second position of stability. This position is when it is totally upside down. Measures can be taken to prevent, avoid and alleviate such a happening, but it remains the basic multihull problem. Multihulls have capsized at sea in this way and such incidents are documented by those who have been rescued; there have also been fatalities arising from circumstances not fully known. The multihull designers, Arthur Piver and Hedley Nicholl, were both lost at sea when sailing their own trimarans. Many multihulls have also made fine ocean passages without incident and sailed many hundreds of miles to windward, as well as thousands down wind. None of these events whether tragic or successful prove anything special; among all types of yacht, totally unsuitable craft have made outstanding voyages, while fine vessels have met disaster.

Multihulls demand their own sailing techniques, but for ocean racing they still have to achieve as hard driving as possible to beat the next man. Racing involves manœuvring at times close to the shore and being able to claw off it when the breeze freshens. Imagine an ocean racing picture that happens perhaps once or twice a season; a dark night, wind 20 knots, but gusts to 29 or 30 knots at times and trying to weather a headland, the tide causing the inevitable confused sea off it; it is then that the conventional yacht is sometimes overpressed and hove down by a squall yet makes to windward, whatever ill-treatment is meted out to her. This is the situation where the multihull will not take *any* treatment. She will be on the knife edge of stability between optimum performance and a serious capsize situation. Too much reduction of sail may result in being unable to sail to windward, nor is bearing away in a squall (which is difficult to anticipate in the dark) sound practice navigationally. If she has sea room she can up helm and run out of it, but when racing this may involve disastrous loss of time.

A possible approach Michael Henderson of Cowes, built his own JOG yacht in the 1950s, and as a result wondered how he could overcome the slow absolute speeds of a boat of some 17 ft. WL. He designed and built several sailing catamarans for ocean racing, fully conscious of the problem which is summarized by the graph of Fig. 137. The lack of stability of the multihull after its peak righting moment, achieved somewhere around 20 degrees, is in striking contrast to the gradual but continuing stability of the ballasted yacht. The Michael Henderson designs sought to change the pattern of this graph by fitting ballast keels to each hull and—a masterly innovation—by fixing a buoyant float at the masthead. These additions made it impossible for the catamaran to capsize beyond 90 degrees. *Misty Miller*, a 24 ft. WL design of this type, could capsize to 90 degrees, but it was possible for the crew to right her by climbing out on to the keel. She was built in 1961 and was sailed for more than two seasons. In 1963 she followed (or was it led?) the Fastnet fleet in an unofficial race with a Piver-designed trimaran, completing the course in 126 hours. The sailing was mostly either to windward or running. Yet at the end of this experience of designing and sailing multihulls offshore, the designer knew the problem was still unsolved, for even a 90 degree capsize at sea is no joke. At the time few other people in Europe were prepared to tackle seriously the development of multihulls for ocean racing and without the regular pressure of offshore courses the boats could not progress.

Racing progress Cruising multihulls have appeared in a number of forms, though without ballast, the promoters claiming that the capsize problem was over-emphasized. The sport is well developed on the west coast of the United States, but the craft are large

s

ones, very suitable with their deck space for the hot weather in that area. They race regularly as far afield as Honolulu, though this route from San Francisco is invariably downwind, and the lee shore problem mentioned above does not arise. Many of the early cruising multihulls in England were under-canvassed, which provided one way of avoiding an unsafe heeling force but contributed nothing to racing. Others did attempt to get speed and considerable claims were made, but I do not know of the graph of Fig. 137 being refuted. Presumably the way to query this is to agree with the behaviour of the unballasted multihull, but dispute the heeling force which is also shown. Whether heeling force A, B or C is true depends on the wind strength in relation to the heeling moment, but the designers of the unballasted boats could say that the heeling moment in a 30-knot wind was shown as C or even in very heavy weather never became greater than B. Therefore the craft in question never reaches the capsizing point at the top of the curve. Others would reply that curve A more accurately shows the situation in a 30-knot wind, and thus the heeling force remains greater than the righting moment at all angles of heel. The size of the vessel has a bearing on the appearance of the graph for heeling versus righting force is proportional to the square of the scale for multihulls of similar proportions. Over 40 or 50 ft. overall the capsizing problem, for this reason alone, becomes less important.

By 1967 interest was high enough for the Royal Yachting Association to arrange a race solely for multihull craft of 20 ft. LWL and over in the English Channel from Cowes to Plymouth, round a buoy off Cherbourg and the Wolf Rock Lighthouse, a distance of 284 miles. This major event for multihulls offshore is known as the Crystal Trophy and is now an annual event. It has been made possible to organize by the introduction of a rule of measurement and rating for multihulls which works the results by a time correction factor derived from the rating. In 1967 there were seventeen starters. The yachts ran from Cowes towards the eastern end of the Isle of Wight before rounding it and coming on to a reach for the leg across the English Channel to the CH1 buoy off Cherbourg. The wind was Force 5 (I was sailing at the time several miles away) and the multihulls began to put up very fast times on their favourite point of sailing. Then the 43 ft. (LOA) Rudy Choy design *Golden Cockerel* experienced a 25-knot gust, which is normal during a Force 5 wind. The crew were about to reduce sail, but they were too late because she was blown on her side and then turned completely upside down. They were rescued by helicopter and a naval vessel, after waiting calmly on the upturned hull. It was fortunate that the incident occurred in daylight and close to land. Later in the race the wind fell right away and the winner was *Tomahawk*, a standard 30 ft. Iroquois design by Rod Macalpine-Downie (Fig. 138), which completed the course in 2 days 22 hours 39 minutes 4 seconds. In 1968 a dozen boats started and there were winds up to Force 7 on parts of the course. *Tomahawk* won again, but covered the distance in half the time of the previous race. Such speeds over an offshore course of 300 miles in dirty weather must be an encouragement to the development of multihull racing.

The boats in the Crystal Trophy have been very varied in shape and concept and none could really be said to be "designed to the rule". Until there is regular multihull racing in European waters, the breed as far as ocean racing is concerned will not be under enough pressure to produce really good sea-going boats. It is therefore not possible to point out a successful type of multihull under the RYA rule. Some of the secondary problems have been tackled and these include the slamming of bridge decks in catamarans, which has resulted in giving more buoyancy forward and keeping solid structure out of the forward

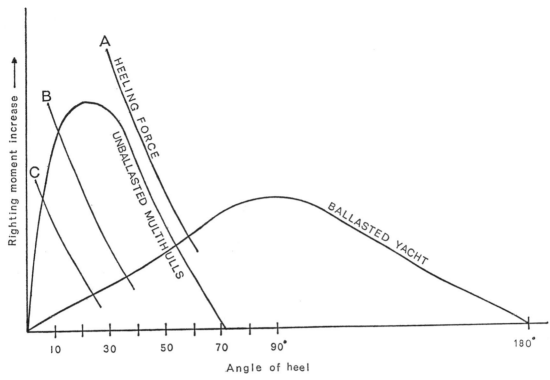

FIG. 137. *The stability of an unballasted multihull and a ballasted single hull.*

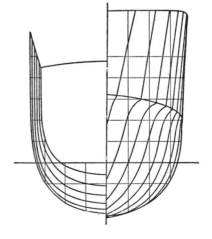

FIG. 138. *Hull lines of one hull of the Iroquois catamaran designed by Rod Macalpine-Downie. Underwater it approaches a semi-circular form thus giving minimum wetted surface. Forward there might be lack of buoyancy, but this potential failing of multihulls is offset here by the pronounced knuckle.*

part of the hull, using struts and netting. Any lack of buoyancy in the forward part of the hull may cause difficulties in steep seas. The 31 ft. LOA catamaran, *Haxted Argo II*, designed by Prout, was capsized in the mouth of the River Elbe after the bows had driven right into a sea and failed to rise; she was running before a gale of perhaps Force 8, and carrying only a storm jib. Total disaster was avoided because the multihull had a masthead float and she lay on her side, enabling the crew to release the life-raft. A contribution to the capsize, which resulted in total loss of the yacht, though the crew were all rescued, was lack of buoyancy in the hulls forward.

The masthead float was non-standard, but should definitely be carried by any multihull going offshore unless she has some other method of preventing total capsize. There are types of these which will inflate in an emergency, thus preventing windage during normal sailing, but an owner would have to be fully satisfied about the reliability of such a device. Some boats have fitted mainsheet jamb cleats which release when the angle of heel goes beyond a certain point, but how the sheet is certain to run out without snarling is not known. If this snag can be overcome it could provide a real aid, as many designs take a long time actually to "flip" and hover long enough for the release of sail pressure to act. Another safety point on multihulls is to have the life-raft secured where it can be released with the vessel completely capsized. It can be lashed on a netting foredeck, for instance. One item that is less trouble on a multihull than on a single-hulled yacht is the spinnaker. Not only is there a wider and steadier deck platform for handling this sail and its gear, but the difficulties associated with rolling are largely eliminated. In light weather the higher speed of the multihull rapidly brings the apparent wind away from astern.

Future developments   For many years the JOG have had a multihull class available, but only occasional boats have turned up to race with the fleet of conventional ocean racers. The same pattern has occurred elsewhere when clubs have announced separate multihull divisions. The exception in England is the Island Sailing Club Round-the-Island race, where a dozen or so multihulls start every year after the fleet of more than four hundred yachts. In Europe the habit of racing multihulls regularly has yet to be established. The Crystal Trophy, interesting though it is, is sponsored by a petrol company and cannot be said to represent a trend in racing. Many of the entries have been backed by their builders or designers. What is needed is for a number of yachtsmen to race multihulls on their own programme for several seasons in the same way as any other class or club to show that good racing is to be had, and despite the efforts of individuals this has not yet happened.

The way multihull ocean racing would seem to be developing is to produce exciting craft with expert crews who will enter for specific events. Such crews will be able to fly the weather hull and ride the boat on the knife edge with a knowledge of how to avoid capsizing or what to do if it should happen. The family cruising catamaran or trimaran will tend to lack sail area, though by reason of her hull from will be reasonably fast compared with single hulled yachts and will have ample deck space and accommodation. The weight and cabin structure required will make it unwise to drive her and she will be advised not to be caught out in a difficult position such as a lee shore. In more settled climates than north-west Europe it should be possible for multihull races to be arranged, particularly if the courses have a good proportion of downwind work and the craft are large, say 40 to 50 ft. LOA and above.

One hopes that this analysis is not too close to the picture, because the development

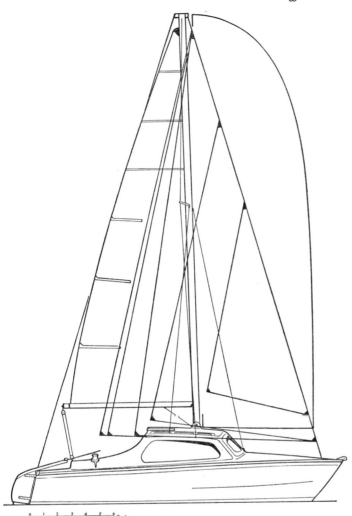

FIG. 139. *Sail plan of Hirondelle Class. The length of mainsail batten is not restricted by any rule. The shrouds are secured to the coachroof. Sail areas: Mainsail 118 sq. ft., 175% genoa 227 sq. ft. 170% genoa 220 sq. ft., 150% genoa 190 sq. ft., No. 1 jib 132 sq. ft., No. 2 jib 52 sq. ft.*

(Below). *Accommodation of the Hirondelle catamaran. The galley and chart table are in different hulls and the dagger boards can be seen near them. Though not shown there are twin rudders, one on each hull, linked for steering. The weight of anchor and chain, if carried, would be better out of the end of the boat. The dimensions are LOA 22 ft. 8 in., LWL 20 ft., beam 10 ft., draft with boards down 4 ft., displacement 1·15 tons.*

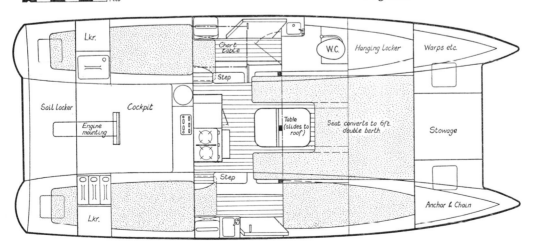

of all-round racing cruising multihulls would better the sea-going properties of the type as a whole in the same way as ocean racers have benefited the modern cruising yacht. One attempt at a cruising boat, which is at the same time aimed at racing under the RYA multihull rule, is the Hirondelle Class designed by Chris Hammond. She is designed to the minimum size allowed under the rule and the rig and fittings follow normal offshore practice. She is constructed in GRP and for what one would expect to pay the cruising range would be greatly in excess of a conventional yacht. With dagger boards, which in many catamarans need to be of large area, the sailing performance in normal conditions is good, but she is, of course, not immune from the multihull problem and for some reason the standard boat is not supplied with a masthead float (Fig. 139).

The RYA multihull rule   The rule was introduced by the RYA as there was no precedent for a rating rule for yachts other than those with a single hull. It is based on the ideas of the 1957 RORC rule, though very different in appearance. At the moment it remains simple as are all rating systems when they are first created, and there will have to be much more design and exploitation of the rule before it reaches the complication of a developed rule. The rating is given as follows:

Rating = MR + (Scantling component + Mast Component + Fin Components + Propeller component)

in this formula
$$MR = \frac{\cdot 2L\sqrt{S}}{\sqrt{A}} + \cdot 2(L + \sqrt{S} + \tfrac{1}{2}B)$$

The factors taken into account are length (L), sail area (S), cross-sectional area at maximum position of the complete boat (A), and beam (B). There is no attempt to measure displacement, weigh the vessel or to try to find the immersed depth as is done with single-hull craft. The B measurement is the greatest overall beam wherever found: wherever $\tfrac{1}{2}B$ occurs in the formulae, it applies to catamarans and when trimarans are being measured $\tfrac{1}{3}B$ is used instead. Length is obtained by simple formulae which take into account the lengths of the different hulls in cases where they vary. The sail area uses the RORC measurement of sail area, but it will make no difference to the principle of the rule if the CCA or IOR system of sail measurement is applied. Two interesting points are that there are no restrictions on batten length or revolving masts. The mast height is restricted to $L + B + \sqrt{A}$. In 1967 the IYRU adopted the RYA rule on an experimental basis for international use, but so far there does not seem to be any great use of it.

RYA racing regulations   Linked to its rating rule the RYA created racing and safety regulations for multihulls and once again these are in form based on the rules of the RORC and JOG. Many of the rules could equally apply to single-hulled vessels and are to do with matters like sail numbers, recalls and the use of radio. The safety rules are also in most respects unexceptional calling as they do for handholds, lifebuoys, fire extinguishers and a guard rail of 24 in. "continuously round the deck area". There are, however, several care-fully thought out rules which apply specially to multihulls. Before racing, the current rules should be obtained from the RYA and studied, but some of interest are as follows:

"The crew should know where the gear is stowed and be trained in its use, and in fire, capsize and man overboard drills. (This last is especially important in the case of multihulls where speeds may be high and special techniques of handling may be necessary.)"

"A vessel should possess sufficient windward ability to enable her to get off a lee shore in bad conditions and, as a guide, it is considered that boats having no salient fins, keels or centre-boards are very likely to be deficient in this ability unless of exceptional type, and owners should make every effort to assure themselves of their boat's weatherliness before racing offshore."

"The cockpit or cockpits must be self-draining outboard of the hulls by means of adequate scuppers, and companionway openings must be provided with suitable weatherboards. As a guide it is considered that a cockpit well area exceeding 20 per cent of LOA × B is verging on the excessive."

·20·

MAINTENANCE FOR RACING

*0730. The main boom is broken!! Of all the son-of-a-bitching luck. It's dispiriting to be brought out of sleep with this kind of news. It gave way under the strain caused by a makeshift vang strop. This probably means that our chances for winning this race are blown. It's pretty hard to recover from a lousy break like this one. Damn it to hell. And the worst of it is that the break was probably avoidable—*WILLIAM SNAITH *on board* Figaro

ENOUGH has been said in the preceding chapters to emphasize the importance of pains-taking preparation needed for success in ocean racing. So for the racing boat maintenance is a continual process and not something which is done during the winter in the hope that the season will then be left free for sailing! During a racing season the commitment of maintaining the yacht between races will be heavy, but it does mean that as she is kept at one hundred per cent, too much work does not accumulate for the laying-up period. Keeping even a wooden ocean racer up to standard in this way, I was surprised how little fitting out work was required at the start of a new season.

Weekly work   Assuming the type of programme which involves regular week-end races, the most important aid to maintenance is a defect list. Ensure that the mates or all the crew are trained to enter any defects or breakages during a race in a book readily available. The most practical plan in a small yacht is to write these in the log book, perhaps always in block capitals or some way in which they can be picked out of the other entries after-wards (Fig. 42). Usually someone will draw the skipper's attention to the trouble and after trying to deal with it or effecting a temporary repair, it is he who will enter the defect. The list of these is one of the jobs to be done before going ashore. The work must then be undertaken early in the week if the yacht is racing the following week-end. Inevitably, materials or spares will take a little longer to obtain than expected and early completion saves the disturbing effect of "last minute" work on the yacht before the next race. More time is spent up the mast of the highly tuned ocean racing rig, than on other types of yacht. A comfortable bosun's chair which is light in weight but also can be used at sea with security in shown in Fig. 140. It was found satisfactory by Dudley Pope on his Atlantic crossing in the yacht *Golden Dragon*.

One part of the equipment that frequently requires attention is the sail locker. Due to handling or chafe, some sail or other will probably need to go ashore for repair. The crew should be trained to check for small holes, while a sail is aloft and easily seen, and to watch for small breaks in stitching. This is the most common fault in synthetic sails and the problem of the stiching standing proud from terylene has not been solved. In some cases the wear of stitching has to be accepted and the sail restitched several times during the season. I had considerable trouble with the batten pockets of a mainsail until we finally used hand-stitching on this particular part of the sail. Spinnakers are particularly prone to small tears, though the modern "rip-stop" cloths are woven to try to halt this, If the rip is more than a few inches it has to be sewn up on board, until such time as it can be taken to a sailmaker, but small holes are very adequately temporarily mended with self-adhesive tape which can be obtained for this purpose. When a JOG boat split her spinnaker quite badly just before the start of a night passage race on a recent occasion, the skipper did a very large repair job putting adhesive tape in a number of places on the sail. The spinnaker was actually used for some thirty miles in a fresh breeze without it parting again: when I saw the sail afterwards, it appeared to be constructed entirely of adhesive tape! Terylene twine ready waxed and plenty of sail needles (in practice carpet needles being better for yacht sails than the traditional needle, which tend to get broken), together with a sail-maker's palm should be carried in a special sailmaker's kit. The various twine and needles can also be used for work on other canvas equipment or ropework during a race.

Hull surface Wherever the hull surface is in contact with the water it must give the least possible resistance. Once the yacht is sailing towards the start of the race nothing more can be done about this vital speed factor, so it is one of the most important of all

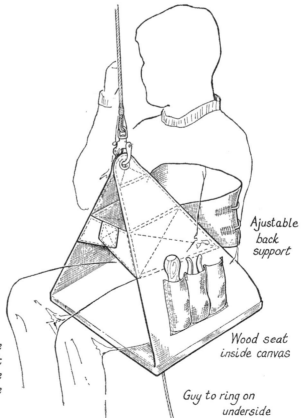

FIG. 140. *Suitable bosun's chain for offshore work, as used on* Golden Dragon. *The back support gives more than usual security and the tool pockets solve a common difficulty. The material used is 11-oz. terylene.*

Ajustable
back
support

Wood seat
inside canvas

Guy to ring on
underside

aspects of maintenance. My attempts over the years to obtain reliable data on the frictional properties of different paints have surprisingly met with a wall of silence and there does not seem to be quantitative information on the comparison of bottom paints. I believe the most important factor is to have a fair hull without ripples which would break any flow that is achieved. Special attention should be paid to fairing in any skin fittings, which should be kept to a minimum. Other uneven places can occur where the rudder and trim tab hinge. After the join has been made as fair as possible in the construction, thin rubber fairing pieces should be mounted to obviate any gap. These will need renewing from time to time. Not only does a gap between rudder and its skeg break up flow, but it renders the blade less effective and less able to be of minimum feasible size. The propeller question has already been discussed and, assuming a folding screw is used, it is thought by many skippers that a solid support for the shaft, suitably faired off, causes less resistance than a strut.

All the firms specializing in yacht paints offer forms of "racing anti-fouling" and this is usually copper based and dries hard so that it can be scrubbed and burnished. Variations are based on mercury and tin. One will not go far wrong with this type of coating and the emphasis should be on having a paint that can be maintained in good condition, rather than something that will stay clean. Such racing anti-foulings do not resist growth as long as the leeching type, but the latter are too soft and will not polish up. It is best to arrange a scrubbing programme so that the yacht comes out before the important races in a season. A couple of weeks is as long as is acceptable to leave the hull without cleaning even if there is no apparent sign of fouling. In most waters it will be unusual if there is not even a slightly slimy feel in a few places and it is this that has to be prevented. Whether it is factual or psychological, I do not know, but to have a yacht which has been burnished within a day or two before the start of race, seems to give her a slight edge. As skipper you know then the bottom is perfect.

Some paints are now made with a graphite content and graphite has long been thought of as giving a low friction surface. The high graphite content paints are only suitable for yachts not kept in the water; for ocean racers a modified form with some anti-fouling properties is usual. It is possible to achieve an excellent surface with one of these known as "Graph-killer" and it is also easy to apply smoothly. The question arises whether small yachts are best kept out of the water and there is no doubt that as far as the hull is concerned, it is advantageous. For wooden yachts there is the additional factor of less soakage.

Keeping out of the water is not a common practice with offshore yachts for practical reasons, though many boats before big events or an important series are kept on the slip for an appreciable period and until it is absolutely necessary for them to be sailing. In the Half Ton Cup a rule was introduced in 1968 to prevent hauling out of yachts once the series, lasting about a week, had started. This was to stop a scramble for the limited facilities, which might be in favour of a home team. Racing men are nothing if not resourceful and I remember that before the long race of the series a diver was offering his services to rub over the immersed area of the yachts! The idea of using underwater equipment is not far-fetched and quite practical at times: if there is only time to check over part of the hull, the area to concentrate on is the leading two feet of the keel, which is the most likely area of laminar flow, followed by the trailing edges of keel and rudder. This consideration also applies when the yacht is being prepared ashore.

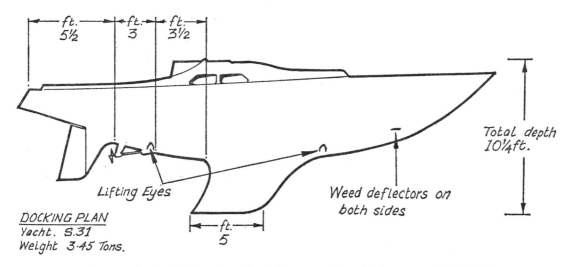

ft. 5½ ft. 3 ft. 3½

Total depth 10¼ft.

Lifting Eyes

Weed deflectors on both sides

DOCKING PLAN
Yacht. S.31
Weight 3·45 Tons.

ft. 5

FIG. 141. *An example of a docking plan. Simple but extremely useful data are available by this means.*

The yacht on shore Various means are employed to haul a yacht out, the most conventional being the slipway with a cradle; for a small amount of work or a scrub, the yacht can stay on the slip to be refloated when the work is done. In tidal water, there are often gridirons where the yacht can be laid alongside for inspection at low water and this is the cheapest method of scrubbing. Many are the nights that ocean racers have spent prior to a race waiting for the tide to refloat them after the previous evening's work on the bottom.

For the smaller boats craning out is a useful method of putting her on the quay quickly and for this purpose lifting eyes should be considered when the yacht is built. Another system is by "Travel-lift", with which more and more yards are now equipped. It is possible the designers had motor boats in mind when they introduced these, but provided the slings are carefully placed an ocean racer can be hauled out safely and rapidly transported around the yard. As the structure of the Travel-lift is above the boat, it is usually necessary to disconnect the backstay and any other rigging that would touch it. When using slings any projecting skin fittings must be remembered and it is best to have a docking plan (Fig. 141). Apart from showing the important matter of hull profile, it gives the position of skin fittings, lifting eyes and certain dimensions.

The increase in international events has led to more yachts being transported from one country to another and it is quite possible to obtain practical trailers for yachts up to 35 ft. length overall. This is one of the advantages of yachts of Half Ton and Quarter Ton size. For instance, *Shewolf* was transported overland from Cherbourg to La Rochelle on her own trailer and towed by a long wheel base Land-Rover. The moderate displacement of modern boats helps in this and crane or Travel-lift facilities are the best way of loading and unloading from the trailer. The ownership of a trailer of this type gives flexibility to offshore racing. It will help pay for itself, if the yacht is laid up using the trailer to take her somewhere where the work can be done perhaps more cheaply than a yard on the coast. (Fig. 142). For the same races, the Swedish competitors, mostly around 22 ft. waterline, were transported 1,400 miles overland across Europe on lorries, whose bodywork had been

FIG. 142. *Satisfactory trailer for transporting an ocean racer of 4 or 5 tons displacement and about 30 ft. LOA. This design is by Tollbridge Trailers Ltd. of Lymington and can be towed behind a heavy Land-Rover or similar vehicle. Air brakes are fitted. Length of trailer is 23 ft. 9 in. widest part of structure (inside wheels) 6 ft. 6 in., centre support girder 12 in. wide with 1 in. thick plank on it.*

cut away to accommodate the fin keels of each boat. This seemed even more suitable than a trailer for a continental journey, being in places easier to manœuvre and not liable to some speed limits. One enterprising crew camped in a tent on the lorry when the boat had been put in the water. However, it is not so easy to work on the outside of the yacht on a lorry and there is no towing vehicle available for use as a car. Before travelling with loads of this type in foreign countries all the regulations in force at the time must be known in advance. For instance, in France there are certain critical widths to which different rules apply, including the banning of transport at the week-end. As such laws change from time to time the current ones should be ascertained through a motoring organization; a commercial boat-transporting company may be able to help with advice.

Tools and spares   It is in the spirit of ocean racing that each yacht should be self-reliant and not to have to call on outside help in the event of accidents or damage unless it is so serious as to be unavoidable. In this respect ocean racing men can encourage the cruising men and newcomers to their ranks. But the difficulty lies in drawing a line on the amount of such equipment carried round the course and seldom used. The tools carried will be much the same whatever the length of the race up to five or six days. Screwdrivers (a selection), gripping and wrenching tools (e.g. pliers, adjustable spanners, wrenches), a hammer, cutting tools (chisel, hacksaw and knives, with a larger wood saw for emergencies only) will be the basis of the tool kit and some ways for it to be stowed have been mentioned in Chapter 6. Engine tools and special tools for electronic instruments or the cooking stove should be kept separately. Spare parts must be held for those items most likely to suffer damage, normal replacement items and material for repair of general damage. In the first category come spare stove burners, a spare ferrite rod for the direction finder, sail battens, spare tiller (compulsory under RORC rules), blocks and cordage. The second type are often electrical and mechanical: replacements for dry batteries, bulbs of all sizes used on board, plugs for the engine, galley towels of paper or cloth and a good assortment of nuts, bolts and screws. The third type are for serious repairs for which canvas, wood and seizing wire in quantity can be useful. Boards ready made up to cover broken coachroof windows are required in some instructions: make sure these have prearranged methods of fixing.

It is on the longer races where the equipment needed for serious damage has to be more elaborate: in races not more than 50 miles from the coast it is usually possible to reach port with a very temporary jury rig. Some aspects of more serious damage at sea are mentioned in the next section and in thinking about these situations before going to sea, a list of equipment needed to rectify them should be made. If the yacht is going away from her home port for a series of races based somewhere else, several types of spare can be taken that can then be left ashore until required. These might include spare sails and components such as spreaders. If the mast is going to be unshipped for transport, plenty of spare split pins and small rigging pieces, including masses of adhesive tape, are useful, and perhaps a spare rigging screw. Anti-fouling or other paint for touching up can be taken, though I would never recommend it to be left on board when sailing. It is messy and heavy and can hardly be applied when racing! Perhaps we have found here a way of distinguishing cruisers and racers: "cruisers carry paint in the lazarette". It is useful to list each spare carried with its location. Nothing is more annoying than to make a skilful jury repair after the carrying away of some component, only to find on return to harbour that a spare for it was secreted on board all the time. To distribute weight fairly and find enough stowage space in a small yacht, emergency items will have to be carried in different places and it should only be necessary for a member of the crew to get hold of the spares location list kept in a waterproof folder to find the required material. An example of a useful list which we had in *Summertime* is as follows:

SPARES AND EMERGENCY EQUIPMENT

LOCKER PORT SIDE OF MAST	Lifejackets
	Heavy canvas for repairs
LOCKER UNDER DECK STARBOARD	Spare reefing handle
FORWARD	Spare ferrite rod (RDF)
	Spares for Primus stove
	Reserve sealed matches
CHART DRAWER	Chart list
	Engine instruction manual
UNDER CHART TABLE	Spare dry batteries
	Fog horn
	Sail number on white canvas
	White flares
BOOK CASE	First-aid manual
NAVIGATOR'S LOCKER	Spare bulbs, small electrical pieces

GALLEY DRAWER	Spares for fresh water pump
	Matches
UNDER GALLEY	Saw
UNDER PORT SALOON SETTEE	Bolt croppers for wire rigging
	Sail and rubber dinghy repair kits
UNDER AND AFT OF PORT	Radar reflector
QUARTER BERTH	Spare wood for repairs; emergency tiller
UNDER CABIN SOLE	Second bilge pump
AFTER LOCKER	Distress flares, rockets, smoke
	Second lifebuoy
	Hose for second bilge pump

Tools, harnesses, navigational and other important equipment which is in normal use are not on this list.

Damage at sea The most likely part of a yacht to suffer major damage is the rig—spars and sails. Sails have been mentioned above as in need of continual attention. The most likely spar to appear in the defect list is the spinnaker pole and if the race is not unduly long, the yacht will get by using the second pole. For long races a ready aid to spar repair is the carrying of wooden plugs of the correct dimensions for the aluminium extrusions. Such plugs are a strong basis for joining up a severed spar. Battens on the outside will lend rigidity, and even better than seizing wire are metal bands of the type used to secure packing cases and which with the right equipment can be compressed round the repair.

If a forestay carries away it seldom seems that the mast is lost and the luff of the jib provides support. For rigging failures, several U-shaped "bulldog grips" give a quick method of setting up wire without rigging screws. If there is lower shroud failure the spinnaker boom topping lifts can be pressed into service for temporary support and if the upper shroud goes, when on the wind, the spinnaker halyard should be taken down to the side required. Spinnaker halyards themselves are the most likely among the halyards to part and as explained earlier, it is not advisable to have them internal for all their length. Spreader damage on yachts is often caused by a brush earlier in harbour with another boat or dock installation. It may be this was not noticed or the spreader was not checked after the incident. Bad sail handling can occasionally result in damaged spreaders. If they are streamlined and shaped as a pair two spares should be carried otherwise one will do, but if the mast and its equipment is inspected before sailing, such a spare is not necessary in races under 250 miles. For one reason or another masts are lost at sea and the action which follows depends on the inventiveness of the crew and the power and fuel capacity of the engine installation.

When dismasted the first task is to prevent the spars damaging other parts of the yacht and the light weight of modern alloy spars helps to bring them inboard quickly. Unless in a perilous position do not hurry to start the engine as it has frequently happened that a piece of rigging has become entangled with the propeller. It is also better to check the fuel supply and keep the motor in reserve for when nearing the shore later on. A jury rig is more easily made if the mast is deck stepped, but what is constructed depends on the sections of spar left and the state of the sea. When I was dismasted in a 24-ft. yacht, we stowed the wreckage of the mast on deck (the pulpit spinnaker rests were helpful!) and used a spinnaker boom in the mast step with a jib on its side, so that its area was spread along the length of the boat: this sailed within 80 degrees of the wind. The main lesson learnt on that occasion was to carry an adequate quantity of fuel, our racing keenness having led us to leave only just enough for picking up the mooring when the race was over. One problem which came to light not so long ago in the USA where more yachts carry radio telephones, was that dismasting involved losing the transmitting aerial; the solution is a whip aerial mounted aft on the counter.

Rudders have become more of a problem as foretriangles have increased in area, bringing bigger spinnakers which in turn are carried longer on a reach. Broaching puts an extreme strain on steering gear and there have been a number of recorded rudder failures in ocean racers on downwind legs. It is usually the connection between rudder and tiller or wheel that is vulnerable and the quadrants of the wheel system have sheared. Trim tabs can be of assistance and more than one yacht has returned safely by using the trim tab for steering after the main rudder has failed.

There are now systems whereby the rudder and trim tab can be locked together for steering and in this case they should be arranged so that they can also act quite independently when required. Some trim tabs merely lock in position using a lever flush with a bulkhead, but it can be seen there are advantages in the tab having its own tiller or secondary wheel. When an emergency tiller is carried either for wheel or tiller steering yachts, thought should be given to the fittings on it and the steering gear so that it can be fitted with minimum delay, enabling the yacht to race on unhindered, apart from the safety aspect. Cases have occurred of rudders simply dropping off and, without a trim tab, a strong jury rig has to be constructed.

The first may be a spar (spinnaker pole) with flat boards (cabin sole) lashed on to make a steering oar. Small yachts which carry a stern rowlock for sculling, a common fitting in France for yachts up to about 25 ft., are nearly able to steer immediately, though the size of an oar blade will not be enough for more than a light breeze. Another thing to try out is a double steering system with a spar and plank on each quarter, or rigged rather like paddle-wheel blades to dip into either side of the yacht as needed. One precaution that can be taken in advance is to drill a hole in the after part of the rudder blade and then insert filler and flush off. In the event of steering failure which otherwise leaves the rudder itself on the yacht, it may be possible to go over the side, force out the plug and pass through a line which when rigged on both quarters will control it. Whether this is practical depends on the shape of the stern in relation to the rudder and is easier in the smaller yachts.

Out of season maintenance Routine winter work is really an extension of the weekly tasks on the boat and in the same way depends on an efficient defect list being kept, especially towards the end of the season. But with the yacht kept up to racing standard the off season is more the time to deal with modifications. If the boat has been going well, the rule wisely made by Don McNamara Jr. is: "Don't tamper with a going concern." This was his feeling when the 12-metre *Nefertiti*, after a good series, had alterations made to her which in his opinion only lowered the calibre of the boat.

If performance has not been as good as hoped, see if this can be accounted for first by faulty tactics and sails, though the latter should have been dealt with in a continuous manner during the season. If it is felt that it is worth the considerable expense to make structural alterations to the hull for performance this will follow close consultation with designer and builder. Alterations are more advisable when there is a definite hull fault, such as lack of balance or poor steering. Then modifications to the keel profile or rudder size follow as a particular cure.

Amendments to rating and safety rules are other reasons for alterations. Things like stanchion height or spacing, cockpit structure and heights and lengths of main boom positions and spinnaker boom tracks come in for the rule makers' attention from time to time. One can recall yachts which have been converted from yawls to sloops after finding the two-stick rig did not pay and more severe structural work when yachts have been changed from the old triangular keel profile to the modern system with separate skeg. Sometimes in these operations the old rudder, reduced in area, has been left on as a trim tab. There have also been a few yachts which have never been quite right despite changes to keel and rudder every winter and they have remained chronic patients.

· 21 ·

RUNNING AN OFFSHORE RACE

SEVERAL clubs which normally have a regular programme of inshore and open meetings have looked into the proposal to run an offshore course, only to find that the organization involved was greater than they had imagined. In regatta-type racing, the start and finish is the same line, with race officers manning it for the several hours that the race is in progress. The competitors themselves are at the club before the race to obtain any sailing instructions and they return there afterwards to sign declarations and file any protests, and before long to see the results on the club notice board. These conditions seldom obtain in ocean racing which is usually on handicap, so that it is not surprising that crews complain that they race without seeing any boats, finish across the line in the dark and, if they are lucky, find out the result of the race a couple of weeks later, by which time they have sailed two more events!

A number of offshore events do finish at the same place that they began and may have the additional advantage of a club house as a base. For instance, every July the Royal Southern Yacht Club of Hamble runs a race of about 90 miles, which goes beyond the Isle of Wight, but starts and finishes off the mouth of the Hamble River. When the yachts finish, they can enter the river and bring up near the club house, where things are so arranged that there is enough of the week-end left for the competitors to contribute to the bar profits. While doing so they can usually catch a glimpse of the tabulated results. The Royal Ocean Racing Club's Channel race also begins and ends at the same point, but being a triangle in the English Channel of 240 miles, the time of finish is much less certain and yachts may finish in darkness and then disperse to home ports of which there are several within a few miles of the finish. Many races, including the most enjoyable, start and finish at different ports. When organizing an ocean race the sailing committee of the club or association should not try to force regatta conventions, such as reporting or collecting programmes, on the offshore boats. It should be possible to turn up in time for the start with all the instructions needed and after the finish the yacht must be allowed freedom to land her crew at a convenient point. The method of organization depends to a great extent on the geography of the area and whether the event is part of a long series or a week-end event.

Advanced notice Offshore races are nearly always "open" and the club (the term I will use for the organizing authority) will take care to announce the event well before the season to attract the owner who is arranging his programme. The avenues for this are national and regional fixtures lists, the yachting press and circulating individuals by mail. If the event is an international one, plenty of notice should be given and I would say twelve months is the minimum, if boats are to be shipped from overseas and crews expected to arrange vacations. Quite an amount of information should be given in the advance

T

notice, including the start time and distance and the approximate course, so that the nature of the race is appreciated in advance and owners can plan accordingly.

There are one or two points about the entry form. It should have a paragraph above the competitor's signature in which he acknowledges that the race is at his own risk and that the club is not responsible for any accidents to yacht and crew. If there is a rating figure to be entered it should be supported by the certificate or obtained independently from the rating authority. My experience is that entry forms sometimes have mistakes in the rating given, which if used would make any result pointless.

The form should also contain a declaration that the yacht will comply with all the safety regulations of the club. A number of offshore clubs now inspect yachts, though this is far from the sort of lengthy scrutineering that occurs before motor-boat races. Such inspections show that they are useful because they often raise points of doubt about rules as well as keeping the careless owner up to scratch. Beginners to ocean racing usually welcome an inspector to see if their equipment is suitable and to talk about points of doubt. The system of inspection varies: the RORC do spot checks before a race and may come back to the same boat later in the season. The JOG inspect all yachts before taking part in any race and the inspection certificate remains valid until the yacht changes ownership.

Sailing instructions The sailing instructions should be sent out to reach the skipper three or four days before the start. With them may be a crew list and analysis form. The analysis is to build a picture of the race from competitors' reports; it is dealt with in more detail below. Crew lists are required by some clubs from skippers in the form of a list of names and addresses. This is partly a safety measure in case the name of those on board are requested by the authorities in an emergency and sometimes a race restriction, where in a series there are rules about changing crews. Where the safety regulations and conditions of the club have not previously been issued, these can conveniently accompany the sailing instructions.

Race officials In deciding how many people are required for the immediate staffing of the race, there are a number of tasks to be done. At the start these include checking the starters, not always an easy job, and recording them as well as timing and making the starting signals and dealing with any recalls. Unlike an inshore race there is no opportunity after the start to check again who is in the race and it is desirable to know who has gone offshore. At the finish, even with boats of the same or close rating, experience shows that with a course of 100 miles or more the time between the first and last yachts can be long. A roster of watchkeepers may be needed. At the report centre for results, one or two people, depending on the size of the race, will be needed to work out the corrected times and a further official to shield them from outside enquirers, by taking times over the telephone or receiving owner's representatives who arrive with declarations. All this means that to deal with a race of fifty boats, with the benefit of shore-based starting and finishing times, two officials are needed at the start in addition to those making the starting signals and at least three over a period of time at the finish. If a committee boat is used more helpers still will be needed to cope with arrangements both ashore and afloat.

Sailing instruction details IYRU rules give a guide to the points to be covered in sailing instructions, but offshore the following also require attention:

JUNIOR OFFSHORE GROUP

Race .... Entry fee received/not received

DECLARATION

BOAT ....

SAIL No. .... R.O.R.C. T.C.F. ....

I hereby declare that all the Safety Rules & Racing Instructions were obeyed during the race and that my **finishing time was** :—

.... hrs .... mins .... secs on 1968

(I retired at .... hrs .... mins .... secs on .... day)

Signed .... Skipper

Date 1968

NOTE : This Declaration must be in the hands of the Sailing Secretary NO LATER THAN first post on Tuesday following the race. Non-receipt will assume that you did not start.

FIG. 143. *A declaration form suitable for use in an offshore race.*

Recalls. Recall numbers are not used in ocean racing and it is usual, if anyone is over the line, to fire a gun and hoist a prearranged signal. It is then the responsibility of the yacht to return. General recalls are unusual but have occurred in the One Ton and Half Ton series at times. I do not think they are appropriate for ocean races.

Course. The course is given in the usual way, stating whether marks are to be left to port or starboard. With offshore marks it is essential to define them clearly and the instructions should contain the latitude and longitude of the mark, together with its light characteristic. The club should check with the buoyage authority that the marks in the chart and almanac are indeed on station.

Class flags. It is sometimes useful when several classes by size are to go off at intervals to specify a code flag to be worn by each class. If possible these should not spell out a message, numeral pennants or substitutes of the international code of signals being suitable. It should be specified that these are shown at the start and finish of the race.

Declaration. It should be stated where the declaration form should be handed in or sent and a time limit given for this. If the yacht gives up the race it should be mandatory that she reports as soon as she reaches harbour and the place to telephone or telegraph should be given in the instructions (Fig. 143).

Navigational warnings. These are not really part of the instructions but if there is a recent wreck or buoyage change, it is a useful courtesy to competitors to mention it. Some times yachts are ordered or requested by shipping authorities to keep clear of certain areas and if this is emphasized it will obviate possible difficulties with such bodies after the race.

Sighting marks. From time to time, due to fog and heavy weather, a yacht does not actually see a mark although the skipper is sure, because of the navigational data, that he has rounded it. He may have seen a series of other buoys or taken soundings which mean that he must have cleared the unseen mark. The RORC cover this in their sailing instructions by saying: "If a mark is not seen, the race committee will require with the declaration satisfactory evidence that the mark has been passed correctly. The onus will fall upon the competitor to satisfy the committee and to appear before it, if requested to do so, within 72 hours of finishing the course, failing which the yacht may be disqualified."

Starting and finishing lines. Starting and finishing lines seem to raise their own crop of problems and a club can save itself trouble by taking care in the arrangement of these. If the entry is a large one, it is probably divadided into classes, which are started at ten-minute or quarter-hour intervals. Taking this further, there is a case for starting the groups of different sized yachts at longer intervals, staggering them for reasons of weather and tide. Different sized boats starting approximately together, will be spread out over many miles at the end of twenty-four hours, or even twelve. They will be sailing in different weather, and if there are strong tides the timings will be even more affected. A partial solution is to start the boats so that they will all be in the same area at about "half way through" the race. This is never quite possible, but can mean that the finishing times are closer together. A number of experienced yachtsmen dismiss this idea, sometimes because it has been found not to work after a single experiment. There is also the inconvenience of starting the classes over a long period of time. However, I feel the system has not been given a fair trial in important races and clubs could well think more closely about it.

It is not necessary to start ocean races to windward as is done in inshore racing. A line of suitable length and good control is more important and as the first mark is probably well over the horizon there is not the need to spread out the fleet with windward sailing before reaching it. As the wind will almost certainly change during the race, there is little point in trying to arrange windward legs in advance. This might not be the case in areas of very predictable weather, though I have yet to meet such an area, whatever the inhabitants may say. Flag signals are usual in Europe—why, I do not know. Even if the flags are big enough they are often impossible to identify because they are blowing towards or away from the yachts. The American system of shapes and colours is better. Guns must be louder than would be used with inshore boats on which the noise of crew, winches and sail handling are not so great. It has already been mentioned that the checking and controls needed for an offshore event are best done from a shore starting line, but for international events it is better to start the race simply between two marks. The outer distance mark of a transit may be difficult to keep on the line and can cause confusion. It is quite possible to have the line between a single shore mark (post) and the outer distance mark. It is advisable to have an inner distance mark, which has to be left on the prescribed side and which should be a few yards ahead of the line to avoid crowding near the shore.

The finishing line in an ocean race should not be too close to the shore. If it is placed inside an estuary or at the mouth of a harbour, local vagaries of wind and current can often invalidate many hours of racing. But with the finish well out, say at a lightship a few miles from the harbour, control becomes difficult. The line may be a bearing from a mark with a close distance, say 200 yards, given as its length, leaving the skipper to judge that he is close enough. This is not always satisfactory and one solution is to make the line "behind" the mark as the yachts come from the expected direction (Fig. 144). This is popular in tidal waters because it may be stated that the yacht can cross the line in either direction, which makes it fair in light airs when yachts arrive at different states of tide. Better than both these is a line between two points and the best of all is where a committee boat can be on station. The marks of the finishing line like all marks other than those for a daylight start in ocean racing must be lit.

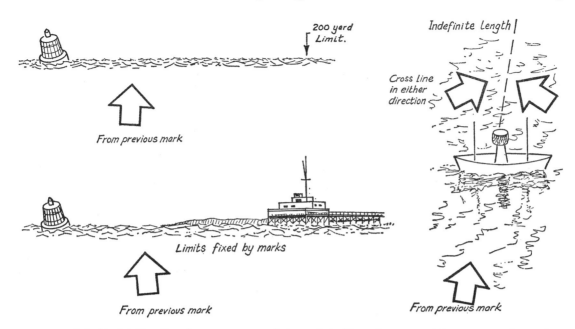

FIG. 144. *Suitable finishing lines for an ocean race. It is not desirable to choose a mark in an area such as a harbour entrance, affected by fluky conditions. The mark must be lit. The line may be given as a fixed bearing and distance, or if possible should be between two lit objects. A line "behind" a mark ensures yachts finish close to it and no critical distance is involved. By being able to cross it either way there is no advantage in arriving at different states of tide in light air conditions.*

If there cannot be anyone on the finishing line competitors must take their own time. This is often not satisfactory due to human error in taking a bearing of the finish mark, reading the watch or checking the watch error, especially at the end of a tiring race. It is used in many races but with the increasing intensity of competition, it becomes less desirable. One way of making it more accurate is to have a master chronometer at the finishing club, for competitors to check watches, but this can only be used if boats come in to a central point. My experience is that when yachts finish near each other and take their own times, these as given can often reverse the true finishing time, showing there is an inaccuracy somewhere. The club should give close thought to the finishing arrangements. Some of the elements are shown in this instruction issued by the RORC for its Channel Race:

"The finishing line extends to the westward at 290 degrees magnetic from the centre of Horse Sand Fort. The yacht *Transit* will be anchored about ¼-mile from the fort and approximately on the line. Cross the line leaving *Transit* to port. By day—show the class flag in the port rigging. By night—illuminate the sail number brightly when approaching and crossing the finishing line. After crossing the line, round up and make sure that the yacht has been identified. If *Transit* is not on station, cross the line and leave the Saddle Buoy to port.

"Each competing yacht must take her finishing time when the centre of Horse Sand Fort bears 110 degrees magnetic, and report this to the Secretary RORC at Combined

Clubs Headquarters (Cowes 2193) as soon as practicable after the race. The time should be taken accurately and time keeper should get another member of the crew to check this and certify on the declaration form that the time entered is correct. The ship's watch should be checked as close to the finish as possible."

Points systems　　A seasonal points system is a reward for consistent sailing and provides an incentive for a yacht to take part in a number of races. The difficulty with points for ocean races over the season is in the widely differing numbers involved and the variation in distances. In inshore clubs these variations are not so great. So it is difficult to find a suitable points system to keep everyone happy and it may have to be changed as numbers and courses vary from season to season. So as to encourage owners to turn up for as many races as possible, but without giving an advantage to the man who is able to spare far more time than anyone else, a certain number of best races should count for points. If there were ten races in the season, a yacht could count her best five races for points. If she only competed in four races she would count all of those. A way of coping with the varying numbers is contained in the Cox-Sprague scoring system used in some of the MORC stations: this is shown in Fig. 145. It is usual to apply factors for the longer races and these can be arranged in accordance with the club's programme. A fair factoring would be 1·5 for races over 70 miles, 2·0 for races over 120 miles and 2·5 for 200 miles. This is for a JOG programme: with proportionally bigger distances, where the yachts are larger, increase the nominated mileages.

Analysis　　Because an ocean race is sailed so much out of sight of other competitors and in the dark, it is very interesting if an accurate analysis of the place changes and the corrected time round marks can be made. The work is considerable with a big entry and it is best to find a volunteer outside the club officials who has the facilities for doing this. Skippers are asked to fill in a form such as that shown in Fig. 146. From these reports the compiler is able to work out the order on corrected time round each mark and the places lost and gained on each leg. From the report columns like "wind" and "sea", he can build up a story of conditions, list gear failures and finally he can add the skipper's remarks which are sometimes the most illuminating part of the analysis.

Dealing with the results　　When the race is of the type in which yachts disperse, perhaps late on a Sunday night, with crews scrambling to get to work on Monday morning, lasting interest depends on early notification of results. Clubs should try to explain to newspapers that offshore events depend for publication of results on them unlike the reporting of regatta racing, the results of which are already known by competitors. Apart from a few good yachting correspondents the significance of ocean racing is not understood, and it is difficult for the sports pages to carry up-to-date accounts of the doings of yachts sailing beyond the horizon and returning to shore in the dark! So it is necessary to persuade them to show results a few days later, the anxious crews knowing that the news will be in that particular paper! To get these results out to the press and sent in detail to skippers in a reasonable time, the sailing instructions must insist that the time of finish is telephoned without delay (unless they are being timed in by the club). With corrected times being worked out as they come in either by special tables, logarithms, calculating machine or computer, it may be evident before all the yachts have finished

Number of Starters

2	3	4	5	6	7	8	9	10	11	12	13	14	15	16	17	18	19	20 or more	Place
10	31	43	52	60	66	72	76	80	84	87	90	92	94	96	97	98	99	100	1
4	25	37	46	54	60	66	70	74	78	81	84	86	88	90	91	92	93	94	2
	21	33	42	50	56	62	66	70	74	77	80	82	84	86	87	88	89	90	3
		29	38	46	52	58	62	66	70	73	76	78	80	82	83	84	85	86	4
			35	43	49	55	59	63	67	70	73	75	77	79	80	81	82	83	5
				40	46	52	56	60	64	67	70	72	74	76	77	78	79	80	6
					44	50	54	58	62	65	68	70	72	74	75	76	77	78	7
						48	52	56	60	63	66	68	70	72	73	74	75	76	8
							50	54	58	61	64	66	68	70	71	72	73	74	9
								52	56	59	62	64	66	68	69	70	71	72	10
									54	57	60	62	64	66	67	68	69	70	11
										55	58	60	62	64	65	66	67	68	12
											56	58	60	62	63	64	65	66	13
												57	59	61	62	63	64	65	14
													58	60	61	62	63	64	15
														59	60	61	62	63	16
															59	60	61	62	17
																59	60	61	18
																	59	60	19
																		59	20

Place	Pts.	Place	Pts.	Place	Pts.	Place	Pts.
21	58	27	52	33	46	39	40
22	57	28	51	34	45	40	39
23	56	29	50	35	44	41	38
24	55	30	49	36	43	42	37
25	54	31	48	37	42	43	36
26	53	32	47	38	41	44	etc.

COX-SPRAGUE SCORING SYSTEM

FIG. 145. *The Cox-Sprague scoring system, which takes into account the number of boats in a race and gives bonus points to the leaders. The use of the table avoids the possibility of errors in calculating under other systems. Additional factors are introduced for multiplying the points to give higher figures for long distances. A boat is only allowed to use so many of her races for assessing the season's results (e.g. her four best scores). For yachts giving up or being disqualified there should be a token few points, but these should never be higher than even a low finisher in a race with few starters.*

who are the leaders. With no compulsory report centre, it may be another twenty-four hours before all the declaration cards with the finishing times are in and then has to follow the checking against the telephoned times, drafting and the production of duplicated copies. If an owner is sent several it will help him to keep his crew's interest. The earliest such results can be distributed will be three or four days after the race finishes, depending on the postal service of the country concerned.

JUNIOR OFFSHORE GROUP

RACE:- SOUTHSEA – NAB TOWER – WEYMOUTH

YACHT........................... TYPE..................... T.C.F.................

L.W.L............................. DATE...................................

FOR OFFICE USE		Time (B.S.T.)	Mark	Dist. off	Wind Direction and Strength	Sea	Next Boat		Remarks
E	C						Ahead	Astern	
			NAB TOWER						
			ST.CATHER-INES POINT						
			FINISH						

TACTICS EMPLOYED AND COURSES STEERED

Start to Nab Tower

Nab Tower to St. Catherines Point

St. Catherines Point to Finish

GEAR FAILURES

SKIPPER'S REMARKS.   (To include any comments on weather, material or
                    personnel factors affecting yacht's performance.)

Please complete and forward as soon as possible to:-

THIS IS NOT A DECLARATION.   DECLARATIONS SHOULD BE SENT TO THE HON. SAILING
SECRETARY.

Please write the name and address to which you wish the completed analysis
to be sent on the back of this form.

These circumstances are the most awkward, and if the yachts are in part of a series or coming into the same harbour for festivities after the race, the problem is eased. Best of all if the races are sailed without handicap, much of the work mentioned is eliminated, and when the race ends the skippers of the yachts will usually have a clearer idea of their placing in relation to other competitors on the course.

FIG. 146 (opposite). *A race analysis form issued with the sailing instructions. From this an account of the race is compiled, showing in particular the corrected time of the yachts at each reporting point and the gains or losses of places on each leg of the course.*

APPENDICES

STANDARD OCEAN RACERS

THIS list of a number of standard yachts suitable for ocean racing is intended to indicate the names and characteristics of some of the boats racing today. It also acts as a reference for yachts mentioned as they occur in the book. Standard reference books of various types are published in all countries, giving brief details of all the yachts available each year. These, of course, do not differentiate between boats suitable for offshore racing and others. Two details not given here because of their liability to change are the price and the rating. If seriously interested in any boat a potential buyer would need to examine these two matters more than superficially. It should be appreciated that the designs most favoured for racing change as the years pass. However, if an approach is made to the designer of a yacht in the list, he can indicate if the design is current or if he has a development of it.

BRITISH BUILT

Name	LOA ft.	in.	LWL ft.	in.	Beam ft.	in.	Sail area sq. ft.	Designer
Corribee 21	21		16		6	10	175	Robert Tucker
Hurley 22	22		17		7	5	240	Ian Anderson
Splinter	21		17		6	10	181	E. G. van de Stadt
Galion	22		18		7	3	240	Ian Hannay
Elizabethan 23	23		18	2	7	1	276	Peter Webster
Arden 4	23	6	18	6	7	3	242	Arden Yachts
Trotter	21	6	18	9	7	1	195	E. G. van de Stadt
Trident	24		19		7	5	245	Alan Hill
Bowman	26		19	10	8		287	Ian Anderson
Folkboat	26		19	11	7	3	258	Scandinavian YRU
Contessa	25	6	20		7	6	260	David Sadler
Nicholson 26	26	7	20		7	9	380	Camper & Nicholson
T24	24		21		8		279	Guy Thompson
Merle	26	6	21		8	2	240	Illingworth & Associates
Twister M2A	28	3	21	6	8	1	424	Holman & Pye
Trapper 28	28	2	22		8	4	292	Cuthbertson & Cassian
T31	31		22		9	3	357	Guy Thompson
Legend	28	9	22	2	8	10	273	E. G. van de Stadt
Westerley 28	28		22		9		379	John Butler
S31	31		22		8	10	333	Sparkman & Stephens
Hustler 30	30	4	22	6	9	2	336	Holman & Pye
Galion 27	27	7	22	8	8	11	341	Ian Hannay
Spinner	27	5	24		9	3	340	Michael Henderson
Elizabethan 9 metre	29	4	24		9	8	450	David Thomas
Pioneer	30		24		8		451	E. G. van de Stadt
Rival	31		24		9	8	410	Peter Brett
Harmony 31	31	2	24		9		500	E. G. van de Stadt

Name	LOA ft.	in.	LWL ft.	in.	Beam ft.	in.	Sail area sq. ft.	Designer
Nicholson 32	32		24		9	3	557	Camper & Nicholson
Northney 34	33	10	24		9	1	538	Holman & Pye
S. & S. 34	33	7	24	2	10	1	466	Sparkman & Stephens
Strider 35	35	2	25	5	9	6	533	Holman & Pye
Swan 36	36		25	6	9	8	538	Sparkman & Stephens
Excalibur 36	36		26	3	10		539	E. G. van de Stadt

FRENCH BUILT

Name	LOA ft.	in.	LWL ft.	in.	Beam ft.	in.	Sail area sq. ft.	Designer
Corsaire	18		16		6	4	172	J. J. Herbulot
Midjet	18	8	16	10	7	5	215	G. A. Brenneur
Muscadet	21		17	9	7	5	210	Philippe Harlé
Sylphe	21	6	18	9	7	11	220	Michel Dufour
Challenger 15	24	2	18	5	7	10	220	André Mauric
Cognac	24	2	19	5	8	11	313	Philippe Harlé
Samourai	24	4	19	1	7	10	227	Michel Bigouin
Defender 15	26	6	19		8	4	285	André Mauric
Emeraude	26	10	18	11	8	7	306	Dominique Presles
Rafale	27	3	20		8	11	226	Dominique Presles
Super Challenger	29	7	22		8	11	323	André Mauric
Defender 18	31	6	22	8	9	10	385	André Mauric
Arpege	29	6	22		9	11	399	Michel Dufour
Scotch	30	10	22	7	9	1	323	Philippe Harlé
Coqueliot	31	8	24	7	9	11	320	Philippe Harlé
Centurion	31	9	24		9	9	402	Holman & Pye
Karate	32	7	24	5	9	6	540	Michel Bigouin
Giraglia	35	6	26		9		440	André Mauric
Tina	37		26	8	10	5	586	Dick Carter

SWEDISH BUILT

Name	LOA ft.	in.	LWL ft.	in.	Beam ft.	in.	Sail area ft. sq.	Designer
Viggen	23	4	19	8	7	4	215	Per Bröhall
Fingal	27		21		7	6	275	Knud Reimers
Magnifik 30	30		22		8	6	326	Bruno Bostrom
Vega	27	1	23		8		295	Per Bröhall
Mistral	33	2	25		9	10	343	Olle Enderlein

DANISH BUILT

Name	LOA ft.	in.	LWL ft.	in.	Beam ft.	in.	Sail area sq. ft.	Designer
Sagitta 20	20		17	6	7	8	225	Sparkman & Stephens
Sagitta 26	25	6	19	8	8	2	312	Sparkman & Stephens

AMERICAN AND CANADIAN BUILT

Name	LOA ft.	in.	LWL ft.	in.	Beam ft.	in.	Sail area sq. ft.	Designer
Cal 20	20		18		7		196	Bill Lapworth
Outlaw	26		19		8		291	Philip Rhodes
Cutlass	23	9	19	1	7	1	242	Richard Carlson
Shark	24		20		6	11	190	George Hinterhoeller
Cal 25	25		20		7	9	274	Bill Lapworth
Capri 26	26	3	20		8	2	301	Sparkman & Stephens
Morgan 24	25		21	6	8		310	Charles Morgan
Tartan 27	27		21	5	8	7½	372	Sparkman & Stephens
Excalibur 26	25	11	21	8	7	9	302	Bill Crealock
Redwing	30	3	21	9	11	3	375	Cuthbertson & Cassian
Columbia 29	28	6	22	6	8		381	Sparkman & Stephens
Sovrel 28	28	9	24		8	4	480	McCarthy & Sorrel
Luders 33	33		24		10		529	A. E. Luders
Medalist	33		24		10		467	Wm. H. Tripp
Alberg 35	34	9	24		9	8	545	Carl Alberg
Cal 2–30	30	1	25		9		480	Bill Lapworth
Nantucket 33	33		26		10	2	488	Alan Gurney
Black Watch	37		25	6	10	6	618	Ted Hood
Cal 36	35	6	27		10	4	600	Bill Lapworth
Columbia 40	39	2	27		10	8	673	Charles Morgan

A SYSTEM FOR HANDICAPPING SMALL CRUISERS

"FAIR COMPARISON"
Reprinted from an article by the author in *Yachting and Boating Weekly*, April 18, 1968.

THERE is not an unnatural tendency today to try to obtain the best of all worlds in one boat. "Fully powered but excellent sailing performance", or "Roomy cruiser but unbeatable racer . . .". Yet it does seem that when the fairly common transition is made from racing dinghy to pocket cruiser, the competitive element is accepted as one of the losses in such a change.

By pocket cruiser is meant a sailing yacht between about 17 and 25 feet overall with a cabin. Certainly the owners of such boats like an occasional club race or even a rally. They are not pot-hunters, but what they do like is to compare the performance of one class of pocket cruiser (their own!) against another. The result, serious or not-so serious, is handicap racing.

Clubs can build up their own handicap records on the performances of the cruisers in their races, but such a system reflects the sailing ability of the owners and penalizes those who sail well.

What we are trying to find here is a ready system of fair handicapping that can be applied, when a club member arrives with, say, a brand new "Easterly 23" at the beginning of June. He missed the club's opening race in May, but is keen to join the midsummer race to Muddy Creek and back. How does the club committee fit him in fairly?

Apart from guesswork, three ways are available today:

PORTSMOUTH YARDSTICK. Several small cruisers have Secondary Yardsticks and Portsmouth numbers. It is significant that there are no primary yardsticks for small cruisers. Dinghies are governed by their own class rules so that the performance of individual boats in separate areas is comparable. There is no such control over cruisers. The majority of cruisers have no Portsmouth number owing to scarcity of data, which can only be obtained from race results.

RYA 1959 SYSTEM. This is based on the pre-1957 RORC rule and involves taking figures from Lloyd's Register and a few simple measurements. The disadvantages are that it involves the club committee in obtaining measurements, few pocket cruisers are in Lloyds and it is based on an obsolete rule.

RORC RULE. This can be applied to any boat, but the fee for measurement in proportion to the value of a pocket cruiser and the number of races she will sail is high.

None of these methods of handicapping was devised with the present situation in mind of hundreds of small cruisers of standard design and identical hulls, increasingly of glass-fibre. Yet without any great administrative problem and with co-operation between existing organizations I am putting forward a suggested system which has these advantages:

1. The rating will be known before the yacht is acquired.
2. It will be fair and not in doubt in comparison with any other class.
3. The system can be applied by any club and can be as stringent or as light-hearted as the members require.
4. It will not be costly to the individual so there will be every incentive to use it.
5. It links up with any existing system of measuring individual cruising and offshore racing yachts.

STANDARD CLASS RATING CHECK

CLASS NAME .... DESIGNER....................................
LOA .... BUILDER....................................
RIG...................................... SALES AGENT ....
Rating .... ft. T.C.F....................................
Rating certificate issued by...(organization)
Measurer ....Dated ....

Measurement check data
Hull mould (number and builder) ....
Ballast keel details ....
Sail plan:

Mainsail   *Spinnaker*
Foot............................ Maximum width ....
Luff............................ Maximum height.............................
Foretriangle: Length of pole ....
Base............................ Genoa:
Height............................ Maximum foot length ....

Standard boat equipment when measured   CLUB
Spars material ....   CHECK
Propeller type...........................
Engine............................
No. of berths............................
Bedding on board ....
Sails on board............................
Safety equipment ....
    Safety equipment on board refers to harnesses, lifebuoy, life-jackets, fire extinguishers, distress signals, fog signal and radar reflector.
    No form of dinghy was on board during measurement.
Lifeline or handholds fitted ....
Anchors and cable.......................

As soon as a standard design becomes available to the public, the builder or sales organization in this country would submit one of the boats to the authority responsible for the measurement of cruising yachts.

The proposed system does not depend on the existing RORC rule, but is applicable to any rule of measurement. Again this can be the RORC, CCA or any future rule which depends on the measurement of the yacht. The loading of the boat when measured afloat would be strictly laid down—as it is at the moment—but in these small cruisers displacement and trim are very sensitive to any alterations. For instance, crew would not be aboard, but standard sails and bedding would be.

So our standard design would be issued with a rating certificate, which we will call the "Standard Class Rating".

With the issue of the rating would be a sheet showing a list of essential dimensions which should be maintained, by any other boat in the class which wishes to race under the "Standard Class Rating". As well as key dimensions, this "S.C.R." Check (as in the example illustrated above) gives items of equipment and other particulars of the boat under which it is valid. The builder would pay for this certificate.

Now club officials would have a rating for every class however new or old, but the flexibility of this scheme is such that they can use the S.C.R. check to ensure either strict compliance to its specification, or show more tolerance. It depends how keenly the racing of this type of boat is conducted.

If a boat departs further than is acceptable to the club from the S.C.R. conditions, then the owner would have to be measured individually.

With S.C.Rs for all boats it only remains for individual clubs to use them for handicap racing in any way they wish: time-on-time, time-on-distance, or some other method.

There may be objections that pocket cruisers will be influenced by the rating rule to the detriment of their primary purpose—whatever that may be. If this is so it would be a criticism of the current measurement rule and not the means of applying it to small cruisers. But the promoters of standard boats are always claiming that they are "fast" and by being able to quote an S.C.R. there will be a figure against which to compare the actual performance—and actual performance is a contribution to seaworthiness.

SEASICKNESS

IN 1966 the Royal Ocean Racing Club introduced a new safety regulation which stated: "The safety of a yacht and her crew entered for an RORC race is the sole and inescapable responsibility of the owner, who must do his best to ensure that the yacht is fully found, thoroughly seaworthy and manned by an experienced crew *who are physically fit to face bad weather.*" This important preamble recognized that whatever the excellence of the equipment the most important factor in the safety of the yacht is the ability of the crew to cope with the conditions. Seasickness can decimate the most knowledgeable crew. It is a factor which tends to be overlooked in the excitement of preparations for the season, but should receive serious thought.

The skipper should be aware of the symptoms in his crew. These may include yawning, listlessness and lack of interest, colour of face becoming pale and then "green", desire to "stay in the fresh air" and finally queasiness and inability to eat and drink. Once seasickness has taken a grip with actual vomiting there is no cure except the passage of time and moderation of the motion due to easing of the weather or sailing into more sheltered waters. Mild attacks, especially if the person is an experienced man who knows his job about the deck anyway, need not affect matters, but from the racing point of view some of the "press on" spirit is going to evaporate and a non-sufferer must be available to push the ship along. A serious case who retires to his bunk is difficult to deal with. Generally, I think he should be ordered on deck for his watch even if he can do nothing but sit in the cockpit: he will probably be grateful you did this. Down below he may be occupying the off watch bunks and a spell on deck may even help the sickness.

Even this sort of attack need not prevent the person offshore racing because seasickness is often quite erratic in its attack. I know one transatlantic crew member whose stomach was quite sound for twenty days and who was then sick in sight of land. Mild cases on short races should not be given the wrong food. Hot soup and cups of tea are not good; I can remember two occasions when these came straight back up a good deal faster than they went down. Hot food is not necessarily the right thing; good cold food can be just as nourishing, though hot food is a morale raiser. Fruit and nut chocolate, nuts and raisins, buttered biscuits, these are suitable fare. Barley sugar (glucose type available from pharmacists) replaces energy. "Well, it's a barley sugar for breakfast again" said one of my crew on a hard passage: this man ate little for forty-eight hours but kept his watches without difficulty.

There is no doubt that the motion felt below in heavy weather in a small yacht is shocking, and many people while quite all right on deck will need to get their heads down as quickly as possible on coming off watch. Lying horizontal is certainly a preventive. Queasiness can come on when getting into clothes to go on deck and this is a reason for not having a smock-type oilskin offshore. A button up jacket is better. In this connection there is a danger in trying to leave clothing until in the cockpit: the same applies to a safety harness which should be put on below decks. A vulnerable moment is when the crew emerges from the main hatch.

Extreme cases of seasickness should be kept warm and not allowed to lose too much fluid. Some dehydration is liable at sea apart from sickness, and persons find that they are urinating less than is normal. If this is the case, liquid (e.g. soft drinks) should be taken more frequently than on shore.

Long-term prevention Needless to say general health has a bearing on vulnerability to sickness and there are occasions when a man is seasick because of a "bug". I can remember this happening on an 80-mile race in a wind not above Force 3. The same person was quite all right in much fiercer conditions two days later when the germ had gone. Fatigue is a cause of liability to seasickness and any physical training, especially of those muscles used at sea but not in life on shore, is useful. One thing is certain: resistance is built up during a season of racing. Not so much as if the person were on the yacht continually, but it is built up even when there is a week or a fortnight between races. This may be of comfort to those who find they suffer at the beginning of a season. The person the skipper should watch for signs of seasickness is the one who is on his or her first offshore race of the season. Newcomers to ocean racing who declare that they are never sick should be tactfully asked what is the worst weather they have been out in and what size of boat. Some people cheerfully believe they are immune because they have survived a choppy voyage in a steamer.

Short-term prevention   There are definite measures that can be recommended to prevent this curse of offshore sailing. The first is to have one's digestion in good order and this means avoiding indigestible foods such as fried dishes, highly spiced and sauced fish and meat, cream and some fruits such as strawberries and raspberries and also alcohol in any form. Avoidance of these foods can begin several days before the race, especially early in the season. An aid I have found useful here is to take a mild liver salt such as Alka-Seltzer which does much to counteract any acid in the system. Take the liver salt each day and again a few hours before the race. A simple meal a few hours before the race is the best way to begin the diet on the event itself. The liver salt has the additional effect of counteracting constipation which can make its small contribution to seasickness and is a common complaint in the first day or two at sea.

Travel sickness pills are primarily designed for passengers and their side-effects, notably drowsiness, are a hindrance to the crew of a yacht. If possible they should not be used, but some individuals may find them helpful. There are two main types: those based on hyoscine and those in the antihistamine group. Hyoscine is effective but has serious side-effects, including blurred vision, painful mouth and throat, drowsiness and sometimes dizziness. The dose is critical as it must not be exceeded, yet is ineffective if reduced. Having said all this, it may still suit some persons, who should stick to it if it helps them. The antihistamines have only one side-effect, that of drowsiness. The dosage is not critical and individuals can experiment to see how much they need and can take without becoming drowsy. Individuals differ in response to the various brands of pills containing antihistamine and the recommendation is that you try out various types and then settle on one which suits you.

These pills are preventive and they will not influence seasickness or even queasiness once established. The pill should be taken as prescribed usually four hours before putting to sea and continued until risk of sickness is thought to have passed.

EXTRACTS FROM THE GENERAL RULES OF THE ONE TON CUP 1968

(as issued in English)

1. A Races are sailed under the IYRU International Racing Rules except particular rules to the One Ton Cup so far as they are different to the present instructions. Specifically between 2100 and 0515 navigation lights shall be lit and rules 36 to 43 inclusive of the international racing rules will cease to apply and will be replaced by International Regulations for the Prevention of Collision at Sea (section 2 steering and sailing rules). In addition the 1968 safety regulations of RORC will be applied.

B *Measurements.* Each yacht shall have been measured and her certificate of measurement sent to the Weser Yacht Club, Bremen, Germany, at the same time as her entry. Yachts shall be available for inspection during four days preceding the first race. The following checks will be made by an international measurement committee:

1. Conformity to the accommodation rules of the 8 metre cruiser-racer class.
2. Measurement of all sails.
3. Length of spinnaker booms.
4. Position of black bands on masts and booms.
5. Conformity to the RORC special regulations for seaworthiness and safety.
6. Other measurements by decision of the measurers.

No protest concerning measurements will be admitted after the start of the first race, except in case of subsequent modifications made to a yacht. The rating figures on the list of competitors are only given for guidance.

D *Sail numbers.* Sail numbers allotted by the RORC or national authority must be carried on the mainsail and spinnaker and must not be of smaller size than prescribed by the RORC. The number must be displayed by alternative means, if the mainsail and spinnaker are down.

E *Radio transmission and reception.* Use of the following is prohibited: (*a*) Radar, (*b*) Hyperbolic navigational aids (consol and radio direction finding are permitted), (*c*) Transmitters except for private business or emergency purposes.

M *Owner's flag.* Regarding IYRU rule No. 27, no protest will be considered by the jury.

IV. C *Minimum speed.* 3 knots. The race committee has the right of cancelling the race at the first mark if the average speed of the first yacht on the first leg of the course is less than 3 knots.

APPENDIX 5

EXTRACTS FROM RULES OF THE
HALF TON CUP (1969)

COUPE INTERNATIONALE ATLANTIQUE

THIS series of races, founded by the Cercle de la Voile de Paris and the Société des Régates Rochelaises, is intended for displacement yachts with accommodation.

It is endowed with:

An individual trophy, Le Coupe Internationale Atlantique. The winner of this will entrust it to the club of which he is a member, this club being recognized by the national authority. This club becomes the defending club.

A team trophy, Le Challenge Internation. This is won by the national team of three yachts with the greatest number of points. The national authority or an organization delegated by it will be responsible in each country for selecting and designating the team of three yachts.

1 From 1966 the Cup was presented for a series of international races for yachts under RORC rating and having a rating equal to or less than 18 ft. (in the case of the RORC rule being altered the Committee reserve the right to select a suitable rating).*

4 The defending club can organize the races in its home waters, but if the same country wins three successive victories, the course in the following year should be in the waters of another nation chosen by the founding committee in consultation with the defending club.

6 Before January 31 in the year following its victory, the defending club must make known by all means, the date and place chosen for the next races. No date before April 30 or after September 15 should be selected, and the Cup may not be contended for outside European waters.

9 There is no restriction on the nationality of the design or construction of the yachts.

11 Five races will be run:

    1. 2 inshore courses of between 20 and 40 miles.
    2. 2 Olympic type courses with a 4-mile distance between start and the first mark.
    3. An offshore race of 150 miles, minimum, which will be the last race.

After the four inshore races, a provisional result will be shown which discards the least favourable race for each yacht.

In the Olympic courses the speed of the first yacht to finish must be at least 1·8 knots. In the case of cancellation for this reason, the race must be resailed.

12 The placing in each race will be the order of finishing without corrected time. For the inshore courses a yacht receives one point for finishing and one point for each yacht beaten. The first to finish receives a bonus point of $\frac{1}{4}$.

For the offshore race, the same points are awarded and then multiplied by 2. The final order is the addition of all points gained, the yacht with the most being declared the winner.

* 1970. The rating selected under the IOR rule was 21·7 ft.

14 The crew of each yacht must be a minimum of three persons and a maximum of five; they must be amateurs; the skipper must be a member of the club which he represents.

16 In the case of dispute, only the French language text of these rules shall be considered as authentic.

ANNEXE—SPECIAL REGULATIONS

The yachts must be measured in accordance with the specified rating rule.

2 The height under the coachroof (not under the beams) in the cabin shall be not less than 1·70 m. (5 ft. 7 in.) over a length of 1·2 m. (3 ft. 11 in.) and width of 0·35 m. (1 ft. 2 in.), the area of the surface of the cabin sole being not less than 0·5 sq. m. (5·4 sq. ft.).

4 The accommodation must be equipped with at least the following:

Three bunks complete with mattresses measuring not less than:
> Length 1·85 m. (6 ft. 1 in.)
> Width 0·55 m. (1 ft. 10 in.) at head; 0·30 m. (11·5 in.) at foot.

A swinging stove suitable for use at sea.
A fixed sink with outlet or adequate tank.
Freshwater pump.
50 litres of water in one or more containers.
A fixed marine W.C., or
A chemical closet, fixed and equal in weight to a W.C.
Locker for at least four hangers.
A table, which may be collapsible of horizontal surface at least 0·3 sq. m. (3·2 sq. ft.).
Stowage for 8 plates, 4 glasses, 4 cups and 4 sets of cutlery at least.

All the above must be permanently installed and functioning.

Yachts must carry lights in accordance with international rules. If electric they must be permanently fixed and not less than 5 watts each. They must rely on a source of power situated inside the yacht and must be able to remain alight for twenty hours.

RDF consol, echo sounders and a radio-telephone for private use only are permitted. A radio receiver to obtain weather information is obligatory.

Sails

Only one normal mainsail may be on board. A small mainsail (trysail) may be carried, but the area must not be more than ¾ of the mainsail rated area.

All self-steering systems are forbidden.

Following IYRU rule 1.3, it is the sole responsibility of the person in charge of each yacht to decide whether to start or continue the course.

SAFETY RULES

1. Life-raft

Each yacht must carry on automatic self inflating life-raft of a type approved by the national authority, with a current inspection certificate and able to carry the entire crew. It must be placed on deck in such a way that it can be used in an emergency.

2. Ventilation

3. Construction and general arrangement

4. Compulsory items

(a) Heavy weather sails.

(b) Lifelines: Lifelines, taut and strong in wire or metal tube or a combination of both, must run from the pulpit (outside the forestay) to half way along the cockpit. Stanchions must be bolted and spaced at not more than 1·5 m. (4 ft. 11 in.). The system must be able to support the weight of a man. The height of the pulpit must be 0·45 m. (1 ft. 6 in.) and the lifelines must be at least 0·30 m. (12 in.) above the deck to a position aft, half way along the cockpit.

Where the height of the wire is greater than 0·30 m., if the distance between the top of the bulwark and wire is more than 0·45 m., a second wire must be fitted approximately half way between wire and bulwark. This second wire need not continue in the pulpit.

(c) Lifebuoy.

(d) Life-jackets.

(e) Harness.

(f) Powerful torch.

(g) Distress flares.

(h) Fog horn.

(i) Bilge pump.

(j) First aid set, with facilities for dealing with serious burns, easily accessible and in a clearly marked place.

(k) Fire extinguisher.

(l) Anchors and chain.

(m) Flags which can signal distress under the international code of signals.

(n) Sail number, for when the number on the mainsail or spinnaker cannot be seen, there must be a special screen, with letters and numbers of suitable dimensions to show the yacht's identity.

(o) Radar reflector.

TRANSLATION OF EXTRACTS FROM RULES OF THE QUARTER TON CUP ISSUED BY SOCIÉTÉ DES RÉGATES ROCHELAISES

This series of races instituted by the Société des Régates Rochelaises is intended for small habitable yachts. The donated trophy is:

La Coupe Internationale des 15 Pieds

The number of entries is not limited.

1 From 1968 this cup is awarded for a series of races for yachts under the RORC rule which have a rating equal or less than 15 feet (in the case of the RORC changing, by means of the rule, the dimensions of a yacht of 15 feet, the originating committee has the right to select any other figure or rating).* The sailing and safety rules are those used by the JOG in England, the GCL and Class IV in France, except for amendments which follow.

4 The club of the defending yacht can organize the races in the waters of its own country, but if the same nation gains three consecutive victories, the races in the following year will be in the waters of another country chosen after consultation between the defending club and the originating committee.

6 Challenging yachts must be named by yacht clubs recognized by their national authority not less than two months before the date fixed for the first race of the series.

9 There is no restriction on the nationality of the design or build of any competing yacht.

11 The Coupe Internationale des 15 Pieds will be determined by 4 races:

One inshore race not less than 20 miles.

Two races over Olympic courses.

One offshore course of not more than 100 miles, which will be the last race. For Olympic type races the speed of the first yacht to finish must not be less than 1·8 knots.

12 The result of each race will be given as the order in which the yachts finish and without corrected time.

For the inshore races, each yacht receives one point for finishing the course and one point for each yacht beaten. The first yacht receives a bonus point and the second a bonus of $\frac{1}{4}$.

For the offshore race, the same points are given and then doubled. The final order is obtained by addition of points from all races.

13 The crew of each yacht must be a minimum of three; it must be composed exclusively of amateurs; the skipper must be a member of the club which entered the yacht.

15 In the case of dispute, only the French language text of these rules will be considered authentic.

ANNEXE

Specifications

The height under the beams must be 1·30 m. (4 ft. 3 in.) for a length of 1·20 m. (3 ft. 11 in.) and width of 0·35 m. (1 ft. 4 in.).

* 1970. The rating selected under the IOR rule was 18 ft.

The interior accommodation must consist of:

(*a*) two fixed bunks with mattresses with the following minimum dimensions: length 1·85 m., width at head 0·55 m., at foot 0·30 m.,

(*b*) A cooking stove suitable for use at sea.

(*c*) Lockers capable of retaining stowed items at an angle of 30 degrees, with not less than four rectangular shelves measuring a minimum of 30 cm. × 20 cm. × 15 cm. (12 in. × 8 in. × 6 in.). (Stowage under the cabin sole shall not be included.)

Spinnakers are allowed in the inshore races, but not in the offshore event.

The hauling out of yachts is not permitted once the series has begun without special permission.

From 1969 a yacht will not be allowed to enter unless she is one of a class of at least 3 similar designs, all of which are afloat before the races. Such boats can have variations in accommodation, fittings and rig, but they must be essentially the same hull without any radical alteration.

In any dispute the originating committee and the organizing club will decide, without any appeal, whether the yacht conforms with this rule.

METRIC AND IMPERIAL EQUIVALENTS OF COMMON DIMENSIONS USED IN REFERRING TO SMALL OCEAN RACING YACHTS

LENGTH

inch	*cm.*	
1	2·54	
6	15·2	(sheet lead inboard on boom end)
12	30·5	
18	45·5	(stanchion heights)
24	61·0	
3 ft.	91·5	
ft.	*metres*	
5	1·51	(typical draft)
7	2·13	(stanchion spacing)
8	2·44	
10	3·10	(typical beam)
12	3·65	
16	4·88	(JOG minimum W.L.)
20	6·20	
24	7·42	
30	9·14	(MORC max. L.O.A.)
35	10·34	
40	12·21	

SAIL AREA

square feet	*square metres*
50	4·66
100	9·31
150	14·9
200	18·6
250	23·3
350	32·6
450	42·0
500	46·6

DISPLACEMENT AND BALLAST

In Great Britain both tons and lb. are used, though usually tons for displacement. In the USA lb. are used.

Tons	Lb.	Kilogrammes
0·5	1120	502
1·0	2240	1008
1·5	3360	1524
2·0	4480	2040
3·0	6720	3065
4·0	8960	4070
6·0	13440	6110
8·0	17920	8145

WIND SPEED

In Great Britain and France, it is common to refer to wind speed by Beaufort scale, though speed in knots is also used. Strictly, Beaufort scale implies a mean speed and it is incorrect to say that the wind was "gusting to Force 6". What this probably means was that the wind was Force 4. The increasing use of wind speed indicators is leading to more frequent reference to wind speed in knots and to mention a 20-knot gust is correct. In USA the use of knots for wind speed is common usage. Metres per second is used in Scandinavia.

Knots	Beaufort scale in which this speed is included	Approx. speed in metres per second
5	2	$2\frac{1}{2}$
13	4	7
24	6	12
37	8	19

SAIL CLOTH

British, US and metric equivalents for sail cloth are explained in Chapter 12.

INDEX

Numbers in italics indicate plate numbers